Studies in the History of Medieval Religion
VOLUME XXVII

THE FOUNDATIONS OF MEDIEVAL ENGLISH ECCLESIASTICAL HISTORY

STUDIES PRESENTED TO DAVID SMITH

The work of historians in providing new editions of primary documents, and other aids to research, has tended to go largely unsung, yet is crucial to scholarship, as providing the very foundations on which further enquiry can be based. The essays in this volume, conversely, celebrate the achievements in this field by a whole generation of medievalists, of whom the honoree, David Smith, is one of the most distinguished. They demonstrate the importance of such editions to a proper understanding and elucidation of a number of problems in medieval ecclesiastical history, ranging from thirteenth-century forgery to diocesan administration, from the church courts to the cloisters, and from the English parish clergy to the papacy.

PHILIPPA HOSKIN is an archivist at the Borthwick Institute, University of York, General Editor of the Canterbury and York Society and Co-General Editor of the English Episcopal Acta Series.

CHRISTOPHER BROOKE is Dixie Professor Emeritus, University of Cambridge and Fellow of Gonville and Caius College.

BARRIE DOBSON is Emeritus professor of Medieval History at the University of Cambridge.

Studies in the History of Medieval Religion

ISSN 0955–2480

General Editor
Christopher Harper-Bill

THE FOUNDATIONS OF MEDIEVAL ENGLISH ECCLESIASTICAL HISTORY

STUDIES PRESENTED TO DAVID SMITH

Edited by
PHILIPPA HOSKIN
CHRISTOPHER BROOKE
BARRIE DOBSON

THE BOYDELL PRESS

© Contributors 2005

All Rights Reserved. Except as permitted under current legislation no part of this work may be photocopied, stored in a retrieval system, published, performed in public, adapted, broadcast, transmitted, recorded or reproduced in any form or by any means, without the prior permission of the copyright owner

The right of the Contributors to be identified as the authors of this work has been asserted in accordance with sections 77 and 78 of the Copyright, Designs and Patents act 1988

First published 2005
The Boydell Press, Woodbridge

ISBN 1 84383 169 4

The Boydell Press is an imprint of Boydell & Brewer Ltd
PO Box 9, Woodbridge, Suffolk IP12 3DF, UK
and of Boydell & Brewer Inc.
668 Mt Hope Avenue, Rochester, NY 14620, USA
website: www.boydellandbrewer.com

A CIP catalogue record for this book is available
from the British Library

This publication is printed on acid-free paper

Typeset by Pru Harrison, Hacheston, Suffolk
Printed in Great Britain by
Antony Rowe Ltd., Chippenham, Wiltshire

Contents

List of Contributors	vii
Acknowledgements	viii
Abbreviations	ix

David Smith: the Scholar   1
Christopher Brooke

'The archivist is not and ought not to be a historian.'   9
David Smith and the Borthwick Institute
Christopher Webb

Why Forge Episcopal Acta? Preliminary Observations on the Forged   18
Charters in the *English Episcopal Acta* Series
Julia Barrow

Pastors and Masters: the Beneficed Clergy of North-East Lincolnshire,   40
1290–1340
Nicholas Bennett

The Convent and the Community: Cause Papers as a Source for   63
Monastic History
Janet Burton

Patriarchy and Patrimony: Investing in the Medieval College   77
Charles Fonge

'Above all these Charity': the Career of Walter Suffield, Bishop   94
of Norwich, 1244–57
Christopher Harper-Bill

The Law of Charity and the English Ecclesiastical Courts   111
R.H. Helmholz

Continuing Service: the Episcopal Households of Thirteenth-Century   124
Durham
Philippa Hoskin

The Acta of English Rural Deans in the later Twelfth and early   139
Thirteenth Centuries
Brian Kemp

The Court of Arches and the Bishop of Salisbury   159
F. Donald Logan

Bishops' Registers and Political History: a Neglected Resource 173
    A.K. McHardy

The Vatican Archives, the Papal Registers and Great Britain and 194
Ireland: the Foundations of Historical Research
    Jane Sayers

Bibliography of the Writings of David Smith   211
Index   217
Tabula Gratulatoria   236

List of Contributors

Julia Barrow, University of Nottingham
Nicholas Bennett, Lincoln Cathedral Archives
Christopher Brooke, Gonville and Caius College, Cambridge
Janet Burton, University of Wales, Lampeter
Charles Fonge, Borthwick Institute, University of York
Christopher Harper-Bill, University of East Anglia
R.H. Helmholz, University of Chicago
Philippa Hoskin, Borthwick Institute, University of York
Brian Kemp, University of Reading
F. Donald Logan, Emmanuel College, Boston
A.K. McHardy, University of Nottingham
Jane Sayers, University College, London
Chris Webb, Borthwick Institute, University of York

Acknowledgements

This book is an act of homage, and a token of very warm appreciation, for all that David Smith has given us, as colleague, scholar, editor and friend – from all the editors and contributors.

The editors would also like to express their very warm thanks to the contributors for the readiness with which they agreed to join in this venture, to do honour with us to David Smith and help him to re-lay some of the foundations of historical research. They also thank Richard Barber and Caroline Palmer and their colleagues at Boydell & Brewer for agreeing to publish our book, and their kind help throughout its preparation.

P.M.H.
C.N.L.B.
R.B.D.

We would like to record our special thanks to Philippa Hoskin, who has generously borne the main editorial burden of this volume.

C.N.L.B.
R.B.D.

Abbreviations

Acta Stephani Langton	*Acta Stephani Langton Cantuariensis Archiepiscopi, A.D. 1207–1228*, ed. K. Major (CYS 50, 1950)
Add. Ch.	Additional Charter
Add. ms	Additional manuscript
archbp	archbishop
archdn	archdeacon
BI	Borthwick Institute
BL	British Library
Bodl.	Bodleian Library, Oxford
bp	bishop
BRUO	*A Biographical Register of the University of Oxford to AD 1500*, ed. A.B. Emden, 3 vols (Oxford, 1957–9)
C&S	*Councils and Synods with other Documents relating to the English Church I A.D. 871–1204*, ed. D. Whitelock, M. Brett and C.N.L. Brooke, 2 vols (Oxford, 1981); *II 1205–1313*, ed. F.M. Powicke and C.R. Cheney, 2 vols (Oxford, 1964)
CCR	*Calendar of Close Rolls, AD 1227–1509*, ed. H.C. Maxwell Lyte et al., 61 vols (London, 1902–63)
CChR	*Calendar of the Charter Rolls preserved in the Public Record Office*, ed. R.D. Trimmer, C.G. Crump, C.H. Jenkinson, 6 vols (London, 1903–27)
CFR	*Calendar of Fine Rolls preserved in the Public Record Office*, ed. A.E. Bland, M.C.B. Dawes and H.C. Maxwell Lyte, 22 vols (London, 1911–62)
Chichester Acta	*The Acta of the Bishops of Chichester 1075–1207*, ed. H. Mayr-Harting (CYS 56, 1964)
CPL	*Calendar of Entries in the Papal Registers relating to Great Britain and Ireland: Papal Letters, 1198–1513*, ed. W.H. Bliss, C. Johnson, J.A. Twemlow et al., 19 vols (London, 1901–)
CPR	*Calendar of Patent Rolls, AD 1216–1582*, ed. H.C. Maxwell Lyte et al., 74 vols (London, 1901–)
CRR	*Curia Regis Rolls* (London, 1922–)
CUL	Cambridge University Library
CYS	Canterbury and York Society
DCM	Durham Cathedral Muniments
DEC	*Durham Episcopal Charters 1071–1152*, ed. H.S. Offler (Surtees Society 179, 1968)

EDR Ely Diocesan Records
EEA *English Episcopal Acta*, published by Oxford University Press for the British Academy; i *Lincoln 1067–1185*, ed. D.M. Smith (1980); ii *Canterbury 1162–1190*, ed. C.R. Cheney with B.E. Jones (1986); iii *Canterbury 1193–1205*, ed. C.R. Cheney with E. John (1986); iv *Lincoln 1186–1206*, ed. D.M. Smith (1986); v *York 1070–1154*, ed. Janet E. Burton (1988); vi *Norwich 1070–1214*, ed. Christopher Harper-Bill (1990); vii *Hereford 1079–1234*, ed. Julia Barrow (1993); viii *Winchester 1070–1204*, ed. M.J. Franklin (1993); ix *Winchester 1205–1238*, ed. Nicholas Vincent (1994); x *Bath and Wells 1061–1205*, ed. Frances M.R. Ramsey (1995); xi *Exeter 1046–1184*, ed. Frank Barlow (1996); xii *Exeter 1186–1257*, ed. Frank Barlow (1996); 13 *Worcester 1218–1268*, ed. Philippa M. Hoskin (1997); 14 *Coventry and Lichfield 1072–1159*, ed. M.J. Franklin (1997); 15 *London 1067–1187*, ed. Falko Neininger (1999); 16 *Coventry and Lichfield 1160–1182*, ed. M.J. Franklin (1997); 17 *Coventry and Lichfield 1183–1208*, ed. M.J. Franklin (1998); 18 *Salisbury 1078–1217*, ed. Brian Kemp (1999); 19 *Salisbury 1217–1228*, ed. Brian Kemp (2000); 20 *York 1154–1181*, ed. M. Lovatt (2000); 21 *Norwich 1215–1243*, ed. C. Harper-Bill (2000); 22 *Chichester 1215–1253*, ed. Philippa M. Hoskin (2001); 23 *Chichester 1254–1305*, ed. Philippa M. Hoskin (2001); 24 *Durham 1153–1195*, ed. M.G. Snape (2002); 25 *Durham 1196–1237*, ed. M.G. Snape (2002); 26 *London 1189–1228*, ed. D. P. Johnson (2003); 27 *York 1189–1212*, ed. Marie Lovatt (2004); 28 *Canterbury 1070–1136*, ed. Martin Brett and Joseph A. Gribbin (2004); 29 *Durham 1241–1283*, ed. Philippa M. Hoskin (2005); 30 *Carlisle 1133–1292*, ed. David M. Smith
EHR *English Historical Review*
EPNS English Place Name Society
ER East Riding
EYC *Early Yorkshire Charters*: vols 1–3, ed. W. Farrer (1914–16); vols 4–12, ed. C.T. Clay, and index to vols 1–3 by C.T. and E. Clay (Yorkshire Archaeological Society Record Series, extra series 1935–65).
Fasti John le Neve, *Fasti Ecclesiae Anglicanae 1066–1300*, compiled by D. Greenway *et al.* (London, 1968–); i *St*

	Paul's, London (1968); ii Monastic Cathedrals (1971); iii Lincoln (1977); iv Salisbury (1991); v Chichester (1996) vi York (1999); vii Bath and Wells (2000); viii Hereford, ed. J.S. Barrow (2002); ix The Welsh Dioceses, ed. M.J. Pearson (2003); x Exeter (2005)
Heads	The Heads of Religious Houses: England and Wales i 940–1216, 2nd edn, ed. D. Knowles, C.N.L. Brooke and V.C.M. London (Cambridge, 2001); ii 1216–1377, ed. D.M. Smith and V.C.M. London (Cambridge, 2001)
HMCR	Historical Manuscripts Commission Report
JEH	Journal of Ecclesiastical History
JSA	Journal of the Society of Archivists
LAO	Lincolnshire Archives Office
LRS	Lincoln Record Society
Mon. Ang.	W. Dugdale, Monasticon Anglicanum, rev. edn, ed. J. Caley, H. Ellis and B. Bandinel, 6 vols in 8 (London, 1817–30, repr. 1846)
Norwich Cathedral Charters	The Charters of Norwich Cathedral Priory, ed. B. Dodwell, 2 vols (Pipe Roll Society new series 40, 46, 1974–85)
PRO	Public Record Office (now The National Archives)
PUE	Papsturkunden in England, ed. W. Holtzmann, 3 vols (Berlin and Göttingen, 1931–52)
RS	Rolls Series
TNA	The National Archives
VCH	Victoria County History
WR	West Riding
Worcester Cartulary	The Cartulary of Worcester Cathedral Priory, ed. R.R. Darlington (Pipe Roll Society new series 38, 1968)

Professor David Smith.
Photograph by Mr Trevor Cooper

David Smith: the Scholar

CHRISTOPHER BROOKE

In a lecture delivered nearly fifty years ago I pilloried the dictum of a distinguished scholar, who had told us that 'the archivist is not and ought not to be a historian'. 'He need not,' said I: 'one has heard of cooks of rare genius who had no palate themselves; one has heard of librarians who never opened a book. But the view that any of the barriers which divide our little worlds is desirable in itself is a terrible notion.'[1] David Smith has trampled for thirty years and more on the boundaries which divide the work of archivist and historian. Of his work as archivist, Chris Webb speaks with authority. But we must dwell on it for a moment more; for it has informed all his scholarly work. Even outside the Borthwick Institute his life has been spent pillaging archives and creating new archives: the recesses of innumerable libraries and record offices have been ransacked for the documents of the bishops of Lincoln and others of his victims; and in *English Episcopal Acta* and *The Acta of Hugh of Wells* the records of innumerable English bishops of the late eleventh, twelfth and thirteenth centuries have been brought together, listed, catalogued, indexed and edited with a precision which would have amazed their authors.[2] His scholarly work is not only very impressive in quality and extent, but it is unerringly directed to help other students and scholars in the fields in which he works.

He started young: he sprang from Lincoln (where he was born on 20 July 1946), and after three years in Oxford and three in Nottingham he had by 1970 completed a complex Ph.D. on a notable bishop of Lincoln, Hugh of Wells (1209–35). In the same year he was first appointed to the Borthwick, and within three years had completed the first of his *Guides*, to the archive collections in the Borthwick Institute: the fruit of that power of hard work, that precision, that concentration which has borne such rich fruit in and out of the Borthwick ever since.

A scholar must be in some measure a specialist, who has drilled deep in a mine – or, to vary the metaphor, has pressed forward the boundaries of

---

[1] 'The Dullness of the Past', reprinted in C.N.L. Brooke, *Medieval Church and Society* (London, 1971), pp. 27–8.
[2] Full references to works by David Smith will be found below, pp. 211–15.

knowledge in some small area. But the best scholars combine this with a wider vision; and this is especially necessary in the study of the institutions of the English church – medieval and modern alike – and in gathering, cataloguing and deploying archives. An archaeologist in the modern world has to be ready to identify and interpret finds from the fifth millennium BC (and beyond) to the third millennium AD: he has to be alive to the nature and interest of prehistoric implements, Roman and medieval pottery, and Victorian toilet arrangements – as well as the art and architecture of religious devotion from the age of Stonehenge via medieval shrines to modern cult centres. By the same token, an archivist has to be at home with medieval and early modern records – and all that follows down to and including the electronic revolution of the late twentieth and early twenty-first centuries. The historian of the English church has to see its role in the wider context of church history– the medievalist especially to see it as part of the church of western Christendom; but he also has to see that in the institutions and buildings and records of the Church of England he is observing a palimpsest to which every century from the sixth and seventh (at latest) has contributed. Its history is deeply scored in all manner of likely and unlikely places and artefacts.

A bottle of Theakston's Old Peculier enshrines not only a measure of 'legendary strong ale' but some very curious passages in the history of the church, familiar to David Smith in his role as Churchwarden of Masham, where it is or was brewed. The prebend of Masham was formed from the gift in the 1150s and 1160s by Roger de Mowbray of three churches to York Minster. Their tithes came to support a canon and more than a canon; for in due course the prebend of Masham became one of the most valuable in Christendom, and in 1265 was added by that notable connoisseur of rich benefices, Bogo de Clare, younger son of the earl of Gloucester, to his collection; and in the fourteenth and fifteenth centuries attracted the notice of cardinals and royal ministers.[3] When Henry VIII was nearing the end of his life, his principal colleague as founder of Trinity College, Cambridge, John Redman, plucked the King's sleeve to such good effect that he added most of the prebend to other rich pickings which Redman had gathered for his college from the king's bounty.[4] Like all York's prebends it had been a region of peculiar jurisdiction; and so the fellows of Trinity College became not only the patrons of Masham church but also lords of the Peculiar of Masham, till it was abolished in the nineteenth century – and so became the Old Peculier. Of every stage in this curious story David Smith is well aware, and both as historian and archivist avoids the 'parochialism in time' which inspired even the editors of *Conferences and Combination Lectures in the Elizabethan Church* – one of the most impressive products of the Church of

---

[3] *Fasti* vi, pp. 87–8; B. Jones, *Fasti 1300–1541* vi (1963), pp. 66–8, corr. by J. Horn and D.M. Smith, *Fasti 1541–1857* iv: *York diocese* (1975), p. 47.
[4] Ibid.

England Record Society – to say of the archdeaconry of Middlesex that its 'jurisdiction for some arcane reason snaked north beyond London into Hertfordshire and then into the Essex deaneries of Harlow, Dunmow and Hedingham'. The reasons are indeed not fully known, but the context is clear: it was formed at the turn of the eleventh and twelfth centuries when territorial archdeaconries were in the making.[5] It is characteristic of David Smith that he should be one of our leading experts on the institutions of the twelfth and thirteenth-century English church, and also have joined Joyce Horn in compiling the modern *fasti* of the sees of York and Lincoln, and Joyce Horn and Patrick Mussett in a volume covering six other northern sees – in the York volume recording the sad demise of the medieval prebend of Masham.[6]

The heart and core of his work and of this book lies in the mid and late Middle Ages. Just as his work has been inspired by the current need to re-lay the infrastructure – to rebuild the foundations – of our knowledge of the medieval English church, so also it reflects the inspiration and dedication of his most fundamental scholarly work.

His name will always be specially linked with the British Academy's series of *English Episcopal Acta of the Twelfth and Thirteenth Centuries*. David Smith has been General Editor since the project was launched in 1973; the first volume is his – Lincoln 1067–1185 – and in volumes 1 and 4, which took Lincoln to 1206, he showed his colleagues how it should be done. As I wrote, the series was approaching volume 30, his own collection for the diocese of Carlisle: now that this is published, two-thirds of the series is in print, and more than three-quarters of the scholarly effort achieved. It is in the nature of a great scholarly enterprise that it is a work of collaboration. The idea of such a series was proposed in Sir Frank Stenton's celebrated paper in the *Cambridge Historical Journal* for 1929, 'Acta Episcoporum'; it was taken up by a succession of scholars in the following twenty-five years. Of these Kathleen Major was the pioneer: after a systematic trawl of available cartularies – whose fruits formed the foundation of the Borthwick's listings, from which each volume has grown – she herself edited the *acta* of Archbishop Stephen Langton; and she supervised the thesis of David Smith.[7]

This comprised a study of 'The administration of Hugh of Wells, bishop of

---

5 The quotation is from *Conferences and Combination Lectures in the Elizabethan Church: Dedham and Bury St Edmunds 1582–1590*, ed. P. Collinson, J. Craig and B. Usher (Church of England Record Society 10, 2003), p. xxxv. The formation of the archdeaconry is the subject of a rich literature: see F. Neininger in *EEA* 15, p. xl, indicating the kind of way in which the vested interests of the early archdeacons of the see were respected.
6 J. Horn and D.M. Smith, *Fasti 1541–1857 iv: York Diocese* (1975), p. 47. See also *ix: Lincoln Diocese* (1999) and *xi: Carlisle, Chester, Durham, Manchester, Ripon and Sodor and Man Dioceses* (2004).
7 F.M. Stenton, 'Acta Episcoporum', *Cambridge Historical Journal* iii, 1 (1929), pp. 1–14; *Acta Stephani Langton*, ed. K. Major (CYS 50, 1950).

Lincoln, 1209–1235', including an edition of his *acta*, completed in 1970, one of many reminders that David was a Lincoln boy. I first came to know David when the thesis was nearing completion, and recall most vividly the impression of confident energy and scholarly grasp he already showed. Hugh's relics combine a formidable collection of about 450 *acta*, to be gathered from over thirty repositories, and the first episcopal register, comprising Hugh's fourteen surviving rolls and the *Liber Antiquus* – a register of vicarages and related documents – in all 'a formidable archival source' in David's own words, a powerful challenge to a young scholar, and an ideal starting-point for his adventures in the episcopal administration of the twelfth and thirteenth centuries. For Hugh of Wells was not only a very active bishop and exceptionally well documented: he lived and worked at the fulcrum between the earlier period documented by episcopal *acta*, and the later Middle Ages for which first a few, then many, sees have preserved bishops' registers. The Canterbury and York Society – of which David is currently Chairman – had long existed to publish bishops' registers; in 1950 it had published Kathleen Major's edition of *The Acta Stephani Langton*, in 1964 Henry Mayr-Harting's edition of *The Acta of the Bishops of Chichester 1075–1207*; by the early 1970s it was clear that the Society alone could not publish both bishops' registers and the earlier *acta* – and that a separate enterprise was needed. Norah Gurney, then Director of the Borthwick Institute of Historical Research (recently incorporated in the University of York) proposed that her Institute should house a central index of post-Conquest episcopal *acta* – and Christopher Cheney requested the Council of the British Academy to undertake the publication of the *Acta* as a major Academy project.

Ironically, David Smith's edition of Hugh of Wells was to appear neither among the *Acta* nor in the Canterbury and York Society – much as he has contributed to both. The *Acta* project had to find a limit, and it was set at the point at which each see could boast its first episcopal register: thus Hugh of Wells fell just outside this definition; and from 1973 to 1986 David Smith was deeply involved with earlier Lincoln material, issuing in volumes 1 and 4 of the *Acta*. In 2000 he celebrated the millennium by issuing *The Acta of Hugh of Wells* in the Lincoln Record Society – another of the societies in which he has played a leading role.

Thus the *Acta* owes much to several pioneers, Sir Frank Stenton, Kathleen Major, Christopher Cheney, and half a dozen others; and it has been created by a group of twenty editors collaborating in the work. But its achievement is unthinkable without the creative example and energy of David Smith. He has been an editor, and more than an editor. First and last, he has recognised the vital importance of accurate texts if medieval documents are not to mislead. Canon Capes of Hereford wrote an imaginary chapter of papal history when he dated a bull of Pope Alexander III of 1178 at Avignon instead of Anagni;[8] and it is evident that errors in transcription

---

[8] *Charters and Records of Hereford Cathedral*, ed. W.W. Capes (Cantilupe Society, 1908),

can render a text useless. Thus David has had to be an immaculate editor of texts. His *anni mirabiles* of 2000–1 saw the publication of *The Heads of Religious Houses II*, not to mention Hugh of Wells and five volumes of *EEA*; and I recall my stupefaction when *The Bolton Priory Compotus 1286–1325* appeared, in collaboration with Sir Ian Kershaw. I vividly remember Ian Kershaw – when a third-year undergraduate at Liverpool – anxiously enquiring whether I thought this Compotus (in effect, his own discovery) might form the basis of research for a Ph.D. From what he told me of it, I thought it a marvellous find, and it duly founded Ian's first career, as a medievalist.[9] Though now better known as the historian of Hitler, he has never lost his interest in medieval economic history, nor in Bolton; and when other schemes had failed to produce what was needed, he found a *Deus ex machina* in David Smith, who 'volunteered to produce a full transcription of the text of the *Compotus*, and, with skill and energy, accomplished this (alongside his other commitments) within nine months'.[10] Editing charters and episcopal *acta* is exacting work – exceedingly exacting if one is determined to get it right. But anyone who has edited a medieval account book knows that can be more exacting still: the book is a monument to David's lifelong capacity for concentrated, precise, enthusiastic and selfless effort. Like many of the great scholars of the past he is a fast worker – there are 570 pages in the *Compotus* – aided by an incapacity to make mistakes such as few of us can boast.

Sound texts are the basis of it all; but there is much more to laying foundations than that. The best of the scholars who created the science of medieval history in the late seventeenth and early eighteenth centuries – in the age of Newton and Bentley – were both editors and technicians. Mabillon set beside the stately folio volumes of Benedictine texts and history his *De re diplomatica* (1681) in which the sciences of palaeography and diplomatic came to birth – and which early found its way into the libraries used by the great English medievalists of the age, Brady and Wanley in particular.[11]

---

p. 28; cf. M.G. Cheney, *Roger Bishop of Worcester 1164–1179* (Oxford, 1980), p. 261. Capes's error was noted by Z.N. and C.N.L. Brooke, 'Hereford Cathedral Dignitaries in the Twelfth Century – A Supplement', *Cambridge Historical Journal* viii, 3 (1946) pp. 179–85 at p. 181.

9   I. Kershaw, *Bolton Priory: The Economy of a Northern Monastery 1286–1325* (Oxford, 1973); *The Bolton Priory Compotus 1286–1325*, ed. I. Kershaw and D.M. Smith, with the assistance of T.N. Cooper (Yorkshire Archaeological Society Record Series 154, 2000).

10   *The Bolton Priory Compotus*, p. vii (preface by Ian Kershaw).

11   On Mabillon's *De re diplomatica*, see D. Knowles, 'John Mabillon' in Knowles, *The Historian and Character and Other Essays* (Cambridge, 1963), chapter 10. His influence on Humphrey Wanley is illustrated by Wanley's ambition to write a *De re Anglorum diplomatica* (D.C. Douglas, *English Scholars 1660–1730*, 2nd edn (London, 1951), p. 110) and on the copy in Brady's college library, see C. Brooke in V. Morgan, *A History of the University of Cambridge II, 1546–1750* (Cambridge, 2004), pp. 483–4.

These names are (or should be) daily on the lips of medievalists in the twenty-first century; the narrative historians – the authors of fashionable monographs – have long since gathered the dust. David Smith has not written large theoretical treatises, but taught us all by example. In *English Episcopal Acta* he has shown the way in which documents of common origin which have now to be reclaimed from widely scattered sources can be made to provide the foundations for an understanding of how the English church actually worked in the period before the registers begin; and how comparative study of terminology and diplomatic reflects the stages in the development of every aspect of diocesan life, from the building of cathedrals to the appropriation of benefices, and the formation of vicarages.[12] The picture which slowly emerges as the volumes spread along our shelves is an exciting one: for this was a notably creative period in the history of the English church: full of scandals, indeed, and the golden age of medieval forgery; it was a period of able and worldly prelates and developing legal structures, but also of new spiritual aspiration, and of St Hugh of Lincoln, the central character in *English Episcopal Acta* volume 4.

In 1973 David became General Editor of *English Episcopal Acta*, and in the same year, at Norah Gurney's suggestion, began work on his *Guide to Bishops' Registers of England and Wales*, published in 1981 after a mighty labour compassing the whole series from Hugh of Wells to the abolition of episcopacy in 1646 – an event for which he was perhaps (though a loyal Anglican) profoundly grateful.[13] By 1981, as Director of the Borthwick Institute, he was archivist to the archbishop of York (and others besides), and here the York registers are planted out in their natural habitat, surrounded by all their fellows from other sees. It is hard to imagine now the plight of medievalists who depended on R.C. Fowler's pioneer pamphlet in 1918; and David characteristically made his book a guide not only to the registers themselves – with details sufficient to reveal the very varied shape and structure of the individual books and rolls – and any documents which might possibly qualify as such, but in a very succinct way to the shape and history of the dioceses.

Bolton apart, these books primarily illustrate the institutions of the medieval secular church. His largest book (so far) lays foundations for the history of the religious orders in the thirteenth and fourteenth centuries: David Smith and Vera London's *The Heads of Religious Houses: England and Wales*,

---

[12] For general accounts, see C.R. Cheney, *English Bishops' Chanceries* (Manchester, 1950); C.N.L. Brooke, 'English Episcopal Acta of the Twelfth and Thirteenth Centuries', in *Medieval Ecclesiastical Studies in Honour of Dorothy M. Owen*, ed. M.J. Franklin and C. Harper-Bill (Woodbridge, 1995), pp. 41–56; J. Barrow, 'From the Lease to the Certificate: The Evolution of Episcopal Acts in England and Wales c.700 to 1250', in *Die Diplomatik der Bischofsurkunden vor 1250*, ed. J.C. Haidacher and W. Köfler (Innsbruck, 1995), pp. 529–42.

[13] It was published by the Royal Historical Society in 1981; a supplement by David Smith, in honour of the centenary of the Canterbury and York Society, was published in 2004.

II, 1216–1377 (Cambridge, 2001). The first volume was published in 1972 – but had its origin in the 1930s, when David Knowles compiled lists for the late eleventh and twelfth centuries to form the bone structure of his reconstruction of *The Monastic Order in England, 943–1216*, first published in 1940.[14] In the 1960s David Knowles and I were joined by Vera London, and after immense toil *Heads I*, was published in 1972, a book of 326 pages and many thousands of references. In the years after 1972 Vera London worked steadily away preparing the ground for another volume; but she and I knew well she could never complete the work alone. In 1985, on a visit to Masham, I told David I was in search of a colleague for her; and he immediately expressed an interest. I thought at the time that it was a miraculous solution, and so it proved. For all Vera's dedicated work, which rightly earned her a place on the title-page, *Heads II* is essentially David's work: it was published in 2001, and David and I were able to visit Vera, then aged 97, in a home in Shropshire and delight the closing months of her life by giving her a copy of volume II – and also of the revised edition of volume I, which I had prepared to accompany it. Since 1216 a certain inflation had taken place: volume II is a book of 798 pages.

Both David and I are addicted to dates: the idea of providing a precise chronology of abbots and priors to help us date undated documents, and lend precision to innumerable careers (so far as is possible) played an important part in our interest in *Heads*; and it is beyond question that dates are the most crucial of all foundations for a historian's work. Not all historians share our addiction – to put it mildly. I recall a distinguished scholar declaiming the ages at which the various steps in John Fisher's career occurred, in ignorance or innocence of the fact that we do not know in what year he was born.[15] But many historians have shared our passion for dates, and David would be the first to acknowledge that many good lists of Heads were to be found in print before he began – notably in the more recent volumes of the *Victoria County Histories*, and most especially in the volumes of the new Le Neve covering the monastic cathedrals and the cathedrals in which abbots and priors were prebendaries.[16] For the cathedral priories indeed, Joan Greatrex's *Biographical Register of the English Cathedral Priories of the Province of Canterbury, c. 1066–1540* provides a prosopography of whole communities, a massive achievement to which David Smith made an important

---

[14] 2nd edn 1963, with the dates 940–1216. On its genesis see C. Brooke, C. Holdsworth, R. Lovatt and D. Luscombe, *David Knowles Remembered* (Cambridge, 1991), chapter 3.

[15] Cf. J. Scarisbrick in *Humanism, Reform and the Reformation: The Career of Bishop John Fisher*, ed. B. Bradshaw and E. Duffy (Cambridge, 1989), p. 155; and C. Brooke and M. Underwood, ibid., p. 235 and n. 1.

[16] Especially *Fasti ii: Monastic Cathedrals*, but also *Fasti iv*, pp. 95–7 (abbots of Sherborne who held a Salisbury prebend); *Fasti vi*, pp. 59–62, 95–7 (priors of Nostell and Hexham who had York prebends); *Fasti vii*, pp. 6–8 (priors of Bath) – and the relevant volumes of *Fasti 1300–1541*.

contribution.[17] *Heads II* thus comprises a mass of prosopographical detail which could be gathered in no other way: full lists and outline biographies of some thousands of medieval religious, including all who attained high office. No such lists formed the backbone to David Knowles' later volumes (*The Religious Orders in England*, volumes I–II, 1948–55), and the difference in the depth and quality of his account of the monastic orders in the thirteenth and fourteenth centuries from that of the twelfth and thirteenth is evident – a new interest and a new kind of source makes his third volume, on the Dissolution of the Monasteries (1959), in its own way as notable a classic as *The Monastic Order*.

A natural companion to *Heads*, reflecting David Smith's own exceptional learning in the field, and the quality of help and kindness he has offered to so many scholars, has been his *Monastic Studies Bulletin*. This has been fruitful in keeping fellow-workers in the field in touch, and in stimulating further adventures in the infrastructure. Articles by his former assistant, now fellow General Editor of *English Episcopal Acta* – and an archivist in the Borthwick – Philippa Hoskin, and Nicholas Vincent, showed how many medieval cartularies, fragments and rumours of cartularies had been found since the publication of Godfrey Davis's invaluable catalogue in 1958; and a group of eight, including David himself, his colleague Philippa Hoskin and his former pupil Claire Breay, has been formed to prepare a new edition.

In this and countless other ways David's energy and learning, and friendly and devoted service to other scholars, have helped to lay foundations in our own day comparable in extent, and surpassing in precision and scholarship those laid by the great antiquaries and historians of the age of the scientific revolution. These are the works which will still be in use generations ahead, when the fashionable monographs of our age lie buried in libraries.

The editors of *English Episcopal Acta* have been kept in touch with one another and with David by letter and phone and e-mail, by an occasional Bulletin, and above all by meetings in York and Cambridge which David's kindness and hospitality and exacting standards have helped to make inspiring occasions. The editors are a group of friends; and they have been able to celebrate with him the steady, relentless progress of the series. But perhaps his most triumphant encounter was on a September day in 1995, when representatives from the Humanities Research Board (as it then was) and the Academy's Committee on Research Projects met some of us in the Borthwick Institute; and the visitors, mellowed by a lunch cooked by David Smith himself, put on record their admiration for the project.

What follows is a menu not of his devising, but one designed to reflect and do honour to his tastes; and a tribute of affection and homage from his friends.

---

[17] Joan Greatrex, *Biographical Register of the English Cathedral Priories of the Province of Canterbury, c.1066–1540* (Oxford, 1997), p. vii.

'The archivist is not and ought not to be a historian.'
David Smith and the Borthwick Institute

CHRISTOPHER WEBB

'The archivist is not and ought not to be a historian.' Christopher Brooke has referred to this aphorism in his own article with some scepticism, and not without good reason, for David's career at the Borthwick is evidence of the falsity of the dictum.[1] It was, however, coined with care, in the early days of the professional development of archivists, and in a laudable attempt to draw a distinction between archives and history. History, well established, with a career structure, commonly accepted methods of entry into the profession and characteristic techniques; and archives, very new, with no career structure (unless you include the Public Record Office) and few prospects, no established method of entry, and with few, if any, commonly shared and characteristic techniques. As archivists asserted their professional identity from the mid-1950s onwards, history and archives have apparently drawn further apart, until today the courses that train archivists can contemplate dropping that core discipline, palaeography, and county record offices are commonly bereft of anyone who can read anything in Latin, or earlier than the seventeenth century. The rather bad-tempered recent exchanges in the *Journal of the Society of Archivists* illustrate how entrenched the positions of the two sides have become, in stark contrast to the prevailing ethos at the Borthwick, where, under David Smith, the links between these two branches of the one profession have been strengthened.[2]

The archives have always been at the centre of David's thoughts, not as a quarry for him to exploit (as most historians view them), but as a resource for

---

[1] David's view of this dictum, and the danger it posed for the future of the profession, can be found in 'Archivists and Historical Research: A Personal View of the English Scene', *Archives et Bibliothèques de Belgique* vol. 46 no. 1–2 (1975), pp. 158–63.
[2] Ian Mortimer, 'Discriminating Between Readers: The Case for a Policy of Flexibility', JSA vol. 23 no. 1 (April 2002), pp. 59–67; Stacey Gee, 'A Standard Service for All? The Case for a Flexible Attitude', JSA vol. 23 no. 2 (October 2002), pp. 233–8; Jenny Moran and Martin Taylor, 'Lowering the Drawbridge: Further Thoughts on Discriminating Between Readers', JSA vol. 24 no. 1 (April 2003), pp. 55–64.

others, now and in the future. The Borthwick and its records were, of course, well known before David's arrival. Canon Purvis, the founding director, was a prolific writer and publisher, and established also a series of summer schools, using the archives as teaching material. Purvis's interests, however, were concentrated securely on the Tudor period. His *Tudor Parish Documents* was a ground-breaking source book, and was supported by a number of other publications in the same area.[3] But Purvis, while he worked on the archives of all periods, did not seek to publicise the riches of the York diocesan archive outside his period (although one should except from this generalisation the Leverhulme Project under Purvis to study the church courts at York from the middle ages to the nineteenth century).[4] It would have been easy for David, at the beginning of his career, to focus his work on the period he knew best and devote his time to the medieval bishops' registers. David recognised, however, that as an archivist his task was to make all the archives in his care accessible to others. With characteristic energy, therefore, almost as soon as he arrived in York, he set about the formidable task of providing a guide to all the archives at the Borthwick. Those who knew a younger David will remember how difficult it was simply to keep up with him while walking; and will remember also the speed with which queries were answered. An idle musing would see him scurry off (if he did not already know the answer) and come up with it before the idle musing itself had died away. This could be, and was, an intimidating characteristic to younger staff – and we have to remember that David himself was a very young man (only 28) when he was appointed director of the Borthwick.

The task of compiling a general guide would have been difficult enough even if the archives had been identified and listed properly. As it was, Purvis (or his staff) had misidentified sections of the archives, and the referencing system adopted by him was eccentric. Both problems clearly needed to be put right. Coupled with this, only a dozen or so repositories had at that stage produced and published guides to their holdings, and many of these held no ecclesiastical records. The models for David to use were few in number, and limited in scope.

It is important to spend some time looking at this particular task, because, in many ways, it set the tone for what was to follow. Purvis had established his own referencing system for the records from the diocesan registry. It is not clear why he did not take account of similar work going on elsewhere.

---

[3] J.S. Purvis, *Tudor Parish Documents of the Diocese of York; A Selection with Introduction and Notes* (Cambridge, 1948).

[4] This project produced three studies of the courts: K.F. Burns, *The Medieval Courts* (1962); R.A. Marchant, *1559–1644* (1963); and B.D. Till, *1660–1883: A Study in Decline* (1963). All three studies are available at the Borthwick. An amended version of Marchant's work was published as R.A. Marchant, *The Church under the Law: Justice, Administration and Discipline in the Diocese of York 1560–1640* (Cambridge, 1969).

He had worked on the diocesan archives since the late 1930s, and might with justification have felt that he was as well placed as anyone to establish a framework for the archives. Moreover, when he began work it was not at all clear that the system devised by G.H. Fowler for use in the fledgling Bedfordshire County Record Office would come to be so widely accepted.[5] At the same time, concordance with other systems was not so necessary as it later became. Few scholars worked on ecclesiastical archives (as Purvis himself pointed out), few diocesan registries had appointed capable people to look after their archives, and the development of a national network of archive repositories was only a dream. For whatever reason, therefore, Purvis devised his own system for the diocesan archives, which he described, some years after he established it, in an early Borthwick publication.[6]

In essence, Purvis divided the archives of the diocesan registry into a number of groups. These groups were somewhat arbitrary and inconsistent, some of them being based on the format of the documents within them (such as marriage licences) and others being based on the organisation that produced them (such as convocation records). Each group was then further subdivided, as necessary, along the same lines as the main groupings. The referencing system he adopted was, as far as I am aware, unique. As an entity the diocesan registry archive was denoted by the prefix R, and each group within it was given a roman numeral as a code letter. Thus parish register transcripts were R.VIII, and convocation records were R.II.[7] It is immediately clear that a researcher would need to know and understand the reference codes in order to work out what kind of document might be hidden in a footnote in a monograph or article. Below the groups were subgroups, each denoted by a letter. Thus the group R.VI (benefice papers) had subgroups A (archiepiscopal books and papers) to F (archdeaconry of Cleveland). Below these a combination of upper and lower case letters, and roman and arabic numerals could bring one down to an individual item. Thus R.IV.L.89.a.i was a note on a paper pinned to one of the pieces in file 89 of the nomination papers (themselves part of the benefice papers group).[8]

This system had the advantage of being hierarchical (which would allow material to be added in the proper place as it came to light) but the disadvantages of impenetrability and complexity (for researchers using it and for other archivists expected to apply it) and, above all, it did not represent either the functional divisions of the archbishop's registry or the administrative origins of the records, but at times the one, at times the other, and even, on occasions, the physical format of the documents created by the registry.

---

5   Patricia Bell, 'George Herbert Fowler and County Records', JSA vol. 23 no. 2 (October 2002), pp. 249–64.
6   J.S. Purvis, *The Archives of York Diocesan Registry: Their Provenance and History*, St Anthony's Hall Publications no. 2 (London, 1952).
7   Ibid., p. 9.
8   Ibid., p. 10.

Purvis's system worked to an extent, and was a good initial attempt to describe and arrange the records, based largely on what he found in the registry building. However, it was not adequate as a basis on which to arrange the records held by the Borthwick, and its eccentricity and uniqueness meant that it could not take its place alongside other schemes of arrangement being brought into common use with the foundation of many local record repositories in the years following the establishment of the Borthwick in 1953.

David began a scheme to rearrange the archives when he arrived at the Borthwick, and, in the words of the then director, Norah Gurney, with 'hard work and dedication' (adjectives that would follow David throughout his career) 'in two years systematically sorted and re-arranged the contents of the strong-rooms'.[9] His task was, always bearing the records themselves in mind, to devise a scheme of arrangement that would reflect the records, and allow them to be described in a logical and consistent manner.

David first of all divided the records into broad sections according to the diocesan officer who was ultimately responsible for their production: archbishop, archdeacons and peculiars. Within each major division he made further subdivisions. The archbishop's records, for example, were divided into three main subgroups (records of administration, records of jurisdiction and records of visitation) and each subgroup was further divided. The records of administration were spilt between their provincial and diocesan functions, and further subdivided as appropriate.[10] In this way David established a framework that led users clearly through the relationships between the often chaotic surviving records, and directed the researcher to the appropriate section for his/her needs. David also adopted a new referencing system. Like the staff of many other record repositories he saw the value of the essentially mnemonic system first applied in Bedfordshire, and later transmitted throughout the nascent records repository network via the Essex County Record Office. Accordingly, faculties, labelled R.IV.F by Purvis, became, simply, FAC (plus a year and a number), and subscription books, labelled R.IV.B.d. by Purvis, became Subs.Bk. (plus a number).

David had the advantage of having worked for some time with Dorothy Owen at the Lincoln Diocesan Archive, and therefore could see how Purvis's scheme could be changed to something more useful. A comparison between Dorothy Owen's *Ely Records* and David's own *Guide to the Archive Collections in the Borthwick Institute of Historical Research* [BIHR] clearly shows how much influence his Lincoln experiences had on his early work at the Borthwick.[11] This willingness to look beyond the boundaries of the records

---

[9] David M. Smith, *A Guide to the Archive Collections in the Borthwick Institute of Historical Research* (York, 1973), p. viii.
[10] Smith, *A Guide to the Archive Collections*, pp. iii–iv.
[11] D.M. Owen, *Ely records: A Handlist of the Records of the Bishop and Archdeacon of Ely* (Chichester, 1971). Dorothy Owen is specifically acknowledged in David's *Guide*.

facing him in the strong rooms, and see and use what others have done before him, is characteristic of David and the ethos he established. He did what scholars have always done, and drew on the findings of others to create something new, but grounded firmly in evidence. In the case of the creation of the guide and the new referencing system, the records he cared for were part of a greater whole; so to treat them as if they had been created in isolation would have been unscholarly and unarchival.

David's work in this area anticipated modern professional developments. Archivists now, sensibly, create their finding aids according to international standards. Long before the standard (ISAD(G)) was published, David's work on the York diocesan archives has almost all the elements needed to comply with it. Indeed, his *Guide* of 1976 has formed the essential basis for the Borthwick's project in 2004 to add descriptions of its holdings to the on-line Higher Education Archives Hub.

The work on the general re-arrangement and re-referencing of the archives was, of course, valuable and necessary in its own right, but was not sufficient in itself to fulfil the main purpose of looking after the archives. Caring for archives is only one part of the duties of an archivist. They exist so that people can use them, and they cannot do this unless the archives are well known. The publication of David's work as *A Guide to the Archive Collections in the BIHR* in 1973 was an event in its own right, and has persuaded many people to visit York to research the records at the Borthwick, but it also heralded the introduction of an ambitious plan to make the archives more widely known through a settled scheme of regular publications about them.

Archival publications were nothing new, of course. In the context of local repositories, the Essex County Record Office, under F.G. Emmison, had been publishing useful works for many years. The Borthwick itself already had St Anthony's Press (its name derived from St Anthony's Hall), and had, like Essex, produced some self-instruction palaeography manuals. David's conception was more ambitious, and drew on these precedents, as well as on the work of county record societies with which he was familiar. The Borthwick embarked on a programme of issuing volumes of guides to and editions of records, aiming at the publication of one every year. In the thirty-one years that have passed since 1973, the Texts and Calendars series has published 29 titles (and 31 actual volumes), ranging from calendars of archbishops' registers and an edition of pre-Reformation churchwardens' accounts to administrative histories of hospitals in the York region.

In choosing what to publish, David set out to cater for those whose needs are strictly amateur, as well the needs of professional scholars. The third volume of the Borthwick Texts and Calendars series was, tellingly, Norah Gurney's *Handlist of Parish Register Transcripts*, published in 1976.[12] In

---

[12] Norah K.M. Gurney, A *Handlist of the Parish Register Transcripts in the Borthwick Institute of Historical Research* (York, 1976).

making this volume such a priority, David set out his stall to show that amateurs are every bit as important as the professionals. Behind the *Handlist* was an enormous amount of work involving cleaning, re-sorting and identifying the transcripts. Originally in annual bundles in groups of deaneries, David set out (with the staff at the Borthwick) to sort the transcripts into parish sets. This was the only way in which the records could be made easily available to the growing numbers of genealogists who wished to use them, and the success of this rearrangement was more or less immediately felt in a substantial increase in their use. This caused its own problems, the solution to which I shall refer later.

For professional historians David sought to concentrate the work of Texts and Calendars on sources that would be valuable, but that were perhaps not so well known. It is interesting to note that his latest publication for the Borthwick is a consolidated guide to the fifteenth-century cause papers and court books.[13] This completely re-works Purvis's pioneering lists of the cause papers, and provides for the first time a means of linking the cause papers with their court book entries. The work has already increased the attention paid to these sources by scholars, and serves to indicate what might be achieved by extending this system beyond the fifteenth century. Similarly, administrative histories of organisations are out of fashion with historians, and little published (except in outline and within their own repositories) by archivists. The Texts and Calendars volume of hospital histories stands as a beacon to guide others, and provides a much-needed context in which the archives can be securely placed and sensibly interpreted.[14] As a result, the hospital archives at the Borthwick are among the more heavily used records, and are exploited to a much higher degree than similar archives elsewhere.

Once the Texts and Calendars series was established new opportunities presented themselves. It became clear that there was a demand for straight archival finding aids and indexes as well as more scholarly editions and calendars. To meet this demand David created the series Borthwick Lists and Indexes. These were simply formatted, sometimes just run off as required, and were generally quick to produce, but met a specific demand from researchers. *Tithe Awards and Maps at the Borthwick Institute: A Handlist*, complemented by *Maps in the Borthwick Institute* are two instances where local historians and present-day administrators (researching rights of way and hedgerows, for example) have benefited from this series.[15] But the greatest products of the Lists and Indexes are the monumental series of

---

[13] David M. Smith, *The Court of York 1400–1499: A Handlist of the Cause Papers and an Index to the Archiepiscopal Court Book* (York, 2003).

[14] K.A. Webb, *From County Hospital to NHS Trust. The History and Archives of NHS Hospitals, Services and Management in York, 1740–2000, Volume 1: History* (York, 2002).

[15] C.R. Fonge, *Tithe Awards and Maps at the Borthwick Institute: A Handlist* (York, 1994); Matti Watton and Debbie Usher, *Maps in the Borthwick Institute* (York, 2000).

indexes to marriage bonds from 1660 to 1839, compiled through the voluntary labour of members of the York and District Family History Society over many years, and the eight volumes of indexes of ordinations at York from 1500 to 1849. This latter series, so useful to the national Clergy of the Church of England project, engaged scholars outside the Borthwick, such as Claire Cross, as well as scholars inside, such as the current office manager, Sara Slinn.[16] It is one example within the Borthwick of the kind of academic archival project outside the Borthwick that Christopher Brooke has described; seemingly too ambitious, but completed through collaborative effort over a number of years, and on completion opening up large intractable archives to new fields of scholarship. Through projects like these the Borthwick, despite its large quantity of genealogical sources, has maintained the level of academic involvement with its archives to a greater degree than elsewhere, and has continued to attract scholars to work on sources that in other places are relatively neglected.

One of the principal aims of this publishing activity was to make the archives more widely known, and the steady increase in the numbers of reader visits (which reached the maximum capacity of the search rooms in the 1990s) and remote enquiries shows that it was undeniably successful. That success, of course, brought its own problems. Some sources, such as the parish register transcripts that were made more accessible through re-arrangement and the publication of a handlist, came under increasing threat from over-handling. The Borthwick was one of the first record repositories to address this problem through the implementation of a comprehensive microfilming programme in partnership with the Church of Jesus Christ of Latter Day Saints. This programme met initial, quite fierce, opposition from users, who did not like the technology, and could not see why we insisted on serving future users (through preserving the records long-term) rather than their own immediate needs. Today, nearly all the Borthwick's most used sources have been filmed, with the originals safe in the strong rooms, and virtually all users accept that it is a sensible way to deal with an intractable problem.

David was a firm advocate of the use of modern transcriptions of parish registers as a means of widening access and securing the long-term preservation of the records. He served for many years on the Yorkshire Parish Register Society, including a stint as chairman, and contributed to the series himself as editor of the parish register of Masham and as a tireless checker of other people's transcriptions. When the Society could not publish a particular volume he persuaded transcribers to donate a copy to the Borthwick library. He also encouraged people to begin transcribing in the first place. Many volumes in the Borthwick library bear the name of Margaret E. Smith, David's mother.

---

[16] Claire Cross, *York Clergy Ordinations 1500–1642* (York, 2000–2002); Sara Slinn, *York Clergy Ordinations 1800–1849* (York, 2001).

When David arrived at the Borthwick it was already well known for its holdings of ecclesiastical archives, particularly of the Tudor period, which Purvis knew best. David's own work has shown to great effect the riches of the medieval ecclesiastical archives, but it is important to understand how far the Borthwick has moved away from being a purely ecclesiastical repository during his time. The archive of the earls of Halifax, with its immensely important nineteenth and twentieth-century political papers, was one of the first non-ecclesiastical acquisitions. At about the same time that the Halifax archive arrived, the archive of the Retreat, the pioneering Quaker psychiatric hospital, was also deposited at the Borthwick. These archives could scarcely differ more from the Borthwick's focus as 'a research institute specialising in the study of ecclesiastical history, in particular that of the Province of York'.[17] These two major acquisitions set the precedent for other important non-ecclesiastical acquisitions. The archive of Rowntree plc, the huge archive of the York Hospitals Trust, and the smaller, but still significant archives of Vickers Instruments and York Waterworks, all arriving in the 1990s, illustrate the growing range of the Borthwick's holdings, and the reputation and public confidence that it built up in David's time as director.

In the twenty-first century the Borthwick has been able to build upon this success through its work with the University's archive. Just as David was always willing to accept modern diocesan records from York (and, indeed, he recently acted as a modern records consultant to Ripon diocese), the principle of acting as the repository for the University's archive was always accepted. In the last few months this activity has been strengthened and consolidated by the appointment of a University records manager and archivist, based in the Borthwick. This appointment serves to throw into relief the main theme of David's career. The new records manager is a medievalist, shortly to publish an edition of a cartulary. His scholarly and forensic abilities as an editor of texts, honed under David himself, are coupled with professional archival training to present a skills set which is singularly appropriate for the formidable task facing him.

The records manager, Charles Fonge, is not the only one of David's pupils to have returned to work with him. Christopher Brooke has mentioned Philippa Hoskin, also now an archivist at the Borthwick, and Claire Breay, working at the British Library but still in partnership with David and Philippa on the revision of Davis's handbook of cartularies. Claire, in fact, held the Borthwick archive traineeship before studying for her Ph.D. with David. This traineeship has been one of the most important professional developments at the Borthwick in the last thirty years. Now past its twentieth trainee, the post was established to supplement the archive assistants and at the same time to address a pressing problem in the profession. There

---

[17] This description of the Borthwick Institute appeared in University of York graduate prospectuses until the late 1990s.

were, in the 1980s, more very well qualified applicants to archive courses than there were places on them. A traineeship for one year would simultaneously assist the Borthwick, help students to discover if archives suited them, inculcate in the trainees the distinctive Borthwick ethos, and provide a series of excellent recruits to the profession. Nearly two-thirds of our trainees attended David's farewell event in the autumn of 2003. They came from all over the country, from local authority record offices, national repositories and university repositories. All of them have published, and continue to publish, works relating to archives, thereby carrying on the Borthwick tradition of scholarship and publication in their respective repositories.

The key to the archival development of the Borthwick under David has been the application of scholarship, the fostering of an academic ethos, and an engagement with the users of the archives in the same activities as they themselves engage in, as an integral part of the duties of the staff. The foundations for this were laid early on. In an article published in *Archives* in 1976, David wrote, 'by the very nature of their work [archivists] are peculiarly competent to deal with particular historical problems illustrated by the records in their custody . . . I am confining my definition of research undertaken by archivists to work of particular relevance to the deposited archives and of benefit to the record office, be it an edition of a text, a comprehensive and scholarly catalogue of an archive collection, or the study of the records and administrative history of a specific institution or body.'[18] In other words, David's aim, right at the beginning of his career, was, in Christopher Brooke's happy phrase, to create the infrastructure of research. He recognised also that in order to do this work properly it was necessary to look beyond the boundaries of one's own holdings, and beyond the chronological constraints of one's own interests as a historian, as exemplified most clearly in his work on bishops' registers.

The products of his publishing activity, the great range of archives held (and catalogued) by the Borthwick, the fostering of this special ethos at the Institute coupled with the assembly of a staff who share his aim, all illustrate how successful David has been. It is fundamental to the appreciation of his achievement to understand that, as technology shifts some of the publishing activity away from print and onto the Internet, and as the Borthwick prepares, with David's encouragement, to leave its medieval past in St Anthony's Hall for a new, purpose-built home on the University's main campus, the aims and ethos fostered by him remain unchanged. In looking to the future, the preservation of the archives and their scholarly exploitation through a partnership between the staff, the rest of the academic community and the wider public, are still centre stage.

---

[18] David M. Smith, 'The Archivist's Personal Involvement in Historical Research', *Archives* vol. 12 no. 56 (Autumn 1976), pp. 167–9, at pp. 167 and 168.

Why Forge Episcopal Acta?
Preliminary Observations on the Forged Charters
in the *English Episcopal Acta* series

JULIA BARROW

'In the eleventh and twelfth centuries social pressures were such that respectable men and respectable communities forged as they had not forged before and would never forge again.'[1] In England, particularly, where the shock of the Norman Conquest had made religious institutions fear that they might lose knowledge of their past and thus control of their possessions, the first half of the twelfth century was, as is well known, a period when the past was reinvented. Closely linked with that process was the forging of charters.[2] However, the practice of forgery had by no means died away in the later twelfth or the thirteenth centuries.[3] We should therefore expect to find examples of forgeries among the thousands of charters assembled in the *English Episcopal Acta* series, and, indeed, such is the case: out of over six thousand episcopal *acta* collected in the series, and in the volumes of *acta* of Archbishop Stephen Langton, the twelfth-century bishops of Chichester and the early twelfth-century bishops of Durham published earlier on in other record series, over 110 documents appear to be forgeries, and question marks hang over another 40 at least.[4] In arriving at these totals I have

---

[1] A. Morey and C.N.L. Brooke, *Gilbert Foliot and his Letters* (Cambridge, 1965), p. 128.
[2] R.W. Southern, 'Aspects of the European Tradition of Historical Writing 4: The Sense of the Past', *Transactions of the Royal Historical Society* 5th series 23 (1973), pp. 243–63, especially pp. 247–56; Martin Brett, 'John of Worcester and his Contemporaries', in *The Writing of History in the Middle Ages*, ed. R.H.C. Davis and J.M. Wallace-Hadrill (Oxford, 1981), pp. 101–26; J. Barrow, 'How the Twelfth-Century Monks of Worcester Perceived their Past', in *The Perception of the Past in Twelfth-Century Europe*, ed. P. Magdalino (London, 1992), pp. 53–74, and eadem, 'The Chronology of Forgery Production at Worcester from c.1000 to the Early Twelfth Century', in *St Wulfstan and his World*, ed. Julia Barrow and Nicholas Brooks (Aldershot, 2005), pp. 105–22, especially 114–22.
[3] C.R. Cheney, 'Magna Carta Beati Thome: Another Canterbury Forgery', *Bulletin of the Institute of Historical Research* 36 (1963), pp. 1–26.
[4] EEA; *Acta Stephani Langton*; *Chichester Acta* and *DEC*; for a provisional list of the spurious and possibly spurious charters in these collections, see Appendix I below.

concentrated, for reasons of time and space, on those items marked out as spurious or possibly so by the series editors, and although I have identified some further items as suspect, the list provided here must be regarded as provisional only, the more so since work on this paper has been done while the series was only about two-thirds complete. The *English Episcopal Acta* volumes available to me at the time of writing were 1–30, which means that no consideration could be paid, inter alia, to any of the *acta* of bishops of Rochester or to those of bishops of Worcester from the Conquest up to the thirteenth century. The cathedral priories of these sees were notorious for forging all sorts of documents and are likely to have been among the most active forgers of episcopal *acta*.[5]

Picking out forgeries in this series as an object of study, however, presents us with a difficulty of approach: the forgeries reveal not the ideas of the bishops in whose names they were supposedly issued, but the wishes of the beneficiaries, while the *English Episcopal Acta* series aims to show the development of episcopal chanceries through the edition of episcopal charters. Discussion of diplomatic in the introductions to the volumes concentrates on the evolution of scripts, layout and above all phraseology in the output of episcopal clerks, without devoting much attention to the output of beneficiaries.[6] This approach is essentially justified in the case of England by the limited number of episcopal *acta* in the pre-1120 period, in which beneficiary output was greatest, by the preference shown by most bishops from early on for the simple writ form, and by the steady development of common form from the middle of the twelfth century onwards, but it makes the identification and study of forgeries harder. Forgeries need to be approached by means of studying the archives and scriptoria of beneficiaries.[7] Forging was overwhelmingly carried out by ecclesiastical institutions, mostly monastic houses: of the charters listed below, only three had lay beneficiaries, being in

---

[5] Martin Brett, 'Forgery at Rochester', in *Fälschungen im Mittelalter*, Internationaler Kongress der Monumenta Germaniae Historica, 6 vols (Hanover, 1988–90), iv, pp. 397–412. For Worcester, see D. Styles, 'The Early History of Alcester Abbey', *Transactions and Proceedings of the Birmingham Archaeological Society* 64 (1946 for 1941–2), pp. 20–38 at pp. 20–33; Barrow, 'The Twelfth-Century Monks of Worcester', pp. 56, 60–74; and eadem, 'The Chronology of Forgery Production', p. 120.

[6] For diplomatic analyses, see introductions to individual *EEA* volumes; see also C.R. Cheney, *English Bishops' Chanceries, 1100–1250* (Manchester, 1950), and Julia Barrow, 'From the Lease to the Certificate: The Evolution of Episcopal Acts in England and Wales (c.700–c.1250)', in *Die Diplomatik der Bischofsurkunde vor 1250*, ed. Christoph Haidacher and Werner Köfler (Innsbruck, 1995), pp. 529–42.

[7] Cf. the approach taken by scholars of twelfth-century German and Swiss episcopal diplomatic, e.g. Peter Johanek, *Die Frühzeit der Siegelurkunde im Bistum Würzburg*, Quellen und Forschungen zur Geschichte des Bistums und Hochstifts Würzburg 20 (Würzburg, 1969); Peter Rück, *Die Urkunden der Bischöfe von Basel bis 1213: Vorarbeit zu den Regesta episcoporum Basiliensium* (Basel, 1966).

favour of Durham episcopal tenants, and one is a literary forgery, but also produced in a monastic environment, St Albans.[8]

Searching for forgeries in the *English Episcopal Acta* series means, therefore, switching attention away from the bishops and their clerks and onto the institutions that sought the benefits of episcopal *acta*. However, we do not need to lose sight of bishops altogether. An important issue is the question of why episcopal *acta* mattered to beneficiaries. What could bishops, fictively or factually, do that other issuers of charters could not?[9] But I wish to begin with an examination of the variations in the numbers of forgeries over the different dioceses, and then to proceed to a study of the individual beneficiaries, before looking at the aims of the forged charters with a view to discovering which aspects of episcopal activity were most valued by twelfth and thirteenth-century forgers, and in which circumstances.

Even a cursory glance at the appendix will show marked differences in the numbers of forgeries attributed to bishops of different dioceses. Three trends are apparent. First, and unsurprisingly, forgers from various dioceses were anxious to have documents in the name of the archbishop of Canterbury. Second, forgers produced a significant number of forgeries in the names of archbishops of York and bishops of Durham, to the extent that the forgeries supposedly issued by these prelates are rather more numerous, in proportion to the total numbers of *acta* from the northern province, than are the forgeries issued in the names of bishops of the province of Canterbury in relation to overall numbers of *acta* there. Last, forgers were much more eager to ascribe their work to bishops of dioceses with monastic chapters than to bishops of dioceses with secular chapters, with the noticeable exceptions of York and Chichester. This difference is likely to become even more noticeable once editions of *acta* become available for Rochester and for twelfth-century Worcester. At first sight the last two trends appear to be somewhat contradictory, but closer examination of the houses which were responsible for the forgeries helps to resolve the apparent problem.

Very few secular chapters can be accused of forging charters: the canons of Wells seem to have forged two charters of their bishop Robert of Lewes,[10] and it is just possible that the canons of Chichester may have forged a charter of Seffrid I establishing the right of the heirs and executors of

---

[8] The charters for Durham episcopal tenants are *DEC*, no. 23 and *EEA* 24, no. 6 and 25, no. 188; the literary forgery, *EEA* ix, no. 133, is the work of Roger of Wendover.

[9] Most attention has so far been paid to the forging of royal charters, though with some observations on episcopal *acta*: Morey and Brooke, *Gilbert Foliot*, pp. 124–7; Eleanor Searle, 'Battle abbey and exemptions', *EHR* 83 (1968), pp. 449–80; Nicholas Vincent, 'King Henry II and the Monks of Battle: The Battle Chronicle Unmasked', in *Belief and Culture in the Middle Ages: Studies Presented to Henry Mayr-Harting*, ed. R. Gameson and H. Leyser (Oxford, 2001), pp. 264–86; David Bates, 'The Forged Charters of William the Conqueror and Bishop William of St Calais', in *Anglo-Norman Durham, 1093–1193*, ed. David Rollason, Margaret Harvey and Michael Prestwich (Woodbridge, 1994), pp. 111–24.

[10] *EEA* x, nos 46, 50.

deceased canons to have a year's income from the latter's prebend.[11] Frank Barlow has cast doubt on a charter of William de Warelwast for the canons of Crediton because it gave them the right to elect their provost and to complain to the bishop if he did not satisfy them,[12] but this preoccupation with the misbehaviour of provosts and their propensity to withhold prebendal income from their fellow-canons was a current one in the 1130s.[13] The canons of Lichfield probably reworked a charter of Bishop Walter Durdent in the thirteenth century.[14] The cathedral chapters of York, Lincoln, St Paul's, Salisbury, Exeter and Hereford, for all of which numerous episcopal charters survive, do not appear to have resorted to forgery.

Hospitals were also little involved in forgery. The Hospital of St John the Baptist in Canterbury claimed to have an indulgence of Lanfranc, and God's House in Southampton may have forged one episcopal charter,[15] though this does not survive. Although Frank Barlow suspected that the hospital of St Mary Magdalene in Liskeard forged a sequence of thirteenth-century episcopal indulgences, now lost, there is no special reason to doubt their authenticity: some other hospitals, notably St Ethelbert's Hospital in Hereford, obtained numerous indulgences from bishops in the thirteenth century.[16]

Monastic houses were responsible for the overwhelming majority of forgeries, and Benedictine foundations were far ahead of all other orders. Twenty-eight male Benedictine houses (one of them French) managed to produce about 90 forged episcopal *acta*, and the total rises to well over 90 if forgeries in the names of Welsh bishops produced by Gloucester abbey and

---

[11] *Chichester Acta*, no. 15, see also p. 46, and *Papsturkunden in England*, ed. W. Holtzmann, 3 vols (Berlin and Göttingen, 1931–52), ii, nos 70, 113. It is by no means impossible that such a system had existed under Seffrid and that his successor, Hilary, transferred these revenues, sharing them between the whole body of canons and the fabric, because Chichester was rebuilt in his time.

[12] *EEA* xi, no. 15.

[13] Cf. Wells, discussed by J. Barrow, 'Cathedrals, Provosts and Prebends: A Comparison of Twelfth-Century German and English Practice', *JEH* 37 (1986), pp. 536–64 at p. 554, and also Chartres: L. Amiet, *Essai sur l'organisation du chapitre cathédral de Chartres (du XIe au XIIIe siècle)* (Chartres, 1922), pp. 112–22.

[14] *EEA* 14, no. 64, editor's comment.

[15] *EEA* 28, no. 2, and ix, no. 55.

[16] *EEA* xii, nos 202, 218, 280, 323. For a list of the episcopal indulgences for St Ethelbert's Hospital in Hereford, see J. Barrow, 'The Canons and Citizens of Hereford', *Midland History* 24 (1999), pp. 1–23, at p. 23 n. 106; of the charters listed there, Hereford Cathedral Archives nos 2040 and 2039 are now published respectively as *The Acta of Hugh of Wells, Bishop of Lincoln, 1209–1235*, ed. D.M. Smith (Lincoln Record Society 88, 2000), no. 257, and *EEA* 30, no. 85. Cf. also indulgences for Ospringe Hospital in Kent: Archives of St John's College Cambridge, D9.4; *EEA* xiii, no. 137; *EEA* 22, no. 162; *St Davids Episcopal Acta, 1085–1280*, ed. J. Barrow (South Wales Record Society 13, 1998), no. 116. In general on indulgences in twelfth and early thirteenth-century England, see Nicholas Vincent, 'Some Pardoners' Tales: The Earliest English Indulgences', *Transactions of the Royal Historical Society* 6th series 12 (2002), pp. 23–58.

its satellite priories are included.[17] Nineteen of these houses were post-Conquest foundations, mostly set up in the three decades immediately following the Conquest, and were particularly active in forging episcopal *acta*.[18] Perhaps also to be associated with this group is Gloucester, which, although it was refounded as a Benedictine house as early as 1022, owed its real growth in endowments, wealth and numbers of monks to Abbot Serlo (1072–1104), who, among other opportunities, was keen to exploit the possibilities of Norman penetration into south Wales at the end of the eleventh century.[19] Prominent within the group of post-Conquest Benedictine foundations are the cathedral priories of Rochester, Durham and Norwich.[20] What is striking about the Benedictine houses is that several major foundations of the tenth and early eleventh century known otherwise to have forged prolifically, especially charters purporting to be issued by Anglo-Saxon kings, do not appear to have forged post-Conquest episcopal *acta*: St Augustine's Canterbury, Malmesbury and Westminster, for example, are missing from the list, and Christ Church Canterbury and Glastonbury feature only once each.[21]

---

[17] Appendix II: Bath cathedral priory, Battle abbey, Canterbury cathedral priory, Chester abbey, Colchester abbey, Colne priory, Durham cathedral priory, St Nicholas' priory, Exeter, Eye priory, Glastonbury abbey, Gloucester abbey, Goldcliff priory, St Guthlac's priory, Hereford, Norwich cathedral priory, Rochester cathedral priory, St Neots priory, St-Valéry abbey, Selby abbey, St Michael's Mount priory, Shrewsbury abbey, Tavistock abbey, Wallingford priory, Whitby abbey, Winchester cathedral priory, Worcester cathedral priory, St Mary's abbey, York and Holy Trinity priory, York.

[18] Appendix II: Battle abbey, Chester abbey, Colchester abbey, Durham cathedral priory, St Nicholas' priory, Exeter, Eye priory, Goldcliff priory, St Guthlac's priory, Hereford, Norwich cathedral priory, Rochester cathedral priory, Selby abbey, St Michael's Mount priory, Shrewsbury abbey, Wallingford priory, Whitby abbey, St Mary's abbey, York and Holy Trinity priory, York.

[19] Emma Cownie, *Religious Patronage in Anglo-Norman England 1066–1135* (Woodbridge, 1998), pp. 54–65; *Original Acta of St Peter's Abbey, Gloucester, c.1122–1263*, ed. R.B. Patterson (Gloucestershire Record Series 11, 1998), pp. xxi–xxxii; see also Julia Barrow, 'Wulfstan and Worcester: Bishop and Clergy in the Early Eleventh Century', in *Wulfstan of York*, ed. M. Townend (Turnhout, 2004), pp. 141–59.

[20] Previously secular communities were refounded as Benedictine ones at Rochester in the early 1080s and at Durham 1083; Norwich cathedral priory was founded 1095 x 1101. See M. Brett, 'The Church at Rochester, 604–1185', in *Faith and Fabric: A History of Rochester Cathedral 604–1994*, ed. Nigel Yates with P.A. Welsby (Woodbridge, 1996), pp. 1–27, at p. 15; W.M. Aird, *St Cuthbert and the Normans: The Church of Durham, 1071–1153* (Woodbridge, 1998), pp. 104–41; Barbara Dodwell, 'Herbert de Losinga and the Foundation', in *Norwich Cathedral: Church, City and Diocese 1096–1996*, ed. Ian Atherton, Eric Fernie, Christopher Harper-Bill and Hassell Smith (London, 1996), pp. 36–43.

[21] On St Augustine's, Canterbury, see Wilhelm Levison, *England and the Continent in the Eighth Century* (Oxford, 1946), pp. 209–23, and S.E. Kelly, 'Some Forgeries in the Archive of St Augustine's Abbey, Canterbury', in *Fälschungen im Mittelalter*, 6 vols (Monumenta Germaniae Historica, Schriften, 33, 1988–90), iv, 347–69; on West-

The figures given for Benedictine forgeries above omit forgeries by Cluniac houses. Lewes and Pontefract, founded in the late eleventh century, both produced several forged episcopal *acta*, while the later foundations of Thetford, Barnstaple and Monkbretton were less productive.[22] Fourteen houses of Augustinian canons produced forged episcopal charters, but among them only Guisborough, founded in 1119, was prolific.[23] Cistercian monks were more restrained, with seven forged episcopal *acta* produced by six houses.[24] Nunneries also forged relatively little: the priories of Catesby and Nuneaton produced one forged episcopal *actum* each, while St Bartholomew's priory in Newcastle and the Hospitaller nuns of Buckland produced two each. Quite exceptional were the nuns of the priory of Wix, in Essex, who at the end of the twelfth century produced a large dossier of forgeries, including five spurious episcopal charters.[25]

As far as the north of England is concerned, the high number of forgeries attributed to the archbishops of York and the bishops of Durham largely reflects the activity of monastic houses founded in the last three decades of the eleventh century: Durham, Whitby, Selby, Pontefract and Holy Trinity York. Durham cathedral priory was almost single-handedly responsible for the high number of forgeries attributed to Durham bishops from the time of William of St Calais to the death of William of Sainte Barbe in 1152; it also forged charters of archbishops of York to protect its numerous interests in the diocese of York.[26] In the northern province, which had had no Benedictine foundations in 1066, several major Benedictine monasteries had been estab-

---

minster, see Pierre Chaplais, 'The Original Charters of Herbert and Gervase, Abbots of Westminster (1125–1157)', in *A Medieval Miscellany for Doris Mary Stenton*, ed. P. Barnes and C.F. Slade (Pipe Roll Society new series 36, 1962 for 1960), pp. 89–110, and T.A. Heslop, 'Twelfth-Century Forgeries as Evidence for Earlier Seals: The Case of St Dunstan', in *St Dunstan: His Life, Times and Cult*, ed. N. Ramsay, M. Sparks and T. Tatton-Brown (Woodbridge, 1992), pp. 299–310; on Christ Church Canterbury see Heinrich Boehmer, *Die Fälschungen Erzbischofs Lanfranks von Canterbury* (Studien zur Geschichte der Theologie und der Kirche 8, 1902); C.N.L. Brooke, 'The Canterbury Forgeries and their Author', *Downside Review* 68 (1950), pp. 462–76 and 69 (1951), pp. 210–81; R.W. Southern, 'The Canterbury Forgeries', *EHR* 73 (1958), pp. 193–226, and see also *EEA* ii, no. 6; Margaret Gibson, *Lanfranc of Bec* (Oxford, 1978), pp. 231–7; on Glastonbury, see L. Abrams, *Anglo-Saxon Glastonbury; Church and Endowment* (Woodbridge, 1996), and see also *EEA* 28, no. 4.

[22] Appendix II: Lewes, Pontefract, Thetford, Barnstaple and Monkbretton.
[23] Appendix II: Darley abbey, and the priories of Barnwell, Bridlington, St Gregory's in Canterbury, Great Bricett, Guisborough, Launde, Leeds, Llanthony Secunda (Lanthony by Gloucester), Nostell, St Mary Overy in Southwark, St Thomas' in Stafford, Thurgarton and Twynham.
[24] Appendix II: the abbeys of Buildwas, Combermere, Fountains, Kirkstall, Newminster and Stanley.
[25] C.N.L. Brooke, 'Episcopal Charters for Wix Priory', in *A Medieval Miscellany for Doris Mary Stenton*, ed. P.M. Barnes and C.F. Slade (Pipe Roll Society new series 36, 1962 for 1960), pp. 45–63, especially pp. 48–50, and plates iii–iv.
[26] *EEA* v, nos 3, 43; 20, no. 16; *DEC*, nos 3–7, 10, 36–7.

lished by 1100. A similar pattern emerges in the diocese of Chichester, dominated in monastic terms by Battle, founded one year after the Norman Conquest, and Lewes, established a decade later.

The factors which led monasteries founded in the late eleventh century to forge, and especially to forge episcopal *acta*, were twofold: on the one hand their endowments often included numerous parish churches, which meant that they needed confirmation of their rights to these from their diocesan, and on the other hand the period of their foundation coincided with a low point in the production of private charters, which meant that they often had no written title from their benefactors for their endowments. Monasteries founded in the pre-Conquest period had usually been endowed with estates on which parish churches had been subsequently founded. Their rights to such churches were fairly secure, even without episcopal confirmation, and, in any case, the estates themselves were their main source of wealth. Monasteries founded later than 1100 which resorted to forgery might do so because their genuine episcopal charters confirming grants of churches or tithes had suffered damage, a predicament postulated by Christopher Brooke in the case of Wix, founded 1123 x 1133.[27]

The most frequent themes which occur in forged episcopal *acta* are confirmations of grants of tithes and churches. In several of these charters the forgery is seeking no rights beyond what might be found in hundreds of genuine episcopal *acta*, and the purpose of the forgery is to obtain or preserve a right to a particular church or parcel of tithe to which the proprietor might have a weak title.[28] But many of the forgeries go further and claim much more. There were two areas of ecclesiastical rights in particular where forgers sought to prove episcopal intervention. One of these was the right to appoint, and quite often also to depose, priests in parish churches belonging to or claimed by the beneficiaries. Durham cathedral priory wanted to claim that it had been granted the right to appoint the vicars in its own churches already in the late eleventh century;[29] Gloucester abbey sought the right to enter its churches and remove vicars;[30] Bath cathedral priory wanted to be able to appoint and depose its chaplains (by using the term 'chaplains' it was trying to deprive them of rights)[31] and St Nicholas' priory Exeter wanted to present its choice of incumbents to the bishops of Exeter by written documents.[32] The Augustinian canons of Twynham priory, in their forged foundation charter, wanted to prevent hereditary succession by priests to its

---

[27] Brooke, 'Episcopal charters for Wix', pp. 57–8.
[28] E.g. two of the Wix forgeries: *EEA* iii, no. 650 and vi, no. 158; similarly *EEA* v, no. 37 for Bridlington.
[29] *DEC*, no. 4; *EEA* v, no. 3.
[30] *EEA* vii, no. 7, and *St Davids Episcopal Acta*, nos 1, 9, and probably also nos 10, 14, 16: see review by Nicholas Vincent in *History* 84 (1999), pp. 511–12, at p. 512.
[31] *EEA* x, no. 10.
[32] *EEA* xi, no. 4.

churches in order to secure its own rights of patronage.³³ A similar disrespect for parish clergy is suggested by the phrase 'when priests die or are degraded' in the charter just mentioned for St Nicholas' priory. These preoccupations on the part of monastic houses disturbed bishops, who worried that parish clergy might be too easily deprived of livings, and who ensured from the later twelfth century onwards that vicars would have secure tenure and sufficient income.³⁴

The other main area which interested forgers was ecclesiastical jurisdiction. Northern monasteries were especially active in this field. Durham demanded freedom from the exactions and demands of archdeacons and other episcopal officials in the diocese of York, and insisted that the vicars of its churches should not be summoned to York synods but that they should only be made to appear in court at Durham.³⁵ Holy Trinity York also claimed freedom from archidiaconal exactions.³⁶ Selby more vaguely claimed freedom from ecclesiastical customs in a forged variant of a genuine charter which had reserved ecclesiastical causes to the archbishop.³⁷ Whitby demanded the right to hold ordeals and freedom from synodal dues.³⁸ Outside the northern province, Norwich cathedral priory claimed the right to enjoin penances at Lynn, and Canterbury cathedral priory urged that its monks should be able to censure malefactors.³⁹ In all these cases monks were going some way beyond what bishops thought was appropriate for them.

Cathedral priories had particular preoccupations of their own: they needed to ensure a division of properties between bishop and monks which was favourable to the latter,⁴⁰ to secure funds for particular needs,⁴¹ and to claim dues from priests attending diocesan synods.⁴² Durham wanted its prior to take precedence over the archdeacon,⁴³ while some Winchester monks wished the behaviour of their prior and obedientiaries to be regulated to protect the monks' interests.⁴⁴ The Canterbury monks demanded that all

---

³³ EEA viii, no. 116. This demand is presented as a moral imperative, and follows a disparaging reference to the 'secular canons' who had served the minster before its conversion to an Augustinian house. On the origin of the term 'secular clergy' as a disparaging way of separating them from 'regular clergy', see Alain Boureau, 'Hypothèses sur l'émergence lexicale et théorique de la catégorie de séculier au XIIe siècle', in Le clerc séculier, XXIIe Congrès de la S.H.M.E.S., Amiens, juin 1991 (Paris, 1993), pp. 35–43.
³⁴ U. Rasche, 'The Early Phase of Appropriation of Parish Churches in Medieval England', Journal of Medieval History 26 (2000), pp. 213–37, and literature there cited.
³⁵ EEA v, nos 3, 43; 20, no. 15.
³⁶ EEA v, no. 24.
³⁷ EEA v, no. 5, based on genuine no. 4.
³⁸ EEA v, no. 68.
³⁹ EEA vi, no. 15; ii, no. 6.
⁴⁰ EEA vi, nos 11, 12; viii, no. 20; see also DEC, no. 3a.
⁴¹ EEA x, no. 10.
⁴² EEA vi, no. 39.
⁴³ DEC, no. 4.
⁴⁴ EEA viii, no. 131.

their archbishop's suffragans be consecrated at Canterbury or else obtain their consent to be consecrated elsewhere.[45]

One final point needs to be raised, though only briefly here since full examination must await the completion of the *English Episcopal Acta* series: the issue of when the forgeries were made and how they were transmitted. Many survive only in copies and it is possible that 'originals' were not made in all cases, because of the cost of seals. It is also clear that many forgeries were made in order to be confirmed in charters of inspeximus and exemplifications.[46] The thirteenth century turns out to be a lively period for forgeries, at any rate of episcopal charters. Canterbury's Magna Carta of Thomas Becket (in fact 1235 x 1236), the forged charters of Ralph Luffa and Hilary for Lewes, Leofric of Exeter's confirmation of the foundation charter for St Michael's Mount (1224 x 1244) and Gerard of Hereford's elaborate confirmation for Gloucester can all be dated within the earlier decades of the thirteenth century.[47] Roger de Clinton's confirmation of pensions for Shrewsbury abbey was created in the thirteenth century; a forgery of Bartholomew of Exeter for Tavistock is probably from late in the thirteenth century.[48] Much of the output of the Rochester cathedral forgers is thirteenth-century, often late in that period.[49] Forgery in several areas continued into the fourteenth century.[50] Certainly the twelfth century saw sustained programmes of forgery, with some spurious episcopal *acta* as early as the reign of Stephen;[51] the Durham atelier was very active from the mid 1160s to the 1170s,[52] and the nuns of Wix created or recreated their archive between 1196 and 1199.[53] Nonetheless, the thirteenth century seems to have been much more productive.

Preliminary findings suggest, therefore, that in England episcopal charters were forged principally by those Benedictine houses which had been founded in the first three decades after the Norman Conquest. The forgers' principal intentions were to claim or to preserve grants of churches and tithes, and in

---

45 *EEA* ii, no. 6.
46 E.g. *EEA* vii, no. 4; 26, no. 4.
47 Cheney, 'Magna Carta Beati Thome', especially pp. 14–22 (*EEA* ii, no. 6); *Chichester Acta*, pp. 66–8; *EEA* xi, no. 2 and vii, no. 4. Battle's forged Stigand *actum* is early thirteenth century: see Searle, 'Battle', pp. 465–6.
48 *EEA* 14, no. 36; xi, no. 136.
49 *EEA* ii, nos 193–5, 304–5, and iii, nos 591–5 were forged in the thirteenth century; in *EEA* 18 this is also true of nos 7, 8, 27–30, 54, 89–90 (a few of these may be even later).
50 *EEA* ix, no. 63 and 16, nos 93 (version b) and 94.
51 *EEA* 15, no. 10; Barrow, 'How the Twelfth-Century Monks', pp. 60–9.
52 Bates, 'The Forged Charters', pp. 119–21.
53 Brooke, 'Episcopal Charters for Wix', especially pp. 52–8. Also twelfth century are *EEA* v, no. 29 (hand suggests last decade or so of the twelfth century: see plate I (b)), and *EEA* 28, nos 3, 21, 24, 32, 33, 43, 87, 88, and also the reworked version of no. 5. Searle dated Battle's forged Ralph Luffa charter to the third quarter of the twelfth century (Searle, 'Battle', pp. 461–2, 475–6).

more extreme cases the right to appoint and remove vicars from their churches without interference from the diocesan. Some monasteries, notably Benedictine houses situated in, or with endowments in, the diocese of York, claimed rights of ecclesiastical jurisdiction. Forgeries of post-Conquest episcopal *acta* began at least in the reign of Stephen, but became much more numerous in the last decade of the twelfth century and the early part of the thirteenth, and continued into the fourteenth century. They thus belong to a somewhat later generation than the productions of faked royal and Anglo-Saxon charters for which the older and wealthier Benedictine houses, such as Westminster and Malmesbury, are renowned.

Appendix I: List of forged episcopal *acta*

The views of the editor of each volume are given after the number of each *actum*; + refers to a charter which is spurious, ? + to a charter which is possibly spurious, and ed. to the editor. An asterisk indicates that the text of the charter no longer survives. In the first seven volumes of the *EEA* series it was editorial practice simply to calendar charters surviving only as copies of which accessible editions already existed, and in these cases references to the most recent editions are given below. Readers are referred to the apparatus and endnotes to each charter for explanation of the origins of the document in question; a few references to more recent publications are supplied here. *EEA* xi, no. 15 and xii, nos 202, 218, 280 and 323 and *Chichester Acta*, no. 8, occurring in the list below because their editors believed them to be spurious, are probably all genuine.

EEA i: *Lincoln 1067–1185*, ed. David Smith (London, 1980)
no. 2 (+ ed.); for text see J.W. Clarke, ed., *Liber memorandorum de Bernewelle* (Cambridge, 1907), p. 44, no. 14.

EEA ii: *Canterbury 1162–1190*, ed. C.R. Cheney with B.E. Jones (London, 1986)
no. 6 (+ ed.) Archbishop Thomas Becket for Christ Church Canterbury; for text, see Cheney, 'Magna Carta Beati Thome', pp. 22–4.
no. 14 (+ ed.); for text see A. Morey, *Bartholomew of Exeter, Bishop and Canonist: A Study in the Twelfth Century* (Cambridge, 1937), p. 154, no. 35.
no. 193 (+ ed.)
no. 194 (+ ed.)
no. 195 (+ ed.)
no. 232 (ed. questioned the validity of this charter, but identified the writing as that of a Christ Church scribe)
no. 304 (+ ed.)
no. 305 (+ ed.)

EEA iii: *Canterbury 1193–1205*, ed. C.R. Cheney with E. John (London, 1986)
no. 484 (+ ed.)
no. 591 (+ ed.); for text see *Registrum Roffense*, ed. John Thorpe (1769), pp. 444–5.
no. 592 (+ ed.); for text see *Registrum Roffense*, ed. John Thorpe (1769), pp. 441–4.
no. 593 (+ ed.)
no. 594 (+ ed.)

no. 595 (+ ed.); for text see *Registrum Roffense*, ed. John Thorpe (1769), pp. 104–6.

no. 650 (? + ed.)

EEA iv: *Lincoln 1186–1206*, ed. David Smith (London, 1986)
No apparent forgeries.

EEA v: *York 1070–1154*, ed. Janet Burton (Oxford, 1988)
no. 3 (+ ed.)

no. 5 (ed. thinks genuine) Archbishop Thomas I for Selby. Although the ed. does not comment on this, no. 5 appears to be essentially a copy of no. 4, also an act of Archbishop Thomas for Selby, with the addition of Hillam among the lands being granted, and the omission of the phrase *excepta Christianitatis causa* by which the archbishop retained ecclesiastical jurisdiction. No. 4 is presumably genuine. No. 5, a reworking of no. 4, is suspect. No. 4 is on left side of table below, no. 5 on right.

Notum volo fieri omnibus sancte matris Dei ecclesie cultoribus quod ego Thomas Eboracensis ecclesie Dei gratia archipresul, *de salute anime domini mei regis Willelmi pariterque mei necnon omnium* (?) *in Christo fidelium in futurum previdens, has terras Friston' et Salebyam* ab omni consuetudine liberas et quietas, *clericorum meorum consensu consilioque comuni, ecclesie que in honore beatissimi confessoris Germani in diocesi mea fundata est donaverim* ita *liberas* sicut superius dixi, excepta Christianitatis causa et celebratione anniversarii quod celebraturi sunt eiusdem ecclesie fratres per singulos annos pro peccatorum meorum remissione; *hoc autem rogo et humiliter meos successores* admoneo *ne hanc caritatis donationem violare vel adnullare aliquatenus presumant, set imperpetuum supradicte ecclesie eiusque servientibus pro remunerationis eterne gloria adiacere permittant. Huius donationis testes sunt* Odo Baiocensis episcopus *et alii*	*Notum volo fieri omnibus sancte matris ecclesie cultoribus quod ego Thomas Eboracensis ecclesie Dei gratia* archiepiscopus, *de salute anime domini mei regis Willelmi pariterque mei necnon omnium in Christo fidelium in futurum previdens, has terras,* Friston, Hillum, Salebiam, *clericorum meorum consensu consilioque comuni* ecclesie Sancti Petri Eboracensis, cenobiali *ecclesie* Salebiensi *que in honore beatissimi* Germani *confessoris in diocesi mea fundata est*, ab omnibus consuetudinibus tam ecclesiasticis quam aliis *liberas* et quietas in puram elemosinam *donaverim; hoc autem rogo et humiliter successores meos* commendo *ammonens* auctoritate divina pontificalique qua possum precipio *ne hanc caritatis donationem* a se vel a qualibet subposita persona minorari, *violari vel adnullari aliquatenus* pati *presumant, set* inperpetuum supradicte ecclesie et eius servientibus pro remunerationis eterne gloria et pro remissione peccatorum meorum *adiacere permittant. Huius donationis sunt* tam commonitores quam *testes* Willelmus de Percy, Erneis de Buron, Osbernus de Arches *et alii*

no. 17 (? + ed.); for text see *EYC* iii, no. 1465.

no. 21 (ed. accepts as genuine) Archbishop Thomas II for Selby; for text see *EYC* i, no. 46. This charter has some diplomatic features, for example a general address, that foreshadow later forms.

no. 23 (ed. accepts as genuine) Archbishop Thomas II for Worcester cathedral priory; for text see *Worcester Cartulary*, no. 264. This charter does not have anachronistic diplomatic forms, but it forms part of the dossier of documents built up by the monks of Worcester to make their claim to the church of Wolverhampton, and as such is not above suspicion.

no. 24 (ed. accepts as genuine) Archbishop Thomas II for Holy Trinity priory, York; for text see *EYC* vi, no. 8. Archbishop Thomas's order that his archdeacons and *ministri* should not interfere with Holy Trinity's possession of the church of Leeds is suspect. The probable occasion for the forgery of both this document and no. 29 below is a claim (see note to no. 24 for details) by Maurice de Gant of one third of the advowson of the church of Leeds against the priory of Holy Trinity in 1205.

no. 28 (? + ed.); for text, see *EYC* iii, no. 1468. The use of papally-inspired formulae in the arenga and narratio ('Iustis postulationibus celerem debemus prebere assensum. Inde est quod ad piam petitionem . . .') is noteworthy.

no. 29 (ed. accepts as genuine) Archbishop T(homas II) or T(hurstan) for Holy Trinity priory, York. The hand (see facsimile, ibid., plate I b), with its Gothic double-strokes for majuscule letters, cannot be earlier than the last two decades of the twelfth century. The reference to 'saving a competent vicarage' (*salva . . . competenti vicaria*) is too late for Thomas II, and probably also for Thurstan.

no. 37 (ed. notes doubts about royal charters closely linked with this one); for text see *EYC* ii, no. 1152.

no. 43 (? + ed.)

no. 50 (ed. accepts as genuine) Archbishop Thurstan for Guisborough priory; for text see *Cartularium prioratus de Gyseburne* ed. W. Brown (Surtees Society 86, 89, 1889–94), i, no. 5. For discussion see notes to *EEA* 20, nos 39, 43.

no. 57 (? + ed.). The wording of this charter is close to that of *EEA* 20, no. 74.

no. 67 (+ ed.); for text see *EYC* ii, no. 875.

no. 68 (? + ed.); for text see *EYC* ii, no. 876.

no. 69 (? + ed.); for text see *EYC* ii, no. 877.

no. 104 (? + ed.); for text see *EYC* ii, no. 879.

no. 121 (? + ed.)

no. 130 (ed. is hesitant); for text see *EYC* ii, no. 878. For comment, see notes to *EEA* v, no. 104 and 20, no. 107.

no. 131 (? + ed.); for text, which is a clumsily amplified version of no. 130, see *Cartularium abbathiae de Whiteby ordinis S. Benedicti*, ed. J.C. Atkinson, 2 vols (Surtees Society, 69, 72, 1879–81), i, no. 296.

EEA vi: *Norwich 1070–1214*, ed. Christopher Harper-Bill (Oxford, 1990)
- no. 4 (probably redrafted, ed.); for text see J.L. Fisher, ed. *Cartularium prioratus de Colne* (Essex Archaeological Society Occasional Publications 1, 1946), no. 14.
- no. 7 (probably redrafted, ed.)
- no. 11 (ed. accepts as genuine) Bishop Herbert Losinga for Norwich cathedral priory; for text see *Norwich Cathedral Charters*, no. 112. No. 11 has the same text as no. 12 below, but is acephalous, lacking the latter's invocation and *intitulatio* (the lack of the latter is unusual for an episcopal charter); no. 11, unlike no. 12, has no date and a much shorter witness list than no. 12, but including Waldric as royal chancellor rather than Roger, who occurs in no. 12. The arenga shared by nos 11 and 12 uses the same biblical quotations as the arenga to no. 13 (*Norwich Cathedral Charters*, no. 115, with facsimile of original, ibid., plate 3), which is genuine, though presumably a beneficiary production.
- no. 12 (ed. accepts as genuine) Bishop Herbert Losinga for Norwich cathedral priory, dated Windsor, 3 September 1101; for text see *Norwich Cathedral Charters*, no. 113. For discussion, see no. 11 above.
- no. 15 (ed. accepts as genuine) Bishop Herbert Losinga for Norwich cathedral priory; for text see *Norwich Cathedral Charters*, no. 107. This is a longer and suspect version of genuine no. 16 (*Norwich Cathedral Charters*, no. 108); it grants to a monk of Norwich cathedral priory the right to enjoin penances in the church of St Margaret, Lynn.
- no. 18 (ed. accepts as genuine) Bishop Herbert Losinga for Norwich cathedral priory; for text see *Norwich Cathedral Charters*, no. 110. It shows use of nos 14 and 17 (respectively *Norwich Cathedral Charters*, nos 111, 109)
- no. 21 (+ ed.)
- no. 22 (+ ed.)
- no. 39 (ed. accepts as genuine) Bishop Everard for Norwich cathedral priory; for text see *Norwich Cathedral Charters*, no. 119. There is a serious problem with the dating, commented on by the ed.
- no. 45 (ed. accepts as genuine) Bishop Everard for the abbey of St-Léonard-de-Noblat (Great Bricett priory). See review by M. Brett in *Journal of Theological Studies* new series 43 (1992), pp. 728–31, at pp. 730–1.
- no. 48 (ed. accepts as genuine) Bishop Everard for St Mary's priory, Thetford; charter is consistently in first person plural and the general address precedes the *intitulatio*, both rather unusual for a charter of the first half of the twelfth century (M. Brett, pers. comm.).
- no. 158 (+ ed.)

EEA vii: *Hereford 1079–1234*, ed. Julia Barrow (Oxford, 1993)
- no. 4 (+ ed.)
- no. 7 (+ ed.)

no. 10 (? + ed.)
no. 155 (+ ed.)

EEA viii: *Winchester 1070–1204*, ed. M.J. Franklin (Oxford, 1993)
no. 19 (ed. expresses hesitancy)
no. 20 (ed. thinks unlikely to be genuine)
no. 116 (+ ed.)
no. 118 (ed. thinks clause about free election of prior interpolated)
no. 131 (ed. raises questions about clauses concerning office of prior)
no. 132 (ed. hesitant: see note to no. 131)

EEA ix: *Winchester 1205–1238*, ed. Nicholas Vincent (Oxford, 1994)
no. 55 (* + ed.)
no. 63 (+ ed.)
no. 133 (ed. suggests that these letters are historical forgeries); for text see Roger of Wendover, *Chronica sive Flores Historiarum*, ed. H.O. Coxe, 5 vols (English Historical Society, 1841–4), iv, pp. 292–3, and Matthew Paris, *Chronica Majora*, ed. H.R. Luard, 7 vols (RS, 1884–9), iii, pp. 265–6, copied from Wendover.

EEA x: *Bath and Wells 1061–1205*, ed. Frances M.R. Ramsey (Oxford, 1995)
no. 10 (ed. accepts as genuine) Bishop Robert of Lewes for Bath cathedral priory, 1135. For discussion, see *Fasti* vii, p. 117.
no. 46 (ed. accepts as genuine) Bishop Robert of Lewes for Wells cathedral. For discussion, see *Fasti* vii, p. 119.
no. 50 (ed. accepts as genuine) Bishop Robert of Lewes for Wells cathedral, Wells, 4 November 1159. There are problems with the dating of this document, raised by the ed. in her note.
no. 98 (+ ed.)
no. 207 (+ ed.)

EEA xi: *Exeter 1046–1184*, ed. Frank Barlow (Oxford, 1996)
no. 2 (+ ed.); for text see *Mon. Ang.* vi pt ii, p. 989, and *The Cartulary of St Michael's Mount*, ed. P.L. Hull (Devon and Cornwall Record Society 5, 1962), pp. 2–3, no. 2.
no. 4 (ed. notes problems with document, and suspicions raised against it by other scholars)
no. 12 (ed. accepts as genuine) William de Warelwast for Barnstaple priory. The position of the address and the form of the notification look much later than the proposed dating limits of 1113 x 1119 and are not paralleled in any of William's other *acta*.
no. 15 (? + ed.) Quite possibly genuine: see article above at n. 13.
no. 136 (+ ed.); for text see *Mon. Ang.* ii, p. 498.

EEA xii: *Exeter 1186–1257*, ed. Frank Barlow (Oxford, 1996)
no. 202 (* ? + ed.)
no. 218 (* ? + ed.)
no. 280 (* ? + ed.)
no. 323 (* ? + ed.)
(Note: all four lost charters above may well have been genuine: see article above at n. 16).

EEA 13: *Worcester 1218–1268*, ed. Philippa M. Hoskin (Oxford, 1997)
No apparent forgeries.

EEA 14: *Coventry and Lichfield 1072–1159*, ed. M.J. Franklin (Oxford, 1997)
no. 4 (interpolated, ed.)
no. 11 (+ ed.)
no. 15 (+ ed.)
no. 35 (+ ed.)
no. 36 (+ ed.)
no. 64 (ed. thinks reworked in early thirteenth century)

EEA 15: *London 1076–1187*, ed. Falko Neininger (Oxford, 1999)
no. 10 (+ ed.)
no. 56 (+ ed.)
no. 76 (+ ed.)

EEA 16: *Coventry and Lichfield 1160–1182*, ed. M.J. Franklin (Oxford, 1998)
no. 80 (+ ed.)
no. 92 (+ ed.)
no. 93, version *b* (+ ed.; version *a* is genuine). For partial facsimiles of the two pretended original exemplars of version *b*, see ibid., plate III.
no. 94 (+ ed.). For a partial facsimile of the pretended original, see ibid., plate III.

EEA 17: *Coventry and Lichfield 1183–1208*, ed. M.J. Franklin (Oxford, 1998)
no. 22 (+ ed.)
no. 58A (+ ed., though noting that it may instead be a genuine charter of Bishop Hugh de Pattishall)
Appendix: no. VI (+ ed.)

EEA 18: *Salisbury 1078–1217*, ed. Brian Kemp (Oxford, 1999)
no. 21 (? + ed.); for text see *Worcester Cartulary*, no. 266, and F.J. Kealey, *Roger of Salisbury Viceroy of England* (Berkeley, Los Angeles and London, 1972), pp. 264–5.
no. 142 (+ ed.)
no. 147 (+ ed.)

EEA 19: *Salisbury 1217–1228*, ed. Brian Kemp (Oxford, 2000)
No apparent forgeries

EEA 20: *York 1154–1181*, ed. Marie Lovatt (Oxford, 2000)
no. 15 (+ ed.)
no. 31 (? + ed.)
no. 39 (? + ed.)
no. 41 (ed. expresses suspicion)
no. 43 (? + ed.)
no. 44 (? + ed.)
no. 73 (? + ed.)

EEA 21: *Norwich 1215–1243*, ed. Christopher Harper-Bill (Oxford, 2000)
No apparent forgeries.

EEA 22: *Chichester 1215–1253*, ed. Philippa M. Hoskin (Oxford, 2001)
No apparent forgeries.

EEA 23: *Chichester 1254–1305*, ed. Philippa M. Hoskin (Oxford, 2001)
Appendix I: Acta of the Bishops of Chichester 1091–1207
no. 3 (ed. notes the possibility that this is spurious)

EEA 24: *Durham 1153–1195*, ed. M.G. Snape (Oxford, 2002)
no. 6 (* + ed.)
no. 60 (* + ed.)
no. 103 (+ ed.)

EEA 25: *Durham 1196–1237*, ed. M.G. Snape (Oxford, 2002)
no. 188 (* + ed.)

EEA 26: *London 1189–1228*, D.P. Johnson (Oxford, 2003)
no. 4 (ed. notes that the diplomatic is not paralleled in the *acta* of the three bishops issuing the charter)

EEA 27: *York 1189–1212*, ed. Marie Lovatt (Oxford, 2004)
no. 8 (? + ed.)
no. 36 (?+ ed.)
no. 38 (? + ed.)
no. 45 (ed. notes unusual combination of witnesses)
no. 95 (? + ed.)

EEA 28: *Canterbury 1070–1136*, ed. Martin Brett and Joseph A. Gribbin (Oxford, 2004)
no. 1 (+ ed.)
no. 2 (* + ed.)

no. 3 (+ ed.)
no. 4 (* + ed.)
no. 5, reworked version (+ ed.)
no. 7 (+ ed.)
no. 8 (+ ed.)
no. 20 (+ ed.)
no. 21 (ed. notes relationship of this text to a suspect charter)
no. 23 (ed. voices suspicion: this text is closely linked with EEA vi, nos 11–12)
no. 24 (ed. is uneasy)
no. 27 (+ ed.)
no. 28 (+ ed.)
no. 29 (+ ed.)
no. 30 (+ ed.)
no. 31 (ed. is uneasy)
no. 32 (+ ed.)
no. 33 (+ ed.)
no. 43 (+ ed.)
no. 54 (+ ed.)
no. 60 (* ed. voices suspicion)
no. 75 (ed. is suspicious)
no. 76 (+ ed.)
no. 87 (ed. expresses unease)
no. 88 (+ ed.)
no. 89 (+ ed.)
no. 90 (+ ed.)

EEA 29: Durham 1241–1283, ed. Philippa M. Hoskin (Oxford, 2005)
No apparent forgeries

EEA 30: Carlisle 1133–1292, ed. David M. Smith (Oxford, 2005)
No apparent forgeries

Acta Stephani Langton
No apparent forgeries

Chichester Acta
no. 1 (+ ed.). See also Searle, 'Battle', pp. 465–6, 478–80.
no. 5 (ed. accepts as genuine) Bishop Ralph Luffa for Battle abbey [1107 x 1123]. The way in which the various items being confirmed are introduced, including the position of the clause about the appointment of a vicar after a *volo et precipio* clause, suggests interpolation.
no. 6 (+ ed.). See also Searle, 'Battle', pp. 465–6, 475–6.
no. 8 (ed. notes that this is unusually early for an indulgence) Bishop Ralph Luffa for Chichester cathedral [1091 x 1123]. In a charter whose

diplomatic forms are those of the thirteenth century Bishop Ralph grants remission of 40 days' penance to all those visiting the cathedral at Pentecost and on the feast of St Faith and on the octaves of these feasts. In fact this is likely to be a genuine indulgence issued by Bishop Ralph de Neville (1224–44) for Chichester cathedral granting remission of 40 days' penance to all those visiting the cathedral on the Feast of Relics, which at Chichester was held on 13 October (*EEA* 20, no. 61, where described as lost), since the octave of St Faith's day (6 October) is 13 October.

no. 10 (+ ed.). See also *Fasti* v, pp. 7, 12, 20.

no. 11 (+ ed.)

no. 14 (ed. accepts as genuine) Bishop Seffrid I for Battle abbey [1125 x 1145]. This charter is similar in form to no. 5 above. The witness list is very similar to that for no. 13, also of Seffrid I for Battle, which E. Searle judged to be a forgery because she thought it granted exemption, though in fact it does not (Searle, 'Battle', 464–5); she considered that the witness list of no. 14 might have served as a basis for that of no. 13, though it is equally possible that it was the other way round.

no. 15 (ed. expresses some doubts)

no. 39 (+ ed.)

no. 40 (+ ed.)

DEC

no. 3, with later variant version no. 3a (both + ed.)

no. 4, with later variant version no. 4a (both + ed.)

no. 5 (+ ed.)

no. 6 (+ ed.)

no. 7 (+ ed.)

no. 10 (+ ed.)

no. 23 (ed. thinks possibly reworked; diplomatic is poor)

no. 33 (ed. thinks problematic). See also note to *EEA* 24, no. 103.

no. 36 (ed. thinks problematic)

no. 37 (ed. thinks problematic)

no. 38 (ed. thinks sealing attachment anachronistic)

no. 39 (ed. thinks sealing attachment anachronistic)

Appendix II:
Alphabetical list of ecclesiastical beneficiaries and their forgeries

Barnstaple priory (Cluniac; daughter house of St-Martin-des-Champs; founded c.1107) (*EEA* xi, no. 12)

Barnwell priory (Augustinian; founded at Cambridge according to an unreliable tradition c.1092; moved to Barnwell 1112) (*EEA* i, no. 2; 28, no. 60)

Bath cathedral priory (Benedictine; founded c.963 as abbey and 1090 as cathedral priory) (*EEA* x, no. 10)

Battle abbey (Benedictine; founded 1067) (*EEA* 23, App. 1, no. 3; 26, no. 4; 28, no. 33; *Chichester Acta*, nos 1, 5, 6, 14)

Bridlington priory (Augustinian; founded before 1114) (*EEA* v, no. 37)

Buckland priory (originally founded c.1170 for Augustinian canons; dissolved c.1180 and refounded for Hospitaller nuns) (*EEA* x, nos 98, 207, for Hospitallers)

Buildwas abbey (Cistercian; founded 8 August 1135) (*EEA* 16, no. 11)

Canterbury, Christ Church cathedral priory (Benedictine from early 11th century) (*EEA* ii, no. 6)

Canterbury, St Gregory's priory (founded as college of priests before 1086; Augustinian from c.1123) (*EEA* 28, nos 1, 20)

Canterbury, hospital of St John the Baptist (founded before 1086) (*EEA* 28, no. 2)

Catesby priory (nuns; Benedictine in 12th century; Cistercian in 13th century; founded c.1175) (*EEA* 27, no. 8)

Chester abbey (Benedictine; founded 1092) (*EEA* 28, no. 21)

Chichester cathedral chapter (secular foundation) (*Chichester Acta*, nos 8, 15; both genuine)

Colchester abbey (Benedictine; founded 1096/7) (*EEA* 15, no. 10)

Colne priory (Benedictine; founded before 1107) (*EEA* vi, no. 4; 28, no. 43)

Combermere abbey (Cistercian; founded 3 November 1133) (*EEA* 16, no. 15)

Crediton minster (secular) (*EEA* xi, no. 15; probably genuine)

Darley abbey (Augustinian; founded 1137 in Derby; moved to Darley c.1146) (*EEA* 17, no. 22)

Durham cathedral priory (Benedictine from 28 May 1083) (*EEA* v, nos 3, 43; 20, no. 15; 28, no. 3; *DEC*, nos 3, 4, 5, 6, 7, 10, 36, 37)

Exeter, St Nicholas' priory (Benedictine; dependency of Battle; founded 1087) (*EEA* ii, no. 14; xi, no. 4)

Eye priory (Benedictine; dependency of Bernai; founded c.1080) (*EEA* vi, no. 7)

Fountains abbey (Cistercian; founded 27 December 1132) (*EEA* 20, no. 31)
Glastonbury abbey (Benedictine from 940 x 946) (*EEA* 28, no. 4)
Gloucester abbey (Benedictine from 1022) (*EEA* vii, no. 4, see also Hereford St Guthlac's; see also *St Davids Episcopal Acta*, nos 1, 9, and probably also nos 10, 13, 14, 16: see review by Nicholas Vincent in *History*, 84 (1999), pp. 511–12, at p. 512).
Goldcliff priory (Benedictine; dependency of Bec; founded 1113) (*EEA* iii, no. 484)
Great Bricett priory (Augustinian; dependency of St-Léonard-de-Noblat; founded 1114 x 1119) (*EEA* vi, no. 45)
Guisborough priory (Augustinian; founded 1119) (*EEA* v, no. 50; 20, nos 39, 41, 43, 44; 24, no. 60)
Hereford, St Guthlac's priory (Benedictine dependency of Gloucester; founded as priory of St Peter's c.1100; merger with St Guthlac's and move to new site 1143) (*EEA* vii, nos 7, 155)
Kirkstall abbey (Cistercian; founded at Barnoldswick 19 May 1147; moved to Kirkstall 19 May 1152) (*EEA* v, no. 121)
Launde priory (Augustinian; founded 1119 x 1125) (*EEA* 27, no. 36)
Leeds priory (Augustinian; founded 1119) (*EEA* 28, nos 75, 76)
Lewes priory (Cluniac; founded 1077) (*EEA* 27, no. 38; *Chichester Acta*, nos 10, 11, 39, 40)
Lichfield cathedral chapter (secular) (*EEA* 16, no. 64)
Liskeard, hospital of St Mary Magdalene (*EEA* 12, nos 202, 218, 280, 323; all probably genuine)
Llanthony priory (Secunda) (Augustinian; founded 1135/6) (*EEA* vii, no. 10)
Monkbretton priory (Cluniac; founded 1153 x 1155) (*EEA* 27, no. 45)
Newcastle, St Bartholomew's priory (Benedictine nuns; founded by 1086) (*EEA* 25, no. 103; *DEC*, no. 33)
Newminster abbey (Cistercian; founded 5 January 1138) (*DEC*, nos 38, 39)
Norwich cathedral priory (Benedictine; founded 1096 x 1101) (*EEA* vi, nos 11, 12, 15, 16, 18, 39; 28 no. 23)
Nostell priory (Augustinian; founded c.1114) (*EEA* v, no. 17)
Nuneaton priory (Fontevraldine nuns; daughter house of Fontevrault; founded after 1147 at Kintbury; moved c.1155 to Nuneaton) (*EEA* 16, no. 80)
Pontefract priory (Cluniac; daughter house of La Charité-sur-Loire; founded c.1090) (*EEA* v, nos 28, 57; 20, no. 73)
Rochester cathedral priory (Benedictine from 1080) (*EEA* ii, nos 193, 194, 195, 304, 305; iii, nos 591, 592, 593, 594, 595; 28, nos 5 (reworked version only), 7, 8, 24, 27, 28, 29, 30, 54, 87, 88, 89, 90)
St Michael's Mount priory (Benedictine; dependency of Mont-St-Michel; founded c.1087 x 1091) (*EEA* xi, no. 2)
St Neots priory (Benedictine; founded 975 x 984) (*EEA* 28, no. 31)
St Valéry abbey (Benedictine from late tenth century) (*EEA* 28, no. 32)

Selby abbey (Benedictine; founded 1069 x 1070 from Auxerre) (*EEA* v, nos 5, 21)
Shrewsbury abbey (Benedictine; founded c.1083 x 1087) (*EEA* 14, nos 35, 36; 16, no. 92)
Southampton, God's House (hospital) (*EEA* ix, no. 55)
Southwark, St Mary Overy priory (Augustinian; founded 1106) (*EEA* ix, no. 63)
Stafford, St Thomas' priory (Augustinian; founded 1173 x 1175) (*EEA* 16, nos 93 version b, 94)
Stanley abbey (Cistercian; daughter house of Quarr; founded 1151 at Loxwell; moved 1154 to Stanley) (*EEA* 18, no. 142)
Tavistock abbey (Benedictine; pre-Conquest) (*EEA* xi, no. 136)
Thetford priory (Cluniac; founded 1103 x 1104) (*EEA* vi, nos 21, 22, 48)
Thurgarton priory (Augustinian; founded 1119 x 1139) (*EEA* 17, no. 58A; Appendix I, no. VI)
Twynham (Christ Church) priory (Augustinian from c.1150) (*EEA* viii, nos 116, 118)
Wallingford priory (Benedictine; dependency of St Albans; founded c.1087 x 1089) (*EEA* 18, no. 147)
Wells cathedral chapter (secular) (*EEA* x, nos 46, 50)
Whitby abbey (Benedictine; founded as priory before 1077; moved to Lastingham and then Hackness; back at Whitby by early 1090s; abbey from 1109) (*EEA* v, nos 67, 68, 69, 104, 130, 131)
Winchester cathedral priory (Benedictine from 964) (*EEA* viii, nos 19, 20, 131, 132)
Wix priory (Benedictine nuns; founded ?1123 x 1133) (*EEA* ii, no. 232; iii, no. 650; vi, no. 158; xv, nos 56, 76)
Worcester cathedral priory (Benedictine; pre-Conquest) (*EEA* v no. 23; 14, no. 4; 18, no. 21)
York, Holy Trinity priory (Benedictine; dependency of Marmoutier; founded 1089) (*EEA* v, nos 24, 29)
York, St Mary's abbey (Benedictine; founded 1088 x 1089) (*EEA* 17, no. 95)

Lay beneficiaries:
Ranulf Flambard's nephew Richard (*DEC*, no. 23)
John Boteler (*EEA* 24, no. 6; 25, no. 188)

Literary forgery: Roger of Wendover (*EEA* ix, no. 133)

Pastors and Masters: The Beneficed Clergy of North-East Lincolnshire, 1290–1340

NICHOLAS BENNETT

The little nunnery of Greenfield lay a few miles to the north-west of the Lincolnshire town of Alford. Carrying out a visitation here in 1293, Bishop Oliver Sutton found that the prioress, Christine of Owmby, was ill-suited for either the spiritual or the temporal rule of the house. Shortly afterwards, he issued a commission to the prior of Markby and to the rector of Aylesby, Master Simon de Luda, to examine and confirm the next prioress to be elected by the convent. Events did not altogether proceed as planned, however, because Master Simon was ill and unable to travel to Greenfield. To avoid prolonging the vacancy therefore, the prior, with the prioress-elect Elizabeth of Harrington, decided that if the rector could not come to them, they would go to him, and the examination duly took place, in Master Simon's presence, in Aylesby church.[1]

On the surface, this might seem to be a purely routine item of diocesan business. There is, however, an element of what Sherlock Holmes might have called 'the curious incident of the dog in the night-time'. The popular view of the beneficed clergy of late medieval England is that they were ill-educated absentees who abandoned their parishioners for the easier life of a chantry or a prebend. Yet here we find an incumbent who was educated, resident and, despite his temporary indisposition, active. This is a long way from Langland:

> I haue be prest and persoun passynge thretti winter,
> 3ete can I neither solfe ne singe ne seyntes lyues rede;
> But I can fynde in a felde or in a fourlonge an hare,
> Better yan in *beatus vir* or in *beati omnes*
> Construe oon clause wel and kenne it to my parochienes.[2]

This portrait of 'Parson Sloth' encouraged the belief, at one time widely

---

[1] Rosalind M.T. Hill (ed.), *The Rolls and Register of Bishop Oliver Sutton 1280–1299* i (LRS 39, 1948), pp. 199–200; iv (LRS 52, 1958), pp. 118–19; *Heads* ii, p. 566.
[2] J.A.W. Bennett (ed.), *Langland, Piers Plowman: The Prologue and Passus I–VII of the B text*, corrected reprint (Oxford, 1979), lines 422–6.

accepted, that the average incumbent was lazy and ignorant, neglecting his spiritual duties in favour of his rhymes of Robin Hood and his love of the chase. Three complaints in particular recur constantly: the parish clergy were ill-educated, they failed to proceed to the priesthood, preferring to remain in minor orders, and they were absentees, enjoying the fruits of their livings but not performing their spiritual duties in person.

The widespread ignorance of the clergy is a common theme. Langland's image of the unlettered priest, stumbling over his Latin, is echoed by Chaucer and Hoccleve. The Biblical metaphor of 'the blind leading the blind' (Matt. 15:14) was used by many writers, not least by Archbishop Pecham in his tract *Ignorantia sacerdotum* (1281): 'The ignorance of priests casts the people down into the ditch of error, and the foolishness and lack of learning of clerics . . . is all the worse when it leads to error instead of knowledge.' While lack of education made it difficult for unlettered incumbents to say Mass and instruct their parishioners through the sacrament of penance, lack of orders made it impossible for others to perform these duties at all. Episcopal registers reveal how few of those being instituted to rectories in the thirteenth century had proceeded to the priesthood. Dr Moorman calculated that of those instituted by Bishop Richard Gravesend of Lincoln (1258–79), only 16 per cent were priests. Other incumbents, of course, were unable to perform their spiritual functions for the simple reason that they were not present to do so. Absenteeism was indeed another common complaint, and Wyclif's trenchant criticism of those who haunted the Roman curia seeking yet more benefices and privileges while being maintained by the alms of their poor subjects must have fallen on fruitful soil.[3]

Such a picture of the medieval clergy is a gloomy one, but how far is it justified? Much of the evidence for it is impressionistic, consisting of literary stereotypes, or the strictures of reformers seeking to substantiate their criticisms. A more positive view was put forward in W.A. Pantin's Birkbeck Lectures on the fourteenth-century church, published in 1955, and this has been amplified in a number of subsequent studies.[4] At a popular level,

---

[3] John Shinners and William J. Dohar (eds), *Pastors and the Care of Souls in Medieval England* (Notre Dame Texts in Medieval Culture IV, 1998), pp. 18, 127; J.R.H. Moorman, *Church Life in England in the Thirteenth Century* (Cambridge, 1955), p. 36.

[4] The pessimistic view of the medieval clergy colours much of the writing of G.G. Coulton, for example *The Medieval Village* (Cambridge, 1925), pp. 258–61; see also G.R. Owst, *Preaching in Medieval England* (Cambridge, 1926), pp. 25–47, and Moorman, *Church Life in England*, pp. 24–37. Among those suggesting a more balanced picture, see W.A. Pantin, *The English Church in the Fourteenth Century* (Cambridge, 1955); J.H. Denton, 'The Competence of the Parish Clergy in Thirteenth-Century England', in *The Church and Learning in Later Medieval Society: Essays in Honour of Barrie Dobson*, ed. Caroline M. Barron and Jenny Stratford (Donington, 2002), pp. 273–85; and C.N.L. Brooke, 'Chaucer's Parson and Edmund Gonville: Contrasting Roles of Fourteenth Century Incumbents', in *Studies in Clergy and Ministry in Medieval England*, ed. David M. Smith (York, 1991), pp. 1–19.

however, this re-assessment has yet to be noticed. More work needs to be done to examine in detail the wealth of evidence for the careers of incumbents such as Simon de Luda, particularly the copious material surviving in bishops' registers. The aim of this paper is to suggest the value of a prosopographical study of the beneficed clergy of medieval England in attempting to establish a more rounded picture than the traditional view outlined above.

As David Smith's admirable *Guide* makes clear, surviving episcopal registers exist by the end of the thirteenth century for most English dioceses.[5] In the case of the diocese of Lincoln, where the keeping of such registers appears to have originated around 1214, the late thirteenth and early fourteenth centuries saw record-keeping reach new heights of thoroughness and efficiency. Under Bishop Oliver Sutton (1280–99) the practice of registering business on parchment rolls was superseded by the use of the volume or codex. The survival from 1290 of general memoranda in addition to the records of institutions and collations may well be attributed to this development. Sutton's successor, John Dalderby (1300–20) continued this policy, with separate volumes being used for institutions and memoranda. The long tenure of the office of registrar by John de Schalby (described by Rosalind Hill as 'one of the ablest registrars who ever served a bishop'), for eighteen years under Sutton and eight years under Dalderby, contributed in no small part to the high standards with which these registers were maintained. A further refinement in record-keeping at Lincoln was introduced in the episcopate of Henry Burghersh (1320–40), with the classification of the memoranda register by the use of different sections for the various types of licences and commissions most commonly issued.[6]

The three registers of Sutton, Dalderby and Burghersh thus provide a wealth of information about the beneficed clergy for the period 1290 to 1340. They not only establish who held which living and for how long: they also provide, through the grant of licences or specific commissions, much additional detail about the careers of many of these incumbents. Used in conjunction with other sources – the records of central government, papal letters, and local archives – it would be possible to build up a more detailed and perhaps more realistic picture of the rectors and vicars of the period than the traditional view can provide. By looking at a small sample of the evidence of these registers, this paper will attempt to show what such a study might achieve.

---

[5] David M. Smith, *Guide to Bishops' Registers of England and Wales* (London, 1981).
[6] *Rolls and Register of Bishop Sutton* i (LRS 39, 1948), pp. xiii–xv; ibid. iii (LRS 48, 1954), pp. xxviii–xxix, lxxxvi; Smith, *Guide to Bishops' Registers*, pp. 108–11; *The Book of John de Schalby*, ed. J.H. Srawley (Lincoln, 1949), pp. 15, 18.

The Benefices

In order to understand the context in which the beneficed clergy lived and worked, it is essential first to examine the patronage and income of their parishes. The sample used here comprises the incumbents of the three deaneries of Grimsby, Yarborough and Walshcroft, covering the period from 1290 to 1340. These three deaneries were situated at the most northerly point of the vast diocese of Lincoln. One of the largest sees in Western Europe, Lincoln stretched from the Humber estuary down to the River Thames and included within its boundaries 8 archdeaconries, 75 deaneries and approximately 1,928 parochial benefices. The sample deaneries formed part of the large Archdeaconry of Lincoln, with 104 of its 597 benefices made up of 52 rectories, 42 vicarages and 10 curacies in appropriated benefices where no vicarage had been ordained.

The pattern of parish churches in north-east Lincolnshire had developed in a similar way to the rest of lowland England. A small number of Anglo-Saxon minsters – large churches, of which Caistor was undoubtedly one, serving the pastoral needs of a wide area – had been overlaid by the subsequent foundation of numerous 'proprietary' churches by landowners on their own estates. There was normally one church per village as a result of this development, but in some cases divided holdings had caused the benefice to be split into portions. Examples of such division could be found all over the diocese, but there appears to have been something in the structure of land tenure in north-east Lincolnshire that made the practice more extreme here than elsewhere. Division of a church into two parts, as at South Ferriby, or the two-thirds/one-third split at Croxton or at Stainton-le-Vale, was not uncommon. More unusual was the fragmentation of a church into fourths (Thorganby) or even sixths (Nettleton, until its reunion in the possession of Sixhills Priory, and Brocklesby).[7]

Elsewhere, the presence of two landowners in the same village resulted in the foundation of two separate churches, as at Binbrook (St Mary and St Gabriel) or South Kelsey (St Mary and St Nicholas). By the early twelfth century, however, the process of creating new parishes seems largely to have halted. The rights of existing churches to tithes and offerings were jealously guarded, and parish boundaries were more precisely established. Outlying settlements such as Howsham in the parish of Cadney might be provided with a chapel but this would remain dependent on the parish church. The

---

[7] For the number and distribution of benefices in the diocese, see N.H. Bennett, 'The Beneficed Clergy in the Diocese of Lincoln during the Episcopate of Henry Burghersh, 1320–1340' (unpublished York University D.Phil thesis, 1989), chapter II, passim; for Caistor, see D.M. Owen, *Church and Society in Medieval Lincolnshire* (Lincoln, 1971), pp. 1–2. The fragmentation of churches is discussed in *Transcripts of Charters relating to the Gilbertine Houses*, ed. F.M. Stenton (LRS 18, 1922), pp. xxiii–xxiv.

incumbent of Searby was bound to provide a chaplain to celebrate divine service daily in the chapel of Owmby, except on the feasts of Easter, All Saints and Christmas, when all were to attend the mother church. Dependent chapels also fulfilled a role in the spiritual provision of towns. The parish church of St Peter in Barton-upon-Humber was augmented by the substantial chapel of St Mary, and in Grimsby, alongside the two parish churches of St Mary and St James, the gild chapel of St John de la Boure was in existence by 1325.[8]

Although the proprietary origins of most parish churches had placed them in lay ownership, the reform movement of the eleventh century, emphasising the separation of the Church from worldly affairs, gradually brought them much more closely under the authority of the diocesan bishop. During the twelfth century, lay proprietary rights were effectively extinguished by canon law and secular lords, unable to profit directly from their churches, increasingly gave them to ecclesiastical institutions. In 1115 Walter de Gant gave St Peter's church at Barton-upon-Humber to Bardney Abbey. The trend can be traced clearly in the endowment of Newhouse Abbey, founded about 1143 by Peter of Goxhill. His original gift included the church of Habrough and a sixth part of that of Brocklesby. To these were subsequently added the churches of East Halton (granted by Ralph de Halton), Killingholme (by Nicholas d'Arcy) and Kirmington (by Geoffrey de Newhouse), besides other churches further afield.[9]

This transfer of churches from lay into ecclesiastical hands meant that the patronage of benefices in later medieval England was predominantly in the hands of religious houses, cathedral chapters and prebendaries. A survey of benefices in the diocese of Lincoln in 1320 reveals that overall nearly two-thirds (65 per cent) of them were in ecclesiastical patronage. This pattern was closely reflected in two of the three north-eastern deaneries (Grimsby with 64 per cent and Walshcroft with 66 per cent) but in the deanery of Yarborough the proportion of ecclesiastical patrons rose even higher, to 87 per cent.[10]

---

[8] For Barton-upon-Humber, see G. Platts, *Land and People in Medieval Lincolnshire* (Lincoln, 1985), pp. 189–90, 221; for Grimsby, see S.H. Rigby, *Medieval Grimsby: Growth and Decline* (Hull, 1993), p. 5. The chapel of St John de la Boure was being constructed or repaired in 1325 when timber and boards intended to be used for its fabric were stolen from the church of St James (LAO, Bishop's Register V, fol. 383v); for its gild connections, see *Records of Plays and Players in Lincolnshire 1300–1585*, ed. S.J. Kahrl (Oxford, 1974), pp. xxvi, 10 (I am indebted to Professor Jim Stokes for this reference).

[9] Dorothy Owen, 'The English Church in Eastern England, 1066–1100', in *A History of Lincoln Minster*, ed. Dorothy Owen (Cambridge, 1994), p. 8; A. Hamilton Thompson, 'Notes on the History of Bardney Abbey', A[ssociated] A[rchitectural] S[ocieties] R[eports and] P[apers] xxxii (1913–14), pp. 42, 54; H.M. Colvin, *The White Canons in England* (Oxford, 1951), pp. 46–7.

[10] For details of the survey, see Bennett, 'The Beneficed Clergy' i, pp. 166–8.

Among the ecclesiastical patrons, the largest single category was the Augustinian houses, with twenty-four benefices in their gift. Of these, Wellow by Grimsby had the largest number (8), followed by Thornton (5), Elsham (4) and Thornholme (3). Alien priories held 14 advowsons in the district, notably the Premonstratensian abbey of Beauport in Brittany which possessed 9 churches centred on its cell at Ravendale, all of them given by Alan son of Henry, earl of Brittany.[11] English Premonstratensian houses held 8 benefices (of which Newhouse had 6) and houses of nuns held another 8. Other orders represented among the religious patrons in this area were the Gilbertines (7 benefices), Benedictines (6) and the Hospitallers (1).

The lay patrons can be classified into gentry (16 benefices), the baronage (8) and the Crown (4). Gentry families typically held a single advowson, as did John de Heyling (Healing), John Malet (Irby), Nicholas Malmeyns (Rothwell) or John de Lasseles (Swallow). In this class, Richard de Buslingthorp was unusual in holding 3 advowsons – Wrawby, Stainton-le-Vale and (just outside this group of deaneries) Buslingthorpe, where his effigy in brass may still be seen. Among the members of the baronage, Gerard de Chauncy likewise held a single advowson (Swinhope). By contrast, the living of Grainsby was one of 6 (all in Lincolnshire) held by Robert Welles, and the 2 benefices (North Cotes and North Thoresby) of which Thomas, earl of Lancaster, was patron represented a tiny fraction of the 18 livings in his gift scattered all over the diocese, not to mention those beyond its boundaries.

The transfer of an advowson from lay into ecclesiastical hands was frequently, though not inevitably, followed by the appropriation of its rectorial endowment of glebe, tithes and other dues to its new patron. Of the 104 benefices in these three deaneries, exactly half had been appropriated by 1320. In 42 of these benefices, a vicarage had been ordained, providing security of tenure and a guaranteed source of revenue for the incumbent. The remaining 10 livings were curacies – churches that had been appropriated but were not endowed with a vicarage. Such curacies included Melton Ross (appropriated to the prebendary of Scamblesby in Lincoln Cathedral), Usselby (appropriated to Elsham Priory) and East Ravendale (appropriated to the nunnery of St Leonard, Grimsby).

Each parish church having been individually founded and endowed, the values of the benefices naturally varied from one to another. For the period under scrutiny, 1290 to 1340, the principal source for the study of ecclesiastical revenues is the 1291 Taxation of Pope Nicholas IV. The drawbacks of this evidence are well known; all that has been attempted here is to establish the comparative values of the churches of these three north-eastern deaneries in relation to those in the rest of the diocese.[12] Looking at the mean

---

[11] *EEA* iv, pp. 147–8.
[12] J.H. Denton, 'The Valuation of the Ecclesiastical Benefices in England and Wales in 1291–2', *Historical Research* lxvi (1993), pp. 231–50. For the present analysis, the

value of benefices in these deaneries, there is a striking contrast between Grimsby, where it was £12, and the other two deaneries, where the mean value of livings failed to reach the figure (6 marks, or £4) below which a church was exempt from the taxation. The mean value in the deanery of Grimsby was exceeded by only five others among the seventy-five deaneries in the whole diocese. At the other end of the scale, Walshcroft and Yarborough were among the fourteen poorest deaneries in the see. Taking the three north-eastern deaneries together, nearly one-third (34 out of 104) of benefices were assessed at more than £10. All but one of these were rectories (the vicarage of Barton-upon-Humber being the sole exception at £17 6s 8d) and they were divided almost equally between those in lay (18) and those in ecclesiastical (16) patronage. These richer livings can be contrasted with the 42 benefices that fell below the £4 level, of which all save one (a fourth part of Thorganby in the gift of the Kyme family) were in the gift of ecclesiastical patrons.

What can this survey of benefices in north-east Lincolnshire contribute to an understanding of the clergy who served them? Two points in particular emerge from it. First, nearly two-thirds of the patrons were essentially local, either members of the local gentry, such as the Motekan family of Newton by Toft, or religious houses situated in or just outside the area – Wellow by Grimsby, Newhouse, Nun Cotham, Thornton, Elsham or Sixhills. Such patrons were in a position to know whether pastoral care in a parish was not being provided, or whether the incumbent was failing in his duty in some other way. Second, the value of many of the churches in the area was comparatively low. With a mean assessment of £6 13s 4d in the 1291 Taxation, the majority of benefices in these deaneries were unlikely to attract the covetous attention of pluralist clergy seeking to acquire rich livings.

The Clergy

The criticisms of the clergy of late medieval England fall under four heads: there were too many foreigners, too many incumbents failed to proceed to the priesthood and thus lacked the qualification needed for their pastoral duties, they were as a class ill-educated, and there was amongst them widespread absenteeism and pluralism.

The belief that English benefices were being given away to foreign clerks was strongly held. A petition of 1307 at the parliament of Carlisle complained that the pope was granting dignities, prebends and churches to

printed edition of the Taxation, *Taxatio Ecclesiastica Angliae et Walliae Auctoritate P. Nicholai IV c.1291*, ed. T. Astle, S. Ayscough and J. Caley (Record Commission, 1802), has been compared with the late thirteenth-century manuscript of the assessment in the archives of the Dean and Chapter of Lincoln (LAO, D & C A/1/11). See also Bennett, 'The Beneficed Clergy' i, pp. 141–60.

aliens, and prophesied all manner of evils as a result. The king himself wrote to the pope in 1343, claiming that 'Christian worship is diminished, the cure of souls neglected . . . [and] the treasure of our realm is exported to foreigners'.[13] Were these fears and claims justified? Where did the clergy instituted to these benefices come from? It is possible to use the evidence of toponymics, which in the early fourteenth century still referred to the birthplace of the bearer, to throw some light on this question. The main difficulty arises from the more commonly recurring place-names, such as Kirkby or Carlton.[14] This problem can partially be overcome through the gathering of biographical details for individual clergy, some of which may well link a particular individual to a specific place. For example, two successive rectors of Wold Newton possessed the surname Willoughby: Hugh (1279–91) and Philip (1291–1306). The 1334 lay subsidy lists eight places called Willoughby, five of them in Lincolnshire. In 1291, however, Hugh moved to the rectory of Willoughby in the Marsh, near Alford, to which he was presented by William of Willoughby, whose wife, Alice, was the niece of Anthony Bek, bishop of Durham and patron of Wold Newton. This network of patronage and family connections clearly identifies the provenance of these two incumbents. A survey of clergy instituted to livings throughout the diocese during the five years from 1320 to 1325 showed that, of those whose places of origin could be identified, nearly two-thirds (63 per cent) came from within the diocese and two-fifths (41 per cent) from the same archdeaconry in which they held their benefice.[15]

In the three north-eastern deaneries, it has been possible to establish the provenance of 197 of the 361 incumbents who held livings there during the period 1290–1340. Of these, 156 (79 per cent) came from within the diocese itself, 144 (73 per cent) from Lincolnshire and 80 (40 per cent) from the three deaneries under study. Local names abound: successive vicars of Cuxwold were Thomas of Kirmington (1288–1318) and Thomas of Habrough (1318–49); the vicarage of West Ravendale was held by Richard of Great Cotes, Thomas of Fillingham, Lambert of Caistor and John of Barnoldby. Some incumbents were presented by members of their own families, resident in the parish or nearby: Roger Malekak, rector of a mediety of Keelby, by Alan Malekak; William of Healing, rector of Healing, by John of Healing. Two successive rectors of Bigby, John Wacelyn (1285–1313) and

---

[13] Quoted in Pantin, *The English Church in the Fourteenth Century*, pp. 52–3.
[14] P. McClure, 'Patterns of Migration in the Late Middle Ages: The Evidence of English Place-Name Surnames', *Economic History Review* second series xxxii (1979), pp. 167–82.
[15] *Rotuli Ricardi Gravesend*, ed. F.N. Davis (with additions by C.W. Foster and A. Hamilton Thompson) (LRS 20, 1925), p. 87; *Register of Bishop Sutton* i, pp. 140, 153; *The Lay Subsidy of 1334*, ed. Robin E. Glasscock (London, 1975), p. 510; G.E. Cockayne, *The Complete Peerage*, ed. V. Gibbs, H.A. Doubleday, Lord Howard de Walden, G.H. White and R.S. Lea, 12 vols in 13 (London, 1910–53), ii, p. 89; xii(2), p. 657; Bennett, 'The Beneficed Clergy' i, pp. 234–5.

William Wacelyn (1313–44) were kinsmen of their patrons, the Wacelyn family of Brumby.

The essentially local nature of the beneficed clergy here is underlined by the fact that, of the 40 incumbents known to have originated outside the diocese, 13 came from the East Riding of Yorkshire, just across the Humber from the three Lincolnshire deaneries, with which there were close links. There is only one example in the survey of a foreign clerk: Palmer Francisci of Florence (rector of Aylesby, 1324–36), which hardly bears out the suggestion that English benefices were overrun by foreign incumbents. Indeed it is notable that, in all the nine livings in the patronage of the alien Beauport Abbey, not one incumbent during this period can be identified as coming from overseas. On the contrary, the great majority of them came from Lincolnshire, many from the Grimsby area: Waltham, Fenby, Limber, Grimsby, Kirmington, Brocklesby and Croxby.

Another recurring criticism of the late medieval clergy is that many of those instituted to parochial benefices were not yet in priest's orders, and as such could not adequately minister to their parishioners. Bishop Moorman calculated that, of the clergy instituted to benefices in Lincoln diocese during the episcopate of Bishop Gravesend (1258–79), only 16 per cent of the rectors were in priest's orders. By the constitution *Licet canon*, issued at the Council of Lyons in 1274, it was decreed that anyone instituted to a parish must proceed to the priesthood within a year of his institution, on pain of deprivation. The survival of the ordination records from the last ten years of Bishop Sutton's episcopate makes it possible to discover to what extent this constitution was being enforced. Out of 27 candidates instituted to rectories during the year 1291, only 8 were in priest's orders. This nevertheless represented a proportion of 30 per cent, a considerable improvement on the figure from Gravesend's register. Moreover, Sutton's ordination records indicate that another 14 of these 27 rectors from 1291 proceeded to the priesthood within a year, thus complying with the terms of *Licet canon*. This gives a proportion of 81 per cent of priests among these newly-instituted rectors, and the proportion might be found to be higher still if the ordination records from other dioceses had survived.[16]

Some examples can be provided from the three north-eastern deaneries. William of Warminster was instituted to Scartho as a subdeacon on 14 September 1289; by 27 May in the following year, he was ordained to the priesthood. On the same day that Warminster was priested, James of Tankersley, a clerk in minor orders, was instituted to Walesby, having first been ordained subdeacon. Just over a year later, on 16 June 1291, he was presented once more to Walesby, the church being vacant because James had not been ordained priest within a year of his institution. This time he

---

16 Moorman, *Church Life in England in the Thirteenth Century*, p. 36; Shinners and Dohar, *Pastors*, pp. 70–1; *Rolls and Register of Bishop Sutton* vii (LRS 69, 1975).

was ordained priest and instituted on the same day. Another incumbent to go through the same repetition of presentation and institution that day was Master Robert of Kirmington, rector of Brigsley, an indication that Bishop Sutton was very watchful of any incumbent not complying with the canon.[17]

More troublesome was Master William of Dalton, instituted as a subdeacon to St Mary, Binbrook, on 22 December 1291. Whether the delay in Master William's progress through the orders was due to his absence studying abroad, to inertia or simply forgetfulness, Sutton had to institute him a further three times to the living, in 1293, 1294 and 1295, before he finally attained the priesthood on 12 May 1296. Where there was a legitimate cause for the delay, Sutton could be merciful. Alan of Rothwell was ordained subdeacon and instituted rector of Rothwell on 21 September 1297 but it was not until 13 June 1299 that he proceeded to the priesthood, it being noted in the register that he had been legitimately prevented from being ordained priest earlier. What might constitute such a legitimate obstacle to ordination is revealed by letters issued on 1 January 1330 by Bishop Henry Burghersh on behalf of Robert de Braundeston, deacon, the rector of a mediety of South Ferriby. The date of Robert's institution is not known, but it is likely to have been in late 1328. The letters testify to the diligence with which Robert has sought ordination to the priesthood, recounting that he had attended the prebendal church of St Margaret, Leicester, on 23 December 1329, intending to present himself at the ordination due to be celebrated on the bishop's behalf by his suffragan, Matthew, Bishop of Bangor, but although Robert had remained in the church from matins until nones, Bishop Matthew had been prevented from coming.[18]

The lack of ordination records for the episcopates of John Dalderby and Henry Burghersh make it difficult to assess whether Sutton's vigilance in enforcing the constitution *Licet canon* was continued by his successors. Overall, however, the evidence of Burghersh's institution register indicates that, of those instituted to rectories during the years 1320 to 1342 whose orders are specified in the record, 62 per cent were already in priest's orders.[19] The three north-eastern deaneries reveal a similar position. Taking rectories and vicarages together, out of all the 361 incumbents identified in these parishes during the period 1290–1340, 209 (58 per cent) were either priests already or proceeded to the priesthood within a year of institution. Given the gap in the ordination records, the true proportion is likely to have been higher, and it would appear that the legislation of the Council of Lyons was having an ongoing effect in reforming the abuse of beneficed clergy who lacked the priestly qualifications to carry out their office.

The standard of education among the beneficed clergy during this period

---

[17] *Rolls and Register of Bishop Sutton* i, pp. 125, 139, 155; ibid. vii, p. 4.
[18] *Rolls and Register of Bishop Sutton* i, pp. 162, 175, 189–90, 200, 200; ibid. vii, pp. 81, 118; LAO, Bishop's Register V, fol. 427v.
[19] Bennett, 'The Beneficed Clergy' i, pp. 265–7.

has in general been described as poor. This view is not confined to modern historians; as Jeffrey Denton has pointed out, their opinions largely reflect the agenda of the reforming bishops of the thirteenth century.[20] Raising the standard of clerical education was seen by Pope Innocent III as an essential step towards improving pastoral care in the parishes and this perceived need was enshrined not only in the decrees of the Fourth Lateran Council but also in much English provincial and diocesan legislation of the following century. Robert Grosseteste's influential diocesan statutes of 1238–9 attempted to tackle the problem, and it has already been noted that Archbishop Pecham's 1281 constitution *Ignorantia sacerdotum* opens with a dire warning: 'The ignorance of priests casts the people down into the ditch of error.'[21]

Had the reforming zeal of such bishops achieved any improvement in the standard of clerical education by the end of the century? Was Pecham in 1281 describing a situation that was as bad as it had ever been, or did his striking opening flourish, as Professor Haines has suggested, 'owe more to the fervour of the reformer than to the carefully qualified assessment of the administrator'?[22] Examination of the detailed sample of clergy in the present survey may throw some light on their educational attainments, some hundred years after the Fourth Lateran Council.

A simple way of assessing the standard of learning among the sample is by counting the number described as *magistri*, either on their institution or in some other source. Of the 361 incumbents in the sample, a total of 61 (17 per cent) were so described. This figure matches very closely the 18 per cent of East Yorkshire incumbents at a similar period (1306–40) identified as graduates by Dr Robinson.[23] Of the 61 graduates in the present sample, 47 (just over three-quarters) were presented by ecclesiastical patrons, a preponderance even greater than their two-thirds share of the advowsons in the area might suggest. The foreign house of Beauport was particularly active in this respect, presenting 13 graduates to its benefices during the period. One of these churches, Autby was held by four successive graduates, all from Lincolnshire, for a period of fifty years from 1273 until 1323.

Perhaps surprisingly, the living of Autby was assessed at the comparatively low figure of £6 in the 1291 Taxation. The overall number of the graduates in the sample who held benefices valued at over £10 was 36, leaving a substantial minority (just over two-fifths) who were incumbents of churches assessed at £10 or less. This suggests that a university education was by no means regarded as an automatic path to wealth in the Church. Nine of the graduates in the sample were indeed incumbents of vicarages. Some of these

---

[20] Denton, 'The Competence of the Parish Clergy', pp. 273–5.
[21] Shinners and Dohar, *Pastors*, pp. 87, 127.
[22] R.M. Haines, *Ecclesia anglicana: Studies in the English Church of the Later Middle Ages* (Toronto, 1989), pp. 133–5.
[23] David Robinson, *Beneficed Clergy in Cleveland and the East Riding 1306–1340* (York, 1969), pp. 14–17.

men, like Alan de Hotoft (Grasby, 1290–1303) and John de Herpeswell (Tealby, 1299–1329), held benefices too poor to be taxed in 1291 but nevertheless brought a combination of local knowledge and university learning to their pastoral work.

As well as the simple counting of *magistri*, the educational attainments of the beneficed clergy can be assessed by an analysis of the licences and dispensations granted by the bishop for the purpose of study. A licence to be absent for this reason could be granted to a rector who was in priest's orders; those issued by Henry Burghersh occupy more than twenty folios of his register. Twenty incumbents from the sample were granted such licences. In twelve cases, the licence was for one year only, as in the case of John de Herford, rector of West Rasen, given leave to study in England or abroad in March 1332. Longer periods of licensed study ranged from two years (for example, John de Barton, rector of Ashby cum Fenby) to five years in the case of William Skelet, rector of Barnoldby, who was absent for three separate periods (1328–29, 1331–34 and 1340–41).[24]

Rectors could also be granted episcopal permission to be absent for the purpose of study by means of dispensations issued in accordance with the constitution *Cum ex eo* of Pope Boniface VIII (1298). Twenty-one incumbents from the sample received such dispensations, the period of absence varying from one year (in two cases only) to the maximum permitted term of seven years, granted to seven of these rectors. William de Kirkham (rector of Nettleton 1305–25) was granted two successive dispensations for three and four years respectively. He is not known to have attained a degree, however, whereas Philip Daubeney (rector of Claxby by Normanby) was already described as *magister* at his institution in 1318 but was granted three dispensations totalling seven years allowing him to be absent for further study.

Professor Haines has argued that the original purpose of the *Cum ex eo* constitution was not so much to improve the education of the beneficed clergy by granting study leave to young incumbents, as to enable benefices to be used to finance the education of those intending to pursue careers in royal service or in the schools. While this was the theory behind the legislation, the way it was put into practice seems to have been more varied. The careers of some of the clerks in the sample do suggest that dispensations were used as a means of acquiring the educational qualifications required for an administrative or university career. Richard de Ragenhull, provided to Barnoldby in 1319, was granted a dispensation for two years of study before he entered the service of John Stratford, archdeacon of Lincoln and subsequently bishop of Winchester.[25] Philip Frank was already a *magister* when he was instituted to Waltham in 1334. The following year he was granted a dispensation to study

---

[24] LAO, Bishop's Register V, fols 190v (Herford), 179v (Barton), 183r, 187v, 201r (Skelet).
[25] LAO, Bishop's Register II, fol. 326v; Bishop's Register V, fol. 4; *CPR 1317–21*, p. 450. See also R.M. Haines, *Archbishop John Stratford* (Toronto, 1986), p. 102.

at Oxford or Cambridge for three years. On the expiry of this period Frank, who by now had proceeded to the priesthood, was granted two successive one-year licences for further study. In his case, the original dispensation was the prelude to an extended academic career, partly financed by the revenues of Waltham, at the University of Cambridge.[26]

The careers of other clerks in the sample, on the other hand, tell a different story. John de Stretton received five *Cum ex eo* dispensations, amounting to the maximum period of seven years, following his institution to Laceby in 1300. He then appears to have returned to his parish, although his implication in an accusation of assault there in 1315 suggests that perhaps his education may not have improved his pastoral skills.[27] The possibility that a dispensation might equip a young incumbent for a useful career in parish and diocese is suggested by the example of Robert de Tynton. Instituted to Autby in 1308, he received four consecutive dispensations enabling him to study in England for seven years. In 1320 he was back in his parish, and was employed by the bishop of the diocese in commissions relating to testamentary business, the auditing of administration accounts. When he died in 1323, he was described in the institution register as *magister*.[28]

The overall conclusion must be that the standard of education among the beneficed clergy was much more varied than might be suggested by some of the sweeping generalisations made by modern historians in the light of papal and episcopal demands for reform. One in six incumbents in the sample was described as magister, and adding to these those who were granted licences or dispensations for study, nearly a quarter of the beneficed clergy in these three deaneries had spent some time studying at a university. Those involved in the production of the growing number of manuals of instruction for parish priests during this period might well bemoan the low standard of education among the clergy – indeed it was in their interest to do so. It could equally well be argued that the widespread dissemination of such manuals during this period is itself a testimony to the desire of many of the parochial clergy, like those in this sample, to educate themselves and thereby to raise the standard of their pastoral care.

Beneficed clergy who received episcopal permission to study at a university could not of course be resident in their parishes while they did so. Indeed, absenteeism is another criticism levelled against the late medieval clergy. Education was not the only reason for an incumbent to spend time away from his parish and, as with study leave, such absence required in most

---

[26] LAO, Bishop's Register V, fols 28r, 198v, 200r; A.B. Emden, *Biographical Register of the University of Cambridge* (Cambridge, 1963), p. 242.

[27] LAO, Bishop's Register II, fols 1v, 305v, 306v, 307r, 308v, 311r; *CPR 1313–17*, p. 402.

[28] LAO, Bishop's Register II, fols 23r, 315r, 318r, 319v, 321v; LAO, Bishop's Register V, fol. 60r; *The Registers of Henry Burghersh 1320–1342 I*, ed. N.H. Bennett (LRS 87, 1999), p. 13.

cases a licence from the bishop. A desire to go on pilgrimage was one such cause. Guy Breton, rector of Wold Newton, was granted leave to visit Rome in October 1321. Even vicars, sworn to keep perpetual residence, might be permitted to be absent for this purpose. In October 1330, William de Edelington, vicar of Thornton Curtis, was licensed to visit Rome and Compostella. Other incumbents might seek a period of non-residence to restore their health, as with William de Harton, rector of St Mary, South Kelsey, who in 1332 was permitted to leave his church for a year for the purpose of recreation.[29]

Apart from education, however, the most common reason for absence among the beneficed clergy was to be in the service of the king, the bishop of the diocese, or the household of some other great lord. Twelve incumbents in the sample under study were king's clerks, some of them connected with the network of clerical dynasties associated with Archbishop Melton, the roots of which extended into north-east Lincolnshire.[30] Notable among these were the future Archbishop, John de Thoresby (rector of Nettleton 1338–42), a chancery clerk from 1336, and Nicholas de Huggate (rector of Scartho 1309–10), whom Melton himself had introduced into the service of the royal wardrobe. In this group another member of Melton's circle was John de Swanland (rector of Thoresway 1300–15), sub-usher of the wardrobe and possibly one of Melton's kinsmen. Geoffrey de Welleford (rector of Linwood 1307–18) and Thomas de Brayton (rector of St Nicholas, South Kelsey, 1324–26) both served as chancery clerks, each eventually serving as keeper of the Great Seal.[31]

Patronage was an essential element in placing clerks in suitable benefices. Of the twelve king's clerks in the sample, nine were presented to their livings by the Crown, either in full right (there were Crown livings at Bradley, Scartho and St Nicholas, South Kelsey) or because the advowson had fallen to the Crown for that turn. The Crown presented John de Swanland to Thoresway in 1300 and Geoffrey de Welleford to Linwood in 1307 because of its custody of the barony of Bayeux, while the presentation of John de Amwell to West Rasen in 1325 was in the king's hands through his custody of the temporalities of the priory of Holy Trinity, York, during the war with France over Saint Sardos.[32] The Bishop of Lincoln similarly sought to provide his clerks with benefices. The list of rectors of Aylesby, a

---

[29] LAO, Bishop's Register V, fols 39r, 43r, 296r.
[30] J.L. Grassi, 'Royal Clerks from the Archdiocese of York in the Fourteenth Century', *Northern History* v (1970), pp. 12–33; L.H. Butler, 'Archbishop Melton, his Neighbours and his Kinsmen, 1317–40', *JEH* ii (1951), pp. 54–68.
[31] For Thoresby's early career, see Jonathan Hughes, *Pastors and Visionaries: Religion and Secular Life in Late Medieval Yorkshire* (Woodbridge, 1988), pp. 130–1. For the whole group, see T.F. Tout, *Chapters in the Administrative History of Medieval England*, 6 vols (Manchester, 1920–33), ii, pp. 23, 171, 237; ibid. iii, pp. 85–6; ibid. vi, pp. 9, 13–15; B. Wilkinson, *The Chancery under Edward III* (Manchester, 1929), pp. 154–5.
[32] LAO, Bishop's Register II, fols 1v, 20r; *CPR 1324–7*, p. 89.

living in the bishop's gift, includes several members of his *familia*: Thomas de Luda (1310–21) served in the household of Bishop Dalderby and was chancellor in that of Bishop Burghersh; Alan de Lughton (1321–24) acted for Burghersh in a financial capacity and Nicholas de Falle (1336–40) was one of the bishop's clerks from the mid 1320s. The rectory of Great Coates was not in the bishop's patronage but when in 1330 the advowson lapsed to him following a lengthy dispute, Burghersh was able to confer it on his clerk Robert de Stanford.[33]

Other diocesan bishops employed incumbents from Lincoln diocese in their households, though not usually as a result of their own patronage. The Bishop of Durham was able to use the advowson of Wold Newton to secure that living for his clerk, Henry de Lusceby (rector 1306–18). John de Barton, however, was presented to Ashby cum Fenby in 1318 by Thornholme Priory and it was not until 1329 that he entered the service of the Bishop of Hereford, eventually exchanging his parish for that of Eastnor on his appointment as archdeacon of Hereford in 1333. John de Guthmundham (rector of Thoresway 1315–22) was presented by Isabella Beaumont, lady Vescy (herself, as will be seen, a regular employer of Lincolnshire incumbents as her chaplains) but he was not to be found in her service but in that of William Melton, archbishop of York.[34]

Lay magnates frequently appointed chaplains whom they had presented to livings in their own gift: the earl of Lancaster with John de Donyngton (North Thoresby), the countess of Kent with John de Barton (St Nicholas, South Kelsey) and Isabella de Vescy with William de Nedham and William de Bitham (Thoresway) and Thomas de Sonnebury and Hugh de Betun (Linwood). On other occasions, however, they might choose from those holding benefices in the gift of others: the countess of Lincoln with Simon de Wadenho (North Coates, patron Nicholas de Cantilupe) and Roger Malekak (Keelby, patron Alan Malekak).[35]

The crucial question to be asked is: how widespread was such absenteeism?

---

[33] LAO, Bishop's Register II, fol. 32r; *Registers of Henry Burghersh* i, pp. xv, xvii, 6, 16, 33, 62, 84; LAO, Bishop's Register V, fol. 283r. Lughton's career as the bishop's receiver does not appear to have been entirely satisfactory: LAO, Bishop's Register Vb, fol. 239r.

[34] For Lusceby, see *Registrum Palatinum Dunelmense: The Register of Richard de Kellawe, Lord Palatine and Bishop of Durham*, ed. T.D. Hardy, 4 vols (RS, 1873–8), i, pp. 105, 274, 306, 480; ii, pp. 1167, 1190, 1194, 1212. For Barton, see LAO, Bishop's Register II, fol. 75v; Bishop's Register V, fols 37v, 39v, 43v; *Registrum Thome de Charlton, episcopi Herefordensis*, ed. W.W. Capes (CYS 9, 1913), pp. 78, 83. For Guthmundham, see LAO, Bishop's Register II, fol. 56; Bishop's Register V, fol. 4; *Registers of Henry Burghersh* i, p. 7; *The Register of William Melton*, eds R.M.T. Hill, David Robinson, Reginald Brocklesby and T.C.B. Timmins, 5 vols in progress (CYS 70–1, 76, 85, 93, 1977–2002), i, pp. 6, 8, 117; iii, pp. 13, 34; iv, p. 38; v, p. 24, 39.

[35] LAO, Bishop's Register V, fols 6v (Donyngton), 51v, 53r, 55r, 56r (Barton), 14v, 36r (Bitham), 43v, 55r (Nedham), 4v (Sonnebury), 36r, 37v, 39r, 43v (Betun), 56r, 58r (Wadenho), 7r (Malekak).

This can be examined from two angles: what proportion of incumbents was absent for reasons other than study, and was their absence permanent or temporary, and if temporary, for how long? Of the 361 clerks in the sample deaneries, 47 (13 per cent) have been identified with some period of such absence. The length of absence is not always easy to discover. In the case of the 16 royal or episcopal clerks in the sample, where no licence was required, the absence was in many cases clearly a long-term one. John de Thoresby is unlikely to have been at Nettleton much, if at all, during the period of his incumbency there (1338–42) – indeed, he was abroad with the king for part of this period. Likewise, Nicholas de Falle (Aylesby 1336–40) was a long-serving member of Burghersh's household and, like Thoresby, was abroad on royal service with the bishop during these years. William de Dalton (Croxton 1324–71) was a wardrobe clerk by 1336, occupied the posts successively of cofferer and controller, and continued in the royal service until the late 1350s.[36]

The length of absence of the other 31 clerks in the sample can be determined more closely from the evidence of the licences. These licences were normally issued for a fixed term of from one to three years. Where the absence was due to pilgrimage, the date by which the incumbent should return to his benefice was usually specified: Guy Breton, setting out for Rome in October 1321, was ordered to be back at Wold Newton by the Feast of the Ascension following. The leave of absence granted in 1332 to William de Harton for health reasons came when he had held the rectory of St Mary, South Kelsey, for nearly thirty-seven years with no recorded absence. The licence was for one year; it was renewed for a further year in September 1333, but by April 1334 Harton was dead.[37]

Most licences to be absent in the service of a lord were limited to one or two years, renewable on the expiry of that term. In the case of 24 of the 31 incumbents in the sample who were so licensed, the period of absence was three years or less. Some of these men received their licences after a long period with no recorded absence. Gilbert de Suthriston, instituted to Newton by Toft in 1312, was licensed for the service of Peter de Scremby in 1327. Alan de Gresseby, rector of Nettleton from 1325 to 1338, was granted leave to be in the service of Walter de Maydenstan, subdean of Lincoln, in 1334. A few incumbents, however, were absent for longer periods, notably those in the service of Isabella, lady Vescy. William de Nedham, rector of Thoresway, received two licences for absence amounting to six years, and Hugh de Betun, rector of Linwood, was granted five licences permitting him to be in her service for a total of eleven years.[38]

---

[36] Hughes, *Pastors and Visionaries*, p. 131; *Registers of Henry Burghersh* i, p. xvii; *CPR 1334–8*, pp. 417, 531; Tout, *Chapters* iv, p. 96n, 104.

[37] LAO, Bishop's Register V, fols 296r (Breton), 43r, 45r (Harton); *Registers of Henry Burghersh* i, p. 53.

[38] LAO, Bishop's Register V, fols 36v (Suthriston), 47r, 49r (Gresseby). For Nedham and Betun, see note 34 above.

There remains one further cause of absenteeism to consider: pluralism. The holding of more than one benefice by the same clerk inevitably meant that only one of them could be served by the rector in person. Perhaps surprisingly – as this is another frequent criticism of the late medieval clergy – pluralism appears to have been comparatively infrequent. The quantity of dispensations recorded in the pages of the printed calendars of papal letters may have led to the supposition that large numbers of the beneficed clergy in the fourteenth century were pluralists. The evidence of the sample deaneries in the present study, however, suggests otherwise. Further research into the wider careers of some of these incumbents will be necessary before the position can be fully established, but preliminary study indicates that only 3 to 4 per cent of them held more than one living simultaneously.

The typical pattern, repeated in many of these cases, was for the pluralist to hold one parochial benefice having the cure of souls together with one or more prebends in cathedrals or collegiate churches, to which no such cure was attached. The holding of such prebends would not normally have entailed residence, leaving the incumbent free to carry out the duties of his parish church. The returns of pluralists made for Pope Urban V in 1366 confirm this picture. Analysis of the details provided for the diocese of Lincoln shows that, of the 136 clerks included in the returns, only 12 held two or more incompatible benefices, each having cure of souls.[39] In the present sample, Philip de Daventre, rector of Wold Newton, was granted papal provision of prebends in Southwell and in Wells, neither of which need have involved him in absence from his parish. There were some rectors who chose to reside on their prebends instead of in their parishes. Thomas Clifford, rector of Aylesby, kept residence at Lincoln Cathedral as prebendary of Bedford Minor between 1306/7 and 1320/1. At the greater secular cathedrals like Lincoln, however, the residentiaries always constituted a relatively small proportion of the whole chapter. Many clerks who combined parish livings with cathedral prebends were of course already absentees for other reasons – working at a university, or in the service of king or bishop. Nicholas Falle, rector of Aylesby from 1336 to 1340, held in addition the Lincoln prebend of Bedford Minor, but his service in the bishop's household meant that he was absent from both benefices. Similarly, the holding of prebends in plurality by king's clerks such as William de Dalton or Edmund Grimesby would have made no difference to their respective parishioners of Croxton and Grainsby who would have rarely seen them in any case.[40]

---

39 C.N.L. Brooke, 'The Earliest Times to 1485', in *A History of St Paul's Cathedral*, ed. W.R. Matthews and W.M. Atkins (London, 1957), p. 52; A. Hamilton Thompson, 'Pluralism in the Medieval Church', *AASRP* xxxiii (1915–16), pp. 35–73; xxxiv (1917), pp. 1–26; xxxv (1918–20), pp. 87–108, 199–242; xxxvi (1921), pp. 1–14; Bennett, 'The Beneficed Clergy' i, pp. 373–4.

40 *CPL* ii, pp. 272, 312; Kathleen Edwards, *The English Secular Cathedrals in the Middle Ages*, 2nd edn (Manchester, 1967), pp. 330–5; *Fasti* i, pp. 35 (Falle), 44, 65, 70

More serious than these were the cases of clerks who held two or more livings with cure of souls, for here it was clearly impossible to fulfil the pastoral duties of both positions in person. John de Craucumb, instituted to Goxhill in 1288, held a papal dispensation allowing him to retain in addition the rectory of Burton Joyce in Nottinghamshire together with the archdeaconry of the East Riding. Such examples, however, were rare. Of the 361 incumbents in the sample deaneries, only 7 have been identified as falling into this category. As well as Craucumb, there were Geoffrey de Welleford (Linwood and Potterspury), Hugh de Walmesford (Great Coates and Glatton), Henry de Lusceby (Wold Newton, Blyborough, and Wooler in the diocese of Durham), William de Rasen (West Rasen and Gedney), Guy Breton (Wold Newton and Hatton) and Thomas de Sonnebury (Linwood and Bubwith in Yorkshire).[41]

Two points may be noted from this list. First, all of these seven clerks had periods of absence from their benefices for other reasons: Geoffrey de Welleford was a king's clerk, William de Rasen in the household of Hugh le Despenser, Hugh de Walmesford spent some time absent for the purpose of study, Henry de Lusceby was a clerk of the bishop of Durham. Second, five of these cases date from before the papal constitution *Execrabilis* of 1318, aimed specifically against the abuse of pluralism. Welleford and Lusceby both relinquished their additional livings as a direct result of the constitution.[42] The other two examples date from the years immediately after 1318 and neither appears to have endured for more than a few years. Further research may modify this picture of the extent of pluralism but it seems unlikely that it will do so to any significant extent.

Overall, therefore, taking the various causes of absenteeism together – study, service, pluralism – there were 78 incumbents in the sample deaneries who at one time or another did not reside in their parishes. This total, a proportion of just over one in five, is made up of 38 absent for study purposes (including 8 who went on to be absent in the service of a lord), 34 who were absent in service of a lord and 6 absent for other or unspecified reasons. The length of absence varied from a few months (in the case of those going on pilgrimage) to three decades or more in the case of a royal clerk like William de Dalton.

In cases like that of Dalton, it is clear that the parishioners can rarely, if ever, have seen their incumbent. Richard de Ragenhull was one such.

(Dalton); ii, pp. 15 (Dalton), 23 (Grimesby); v, p. 27 (Grimesby); vi, p. 60; x, p. 63 (Dalton). For Grimesby, see also Edward Gillett, *A History of Grimsby* (London, 1970), p. 82.

[41] *Rolls and Register of Bishop Sutton* i, pp. 105–6 (Craucumb); LAO, Bishop's Register II, fols 7r (Walmesford), 16v (Lusceby), 20r, 125v (Welleford), 60v, 75v (Breton), 74 (Sonnebury); Bishop's Register III, fols 100v (Walmesford), 141v (Rasen), 363v (Lusceby); *CPL* ii, pp. 4 (Rasen), 34, 91 (Lusceby), 68 (Welleford); *Registers of Henry Burghersh* i, p. 10 (Sonnebury).

[42] LAO, Bishop's Register II, fols 74r, 75v.

Admitted to the rectory of Barnoldby by papal provision in February 1319, he received a dispensation in the following month to study in England or abroad for two years. Before the expiry of this period, however, he had entered the service of John de Stratford, archdeacon of Lincoln, accompanying his master across the Channel in June 1320, part of the royal entourage as Edward II went to pay homage to Philip V of France. In January 1321 Ragenhull received a licence from Bishop Burghersh regularising the position and permitting him to be absent from Barnoldby in Stratford's service for three years. He was to make four further journeys abroad with Stratford on royal business between 1321 and 1325, to Avignon and elsewhere. In November 1322, he was sent from the curia back to the king's court to seek further instructions, making the journey on horseback from Avignon to York in twenty-three days. It seems unlikely that he found time to visit Barnoldby. Stratford's promotion in 1323 to the see of Winchester was to lead eventually to Ragenhull's appointment to the Hampshire rectory of Burghclere and his resignation of Barnoldby in March 1327. In an incumbency lasting just over eight years, he can have spent little time in his parish.[43]

Another example of long-term absence can be seen in the career of Robert Copgrave or Toft (the latter surname being normally used in the registers). A Yorkshireman, he had graduated Master of Arts at Oxford and in 1317 was granted papal reservation of a benefice in the gift of St Mary's Abbey, York. Accordingly, in June 1318 he was provided to the church of St Mary, Binbrook. In January of the following year, he was granted the first of three dispensations permitting him to study in England or abroad for a period extending to the maximum seven years allowed under the constitution *Cum ex eo*. He was subsequently licensed for a further three years of study in September 1328, having by then presumably proceeded to the priesthood. His next move came in December 1334, when he was granted leave to be in the service of William de Colby (dean of York, 1333–36). A few days after Colby's death in early November 1336, Toft was licensed to join the household of the dean of Lichfield. This was Richard Fitzralph, appointed to the post the previous year and taking his duties of residence and the administration of the cathedral very seriously. When in 1337 Fitzralph travelled to Avignon to promote the causes of the dean and chapter at the curia, Toft remained behind; in January 1338 he was licensed to study in England once more for a period of one year and this permission was renewed twelve months later. His career was thus spent predominantly at university, with a temporary absence in the service of two cathedral deans. Any periods of residence in his parish would have been brief and intermittent.[44]

---

43 LAO, Bishop's Register II, fols 76v, 326v; *CPR 1317–21*, p. 450; Bishop's Register V, fol. 4r; *CPR 1321–4*, pp. 45, 182, 244; *CPR 1324–7*, p. 129; Haines, *John Stratford*, pp. 102, 134; *Registers of Henry Burghersh* i, p. 23.
44 A.B. Emden, *A Biographical Register of the University of Oxford to A.D. 1500*, 3 vols (Oxford, 1957–9), p. 483; LAO, Bishop's Register II, fols 72v, 326v; Bishop's Register

The careers of men like Ragenhull and Toft suggest that there may be some justification for the criticism that the late medieval clergy were all too often absent from their parishes. It must be emphasised, however, that examples such as these, conspicuous and well recorded as they are, represent nonetheless only a minority of the parish clergy. If evidence of absenteeism can be found for 78 of the clerks in the sample deaneries, there still remain 283 others in that sample who cannot as yet be shown to have been absent at all. Among these, above all, it must be remembered that all those who were vicars of their parishes, on their institution, had taken an oath of perpetual residence. Leave of absence might be allowed in exceptional circumstances (as in the case of William de Edelington's desire to go on pilgrimage), but in general it would be fair to assume that vicars, who made up 136 of the 361 clerks in the sample (a proportion of 38 per cent), were resident in their parishes.

It is a fundamental problem in dealing with this kind of issue that the records are biased in a negative sense, in favour of those who, for whatever reason, did not fulfil the duties of the post to which they had been appointed. It is much more difficult to establish that clergy were resident than that they were not. All too often, it appears to have been assumed that, in default of any firm evidence to the contrary, beneficed clergy were as likely as not to have been non-resident. Yet the machinery of episcopal and archidiaconal visitation was in regular operation and any flagrant cases of unlicensed absence would have been brought to light.

Moreover, there are some pieces of evidence that can be used to help to establish a degree of residence on the part of an incumbent. The episcopal registers contain many commissions issued by the bishop for the carrying out of specific business. While many of these were addressed to clerks in the bishop's household, archdeacons or other diocesan officials, there remain a number that were directed to parish clergy. It has already been seen that the presence of Robert de Tynton back in his parish of Autby after a seven-year dispensation for study leave can be inferred from his employment in 1320 on a commission to audit the accounts of the executors of William de Shadeworth, a local knight. Testamentary business of this nature is a recurring concern in the registers; indeed, it occupies a section of its own in Burghersh's classified memoranda. William de Colston, a predecessor of the absentee Richard de Ragenhull as rector of Barnoldby, can be seen resident in his parish by the commission of November 1300 instructing him to audit the accounts of the executors of William de Caples, rector of nearby Laceby. Some incumbents were regularly employed in this way. Master Robert de

---

V, fols 2v, 10v, 20v, 48v, 53r, 198r, 200r; Katherine Walsh, *A Fourteenth-Century Scholar and Primate: Richard FitzRalph in Oxford, Avignon and Armagh* (Oxford, 1981), pp. 109–115.

Kirnington (rector of Brigsley 1291–1304 and of Hatcliffe 1304–23) received four such commissions in 1321.[45]

Local clergy might also be employed on commissions relating to benefice matters (John de Rasen, rector of Claxby by Normanby, was appointed proctor of the rector of West Rasen in 1299 to settle the amount of the dilapidations owed by the previous incumbent) or in matrimonial business (the vicars of Stallingborough and East Halton – both *magistri* – were deputed to act in such a cause in 1330). The residence of particular incumbents can also be established by their employment in penitential responsibilities. Joel de Dunham (rector of Somerby) was appointed to hear confessions in the deanery of Yarborough in 1300, and William de Billesby (rector of Wrawby), who had earlier been licensed to be absent for study, was given the post of penitentiary in the same deanery in 1338.[46]

It has already been seen how Simon de Luda was commissioned to examine the election of the prioress of Greenfield in 1293; other incumbents also found themselves involved in the affairs of local religious houses. Roger Malekak (rector of Keelby) was appointed custodian of Nun Cotham priory in 1318, which suggests that he spent some time resident in his parish before briefly entering the service of the countess of Lincoln in 1321. The rector of Scartho, William Chauncy, was instructed in 1324 to audit the accounts of the vicar of Little Coates as custodian of the nunnery of St Leonard, Grimsby. Although Scartho was a Crown living, held in 1309–10 by the prominent royal clerk Nicholas de Huggate, his successor Chauncy (probably a kinsman of the Swinhope family of that name) was active in local affairs, being employed on two testamentary commissions relating to the wills of local clergy.[47]

When an incumbent became too old or incapacitated to carry out his duties, the bishop would appoint a coadjutor to assist him. In the case of Gilbert de Suthriston, rector of Newton by Toft, the physical infirmity that led to the appointment of a coadjutor in 1316 was evidently of a temporary nature, since he was still in possession of the living in 1327 when he was licensed to be in the service of a Lincolnshire knight, Peter de Scremby.[48] When Walter Savage, rector of Scartho, became blind in 1305, the vicar of Cabourne, Thomas de Limberg, was chosen to assist him. In 1309 William Wacelyn was appointed coadjutor to his kinsman, John Wacelyn (rector of Bigby) who had become blind and feeble; on John's death in 1313, William succeeded to the benefice.[49] John de Manneby, rector of Saxby All Saints,

---

45 Smith, *Guide to Bishops' Registers*, p. 111; LAO, Bishop's Register III, fol. 20v; Bishop's Register V, fols 61r, 62r–v, 63v.
46 *Rolls and Register of Bishop Sutton* vi, p. 182; LAO, Bishop's Register II, fol. 22r; Bishop's Register V, fols 7v, 149r, 435v.
47 LAO, Bishop's Register III, fol. 404r; Bishop's Register V, fols 61r–v, 368r.
48 LAO, Bishop's Register III, fol. 344v; Bishop's Register V, fol. 36v.
49 LAO, Bishop's Register II, fol. 47r; Bishop's Register III, fols 79v, 150v.

was seemingly indestructible. Instituted in 1268, he had served the parish for nearly fifty years when in May 1316, on account of his senility and infirmity, he was given a coadjutor, Hugh de Cumpton. Four months later, it was not the rector but the coadjutor who was dead, and a successor had to be chosen. Three years later, in December 1319, yet another coadjutor was appointed, with John de Manneby still in post.[50]

Another way in which the involvement of an incumbent with his parish can be revealed is through the burial of members of his family in the church, or indeed, after his death, through the burial of his own body there. It has already been seen that Hugh de Walmesford, rector of Great Coates, was a pluralist, and his burial took place in the chapel of St Mary within his other parish church of Glatton in Huntingdonshire. His connection with Great Coates was shown nevertheless, through the burial there of his brother, Peter de Walmesford. A rector of Keelby, Thomas de Stalingburgh, died in 1315; his body was buried in his parish church and an indulgence of thirty days was granted to all who prayed for his soul.[51]

These are all tiny scraps of evidence, many of them relating to humdrum, routine business, far removed from the glittering careers of the royal clerks and other non-resident incumbents. Taken as a whole, however, these piecemeal, almost random references begin to add up to a strikingly different picture of the late medieval clergy than the portrait of the ill-educated and non-resident men which formerly was traditionally, and often unthinkingly, handed down. The present paper is very much an interim report; this prosopographical study of the beneficed clergy of the diocese of Lincoln in the early fourteenth century is in its early stages, and further research will undoubtedly reshape and modify these preliminary suggestions. The initial findings of this small survey, however, indicate that more than 45 per cent of the beneficed clergy in the sample were either resident or engaged in some local activity that implied at least partial residence. In addition, a further 17 per cent of incumbents in the sample, for whom no evidence has yet been found to establish residence or non-residence, can be identified by their surnames as having their origins within Lincolnshire, suggesting some degree of probability that they too lived in their parishes.

From this multitude of incumbents, two portraits must suffice to suggest the type of man the resident incumbent might have been. John de Askeby was vicar of Great Limber from 1281 until his death in 1329. He is not known to have had a university education and no details have yet emerged of his first three decades in the parish. From 1309, however, he became a regular and trusted assistant of the diocesan administration in north-east Lincolnshire. In that year, he was appointed to accompany the bishop's sequestrator, Master William de Hale, to assess the revenues of Goxhill

---

[50] *Rotuli Ricardi Gravesend*, p. 27; LAO, Bishop's Register III, fols 346v, 353v, 429v.
[51] LAO, Bishop's Register III, fol. 417r; Bishop's Register V, fol. 263v.

church and the state of its books and ornaments, as part of the process leading to its appropriation to Bridlington Priory. In 1314 Askeby was involved in proceedings taken against those from the deaneries of Grimsby, Yarborough and Walshcroft who were withholding the tribute known as 'St Mary's Corn' payable to the prebendaries of Lincoln Cathedral. In the following year, he was commissioned to hear a suit relating to tithes in South Ferriby. In addition to all this, he received regular commissions to audit the accounts of coadjutors and of the executors of wills. The business entrusted to him suggests that he possessed legal, administrative and financial skills far removed from the traditional view of the late medieval incumbent.[52]

Finally, to return to the starting point of this paper, there is the career of Simon de Luda. Already described as *magister* on his institution to Aylesby in 1278, he may have served in the household of Bishop Gravesend, who collated the living to him, and he was certainly present in the retinue of Bishop Sutton at the beginning of his episcopate. By 1290, however, when Sutton's memoranda register begins, Luda was clearly resident at Aylesby. During the following decade he provided regular assistance to the bishop in the execution of commissions for testamentary and other business. His involvement in the Greenfield election demonstrates the confidence that Sutton placed in him. Like his bishop, he was tenacious of the rights of his office and he brought suits against those from neighbouring villages who pastured their sheep in Aylesby without paying tithes, and against those who disputed his right to the timber growing in the churchyard. He died some time before February 1306 and his body was buried outside the south door of Aylesby church.[53]

Askeby and Luda may have been exceptional in their involvement, as parish priests, in the administration of the diocese but their histories may serve as a reminder that the condition of the late medieval clergy was a great deal more varied – and arguably more positive – than the traditional picture once suggested.

---

[52] *Rolls and Register of Bishop Sutton* i, p. 10; *Registers of Henry Burghersh* i, p. 31; LAO, Bishop's Register III, fols 148r, 165v, 180r, 291v, 293v, 333r, 429v; Bishop's Register V, fols 61–5.

[53] *Rotuli Ricardi Gravesend*, p. 82; *Rolls and Register of Bishop Sutton* i, pp. 2, 7–8; iii, pp. 39, 41–2, 93; iv, pp. 8–9, 112, 119; v, pp. 55–6, 64; LAO, Bishop's Register III, fols 21r, 23v, 318r.

The Convent and the Community: Cause Papers as a Source for Monastic History

JANET BURTON

Among David Smith's many contributions to making known and making accessible the archives held at the Borthwick Institute, his two volumes of lists and indexes to the cause papers generated by the Consistory Court of the archbishops of York are of special interest for historians working in a number of different fields.[1] First designated 'cause papers' by Canon Purvis, who was responsible for their earliest listing, the files are a rich source for the church's jurisdiction in matters concerning ecclesiastical dues (the payment of tithes and other offerings), matrimonial cases, defamation, and testamentary business, and the workings of the church courts.[2] The York cause papers consist of 252 files from the fourteenth century, and 308 from the fifteenth.[3] They have been used by Richard Helmholz in his studies of medieval marriage and of medieval charity law,[4] and by Jeremy Goldberg to illuminate many aspects of the lives of medieval women, through childhood and adolescence, work, and marriage, to old age and widowhood.[5] Less well investigated has been the potential of cause papers as a source for monastic history, and it seems appropriate here to salute David Smith's achievements as a scholar and his service to the Borthwick Institute, by offering these preliminary observations on how cause papers illuminate monastic life in the later middle ages, and in particular how they allow us to see medieval monasteries

---

[1] D.M. Smith, *Ecclesiastical Cause Papers at York: The Court of York 1301–1399* (Borthwick Texts and Calendars 14, 1988), and *The Court of York 1400–1499* (Borthwick Texts and Calendars 29, 2003).
[2] See also Charles Donahue, *The Records of the Medieval Ecclesiastical Courts, Part II, England* (Berlin, 1994), especially pp. 109–51.
[3] See Smith, *Court of York 1301–1399*, p. vi, and *Court of York 1400–1499*, pp. iii–iv.
[4] R.H. Helmholz, *Marriage Litigation in Medieval England* (Cambridge, 1974), pp. 11–22, and 'The Law of Charity and the English Ecclesiastical Courts', in this volume; see also Frederik Pederson, *Romeo and Juliet of Stonegate: A Medieval Marriage in Crisis* (Borthwick Paper no. 87, 1995).
[5] P.J.P. Goldberg, *Women in England c. 1275–1535* (Manchester, 1995); and *Women, Work, and Life Cycle in a Medieval Economy: Women in York and Yorkshire c. 1300–1520* (Oxford, 1992).

as part of the social fabric of town and countryside, interacting with the local community.[6]

By their very nature, the cause papers that involve members of the religious orders – other than those in which the religious appear as witnesses[7] – are likely to be those that concern their ecclesiastical liberties and rights. Thus we find cause papers relating to tithes, when religious houses are plaintiffs demanding payment,[8] or defendants claiming the right to exemption;[9] there are cases concerning parish churches appropriated to monasteries, or where monasteries held, or claimed, the right of advowson;[10] and cases concerning the provision of chapels and chaplains.[11] Some cause papers comprise a single document, such as the libel, or statement of the plaintiff's case, like that made by the proctor of the prior and convent of Holy Trinity, York, described as *ordinis Maioris Monasterii* ('of the "order" of Marmoutier'), in a case against John, rector of Adel church, for the payment of an annual pension of ten marks (CP E. 241).[12] In other cases the files are substantial,

---

[6] I discussed one such case in my paper 'Priory and Parish: Kirkham and its Parishioners, 1496–7', in *Monasteries and Society in Medieval Britain*, ed. B. Thompson, Harlaxton Medieval Studies, vol. 60 (Stamford, 1999), pp. 329–47. I am most grateful for help in the preparation of the present paper to Judy Frost of the Centre for Medieval Studies at the University of York, and especially to Dr Philippa Hoskin and her colleagues at the Borthwick Institute. I should also like to thank Professor Christopher Brooke for comments, and for his helpful suggestions.

[7] CP F. 104, a matrimonial case, contains evidence that Robert Hertford, monk of St Mary's Abbey, York, was drinking at the Lion in Pontefract with his nephew, John Hertford, at the time John was alleged to have been promising marriage: Goldberg, *Women in England*, pp. 114–17.

[8] See, for example, the case brought by the prior and convent of Nostell against Adam Fraward for the tithes of iron workings in the parish of Birstall, of which they were appropriators of the church (CP E. 98), as well as those cases discussed below.

[9] For example, the case brought by the rector of Thweng against the prioress of Wykeham (CP E. 52), or the rector of Normanby against Thomas of Crathorne, farmer of the grange of Rook Barugh, and the nuns of Yedingham (CP E. 177). The latter contains a list of expenses incurred by the rector in bringing the case.

[10] For example, the case brought by the priory of Bridlington for the appropriation of the churches of Grinton in Swaledale and East Cowton (CP E. 11), or that brought by the abbot and convent of St Mary's, York, against the bishop of Carlisle concerning the abbey's cell at Wetheral and its churches in the diocese of Carlisle (CP E. 58).

[11] In 1371–72 there was a dispute between John de Harwode, rector of Richmond, and the abbot and convent of St Mary's, York, concerning the expenses of providing a chaplain for the chapel in Richmond castle, the abbot and convent being the patrons of Richmond church (CP E. 115). In 1387–88 there was a similar case between the abbot and convent and Nicholas de Harwode, then rector (CP E. 134): see Smith, *Court of York 1301–1399*, pp. 44, 56–7.

[12] Dorothy Owen, 'Ecclesiastical Jurisdiction in England 1300–1550: The Records and their Interpretation', in *The Materials, Sources and Methods of Ecclesiastical History*, ed. Derek Baker (Oxford, 1975), pp. 199–221, notes that the formal libel was not used or preserved at York, and that 'For the substance of the cause it is necessary to rely on the proctor's statement of the positions or articles which he proposes and intends to prove' (p. 212).

containing the appointment of proctors, the positions for proof, that is, the plaintiff's case,[13] the articles,[14] the depositions, and the definitive sentence. The depositions were taken in secret and recorded by a scribe or clerk, to be written up later from notes taken at the time.[15] The language of the record is Latin, though occasionally phrases in the vernacular creep in, creating a sense of immediacy.[16] Not mentioned directly by Helmholz or Owen, but often to be found among supporting papers, are copies of papal and episcopal privileges, and other confirmations, which were produced to support the claims of the plaintiff.[17]

One type of evidence that cause papers yield is quite simply the record of the names, associations, and to some small extent the careers, of male and female religious that are unknown from other sources. CP E. 49 is a case, dated 1344, concerning the tithes of Wressell (ER), more specifically three places within the parish, Loftsome, Brind, and Newsholme. The parties concerned were the rector of Wressell and the prior and convent of the Gilbertine monastery of Malton. Among those who gave evidence was Robert of New Malton, aged over sixty, a canon of Malton.[18] Fellow witnesses, also canons of Malton, were Brother Henry de Rygby, almost eighty years of age (CP E. 49/2, deposition x), and William de Clifton (deposition xxii). Giving evidence on behalf of the canons of Malton were three canons of Ellerton on Spalding Moor, another male Gilbertine house in the diocese of York: Brother William de Ad', aged over eighty, Robert de Burton and Richard de Donnesburgh (CP E. 49/2, depositions xviij, xx and xxi). The priory of Ellerton was itself involved in a case against the prioress and convent of Thicket in 1440–41 (CP F. 221). The records of the case include the names of two nuns of Thicket, Dame Alice Hadilsay, aged over forty, who claimed to have been a professed nun there for 30 years, and Dame Alice Broghton, aged forty-nine, who claimed to have been a nun for 40

---

[13] Owen (ibid.) notes that these can be very long, and that at York they were 'carefully and professionally drawn up', in contrast to Ely, where they were drawn up *oretenus*.

[14] Helmholz, *Marriage Litigation*, pp. 17–18. Helmholz notes that by the fifteenth century the York cause papers often combine the positions, which begin with the phrase *Item pono quod . . .*, and articles, which begin *Item probare quod . . .* . The combined positions and articles are distinguished by the opening: *Intendit ponit et probare intendit quod . . .* .

[15] See Helmholz, *Marriage Litigation*, pp. 19–20; Owen, 'Ecclesiastical Jurisdiction', pp. 213–14.

[16] See, for instance, Burton, 'Priory and Parish', p. 238.

[17] My attention was first drawn to the presence of copies of such documents among the files of cause papers by David Smith, who pointed out to me the act of Archbishop William Fitz Herbert in favour of Kirkham Priory, in a case concerned with the inhabitants of the hamlet of Kirkham Roo, which lay outside the gates of the priory (CP F. 307, discussed in my 'Priory and Parish'), and that of Archbishop Henry Murdac for Kirkstall Abbey, produced in a case concerned with the appropriation to Kirkstall of the church of Barnoldswick (CP E. 243). These appear in *EEA* v, nos 91, 121.

[18] CP E. 49/2, deposition iii; this set of depositions was listed by Purvis under the number E. 256, but recognized by David Smith as a part of CP E. 49.

years (CP F. 221/1). This would suggest that the women had been educated at the nunnery from an early age. Their evidence in turn reveals the names of two canons of Ellerton, Brother John Bolyngton and Brother John Rotcy. These examples give a strong indication of the potential of cause papers for prosopographical research.

The sources for the history of medieval nunneries are notoriously meagre, and although it can be argued that previous studies may have overstated the case, it remains true that records generated by the northern nunneries do not survive in the same quantity as those of many of their male counterparts. The York cause papers therefore provide a welcome addition to the corpus of material available for study. The question of Cistercian nunneries is an interesting case in point. Scholarship is quite rightly now questioning the old maxim that all Cistercian monks were members of an 'obstinately masculine' order, which rejected 'Cistercian nuns' out of hand, and instead emphasizes their ambivalence: some Cistercian monks and abbots were supportive of religious women, others less so. In Yorkshire, Cistercian men seem to have been sympathetic to female religious who wished to follow the Cistercian way of life.[19] However, recent investigation into one Yorkshire Cistercian nunnery, Swine, has shown that arrangements in this one house seem to have been flexible, and experimental, suggesting that to label a nunnery 'Cistercian' may be misleading;[20] and there are still questions to be asked about the date and circumstances in which nunneries became Cistercian.

Two causes from York shed some light on the question of Cistercian nunneries. In 1393 a three-way case was brought, the parties being the prioress and convent of Wallingwells in Nottinghamshire,[21] the prioress and convent of Hampole (WR), lying about fifteen miles north-north-west of Wallingwells, and Hugh Folwod and Henry Holme, whom the prioress and convent of Wallingwells had brought to court for non-payment of tithes in a wood called Brockhole.[22] The proctor's statement indicates that among the

---

[19] Janet Burton, *The Monastic Order in Yorkshire, 1069–1215* (Cambridge, 1999), pp. 146–52. See also my earlier study, *The Yorkshire Nunneries in the Twelfth and Thirteenth Centuries* (Borthwick Paper 56, 1979).

[20] Janet Burton, 'The "Chariot of Aminadab" and the Yorkshire Priory of Swine', in *Pragmatic Utopias: Ideals and Communities, 1200–1630*, ed. Rosemary Horrox and Sarah Rees Jones (Cambridge, 2001), pp. 26–42. Sally Thompson drew attention to the variety of observance and allegiances displayed by women's houses, and the difficulties of defining their association with male religious orders: see *Women Religious: The Founding of English Nunneries after the Norman Conquest* (Oxford, 1991), p. 3, and, on the Cistercians in particular, pp. 94–112.

[21] A Benedictine nunnery, founded 1140 x 1144 by Ralph de Chevrecurt.

[22] CP E. 195; Donahue, *Records of the Medieval Ecclesiastical Courts, II*, p. 128, notes this as a tithe case with a prioress and convent [Hampole] intervening after a sentence by the commissary general for another [Wallingwells]. The 'Brockholes' of the cause paper is to be identified as Brockhole in the parish of Cantley: EPNS, *West Riding of Yorkshire* i, p. 41, where the first recorded occurrence is noted as 1532. Cantley is now part of Doncaster: ibid., p. 39.

many questions to be asked of the witnesses were whether the wood belonged to Hampole Priory, and whether tithes had ever been paid on the property.[23] The articles indicate that the proctor of the prioress and convent of Hampole intended to prove that Brockhole belonged to them, and had done so for over 40 years; and that the prioress and convent were free, by papal privilege, from the payment of tithes on all lands they cultivated themselves, or gave to others to cultivate. The articles end, quite characteristically, with a statement that these things were well known in the city and diocese of York and the parishes of Hampole and Cantley.

The case, then, seems to be fairly routine. The Cistercian nunnery of Hampole, which held the woodland called Brockhole, was claiming tithe exemption granted to it by the pope, against the prioress and convent of Wallingwells, who had demanded tithes from the two named individuals.[24] What are of particular interest in this cause paper, however, are the supporting documents displayed by the nuns' proctor. The roll of privileges began with a bull of Pope Innocent III, dated at the Lateran, 10 Kal. June (23 May) 1204. C.R. and Mary Cheney knew only the abbreviated version of this bull, transcribed by Roger Dodsworth in the seventeenth century, and now Oxford, Bodl. MS Dodsworth 9, fol. 318r, and Dodsworth 118, fol. 45v.[25] CP E. 195 preserves the full version, and from this we learn that the bull was addressed to Prioress Cecily[26] and her sisters, present and future, in the monastery of St Mary, Hampole. It stipulated that the monastic order be kept inviolate there, according to God and the Rule of St Benedict, and the institutes of the Cistercian order. It confirmed the possessions of the house, enumerated as: the place where the monastery was situated; the church of Adwick on the Hill; the church of Melton on the Hill, and the church of Greetwell, all of which the priory had possessed *antequam Cisterciensis ordinis instituta susciperet*. The pope confirmed other possessions, and granted the nunnery immunity from the payment of tithes on lands the nuns cultivated with their own hands.

The third privilege included in this roll is the full text of a papal bull of Adrian IV, dated at the Lateran, 3 Nones February (3 February) 1156, and addressed to his beloved daughters in Christ the nuns of the monastery of Hampole. The pope ordered, *in primis*, that the Rule of St Benedict be kept inviolate; confirmed various possessions; and granted tithe exemption on *novalia* cultivated by the nuns' own hands, and free sepulture for all those

---

[23] The statement ends with the vernacular: 'A dieu meistre Hugo dieu vous garde quod Joh' et Robyn kyng off felaws.'

[24] Cantley church was appropriated to the nuns of Wallingwells in 1272: *The Register of Walter Giffard, Lord Archbishop of York, 1266–1279*, ed. W. Brown (Surtees Society 109, 1904), pp. 36–7.

[25] C.R. Cheney and Mary Cheney, eds, *The Letters of Pope Innocent III concerning England and Wales* (Oxford, 1967), p. 100, no. 602.

[26] Noted in the revised edition of *Heads I*, p. 293.

who wished to be buried there, except for those who were excommunicate. Holtzmann (*Papsturkunden in England*) had available to him only the English abstract in Oxford, Bodl. MS Dodsworth 9, fol. 317v.[27] In this bull, which provides the earliest date for the foundation of Hampole by William de Clerfai and his wife, Avice de Tany, the pope granted Cistercian privileges, but did not explicitly call the house Cistercian. The bull of Innocent III, with its phrase *antequam Cisterciensis ordinis instituta susciperet*, suggests that at a date between 1156 and 1204 Cistercian statutes were more formally adopted. Here the cause paper yields complete texts of bulls previously known only in brief abstracts from other sources.[28]

Further evidence of the Cistercian identity of Hampole, as well as its wider Cistercian contacts, is suggested by the inclusion, on this same roll of privileges, of a bull of Pope Innocent IV for the male abbey of Rievaulx, dated 6 Kal. August in his first year (27 July 1243), ordering that no one was to exact tithes from the monks.[29] This has a marginal note: *Facta est collacio et concordat cum originali*. Thus, the nuns of Hampole were apparently associating themselves not with the nearest male Cistercian house, Roche Abbey, but with one of the two premier Cistercian houses in the North. They were apparently reinforcing their claims to Cistercian privileges by displaying not only their own papal bulls, but those of Rievaulx Abbey as well.

A further cause paper that sheds light on issues surrounding the rights and privileges of Cistercian nuns comes from a tithe case of 1440–41, brought by

[27] *PUE* iii, p. 16: 'Pope Adrian the fourth ordaynes that the nonnys of the monastery of St Mary in the place called Hanapole shole be of the order (*PUE* ordre) of St Benet and doth grant unto them free sepulture and byryeng to all that frely chose (*PUE* these) to bee byried theare. Dated in the yeare 1156'. Holtzmann notes (p. 19) a further copy in MS Dodsworth 118, fol. 45v. Dodsworth 9 was copied by Roger Dodsworth mainly from monastic cartularies, and the note to the copy of this and other Hampole charters, 'Lib. B, fol. 45', suggests the existence of a lost Hampole cartulary. The Hampole charters in MS Dodsworth 118 were copied 'ex evidentiis domini Wassington de Adwik in the West [sic] 3 June 1621' (fol. 44r).
[28] Similarly, CP E. 4, a case brought by the prior and canons of Bridlington against the bishop of Lincoln, concerning the appropriation of the Lincolnshire church of Goxhill, contains a roll of confirmations, among them a bull of Pope Benedict XI confirming bulls of Clement III and Celestine III. The earlier bulls were printed by Holtzmann in *PUE* iii, no. 422 (pp. 517–18) and no. 486 (p. 578) from incomplete copies in the cartulary of Bridlington, which lacked the dating clauses. They were accordingly dated by Holtzmann simply to the pontificates of the two popes. The full copies in CP E. 4/2 allow more the precise dating of 5 March 1190 and 25 March 1194 respectively.
[29] *CPL* i, 199; *Les Registres d'Innocent IV*, ed. E. Berger, Bibliothèque des Ecoles Françaises D'Athènes et de Rome I (Paris, 1884–1911), i, p. 13, no. 47. The second privilege on the Hampole roll is a further bull for Rievaulx, granting tithe exemption, issued by Pope Innocent III at the Lateran, 11 Kal. June in his seventh year (22 May 1204), but I have not been able to locate this among the printed bulls of Innocent III. This was dated the day before Innocent's privilege for Hampole, noted above.

the prioress and convent of Thicket (ER) against the prior and convent of Ellerton, appropriators of the churches of Ellerton and Aughton, and the chapel of East Cottingwith (CP F. 221). The surviving papers in this case comprise a series of five depositions, two, as already mentioned, by nuns of Thicket (CP F. 221/1); a notarial instrument, authenticated by William Byspham, of a statement by Thomas Fosseton, chaplain, proctor of the prioress and convent, showing his authorization, and reciting the appeal, that the nuns were of good reputation, and exempt by Roman privilege from payment of tithes on their lands (CP F. 221/2); a further notarial instrument, by William Morland, again an appeal by Thomas Fosseton, in which the nunnery is described as *prioratus monialium de Thikheued ordinis Cisterciensis et regule Sancti Benedicti*, and as being free from the payment of tithes on *novalia* and on lands the nuns cultivate themselves (CP F. 221/3). The letters patent of the prioress and convent appointing as their proctors Thomas Fosseton and Robert Thomson merely describe the convent as *ordinis sancti Benedicti* (CP F. 221/4), but the bull of Pope Gregory IX (dated at Rieti, 8 May 1228), produced as evidence of the nuns' entitlement to tithe exemption, is addressed to *priorisse monasterii de Thiccheheud Cisterciensis ordinis* and her sisters, and refers to the *ordo monasticus . . . secundum deum et beati Benedicti regulam atque institutionem Cistercien' fratrum* (CP F. 221/5). In the positions, the convent is once again called Cistercian (CP F. 221/6). These state that the nuns are of good reputation, and are immune from the payment of tithes on *novalia* and lands cultivated by their own hands; that they had the right of appeal to the apostolic see; that the prior and convent of Ellerton had caused distress by demanding tithes; that Thicket has appealed for tuition; and that these matters are well known in the city and diocese of York. The bull of Gregory IX in favour of Thicket, produced by the nuns' proctor, does not appear in Gregory's printed register, but there is evidence of his presence at Rieti on 7 May 1228.[30]

This one cause paper builds a compelling argument that in the thirteenth century (CP F. 221/5) and again in the fifteenth (CP F. 221/2 and 3, and 221/8, the nuns' appointment of a proctor) the nuns of Thicket were regarded as Cistercian, following the institutes of the Cistercian order. Like the other northern nunneries, such as Hampole, which followed the Cistercian institutes but were never formally incorporated into the order, the nuns of Thicket may have been attracted as much by the privilege of tithe exemption enjoyed by the order as by other features of the Cistercian observance. Indeed in the thirteenth century the abbot of Cîteaux complained that nunneries that the order did not regard as Cistercian were claiming to be so merely to avoid paying tithes.[31] However, what is notable is that the nuns of

---

[30] *Les Registres de Gregoire IX*, ed. L. Auvray, 4 vols, Bibliothèque des Ecoles Françaises d'Athènes et de Rome 2nd series IX (Paris, 1890–1955), i, p. 144, no. 193.
[31] Thompson, *Women Religious*, pp. 105–6.

Thicket felt confident, within a local context, in claiming to be Cistercian. The evidence of CP F. 221 is even more significant than that of CP E. 195, since Hampole has long been recognized as Cistercian in its observances, while Thicket has traditionally been regarded as Benedictine.[32]

The evidence of the witnesses built up a picture of intimidation of the nuns of Thicket, and concurred with the proposition that they were indeed entitled to tithe exemption. Their testimony also adds to our picture of the endowments of this small priory of nuns. Robert Barker of Wheldrake, aged fifty-three, attested that he had been born in the parish of Wheldrake, and that the priory was scarcely any distance away. The prioress and convent had several pieces of arable and seven acres of meadow, and had, throughout his lifetime, cultivated these at their own expense. He had seen their servants take away sheaves and hay, without any payment of tithe or any contradiction. This had been done from time out of mind and was openly believed by the people of Wheldrake. It was, he claimed, 6 years ago that the canons of Ellerton had first unjustly taken tithes from certain lands. He was not able to depose on the second position, but on the third he had heard tell that the prior had, the previous autumn, gone with one of his canons to the house of Thicket and had threatened the nuns. He was also unable to comment on the fourth point, but on the final article he confirmed that all the matters were indeed well known in Wheldrake. A second witness, Nicholas Darel of West Cottingwith (which he stated to be half a mile from the nunnery), aged sixty-seven, attested in much the same manner. However, he claimed that it was fourteen years ago when the prior and certain canons of Ellerton had taken tithes of sheaves and wheat from a certain close or lands, called *vulgariter* 'intake', and carried them off on their shoulders. He attested that the previous autumn the prior of Ellerton had gone to the conventual church of Thicket and had forbidden the nuns to remove hay, sheaves, or harvest from their lands and meadows. The witness, Nicholas, saw this as – he claims – did John Stillingfleet, William Grayve, John Lange the younger, and Robert Hueson of Cottingwith.

More substance is given to the charge of intimidation by the prior and canons in the depositions of two nuns of Thicket themselves. Alice Hadilsay, examined on 27 September 1441, swore that on an autumn day the previous year she had been present in the choir of the priory church when the prior of Ellerton and others had appeared in person to require the prioress to pay tithes before the removal of hay, sheaves, and harvest from lands within the parish of Aughton, the church of which was appropriated to Ellerton. Later that same day, she alleged, in the prioress's hall (*aula*) two canons of Ellerton, Brother John Bolyngton and John Rotcy, who had been sent by the prior, with the authority of the church of York, had forbidden the

---

[32] D. Knowles and R.N. Hadcock, *Medieval Religious Houses. England and Wales*, 2nd edn (London, 1971), pp. 255, 267.

removal of hay from the nunnery lands of Aughton. Alice's fellow nun, who had also been present in the choir and the hall that day, gave similar testimony.[33]

Cause papers, therefore, add greatly to our knowledge of the nature of the claims made by nunneries to be Cistercian and to enjoy Cistercian privileges. From day to day, however, whether a nunnery was Benedictine or Cistercian may not have been the question uppermost in the minds of prioresses and their nuns. Many nunneries were poorly endowed, and their everyday existence was probably not easy. This is brought home to us through a harrowing episode involving Prioress Ivetta of Handale, a small Benedictine nunnery on the North Yorkshire moors.[34] In 1305–6 Ivetta brought to court three men, Gilbert son of Lecia, Nicholas of Marske, and Humphrey Pex, who, it was alleged, had assaulted the prioress. The file of surviving documents include the articles (CP E. 3/1), positions (CP E. 3/2 and 3), and witness depositions (CP E. 3/4 and 5).[35] CP E. 3/4 is endorsed with the sentence of the court.

The first witness, William de Kirkeby, living in Liverton, stated that he had known the prioress for 3 years, and that he had known the defendants, Gilbert son of Lecia and Nicholas of Marske, for 5 years. He claimed to have been present in the field (*campus*) of Lofthus on the eve of St Matthew in the autumn [20 September] the previous year [1304] after Vespers but before sunset. He stated that he had seen the two men approach the prioress as she was riding, and observed Nicholas say to the prioress that she should have (*haberet*) no common for her animals in Lofthus field. Having said this, Nicholas took the prioress violently by the arm, and the palfrey she was riding by the bridle; the horse pulled back and fell to the ground; Gilbert seized the stick the prioress was carrying in her hand, and beat her on the side with it. While Nicholas held the bridle, Humphrey Pex, with the consent and will of both Nicholas and Gilbert, struck the prioress a blow to the back with his bow as she continued to sit on her palfrey. Asked whether Gilbert and Nicholas ordered Humphrey to strike the prioress, the witness said he did not know, but he did know that Humphrey was the servant (*subiectus*) of Nicholas, and that Nicholas could have stopped the assault had he wished. When the witness was asked what the prioress was doing in Lofthus, William replied that she had ridden to South Lofthus to free her animals that had been impounded, and that it was as she was returning to Handale that the assault took place. Moreover, the witness had seen Nicholas with a drawn sword. Ranulf of Easington, who, like William, was examined on 7 February 1305,

---

[33] In addition to the witnesses whose depositions are discussed here, CP F. 221/1 has a deposition of Henry Queldryke of Thorganby, about half a mile from the nunnery, and CP F. 221/6 is endorsed with the names of these witnesses, plus three others: Thomas Barleby, now of Topcliffe, Robert Hudeson and William Darell, both of Thorganby.

[34] For occurrences of Ivetta, see *Heads II*, p. 568.

[35] These last two are copies of the same four depositions.

made a similar deposition. Richard son of Simon the forester of Hutton (possibly Hutton Lowcross), on the other hand, who was examined on 29 January 1305, only knew of the assault through rumour (*per puplicam famam laborantem in decanatu Cliveland*). Osbert, parochial chaplain of Lofthus, who had known the prioress for over 6 years, gave evidence that he had witnessed no violent assault, but admitted that he had seen Humphrey Pex arguing with the prioress in the field of Lofthus, and heard him call her a liar. He could not recall the day, but thought it was around the feast of St Michael [29 September] the previous year.

The court appears to have been persuaded by the first two witnesses, and the sentence, given on the Saturday after St Michael [1 October] 1306, reveals that the decision was for the plaintiff, and that Nicholas and Gilbert were excommunicated. This case reveals the workings of the court, but also provides a glimpse into the life, and difficulties, of a small nunnery. Prioress Ivetta had set off on an autumn day from Handale to ride to the priory lands in South Lofthus, a short journey, but one that would have taken her across the moor. The purpose of her journey was administrative: to free her animals that had been impounded. She was, apparently, alone when the confrontation, verbal and physical, occurred, the conflict seeming to be about the nuns' right of common in Lofthus.[36] The hour was after Vespers, and it could not have been long before nightfall when she was still some way from home. There is no indication that she was accompanied by a bailiff, or servant, or any of that male assistance on which female religious are said, by historians, to have relied. The depositions indicate that Prioress Ivetta, far from being protected from the outside world, was at risk from it. However, they also show the confidence felt by the prioress that – under normal conditions – she could travel freely and conduct the business of her house unimpeded and in safety.

CP E. 3 shows us a member of the monastic order being brought into contact with the local community in her role as a landowner. For many religious another important source of contact with the wider community came with their possession of parish churches and chapels, and to a greater or lesser degree their involvement with the cure of souls. Like many Augustinian houses, the priory of Newburgh had counted parish churches as part of its endowment from its early days. The canons held the patronage of some of these churches, while others were formally appropriated. It was the chapel of Ness, a dependency of the parish church of Hovingham, which was appropriated to Newburgh, that was at the centre of a case brought in 1357 (CP E.

---

[36] The dispute seems to have been ongoing, for at Trinity term 1319 the prioress of Handale, unnamed, recovered seisin of 30 acres of moor in South Lofthus, common pasture in 300 acres after the corn had been removed, and in moor and pasture, against Galvanus de Tavenge and John de Dighton: *Placitorum in domo capitulari Westmonasteriensi asservatorum abbreviatio temporibus regum Ric. I, Johann., Henr. III, Edw. I, Edw. II.*, ed. W. Illingworth (London, 1811), p. 334.

75).³⁷ This case is of interest for a number of reasons, not least because some of the articles set out by the proctor of the prior and convent are concerned to demonstrate that the witnesses brought by the opposing party were not to be trusted, since they were of servile condition, and subject to John Pert, the other party in the case.³⁸ John Pert and his supporters claimed that the chapel of Ness was a private house (*capellam de Nesse esse domum privatam*) and that the cemetery was a private garden (*ortum*) belonging to John. They also claimed that John, and his predecessors as lords of Ness, had the right to take herbage from the cemetery.

One of the witnesses called, and the one with most to say, was William de Galeway, chaplain. On the first article he attested that William Wolf, Richard Pylks and William Scot were in bondage to John Pert and performed labour service (*opera servilia*), that they had been born in servile tenure, and therefore could not resist John Pert's orders for fear of losing their lands. On the fourth article, the status of the chapel, he claimed that the chapel was not a private house, nor the cemetery a private garden, nor had they been for 30 years past. In all this time he had seen divine office being celebrated and bodies being buried. In times of war he had seen men use the chapel as sanctuary for themselves and their goods, and seek immunity there. He admitted that William of Crathorne, a former lord of Ness, and others, had cut down branches from trees in the cemetery, but insisted that they had done so without the knowledge of the prior and convent, and to the peril of their souls. He further attested that the prior and convent were rectors of Hovingham church, and that the chapel and cemetery were ecclesiastical places, given over to divine service, oblations being made to an image of St Mary, in whose honour the chapel was founded.³⁹ He attested that marriages took place in the chapel, and that he had heard tell from his elders that this had been the case for 80 years, before the time when William of Crathorne was lord of Ness; this William had, he said, been killed at the Battle of Durham.⁴⁰ The witness himself had frequently celebrated mass in Ness chapel with the consent of the prior and convent. The deposition of William

---

37 Donahue, *Records of the Medieval Ecclesiastical Courts*, II, p. 121, notes this as an appeal from a sentence of the commissary general to the official.
38 The admissibility of the witnesses in CP E. 75 is discussed in C. Donahue, 'Proof by Witnesses in the Church Courts of Medieval England: An Imperfect Reception of the Learned Law', in *On the Laws and Customs of England: Essays in Honor of Samuel E. Thorne*, ed. Morris S. Arnold, Thomas A. Green, Sally A. Scully and Stephen D. White (Chapel Hill, 1981), pp. 127–58, at p. 148.
39 The accounts of East Ness and West Ness in the *VCH North Riding* i, pp. 505–6 and ii, pp. 545–6 and 561–2, do not mention a chapel at Ness.
40 The tenant of East Ness in 1284/5 was Sir Gilbert de Louth, who was succeeded by his son, Nicholas. Nicholas's heir, who was lord of Ness in 1316, was William of Crathorne, son of John le Tyghler of York. He was killed at the Battle of Neville's Cross in 1346: *VCH North Riding* i, p. 508 and ii, p. 235. For William of Crathorne's nuncupative will see *Testamenta Eboracensia* i, ed. J. Raine (Surtees Society 4, 1836), p. 21, no. xvi.

de Galeway concluded with a statement concerning the ecclesiastical ornaments used in the chapel. As the chapel was over a mile from the mother church of Hovingham, the chaplains who celebrated mass with the licence of the prior used to leave the key of the door of the chapel, and the chalice, missal, vestments, and other ornaments, in the hands of William Wlfe and other inhabitants of Ness (CP E. 75/3).

Others had a slightly different tale to tell. Richard of Sleightholme (probably Sleightholme Dale, in Ryedale) testified that the church of Hovingham was appropriated to the canons of Newburgh, but, while he was certain of Hovingham's status as a parish church because it had parochial insignia – such as a baptismal font – he was less certain about the status of Ness, although masses and marriages did take place there with the consent of the rector of Hovingham. He was aware that several laymen had been warned for cutting down twenty-four ash trees in the cemetery (CP E. 75/5). William Carter of Holm, a parishioner of Hovingham, stated that he knew that the prior and convent took all the oblations from Ness chapel, and had seen masses performed there, and he claimed that for 30 years the chapel had been closed off and shut off by hedges. He knew that John Pert had sold twenty-four ash trees that had been cut down, on his orders, from the cemetery. However, he believed that the persons who cut down the trees themselves believed the cemetery to be part of the demesne (E. 75/5 and 8).

The case had arisen because John Pert was alleged to have infringed ecclesiastical liberties by taking the property of the church, that is, twenty-four ash trees, and then by claiming that the chapel and cemetery, far from belonging to the church, were private property. The interest, for the monastic historian, lies in the relationship that such cases highlight between religious houses and their appropriated churches, and the way in which pastoral care was – or was not – carried out.

Cause papers have much to offer concerning the relationship between monastery and patron, either in the present, or in the past, through the memory preserved in both local and monastic communities. In 1344 over thirty witnesses were summoned to appear in a case concerning the tithes of Brind, Loftsome, and Newsholme, all in the parish of Wressell (CP E. 49/1),[41] which were claimed by the prior and canons of the Gilbertine house of Malton. Many of the depositions concern the boundaries of the parish of Wressell, which distinguished it from the surrounding parishes of Bubwith, Howden, and Hemingbrough. There is here a wealth of topographical detail.[42] Of the inhabitants of Loftsome, Newsholme, and Wressell who attested, it was John son of Gilbert of Wressell, aged over fifty, who mentioned that Lord Eustace, called Lord de Vescy, conveyed the tithes in

---

[41] See EPNS, *East Riding of Yorkshire*, pp. 242–3.
[42] See in particular the depositions in CP E. 49/1. See also the detailed boundaries in CP E. 50, a case brought by the prior and convent of Thurgarton against Ralph Fisher concerning the tithes of a fishery on the Trent.

question to Malton, because of the foolishness and malice of the then rector of Wressell. Lord Eustace could refer to Eustace Fitz John, founder of the priory of Malton, who married Beatrice de Vescy, or to their grandson, Eustace, son of William de Vescy and Burga de Stuteville.[43] The reeve of Newsholme also mentioned the Vescy connection. He claimed to have learnt from his elders that Eustace de Vescy, at a time when he was in need of money and a horse, asked for assistance from the then rector of Wressell. When the rector refused, Eustace went to the prior of Malton, who indeed obliged him in his request, and in return for the money and the horse Eustace granted two parts of the tithes, mentioned in the third article.[44] This kind of evidence takes us behind the formal language of land grants, as preserved in charters, to local traditions about the reasons that grants were made.

Witnesses whose depositions are entered on the second roll testified less about the boundaries of the parish of Wressell, and more about the recent history of the tithes. On the whole, they supported the canons' case that they were entitled to the tithes, claiming that the rectors until the present had rendered tithes from the three vills, until John Peret, the current rector, had withheld two parts of the tithes of hay from the park of Newsholme for the years 1342 and 1343. With the testimony of Robert of New Malton, a canon of Malton, the church of Wintringham becomes part of the story. The prior and convent, he claimed, were rectors of the church, and had been, time out of mind. He further indicated that he himself had seen the donation of Lord Eustace de Vescy, founder of the monastery (and so Eustace Fitz John rather than Eustace de Vescy) by which he conveyed two parts of the tithes of Wressell to the canons of Malton, to come to them by reason of the church of Wintringham. Another canon, Henry de Ryby, concurred that he had seen the donations of Eustace Fitz John de Vescy, and these included the church of Wintringham.[45] John de Hewyk, aged almost sixty, said that he had seen the religious take the tithes in their name and in that of the church of Wintringham. Brother William de Clifton, canon of Malton, stated that he had seen the grant by Eustace Fitz John in the muniments at Malton. So, while our witnesses from the monastery relied on its written muniments, these were supplemented by the oral traditions preserved in the locality.

Cause papers have potential as a rich source for monastic history. The cases themselves illustrate the kinds of claims and counterclaims that were likely to have brought the monks, canons, and nuns into court. They reveal to us whom the religious chose as their proctors, and details of the supporting

---

43 Eustace Fitz John died in 1157. His grandson, Eustace, was born between 1169 and 1171, and was killed in August 1216: *The Complete Peerage*, ed. G.E. Cockayne and others, 13 vols in 14 (London, 1910–40), xii, pp. 272–81.
44 Unfortunately the articles themselves are missing from the file of papers.
45 Eustace Fitz John did indeed grant the church of Wintringham to Malton. See *PUE* i, nos 112, 154.

documents they produced as evidence to back their claims. Indeed, this paper has shown that cause papers may preserve the best, and indeed the only, copies of documents issued by the ecclesiastical authorities, for example, a papal bull or episcopal confirmation. They reveal something of the way in which monastic houses cooperated, or supported one another, or, on the contrary, reacted against one another's claims. They can give evidence of the perils to which members of the monastic orders were subject, such as the danger faced by a prioress in carrying out the routine administrative tasks of her house, and the actions of a prior in entering the choir of a nunnery church in order to pursue his claims. They can tell us of the provision of pastoral care in churches and chapels appropriated by monasteries and nunneries. In very many ways they can provide detailed pictures of the interaction between monastic houses and the wider communities in which they were located.

Patriarchy and Patrimony: Investing in the Medieval College

CHARLES FONGE

The collegiate church is something of an under-studied phenomenon. Commonly considered to have declined from the early twelfth century, its renaissance was only to come after the Black Death, in the form of the chantry college. Those colleges which existed during the period between the Conquest and the Pestilence of 1348–49 have been considered by historians principally in terms of their role as alternative or additional sources of patronage: for bishops, limited by their cathedral chapters, and likewise for the Crown and some secular lords, fostering similarly burgeoning administrations. The provision of patronage is undoubtedly a pivotal role of the collegiate church and, while it should not be underestimated, its prevalence as a defining motif in the history of these institutions tends to obscure their wider relevance. Aside from colleges' spiritual functions (their performance of liturgical and often parochial duties) and the intercessory value they held for their patrons, it is clear that the medieval college was both a more important and a more vibrant institution in the period 1100–1350 than historians have generally allowed. Indeed, colleges can be seen to have fulfilled other roles – not always created intentionally or codified in statutes or constitutions – which were integral to wider structures and trends and which shaped their development and supported their survival. A more extensive and detailed study of the collegiate church is necessary to identify the true extent and nature of these roles, but consideration of the current available evidence suggests a few areas of interest that highlight the structural significance of the medieval college. In particular, the cartulary of St Mary's, Warwick, a secular college in the diocese of Worcester, founded c.1123 by the earls of Warwick, and edited under the supervision of Professor David Smith, provides valuable examples.[1] More so when considered in relation to the wider range of primary and prosopographical sources (episcopal registers and *acta*, cartularies and lists of *fasti*) of the type sponsored and advanced, in no small part, by David's scholarship. Structurally, the foundation of colleges

---

1 *The Cartulary of St Mary's Collegiate Church, Warwick*, ed. C. Fonge (Woodbridge, 2004).

marked a shift from a system of patriarchy, characterised by the dominance of the household and familial dependents, to one of patrimony, as bishops and diocesan administrations harmonised themselves in line with administrative, political and economic changes.

The collegiate church is often only considered in immediate contexts: the patron's need to provide for clerical staff; the political disposition of patronage; or, for the local diocesan, a requirement to respond to a college's challenge for jurisdictional independence. In the pre-plague period, which this paper takes as its focus, these contexts are perhaps best exemplified by the place of colleges in the aftermath of the Norman re-organisation, where many were reformed as houses of regular canons, with those that remained being endowed with regularised constitutions and commonly attached to diocesan, royal or seigneurial administrations; by projects such as the attempted foundation of colleges at Hackington and Lambeth by Archbishops Baldwin and Hubert Walter of Canterbury; and in the claims for exemption lodged by many cathedral chapters and royal free chapels.[2]

In these circumstances, confined to a particular episcopacy or political context, the medieval secular college is defined essentially as an ad hoc instrument of patronal agency.[3] Accordingly, to safeguard the position of the new cathedral of Exeter, the college at Crediton was re-established on a smaller scale and under direct episcopal control following the cathedral's foundation (the diocese's three other colleges being converted to houses of regular canons).[4] As the need to provide for the expanded ranks of cathedral clergy was recognised, additional prebends were provided at cathedrals such as York and Lincoln, Bishop Samson converted the monastic community at Westbury into a collegiate church and Archbishop Theobald of Canterbury re-erected the college of South Malling.[5] The need for sources of patronage fused with a desire on the part of diocesans to in some way check or subvert the growing authority of cathedral chapters, and projects were initiated whose aim, if not to establish rival chapters, was to reassert the authority and independence of the diocesan. In 1186 Archbishop Baldwin endowed a college of secular canons at Hackington and, although the project was abandoned in 1189, it was revived on Richard I's leaving for the Crusades, when Baldwin attempted to transfer the projected college to recently acquired

---

[2] G.V. Scammell, *Hugh du Puiset, Bishop of Durham* (Cambridge, 1956), pp. 136–7; J.H. Denton, *English Royal Free Chapels, 1100–1300: A Constitutional Study* (Manchester, 1970), pp. 15–22.

[3] A. Hamilton Thompson, 'The Collegiate Churches of the Bishopric of Durham', *Durham University Journal*, 36:2 (1944), pp. 33–42.

[4] EEA xi, pp. xxix, xxxi, xxxiv.

[5] EEA v, p. xli, nos 8, 54–5, 83; EEA 20, no. 135; EEA i, p. xlix; *De Gestis Pontificum Anglorum*, ed. N.E.S.A. Hamilton (RS 52, 1870), p. 290 and n.; *VCH Gloucestershire* ii, p. 107; EEA iii, nos 537–8.

property at Lambeth.⁶ Vociferously opposed by Canterbury's monastic chapter, to whom the college represented a means of devaluing the church of Canterbury, endangering their rights and voice in archiepiscopal elections, the project was nonetheless resumed by Archbishop Hubert Walter. He bought the manor of Lambeth outright and, in 1197, obtained papal approval for the collegiate establishment. A bitter catalogue of appeals and counter appeals by the archbishop and chapter to the pope, king and their peers then ensued and Hubert Walter was eventually compelled to relinquish his plans.⁷ In 1189 Bishop Hugh de Nonant went as far as expelling the monks of Coventry Cathedral and replacing the conventual community with one comprised of secular canons.⁸ This followed the example of Christ Church, Dublin, c.1163, and is later mirrored to a degree in the development of the Culdee community of St Andrews into a collegiate body, separate from the cathedral priory, in the first half of the thirteenth century.⁹ Finally, in 1286 Godfrey Giffard of Worcester applied to the pope to secure a prebend for himself in the collegiate church of Westbury on Trym (a college in his patronage), and, furthermore, to have all the churches in his patronage made prebendal to the Gloucestershire college.¹⁰ In 1287, the annexation of key churches in his collation began and a dispute with the cathedral priory ensued, notwithstanding judgements in Giffard's favour from the king and Court of Arches in 1289 and 1297 respectively.¹¹ Despite the lack of any definitive prohibition, however, presumably having failed to secure the position of any new prebendal churches, the project was not realised beyond Giffard's episcopacy.

These instances reflect a traditional view of the older collegiate churches. They represent the college as a valued source of patronage and a means for the patron of providing for clerical familiars, while gaining added political

---

6   D. Knowles, *The Monastic Order in England* (Cambridge, 1940), pp. 318–29; Scammell, *Hugh du Puiset*, pp. 86–7, 137; *EEA* ii, no. 244; *EEA* iii, no. 370.
7   C.R. Cheney, *Hubert Walter* (London, 1967), pp. 137–57.
8   *EEA* 17, pp. xxxv–xxxvii, no. 6; Knowles, *Monastic Order*, pp. 322–7; G.W.S. Barrow, 'The Cathedral Chapter of St Andrews and the Culdees in the Twelfth and Thirteenth Centuries', *JEH* 3 (1952), p. 37; D.E. Desborough, 'Politics and Prelacy in the Late Twelfth Century: The Career of Hugh de Nonant, Bishop of Coventry, 1188–98', *Historical Research* 64 (1991), pp. 1–14. Bishop Glanvill may have considered a similar scheme at Rochester (N. Vincent, 'Master Elias of Dereham (d.1245): A Reassessment' in *The Church and Learning in Later Medieval Society: Essays in Honour of R.B. Dobson*, ed. C.M. Barron and J. Stratford (Donnington, 2002), pp. 128–59).
9   Barrow, 'St Andrews and the Culdees', pp. 23, 29, 36–8; Scammell, *Hugh du Puiset*, p. 136.
10 *Register of Bishop Godfrey Giffard*, ed. J.W. Willis Bund (Worcestershire Historical Society 15, 1898–1902), pp. 301–3; H.J. Wilkins, *Westbury College from 1194 to 1544* (Bristol, 1917), chapter 1; *VCH Gloucestershire* ii, p. 102.
11 *Reg. Giffard*, pp. 320–3, 336, 340, 343, 347, 361–4, 391, 393, 427, 451, 454, 455, 492, 540, 547–52; *Annales Monastici*, ed. H.R. Luard (RS 36, 1864–69), iv, pp. 495–6, 501–2, 504; Wilkins, *Westbury College*, pp. 22–3, 28–30.

currency from bringing them together in the form of collegiate communities, to be used, for instance, as a counter to capitular authority or as a voice in episcopal elections.[12] The history of St Mary's, Warwick, furnishes similar examples of the centrality of patriarchal authority. The Warwick canons were closely associated with the earl's household, a high proportion of those identified in the twelfth century being the earls' chaplains, witnessing with other members of the family and household.[13] One of the college's earliest prebends was granted to the first earl's chaplain, William, and the dependency of the college's clergy on the earl was not limited to their position in his household but extended to his borough.[14] Richard, son of Azor, first appears as a portioner in the Warwick parish church of St Nicholas 1119 x 1154 and was probably dean of St Mary's c.1144. His father had been one of the borough's *prepositi* and Richard was to have a son, William, who later also became a clerk and was to be a burgess of the town and a familiar of Earl Waleran.[15] The unequivocal dependency on the patron is demonstrated in Richard's case when the archdeacon of Coventry, having been sold rights in St Mary's by the earl at some point before 1144, removed Richard as dean and intruded another.[16]

In addition to securing a return in terms of patronage, investing property in a secular college was a means of safeguarding that property. Shortly after the death of Warwick's first earl in 1119, Geoffrey de Clinton was appointed as sheriff of Warwickshire, a position he certainly held by 1121.[17] The king established Clinton in the county as a counter to the powerful earls of Warwick. Earl Roger, who succeeded to the earldom in 1119, though possibly still in his minority, presented a latent political threat to the king in so far as he was not tied to the *curia* and, at the time of his succession, his brother, Robert, was in open rebellion against Henry I. Clinton was therefore established as a check in nearby Kenilworth and, by 1124, was in receipt of a large estate from Earl Roger, who had been forced by the king to enfeoff the new *curialis* and to estrange a large part of his honour to do so.[18] Although Clinton's rise to power was curbed in 1129, when the Beaumont family returned to royal favour and Earl Roger to the curial fold, the young earl's completion of St Mary's foundation may, in part, have been a

---

[12] Scammell, *Hugh du Puiset*, pp. 136–8; Knowles, *Monastic Order*, pp. 318–27; Barrow, 'St Andrews and the Culdees', pp. 24–6, 37–8; EEA 21, p. xxxiii.
[13] *Cartulary of St Mary's Collegiate Church*, nos 9, 12–13, 16–17.
[14] *Cartulary of St Mary's Collegiate Church*, no. 9.
[15] *Cartulary of St Mary's Collegiate Church*, pp. 440–1.
[16] PUE, i, no. 29.
[17] This paragraph reprises the work of David Crouch, 'Geoffrey de Clinton and Roger, Earl of Warwick: New Men and Magnates in the Reign of Henry I', *Bulletin of the Institute of Historical Research* 55 (1982), pp. 113–24. See also J.A. Green, *English Sheriffs to 1154* (London, 1990), p. 83.
[18] Crouch, 'Geoffrey de Clinton and Roger, Earl of Warwick', p. 118.

means of his protecting his holdings from the king and Geoffrey de Clinton c.1123.[19]

The timing of the college's foundation corresponds with political events. Installed as sheriff by 1121, Clinton did not receive any of his barony until the close of 1124. The open rebellion of Roger's cousins, Count Waleran of Meulan and Earl Robert of Leicester, in October 1123, signalled a dramatic blow to Earl Roger and his relations with the Crown, and hastened the creation of Clinton's barony as a counter to the earl's landed dominance in the Midlands.[20] It is, therefore, highly likely that the threat posed to Earl Roger by Clinton was quite apparent to the earl by 1123, who may well have known of his cousins' complicity with the conspirators in 1122. Of course, Roger may have simply been fulfilling 'the virtuus purpos of his fader' in completing the foundation,[21] but his alacrity is noteworthy. Roger had only recently acceded to the earldom.[22] It was more conventional for such projects to be contemplated in later life, when one's fortunes and position were more secure.[23] The sense of haste is compounded, moreover, in that he was simultaneously completing the foundation of St Sepulchre's priory and possibly beginning that of St Michael's hospital in the town,[24] and all during a vacancy in the see of Worcester which was not to be filled until 1125.[25] This, in spite of the provision of the council of 1102 concerning the necessity of episcopal consent for grants of churches or tithe to clerks or monks (reiterated and enlarged upon in 1125).[26] If these endowments were not to protect his core estates from complete enfeoffment, they would nevertheless consolidate his local connections and affiliations, and may also have been inspired by a desire to harness divine support by securing the prayers of these religious communities.[27] At the same time they could have acted as a sign of political appeasement, demonstrating that the earl was investing in churches, not war – a gesture both of his piety and of peaceable intent.

The question of the proportion of St Mary's endowment that derived from

---

[19] *The Beauchamp Cartulary Charters, 1100–1268*, ed. E. Mason (Pipe Roll Society, new series 43, 1980), pp. 162–3.
[20] D. Crouch, *The Beaumont Twins: Roots and Branches of Power in the Twelfth Century* (Cambridge, 1986), pp. 13–24; G.H. White, 'The Career of Waleran, Count of Meulan and Earl of Worcester (1104–66)', *Transactions of the Royal Historical Society* 4th series 17 (1934), pp. 19–48.
[21] J. Rous, *The Rous Roll*, ed. C. Ross (Gloucester, 1980), c. 32. See also *Cartulary of St Mary's Collegiate Church*, no. 20.
[22] G.E. Cokayne, ed., *Complete Peerage*, XII, pt. 2, p. 361.
[23] For example, Quatford, founded by the Earl of Shrewsbury, *VCH Shropshire* ii, p. 123.
[24] D. Knowles and R.N. Hadcock, *Medieval Religious Houses, England and Wales* (London, 1971), pp. 178–9, 401; *Rous Roll*, c. 32, no. 23.
[25] *Handbook of British Chronology*, ed. E.B. Fryde, D.E. Greenway, S. Porter and I. Roy (Cambridge, 1996), p. 278.
[26] *C&S* i, part ii (Oxford, 1981), pp. 668–88, 739; M. Brett, *The English Church under Henry I* (Oxford, 1975), pp. 143–4.
[27] *Cartulary of St Mary's Collegiate Church*, no. 20.

the town's former minster of All Saints,[28] rather than the earl's honour, and the fact that an episcopal vacancy would be just the time to make such grants, need not diminish the hypothesis for investment on the grounds of protection. The disbandment of All Saints' clerical community meant the potential release of important rights and properties centred on Warwick and its hinterland: territory that the earl could ill afford to let fall into the wrong hands. The best way of protecting these possessions would be to transfer them to another ecclesiastical institution. The episcopal vacancy meant a power vacuum, and the removal of a figure who could potentially side with the king and foil any transfer of property to the new college, by using the legislation of 1102 against the earl and his college. This may be one reason why Roger did not seek to confirm the transfer until the third year of Bishop Simon's episcopate, waiting for tensions to ease, and to gauge the new bishop's stance and affinities.[29] The episode at once highlights the structural significance of the foundation and retention of secular colleges. Whatever the political imperatives, investment carried long-term benefits, obligations and implications.

The marginalised position of collegiate foundations is an impression heightened by the popularity of Augustinian houses and by Gregorian reform from the early twelfth century, the consequent conversion of many early colleges to regular houses in this period, and the later popularity of the chantry college, which blossomed after the mid fourteenth century.[30] The relatively small number of early colleges, particularly if considered aside from secular cathedrals and royal free chapels, can reinforce an impression of colleges' subsidiary significance to wider trends and structures.[31]

Patriarchal authority and the household have a long association, one that resonates most strongly in the early development of some of the secular cathedrals and in seigneurial foundations such as St Mary's and the earl of

---

[28] The church of All Saints had stood on the site of the castle and, in order to allow the castle's development to progress, its canons were translated to St Mary's in 1127/8 and its holdings formed a significant proportion of the new college's endowment (*Cartulary of St Mary's Collegiate Church*, pp. xvii–xxxvi, nos 18, 20–1).

[29] *Cartulary of St Mary's Collegiate Church*, no. 21.

[30] Knowles, *Monastic Order*, pp. 139–41; Brett, *English Church under Henry I*, pp. 138–40; G. Constable, *The Reformation of the Twelfth Century* (Cambridge, 1996), pp. 54–5, 318; K.L. Wood-Legh, *Perpetual Chantries in Britain* (Cambridge, 1965), pp. 4–5; A. Hamilton Thompson, 'English Colleges of Chantry Priests', *Transactions of the Ecclesiological Society* new series 1 (1943), pp. 92–8; Hamilton Thompson, 'Notes on Colleges of Secular Canons in England', *Archaeological Journal* 74 (1917), pp. 139–99; Hamilton Thompson, 'The Early History of the College of Irthlingborough', *Associated Architectural Societies' Reports and Papers* 35:2 (1920), pp. 267–92.

[31] Knowles and Hadcock, *Medieval Religious Houses*, pp. 411–46; J. Barrow, 'Cathedrals, Provosts and Prebends: A Comparison of Twelfth-Century German and English Practice', *JEH* 37:4 (1986), p. 563; Brett, *English Church under Henry I*, p. 199; and see P. Jeffery, *The Collegiate Churches of England and Wales* (London, 2003).

Shrewsbury's foundation at Quatford.[32] From the late Saxon period, for example, English bishops had divided and apportioned lands from the episcopal demesne to their canons for the support of clergy and the better management of the property.[33] At Exeter and Hereford, after the Conquest, the bishops' clerks were synonymous with their canons and a close correlation existed between these bodies and the number of cathedral prebends.[34] At Hereford, clerks and canons were given holdings on episcopal estates, as Hugh the Chanter also records at York.[35] At Salisbury the canons formed an extended *familia* round the bishop while, at Exeter, where the common life was practised more strictly, the familial structure is highlighted by the diocesan's appointment of a steward to look after the chapter and distribute its allocation of food and clothing.[36] Here, the canons' dependence on the bishop was much closer than elsewhere but, even in monastic cathedrals like Winchester, the bishop's command over resources could effectively 'curtail the income and administrative initiative' of the monastic community.[37] However, through the findings of surveys such as the Episcopal *Acta* project and examination of the *mensae episcopales et capitulares*, it is clearer than ever that episcopal households and estates had to adjust as cathedral chapters forged their corporate identities and jurisdictional independence.[38]

Increasingly, collegiate patronage no longer assumed a strictly patriarchal *modus operandi*, with the household as the centre of production, clerks working exclusively for the patron, their fortunes tied to him. It is to be doubted whether this was ever wholly the case, but certainly patronal authority reaped new rewards from the increasingly complex and diverse structural ties that were formed among individuals and institutions. One might posit that the indirect payment of clerics was to change the underlying basis of any patriarchal regime, fragmenting resources (such as the episcopal estates) and dependencies. Separate prebends introduced a new scope for individual enterprise, collegiality a corporate voice which might be at variance with patronal wishes, yet both were necessary to the wider demands of

---

32 C.N.L. Brooke, 'The Composition of the Chapter of St Paul's, 1086–1163', *Cambridge Historical Journal* 10:2 (1951), pp. 111–32; *VCH Shropshire* ii, p. 123; A. Hamilton Thompson and W.G. Clark-Maxwell, 'The College of St Mary Magdalene, Bridgnorth, with some Account of its Prebendaries', *Archaeological Journal* 84 (1927), pp. 1–81; J.F.A. Mason, 'The Officers and Clerks of the Norman Earls of Shropshire', *Transactions of the Shropshire Archaeological Society* 56:3 (1960), pp. 244–57; *EEA* v, pp. xxxii, xxxiii, xxxvi; *EEA* vii, pp. l–liii; *EEA* xi, p. lviii.
33 Barrow, 'Cathedrals, Provosts and Prebends', pp. 563–4.
34 *EEA* xi, p. lviii; *EEA* vii, pp. l–li; *EEA* x, p. xxxix.
35 *EEA* v, p. xxiii; *EEA* vii, p. xxxvi; E.U. Crosby, *Bishop and Chapter in Twelfth-Century England: A Study of the 'mensa episcopalis'* (Cambridge, 1994), p. 285.
36 *EEA* 18, p. xxxvi; Crosby, *Bishop and Chapter*, p. 272 (citing William of Malmesbury).
37 Crosby, *Bishop and Chapter*, p. 222; *EEA* 24, pp. xxxiv–v.
38 *EEA* i, p. xlix.

the social and political aspirations of their holders and patrons and the administrations within which they operated.[39]

While a hierarchical model of patronage continued to satisfy basic needs, such as the provision of clerical personnel and the staffing of positions, in its purest form, such a model was increasingly outmoded within a broader historical context. From the start, bishops had vied with kings and magnates for patronage and, from the thirteenth century, papal provision came increasingly to compete.[40] Viewed as part of the expansion of royal government and diocesan administrations from the thirteenth century, the growing ranks of king's clerks and 'the scramble for preferment' and – besides this more evident clerical careerism – the establishment of chapters' corporate identities and jurisdictions; more complex networks of associations and loyalties were required, offering new opportunities to the patron as much as the cleric.[41] While nobility might still offer a speedier, more assured, path to advancement, there can be little doubt that it was ever more common for clergy to serve more than one master and to move more freely among the administrations and patrons they served.[42]

As the early thirteenth-century career of Elias of Dereham shows, albeit on an extraordinary scale, a significant degree of contact and movement could exist between the households and administrations of bishops, magnates and the Crown – patrons as well as clerical adherents being apt to take advantage of the contacts this mobility offered.[43] In the case of Elias, his particular talents in the field of architecture and construction were recognised alongside his administrative skills and legal training. His extensive service in the households of English bishops saw him act as steward to Archbishop Hubert Walter of Canterbury, Bishop Gilbert Glanvill of Rochester and Bishop Jocelin of Bath, whilst his later patrons included Archbishop Stephen Langton, Archbishop Edmund of Abingdon, Bishop Hugh of Lincoln and Bishop Richard Poore of Salisbury. He was involved in the rebuilding of the cathedrals of Rochester and Salisbury and of Becket's shrine. His career, which included acting as papal judge delegate, and his continued contact with previous patrons and their households, allied to the likelihood that he was loaned from Canterbury to Salisbury c.1220 specifi-

---

[39] Philippa Hoskin, 'Continuing Service: The Episcopal Households of Thirteenth-Century Durham' in this volume, pp. 124–38; *EEA* vii, pp. l–lx; *EEA* 24, p. xli; *Cartulary of St Mary's Collegiate Church*, p. xli, nos 25, 28.

[40] W.R. Jones, 'Patronage and Administration: The King's Free Chapels in Medieval England', *Journal of British Studies* 9:1 (1969), pp. 1–23; D. Lepine, *Brotherhood of Canons Serving God: English Secular Cathedrals in the Later Middle Ages*, Studies in the History of Medieval Religion VIII (Woodbridge, 1995), pp. 27, 35–7.

[41] Jones, 'Patronage and Administration', p. 22; Lepine, *Brotherhood of Canons*, pp. 18–40, 77–9, 83; Brooke, 'Composition of the Chapter of St Paul's', p. 119.

[42] Lepine, *Brotherhood of Canons*, pp. 75, 85–6.

[43] Hoskin, 'Continuing Service', p. 136; *EEA* 24, p. xli; Vincent, 'Master Elias of Dereham', pp. 128–59.

cally for the rebuilding, demonstrates the very great value patrons now placed on experience and ability.[44] Professional contacts and relationships developed by the individual clerk were reinforced, and probably in part prescribed, by a network of interests shared between Church and State.[45]

At Warwick, it was clear by the thirteenth century that, although there remained a close link with the earls' household and affinity, a different dynamic was in operation. As a corporate entity, the canons secured the free election of their dean in 1146 and had corresponded with the Salisbury chapter on matters such as the election of the dean, canonical property, prebendal jurisdictions and capitular customs and freedoms 1155 x 1165.[46] By 1246 the college was exercising its own archidiaconal jurisdiction and was to challenge that of the diocesan from the 1280s.[47] Comital chaplains remained among the prebendaries, but canons were now much more likely to hold additional positions.[48] Richard le Duc, a canon, occurs as a papal judge delegate in 1250 and Dean Thomas de Siddington as an itinerant justice in 1284 and 1289.[49] Ralf de Hengham was already a lawyer and judge when he first appeared at Warwick and was later a canon of St Paul's, Lichfield and Westbury, and a baron of the Exchequer.[50] Just as many diocesans were encouraged to develop or sponsor clerical adherents extraneous to their cathedral chapters, even their households and chanceries, and clergy might work in both ecclesiastical and secular administrations, the formalisation of these spheres and the mutual realisation of the personal and political advantage to be accrued from the situation made themselves apparent at Warwick as elsewhere. The greater complexity of the situation is also attested by Warwick's position in relation to Bishop Giffard's scheme to make the churches in his patronage prebendal to the college of Westbury.

In September 1285, just a year before his annexation of churches to Westbury, Giffard was also actively working with the earl of Warwick to endow Warwick with extra prebends.[51] This initiative continued in tandem with his plans for Westbury, and among Worcester priory's complaints of *sede vacante* losses surrounding the grant of these churches as prebends to his

---

[44] EEA 13, p. xxxiv; Lepine, *Brotherhood of Canons*, p. 81.
[45] Jones, 'Patronage and Administration', pp. 3–4, 21–2; C.R. Cheney, *English Bishops' Chanceries 1100–1250* (Manchester, 1950), pp. 18–19; Lepine, *Brotherhood of Canons*, pp. 83, 85–6.
[46] *Cartulary of St Mary's Collegiate Church*, p. xlix, nos 25, 68. A very similar contemporary correspondence took place between Wells and Salisbury (*Fasti* vii, p. xxiii and n. 19).
[47] *Cartulary of St Mary's Collegiate Church*, nos 53–4; *Reg. Giffard*, pp. 147–8, 151.
[48] *Reg. Giffard*, p. 217; and see *Cartulary of St Mary's Collegiate Church*, Appendix 2.
[49] Warwickshire County Record Office, Z 131/7(sm); *Annales Monastici* iii, pp. 315, 357; *Cartulary of St Mary's Collegiate Church*, p. 443.
[50] *Cartulary of St Mary's Collegiate Church*, pp. 424–5.
[51] A letter from the bishop to the earl concerning the selection of prebends for the church of Warwick. For two of the three prebends yet to be chosen out of the thirteen, the bishop suggests Childs Wickham and Salwarpe (*Reg. Giffard*, p. 266).

clerks and household was the charge that Giffard had made the church of Woodbrook prebendal to St Mary's and instituted Peter de Leicester as its prebendary.[52] The episode is illuminating in several respects. As with Hugh du Puiset's sponsorship of collegiate establishments at Durham,[53] it is unlikely that Giffard intended to fashion a rival chapter from Westbury, however, both bishops had large households and wished to extend the patronage at their disposal.[54] As has long been recognised, clerical provision was not the sole motive for such actions and patronage was used equally to secure influence with clergy operating within one's own and other administrations and with other patrons, such as the earl of Warwick. For Giffard, augmenting St Mary's prebends could represent a useful strategic alliance with the Beauchamp family, a major landowning and political force within the diocese. The inclusion of Warwick within Giffard's scheme warns against confining interpretations to episcopal–capitular relations and demonstrates the interconnections, as well as tensions, that could exist between college and diocese. St Mary's had continued to grow in capitular confidence and was similarly aware of the growing opportunities and demands of these networks of patronage. An indicator of these demands is the incidence of non-residency issues. Bishop Walter de Cantilupe issued an ordinance to the college 1237 × 1266, warning the dean and canons as to their residence and establishing six chaplains who were to be supported from the canons' prebends.[55] Non-residence now appears as a recurrent theme in St Mary's history, Giffard's proctor warning John de Plesset (possibly a relation of the late earl of Warwick, Sir John du Plessis, d.1263) as to his residence soon afterwards, in 1270.[56] The Warwick chapter, perhaps spurred by their success in exercising their own de facto archidiaconal jurisdiction, or by Giffard's excommunication of three of their number in 1275, issued a suit against the bishop, claiming exemption from his right to visit and correct their house, in 1282.[57] The dispute between the college and their diocesan continued until 1285. In the light of the Warwick/Westbury project, it is

---

[52] *Reg. Giffard*, p. 363. The papal bull including these charges was dated 1 June 1289. For the commissions that followed, see *Reg. Giffard*, pp. 363–4.
[53] Scammell, *Hugh du Puiset*, p. 136.
[54] Scammell, *Hugh du Puiset*, pp. 232–9. Interestingly, a later successor of Giffard, Bishop John Carpenter (1444–76), was to rebuild the college and revise its statutes and, indeed, was to style himself 'bishop of Worcester and Westbury' (*VCH Gloucestershire* ii, p. 108; Wilkins, *Westbury College*, pp. 145–53).
[55] EEA 13, no. 162.
[56] *Reg. Giffard*, p. 39. That an apparent increase in non-residence is not wholly linked to the emergence of a fuller written record is attested by the example of St Paul's, where there was relatively little non-residence in the early Norman chapter (Brooke, 'Composition of the Chapter of St Paul's', p. 120). Absenteeism and a traffic in prebends occurs at Penkridge from the early thirteenth century (D. Styles, 'The Early History of Penkridge Church', *Staffordshire Historical Collections* 3rd series (1950–51), pp. 3–52).
[57] *Reg. Giffard*, p. 151.

eloquent of the bishop's ability to separate issues with the dean and canons from those concerning the college and its patron, the canons' awareness of their corporate status and rights, and the greater removal of the earl from most matters surrounding internal governance and some in relation to ecclesiastical jurisdiction. The episode also highlights the complexity of political and patronal networks.

In 1282, amid St Mary's claims for exemption, Giffard issued a petition against the then dean, Robert de Plesset, and canons.[58] He also absolved a priest who had been excommunicated by Dean Robert. In return, the dean refused to consent to the presentation of Peter de Leicester to the college's church of Budbrooke.[59] This may well have been because of Peter's connection to the bishop: if not already, he was soon to be a member of the bishop's household.[60] Peter undoubtedly felt the animosity, immediately applying to the bishop for an indemnity against any suit Dean Robert might lodge against him.[61] By 1283, the bishop's jurisdiction at Warwick remained unresolved and Peter's position did not improve when, in May, he was appointed as the bishop's proctor in a case between the diocesan and Dean Robert and another canon.[62] The following month, Dean Robert found himself excommunicated for failing to fulfil his duties as an executor of the late John du Plessis, earl of Warwick.[63] St Mary's appeal for exemption from episcopal visitation and jurisdiction was to fail the following year, when the dean of Arches also confirmed Giffard's sentence of excommunication on the dean and chapter.[64] Consequently, the bishop instructed the archdeacon to pronounce this sentence on Robert and the canons and to examine the rule of their house. But it is at this point that the earl, William de Beauchamp, intervened as patron and, at his insistence, the bishop superseded this sentence.[65]

The episode demonstrates vividly the complex position of Peter de Leicester within a situation where the variant aspirations of bishop, monastic chapter, college and patron vie for realisation. As the earls' grant of rights in the college to the archdeacon of Coventry in 1144 and presentation rights in its prebends to Archbishop Hubert Walter for his lifetime show, the political ends that could be achieved through the disposition of patronage had been a constant consideration.[66] However, the increasing value patrons

---

[58] *Reg. Giffard*, p. 148.
[59] *Reg. Giffard*, pp. 153, 169.
[60] *Reg. Giffard*, p. 306. In 1284 he was appointed steward of the bishop's estates and in 1287 the bishop conferred upon him 'in charity' a prebend in the college of Westbury. *Reg. Giffard*, pp. 229, 334.
[61] *Reg. Giffard*, p. 169.
[62] *Reg. Giffard*, pp. 188, 199.
[63] *Reg. Giffard*, p. 195.
[64] *Reg. Giffard*, pp. 245, 249.
[65] *Reg. Giffard*, p. 245.
[66] *PUE* i, no. 29; *Cartulary of St Mary's Collegiate Church*, no. 69.

placed on experience, and the greater movement of clergy between administrations, could be viewed as potentially destabilising the position of the patron as the scope for careerism and cross-patronage become more evident. To what extent, then, are we at risk of concentrating on the relationship between patron and individual, or patron and institution, to the exclusion of the broader structural relevance of the collegiate church? In all probability, the collegiate church, whether in lay or ecclesiastical patronage, constituted an important structural presence at the intersection of newly formed and expanding bureaucracies and administrations.

The period from the late eleventh to the mid fourteenth centuries witnessed significant demographic growth, economic changes, administrative expansion and the greater mobility of capital and population as urban societies expanded, investment increased and the agrarian economy slowed. One sees the growth of the cathedral chapter, the definition of its jurisdictions, the separation of episcopal and capitular estates (*mensae*), the formalisation of bureaucracies and structures, the development of procedural and common form and the creation of new offices and judicial fora such as the bishop's official and the consistory court.[67] The medieval administration was one of the few avenues of upward social mobility. Its prestige and opportunities offered scope for advancement and a share in power and resources.[68] But what place did the collegiate church occupy in such a system?

From the eleventh century, in diocesan administrations in particular, increasing value was placed on educational standards and there existed a recognised need for an educated and mobile clergy to meet bureaucratic, liturgical and pastoral demands.[69] Bishops increasingly hailed from more educated and curial backgrounds, their careers demonstrating the close structural links between episcopal administrations and others, such as the royal household.[70] An expansion in the numbers of educated clergy is reflected in the increased number of *magistri*, who became noticeably more prevalent from the close of the twelfth century.[71] With cathedral schools and libraries, the older collegiate churches, like those at Warwick, Hastings, Beverley, Pontefract and Waltham, had schools attached to them and were also part of a system of educational provision.[72]

---

67 These trends are charted by the English Episcopal Acta project and in studies such as Crosby's *Bishop and Chapter* and Cheney's *English Bishops' Chanceries*.
68 Brooke, 'Composition of the Chapter of St Paul's', pp. 121, 123; Lepine, *Brotherhood of Canons*, p. 68–9, 85–6; *EEA* xi, p. lxxi; Jones, 'Patronage and Administration', p. 22; G.P. Cuttino, 'King's Clerks and the Community of the Realm', *Speculum* 29 (1954), pp. 395–409.
69 *EEA* i, p. xxxvii; *EEA* vii, pp. xxxi–xxxiii, xliii–xliv; *EEA* 13, p. xxx.
70 J.L. Grassi, 'Royal Clerks from the Archdiocese of York in the Fourteenth Century', *Northern History* v (1970), pp. 12–33; Cheney, *English Bishops' Chanceries*, pp. 17–19; *EEA* vii, p. xxxiv; *EEA* 21, p. xx; *EEA* 24, p. xxxv.
71 Cheney, *English Bishops' Chanceries*, p. 11; *EEA* 24, pp. xli–xliii, xlvi.
72 *EEA* xi, p. lvi; *Cartulary of St Mary's Collegiate Church*, nos 5, 11, 18, 20–1, 325; A.F.

Colleges like St Mary's could also provide an important career step in advancing canons' administrative experience and contact with other bureaucracies and patrons. Adam de Harvington first occurs as a Warwick prebendary in 1313, at the presentation of the earl. In 1315 he received a commission to appoint chaplains to the local hospital, acted as executor to Earl Guy, who died that year, and was instituted to another prebend in the college. He was soon, however, to become Bishop Orleton's vicar general at Hereford and, following Orleton's translation, at Worcester also. He also served Edward III's government and occurs as a royal clerk. Although he owed much of his later advancement to Orleton, he retained his Warwick prebend for life and commemorated his Beauchamp patrons, Earl Guy and Earl Thomas, in the chantry he established on his death.[73]

The collegiate church not only brought educated and newly mobilised personnel into a formal structure but was, in part, a means of managing the dispersal of power and movement of personnel between and within the structures that supported administrative expansion. In this way, although the individual careers and various posts and loyalties of the clergy introduced potential sources of tension, even instability, as seen in the case of Peter de Leicester at Warwick, the shared interests and interdependency of, for example, royal and diocesan administrations was, at the same time, an important mechanism of control. Not only did the limited number of available prebends provide a visible cap, but colleges offered a range of openings for the lesser clergy. The Crown's ability to present to colleges like Warwick and Westbury during vacancies in the earldom or see, and the clergy's ability to secure occasional papal provisions, meant that colleges were rarely tied to a single administration. They bridged a variety of structures and balanced a range of patronal interests, seeking the achievement of a competitive equilibrium between the needs and aspirations of individual canons and clergy, the college as a corporate body, the patron, and the wider political economy and its associated administrations. In this context, the separation of episcopal households and chapters, the development of capitular dignitaries and the delegation of certain rights or responsibilities on the part of bishops can be seen as marking a structural re-alignment to avoid any sustained conflict of interests as much as any retreat in the face of cathedral corporatism.[74]

Despite impressions to the contrary, the number and incidence of collegiate foundations in the period 1120–1340 is significant. This is particularly so when the episcopal foundation of colleges is viewed in the context of the development of cathedral chapters and mensal divisions. During this period

---

Leach, *Educational Charters and Documents, 598–1909* (Cambridge, 1911), pp. xix, xxi, 54–5, 66–9, 77, 270.
[73] *Cartulary of St Mary's Collegiate Church*, p. 423.
[74] *EEA* i, p. xlix; *EEA* xi, p. lxxv; *EEA* 13, p. xxvi; *EEA* 21, pp. lxii–lxiii; *EEA* 24, p. xxxv, nos 302–9.

bishops founded twenty-three collegiate institutions.[75] The foundations speak eloquently of the mobility of capital and personnel in this period, the growth of administrations and the need for clergy to serve in them, as well as an incipient chantry function. They are also telling of particular political tensions, as at Lambeth, Hackington and Coventry – although not all derive from monastic sees. However, do the foundations also represent a deliberate, strategic investment – a means of channelling resources and protecting the episcopal *mensa* from further division by investing in an institution whose returns were less obviously pecuniary (and thus less vulnerable)?

Bishops had to move to counter the possible erosion or devaluation of their holdings in response to changes in the agrarian economy and the position of the *mensa episcopalis* in relation to the *mensa capitularis*. Episcopal estates had often been used to fund earlier benefactions in endowing cathedrals and chapters, to support the diocesan's requirements respecting the need to increase patronage, sponsor his household and career and to provide hospitality, as systems of patronage extended beyond the realm of family and household. Bishops also had to guard against capitular challenge or encroachment – not only the direct alienation of estates, but the costs they might have to bear in mounting and responding to legal challenges. Moreover, they had to compensate for the loss of a degree of contingency in the form of the *mensa capitularis*, which had been used as a form of fiscal buffer.[76] Investment in a college provided some relief to these concerns and carried a range of benefits.

The most obvious of the investment's 'returns' was patronage (primarily in the form of provision for the bishop's personnel). This effectively comprised a form of currency, patronage rights being capable of being granted away on various bases, and favours issued to others in the form of

---

[75] Bosham (re-founded by William Warelwast, bp of Exeter); Marwell (founded by Henry de Blois, bp of Winchester); Crediton (re-established by William Warelwast, bp of Exeter); South Malling (re-founded by Theobald, archbp of Canterbury); Heytesbury (established by Jocelin, bp of Salisbury); Darlington (constituted by Hugh du Puiset, bp of Durham); St Mary and the Holy Angels, York (founded by Roger de Pont L'Evêque, archbp of York); St Patrick's, Dublin (founded by John Cumin, archbp of Dublin); Hackington (founded by Baldwin, archbp of Canterbury); Coventry (briefly established by Hugh de Nonant, bp of Coventry); Lambeth (founded by Baldwin and Hubert Walter, archbps of Canterbury); college of Culdees (established by bps of St Andrews); Penkridge (granted to archbps of Dublin); Crantock (re-founded by William Brewer, bp of Exeter); St Buryan (re-constituted by William Brewer, bp of Exeter); Glasney (founded by Walter Bronescombe, bp of Exeter); Wingham (projected by Robert Kilwardby, archbp of Canterbury); Llangadock (founded by Thomas Bek, bp of St Davids); Lanchester (founded by Anthony Bek, bp of Durham); Chester-le-Street (re-founded by Anthony Bek, bp of Durham); Llanddewi-Brefi (re-founded by Thomas Bek, bp of St Davids); Wingham (foundation completed by John Pecham, archbp of Canterbury); Auckland (re-built by Anthony Bek, bp of Durham); Ottery St Mary (founded by John Grandisson, bp of Exeter).

[76] Crosby, *Bishop and Chapter*, p. 223; *VCH Staffordshire* iii, pp. 140–1.

preferments, so engendering a network of protection and obligation upon which the bishop could capitalise.[77] By demising a portion of his episcopal demesne or *mensa* to a collegiate body not only was a bishop affording the investment some protection (by its assuming the form of an 'independent' organisation), and financing further staff to meet the needs of a growing bureaucracy, but he was simultaneously delegating much of the management of the property forming the endowment to the institution, thereby relieving his own administration of some of its workload in this respect. Another dividend was that a college could generate further finances which, while the college was by no means wholly answerable to the bishop, would nevertheless still benefit him and his household indirectly, for example in the value or status of its prebends. This is best illustrated in the form of colleges' ability to attract lay investment.[78] There was also a spiritual return for the founder and, stemming from that, a memorial/prestige factor that would be of lasting advantage.[79] Thus, such a college would add to the bishop's standing (in life and death) and would bring a variety of rewards, whilst also securing for at least some of his *mensa* a degree of jurisdictional and financial security and, commonly, further gains in the same areas.

At Exeter there was no noticeable division between the household and chapter of the bishop during the twelfth century, and its bishops, like Henry Marshal (1194–1206), were generous in their support of the chapter, canons and vicars.[80] However, even here, where a patriarchal model persisted longer than in other cathedrals and where there was little overt antagonism between bishop and chapter, the structural significance of the collegiate church remains evident. From the thirteenth century, the association of Exeter's archdeacons with the episcopal household is more markedly absent and the household itself is less apparent as an entity.[81] Even as the chapter fostered its

---

[77] R.M. Haines, *The Administration of the Diocese of Worcester in the First Half of the Fourteenth Century* (London, 1965), pp. 94–7; Crosby, *Bishop and Chapter*, p. 359; Denton, *English Royal Free Chapels*, p. 133; Brett, *English Church under Henry I*, p. 188; P.M. Hoskin, 'The Bishops of Worcester and their *Acta*, 1218–1268' (D.Phil. thesis, Oxford University, 1995), i, pp. 28, 46–7.

[78] Crosby, *Bishop and Chapter*, p. 30; EEA x, p. liii; T.C. Peter, *The History of Glasney Collegiate Church, Cornwall* (Camborne, 1903), pp. 19, 26–39; Hamilton Thompson and Clark-Maxwell, 'The College of St Mary Magdalene, Bridgnorth', p. 20; J.E. Auden, 'The College of Tong', *Transactions of the Shropshire Archaeological Society* 3rd series 6 (1906), p. 201.

[79] These aspects are most evident in colleges such as Marwell (founded by Bishop Henry of Blois of Winchester, 1129 x 1171), the collegiate chapel of St Mary and the Holy Angels at York (founded by Archbishop Roger de Pont L'Evêque of York, 1154 x 1181) and Glasney (founded by Bishop Walter Bronescombe of Exeter in 1265). *Mon. Ang.* vi:3, pp. 1343–4; Hamilton Thompson, 'English Colleges of Chantry Priests', p. 94; Hamilton Thompson, 'Notes on Colleges of Secular Canons', pp. 162, 188–9; Peter, *History of Glasney*, pp. 2–5, 19, 39.

[80] EEA xi, pp. xlv, lviii.

[81] EEA xi, p. lxxv.

independence through prolonged episcopal vacancies and absences, there remained few tensions between it and the diocese.[82] The canons' election of their former precentor, William Brewer, in 1223 compounded this trend, his episcopate (1224–44) seeing the creation of the offices of dean and of chancellor, the granting of additional revenues for the cathedral's vicars and common fund (all financed at the expense of episcopal resources) and an episcopal confirmation of the capitular *mensa*, with an agreement on the part of the diocesan not to alienate property without the permission of the dean and chapter.[83] Although elected as someone pliable and sympathetic to the chapter's aims, and who could break the persistent patriarchal hold over the chapter,[84] even Brewer had to effect some form of strategic realignment in response to the limitation of his authority and the drain on episcopal resources. His response was to create the borough of Crediton 1231 x 1236 around the town's ancient collegiate church (re-established as a smaller college during the early years of the new see).[85] Barlow notes the importance of Crediton to the bishop as he increasingly resided in the college and made use of its patronage, to the extent that he effectively established an alternate power base there.[86] The renewed interest in the college and the foundation of boroughs at Crediton and Penryn (where Glasney College was founded in 1265) also demonstrates a financial as well as political readjustment. The long-term significance of this watershed is attested by the fact that Brewer's earlier grants to the chapter represent some the last direct endowments made to the cathedral's common fund.[87]

Just as much of the Church's thinking was based on a static agrarian economy, and scholars (like Robert Grosseteste, bishop of Lincoln) who defended canonical ideals found themselves at variance with more politically aware pluralist prelates (like Walter Cantilupe, bishop of Worcester), so the foundation of collegiate churches by bishops represented an investment in the political and economic structures of the time. The older colleges contributed to the system of educational provision, allowing secular clergy to form structural links and important associations, and patrons to capitalise on a more educated and mobile body of clerics yet manage the greater scope for individualism and the dispersal of political power by maintaining their influence through a more complex patrimonial system of patronage. Investment could help patrons safeguard something of the secular or ecclesiastical lordship and colleges are associated with the foundation of boroughs (as at

---

[82] EEA xi, p. xlvii; Crosby, *Bishop and Chapter*, p. 277.
[83] A.M. Erskine, 'Bishop Briwere and the Reorganisation of the Chapter of Exeter Cathedral', *Transactions of the Devonshire Association for the Advancement of Science* 108 (1976), pp. 159–71; Crosby, *Bishop and Chapter*, p. 278; EEA xi, pp. xlix–l, lxx; EEA xii, nos 245–51.
[84] EEA xi, pp. xlvii, lxxii–lxxiii.
[85] EEA xi, p. xxix; EEA xii, no. 242.
[86] EEA xi, p. lxxv.
[87] EEA xii, nos 242, 286; Erskine, 'Bishop Briwere', p. 169.

Warwick, Penryn and Crediton) and with the bringing of new land into cultivation (as at Auckland). The colleges, generally founded on their lords' manors, brought significant returns in terms of patronage. At Glasney, the collation of the vicarages of its appropriated churches and portions also went to the diocesan as patron, who reserved the right to increase their number.[88] These collegiate churches were not a post-Conquest anachronism or simply a means of financing clerical adherents, to be used on occasion as a political tool, but otherwise limited in function. Rather, theirs was a presence imbued with structural significance, integral to the development of medieval administrations and the movement of capital and personnel that marked the fortunes of the wider political economy in this period.

---

[88] Peter, *History of Glasney*, pp. 9–15; and see *EEA* 21, pp. lvi–lvii.

'Above all these Charity': the Career of Walter Suffield, Bishop of Norwich, 1244–57

CHRISTOPHER HARPER-BILL

Walter Suffield became well known beyond his own diocese of Norwich and the royal court through his enforced role as chief assessor of the 1254 valuation, for taxation purposes, of the resources of the English church.[1] Some light is thrown on his reputation, and perhaps even on his character, in the pages of Matthew Paris. On one occasion he is criticised for securing from the papacy a privilege by which he might extort money from his diocese (within which St Albans had two dependent priories). Elsewhere, however, he is noted for preaching eloquently at the translation in 1247 of the relic of the Holy Blood to Westminster, and praised for his spirited protest at the curia against papal exploitation of the English church and for his notable charity, most particularly that in a time of great hardship he sold his plate to provide for the destitute. Paris reported, indeed, that after his death he was popularly regarded as a saint.[2] Overall, this is a remarkably positive assessment from a chronicler who generally had little love for bishops and who displayed venomous hostility against those who encroached on the revenues of his own abbey. The aim of this paper is to amplify Matthew Paris's picture by consideration of the bishop's remarkable will,[3] of Norwich synodal statutes which are at least near-contemporary and may well have been issued during his tenure of the see,[4] and of his episcopal *acta*,[5] a category of

---

[1] *The Valuation of Norwich*, ed. W.E. Lunt (Oxford, 1926), esp. pp. 52–95; cf. W.E. Lunt, *Financial Relations of the Papacy with England to 1327* (Cambridge, Mass., 1939), pp. 255–90.
[2] *Matthaei Parisiensis Chronica Majora*, ed. H.R. Luard, 7 vols (RS, 1872–84), iv, p. 642; v, pp. 80, 638; *Matthei Parisiensis Historia Minor*, ed. F. Madden, 3 vols (RS, 1866–69), iii, pp. 58, 309.
[3] Summarised in detail in F. Blomefield and C. Parkin, *An Essay towards a Topographical History of the County of Norfolk*, 11 vols (London, 1805–11), iii, pp. 486–92.
[4] *C&S* part ii, vol. i, pp. 357–64 (statutes additional to those now securely attributed to Bishop William Raleigh). These statutes are there dated, with a high degree of probability, 1240 x 1266, that is, within the episcopates of Raleigh, Suffield and Simon Walton; cf. C.R. Cheney, *English Synodalia of the Thirteenth Century* (Oxford, 1941),

Footnote 5 appears on the opposite page

evidence in the study and publication of which David Smith has been pre-eminent in his generation.

It is clear from various sources that Suffield moved in a milieu of sanctity. He had acted as Archbishop Edmund Rich's official *sede vacante* in Norwich diocese in 1237,[6] and the archbishop left him a cup which, in his own will made nine years after Edmund's canonisation, Suffield left to his foundation of St Giles's hospital. He also bequeathed twenty marks to the completion of the work which he had inaugurated on the saint's feretory at Pontigny, for which house he confirmed Edmund's grant of revenues from Romney church.[7] At the very beginning of his episcopate Suffield was present when archbishop-elect Boniface of Savoy stamped his authority on Christ Church, Canterbury, by unilaterally appointing a new prior and obedientiaries, and in testifying to these proceedings he must have been well aware that this was a vindication of St Edmund's claims to authority over his monastic chapter, although there is no suggestion that such tension was replicated at Norwich in Suffield's time.[8] The bishop's copy of the *Decretum* had come to him from Master John of Uffington, a member of Edmund's *familia* and his proctor at the curia, called by Matthew Paris the most famous clerk in England.[9] In December 1254, while in the North supervising the assessment of taxation, Suffield issued an indulgence to those visiting the chapel of St Edmund at Bearpark, the favourite manor house of the prior of Durham.[10] One of his earliest episcopal *acta* had been a similar remission of penance granted to those praying at the tomb in St Paul's of Roger Niger, bishop of London, another reformer popularly reputed to be a saint.[11]

Walter's closest association, however, was with St Richard Wich, St Edmund's chancellor and subsequently bishop of Chichester.[12] They were contemporaries, Richard being consecrated bishop a month after Suffield and dying three years before him. Their lives overlapped at many points: both were canon lawyers, Richard was the main preacher of the projected crusade for the financing of which Walter was to be the chief collector, the

---

pp. 125–36. They were previously attributed to Suffield by M. Gibbs and J. Lang, *Bishops and Reform, 1215–72* (Oxford, 1934), p. 46, following D. Wilkins, *Concilia Magnae Britanniae et Hiberniae, A. D. 446–1717*, 4 vols (London, 1737), i, pp. 731–6. There can be no certainty, but many of these statutes, although of course reflecting earlier papal and provincial legislation, deal with matters also treated in Suffield's *acta*.

5   To be printed in *EEA Norwich, 1243–66* (British Academy, forthcoming).
6   *CRR* xvi, no. 318.
7   C.H. Lawrence, *St Edmund of Abingdon: A Study in Hagiography and History* (Oxford, 1960), pp. 320, 322; *EEA* 22, no. 167.
8   H. Wharton, *Anglia Sacra*, 2 vols (London, 1691), i, pp. 174–5.
9   Paris, *Chronica Majora* v, p. 230.
10 Durham Cathedral Muniments, 2. 13., Pont. 4.
11 *HMCR*, 9th Report, part i, p. 42; for miracles at the tomb, see Paris, *Historia Minor* ii, p. 493.
12 D. Jones, *St Richard of Chichester: The Sources for his Life* (Sussex Record Society 79, 1955); *EEA* 22, especially pp. xxxvi–xxxix and nos 87–160.

bishop of Norwich issued an indulgence for benefactors of Chichester cathedral,[13] and Wich dedicated Marham abbey in Norfolk, the foundation of the countess of Arundel which Suffield did much to stabilise.[14] Both men, from being initial supporters of Archbishop Boniface, apparently became disillusioned with him.[15] St Richard's biographer asserts that Walter, as good a bishop as he was, became a better pastor through his imitation of the saint, whose regard for him is testified by the fact that the bishop of Norwich, alone among his episcopal colleagues, was a beneficiary of his will.[16] Eighteen months after Richard's death Walter made provision for his friend's soul. He appropriated to the dean and chapter of Chichester the Suffolk church of Mendlesham, of which they had acquired the advowson from Battle abbey through Richard's initiative. A vicarage was now established, valued in 1291 at the generous sum of £12, but the rectorial income was earmarked to fund a priest at Richard's tomb, two lights continually burning there, and the celebration of his anniversary.[17]

Such influences upon Suffield explain in part his Christocentric piety and his veneration of the Eucharist, most obviously manifest in his selection as preacher at the translation of the Holy Blood relic to Westminster abbey in 1247, which to suit the occasion he set in the context of the particular excellence of the English church and realm.[18] He gave to his own monks at Norwich a great silver cup in which to place the crystal reliquary containing the Holy Blood brought from Fécamp in 1171.[19] Reverence for the Eucharist is reflected in a mid-thirteenth-century diocesan statute that no leper or other person should ring a bell in a public street, except a priest carrying the host to the sick, so as to increase devotion.[20] Suffield's *acta* reveal a concern to licence new sites where mass might be celebrated; three chapels were authorised at manors of religious houses,[21] and six lay people were permitted to have household chapels, provided always that they attended the parish church on certain great festivals and that parochial revenues were not diminished.[22]

---

[13] *The Chartulary of the High Church of Chichester*, ed. W.D. Peckham (Sussex Record Society 46, 1946), no. 83.
[14] Jones, *St Richard*, p. 50, no. 87.
[15] Jones, *St Richard*, p. 31, no. 18.
[16] Jones, *St Richard*, pp. 68, 165–6; *EEA* 22, no. 188.
[17] *Chartulary of Chichester*, no. 251.
[18] Paris, *Chronica Majora* iv, pp. 640–4; cf. N. Vincent, *The Holy Blood: King Henry III and the Westminster Blood Relic* (Cambridge, 2001), pp. 69–71.
[19] Vincent, *Holy Blood*, pp. 209–10.
[20] *C&S* part ii, vol. i, p. 361, no. 76.
[21] *Cartularium Monasterii de Rameseia*, ed. W.H. Hart and P.A. Lyons, 3 vols (RS, 1884–94), ii, no. 317 (for the monks at Burwell); Dublin, Trinity College, ms 1208/374 (for the canons of Pentney at Ashwicken); TNA, DL42/5, fol. 55v (for the monks of Bury at Pakenham).
[22] Philip Basset at Soham (TNA, E40/14373); Agnes l'Enveyse at Chediston (TNA, LR14/1107); Reginald le Gros at Stalham (BL ms Cotton Galba E ii, fol. 49r); Roger

The contemporary synodal statutes display determination that the sacraments should be administered by priests worthy of their calling. Rectors as well as vicars should be resident, and would be severely punished if they allowed wanton men to serve their cures. The clergy should be distinguished from the laity by their sober dress, and if they failed to adopt such would be deprived of their benefices. Those ordained in other dioceses should be inducted to livings only after examination by archdeacon or bishop's official. No clergy should make undue demands, beyond the custom of the parish, for any sacrament.[23]

One of the urgent concerns of contemporary bishops was to provide a suitable competent priest in every parish, and as local churches were granted in increasing numbers to religious houses, this need could best be fulfilled by the ordination of endowed vicarages. By the mid thirteenth century this was not a novel solution, but at the beginning of his episcopate Suffield definitively established his policy in this matter. On 8 August 1245, less than a month after the conclusion of the Council of Lyons, which the bishop had attended, Pope Innocent IV responded to a request for the reinforcement of episcopal authority by ruling that, since there were in Norwich diocese many parish churches held by religious in which vicarages were not yet taxed, the bishop might act in this matter as canon law and the custom of the *ecclesia Anglicana* required, as seemed best to him for the good of the churches and the worship of God, saving right of appeal against his decisions.[24] A contemporary diocesan statute reiterates that vicars should serve their cures in person, and that those not yet in holy orders must be advanced thereto at the next ember-day.[25] Individual *acta* reveal how seriously Suffield treated this matter. In January 1248 he learned that at Walden abbey's church of Chippenham the vicarage had been taxed not by one of his predecessors, but by the official of Norwich, and considering that this duty pertained specifically to the diocesan, he proceeded to make a new assessment.[26] There is a hint of exasperation in an actum of 1253, in which Suffield noted with disapproval that although there were various portions in the church of Crimplesham, appropriated to Stoke-by-Clare priory, no vicarage had been ordained there, which deficiency he now remedied.[27] At Wymondham in 1251 he ordered that the vicar should henceforth, in addition to what he

---

of Hales at Hales (Arundel Castle, Duke of Norfolk's Muniments, Hales ch. 104); Almaric Pecche at Great Bricett (Cambridge, King's College, ms GBR 37); Simon of Shouldham at Marham (Norfolk Record Office, Reg 5/10, fol. 93r).

[23] C&S part ii, vol. i, pp. 357–62, nos 59–60, 64, 70–1, 73, 75, 83.
[24] *Norwich Cathedral Charters*, i, no. 299.
[25] C&S part ii, vol. i, 362, no. 84.
[26] BL ms Harley 3697, fol. 50v.
[27] *Stoke by Clare Cartulary*, ed. C. Harper-Bill and R. Mortimer, 3 vols (Suffolk Record Society, 1982–4), i, no. 91.

had before, receive a monk's corrody, so that he might maintain residence.[28] Whereas his predecessors had often allowed the monks of the cathedral priory to serve their churches by the employment of removable chaplains, Suffield, when confirming All Saints, Wicklewood, Hempstead and Worstead, now insisted that vicarages be ordained, as occurred when he himself appropriated to them Marsham church.[29]

Perhaps the most difficult decision for the diocesan was how to strike the right balance between the financial interests of religious houses (the duty of care for which was trumpeted in so many *arengae*), the pastoral needs of the parish and the income and career prospects of individual clergy. An excellent example of this dilemma is provided by an actum of 1252 by which Suffield appropriated Barmer church to Coxford priory. He recognised the canons' excellence in religious observance and hospitality and was prepared to grant their request for appropriation of the church in the future, provided that a vicarage should be established. For the moment, however, he was more concerned with the position of William of Syderstone, the former rector, who had resigned the benefice on being instituted to the vicarage of the cathedral priory's church of Hindringham. The surrender of Barmer was made on the advice of the bishop, who was eager that rectors should be resident, but Suffield was also very conscious that almost seven years earlier William had abandoned his academic studies, on which he had only recently embarked, when the canons had called upon him to serve the cure of Barmer, thus sacrificing both learning and time, than which things nothing is more valuable. Now, since the vicarage of Hindringham could not support him properly, the bishop decreed that he should hold for his lifetime the free lands of Barmer church, paying to the canons merely one mark a year, far less than their true value.[30] In other cases, too, Suffield had a regard for the particular merits of worthy clerics. In adjudication on a tithe dispute between the monks of Norwich and the rector and vicar of Marsham, he awarded the contested tithes to the cathedral priory, but since he considered the incumbent vicar to be worthy of special grace and honour, allowed him to hold them of the monks for 5s a year.[31] Similarly in 1246, in the resolution of a dispute between the monks and vicar of Castle Acre, Suffield ruled that the vicar's stipend should be increased from the customary knight's corrody plus 10s to ten marks a year, but only for the tenure of John of Walton, currently vicar.[32]

Few bishops can have been more heavily burdened than Walter Suffield by the increasing fiscal demands of the thirteenth-century papacy. To the normal pressure on any diocesan was added repeated duty as collector or

[28] BL ms Cotton Titus C viii, fol. 71v.
[29] *Norwich Cathedral Charters* i, nos 205, 207, 214.
[30] Oxford, Bodl. Norfolk ch. 73; Norfolk Record Office, ms SUN/8, fol. 57r.
[31] *Norwich Cathedral Charters* i, no. 259 (16).
[32] BL ms Harley 2110, fol. 131v.

assessor of taxation. His commitments began in the first year of his episcopate, when at the Council of Lyons a group of six English bishops undertook the collection of a subsidy sought by Pope Innocent IV since late 1244, but prohibited by the crown until the *gravamina* to be presented to the Council by the English delegation had been addressed. The lack of a satisfactory response from the pope led to further procrastination, ordered by the great council in Lent 1246. By this time the pope had written an admonitory letter to the six bishops, but he received no reply from them, due to royal intransigence, and he wrote again, shortly before 24 March 1246, to the bishops of Norwich and Winchester, ordering them, if their colleagues failed to cooperate, to act alone.[33] Bishop Raleigh of Winchester, however, also conveniently excused himself, and it was Suffield alone who wrote to the monks of St Albans (and certainly to many other corporations) ordering them to pay their share of the subsidy at the New Temple in London three weeks before Easter.[34] In the event, further royal prohibition delayed payment until late in 1246, when the king was finally coerced by the threat by some bishops to impose an interdict.

Some time before 26 May 1252 Bishop Suffield, with the abbot of Westminster, was apparently added to the commission empowered to collect gifts and legacies for the prosecution of holy war and money paid in redemption of crusaders' vows.[35] On 12 September 1253 the pope mandated these two, with the new bishop of Chichester, to collect clerical taxation according to a fresh assessment, and the following spring, when the collectors consulted with the royal council about procedure, Suffield was allocated the dioceses of Norwich, Ely, Lincoln, Coventry and Lichfield, London (excluding the archdeaconry of London) and the entire northern province. His major role was acknowledged by the grant to him of five hundred marks for salary and expenses, as much as his two colleagues together received.[36] The new Valuation of Norwich was calculated on the basis of self-assessment; mandates are extant from Suffield to the monks of Burton and the Augustinians of Canons Ashby and to the rural deans of Cirencester and Stafford, ordering them to send in their returns.[37] The task involved him in a great deal of work and travel; between mid-July and mid-November 1254 *acta* were issued at Eynsham, Cambridge, Durham and Sulby.[38] Despite threats of excommuni-

---

[33] *Valuation of Norwich*, pp. 31–6; Lunt, *Financial Relations*, pp. 206–19, especially 217–19; *C&S* part ii, vol. i, pp. 388–9.

[34] Paris, *Chronica Majora* iv, pp. 555–7.

[35] Lunt, *Financial Relations*, p. 440.

[36] *Valuation of Norwich*, pp. 52–3; Paris, *Chronica Majora* vi (*Additamenta*), pp. 296–8; *CPR 1247–58*, pp. 164, 370, 377.

[37] *Annales Monastici*, ed. H.R. Luard, 5 vols (RS, 1864–9), i, pp. 325–7; BL ms Egerton 3033, fol. 7v; *The Cartulary of Cirencester Abbey*, ed. C.D. Ross and M. Devine, 3 vols (London, 1964–77), ii, no. 458.

[38] As n. 37 above; also A. Gray, *The Priory of St Radegund, Cambridge* (Cambridge Antiquarian Society, 8°, 31, Cambridge, 1898), p. 79.

cation and damnation, it is not surprising that the 1254 valuation substantially underestimated the resources of the English church. Matthew Paris reports that the bishop made it clear that his sympathies lay with the English clergy rather than with pope and king;[39] and they, not surprisingly, were disappointed by the results achieved.

In late May 1255 the new pope, Alexander IV, appointed Archbishop Boniface and Rostand Masson, a papal nuncio, to supersede the previous collectors and to make a new valuation, which in the face of great opposition was never completed (although where it was, temporalities, so often omitted from the Valuation of Norwich, were generally included).[40] After the king had in June asked the pope to authorise further taxation of the English church for the subvention of his Sicilian enterprise, in late summer Alexander mandated Suffield and the abbot of Peterborough to execute the business of the cross, including the collection of the tenth, apparently in subordination to Master Rostand, who had overall control.[41] So, in the last year of his episcopate, as in the first, Suffield was burdened with the unwelcome task of collection beyond his own diocese.

When in 1248–49 Suffield had been at the curia at Lyons he had, according to Matthew Paris, tearfully lamented the oppression of the *ecclesia Anglicana*, urging the pope to show mercy to the land which, above all others, was loyal to him.[42] Most especially he complained of countless provisions: no English prelate was free to confer even the most modest benefice on poor learned clerks, and the interests of needy kinsmen, *familiares* and worthy friends were sacrificed to the demands of papal nominees. The chronicler's rhetorical outbursts against foreign exploitation of English benefices have frequently been discounted, but recent work has suggested that the situation may have been almost as serious as contemporary English critics claimed.[43] Certainly Suffield's protest at the curia did little to improve the situation. One of the most notorious cases, because reported by Paris, occurred a year later, in 1250, when Innocent IV provided Herigettus, son of a prominent Genoese citizen, to Binham priory's appropriated church of Westley Waterless, in Ely diocese; the provision was, in fact, quashed on

---

[39] *Gesta Abbatum Monasterii S. Albani*, ed. H.T. Riley, 3 vols (RS, 1867–9), i, pp. 368; Paris, *Chronica Majora* v, pp. 451–2.
[40] Lunt, *Financial Relations*, pp. 259–60.
[41] Lunt, *Financial Relations*, pp. 275–6.
[42] Paris, *Historia Minor* iii, p. 58.
[43] *The Letters and Charters of Cardinal Guala Bicchieri*, ed. N. Vincent (CYS, 83, 1996), pp. lxvii–lxxiv; C. Harper-Bill, 'The Diocese of Norwich and the Italian Connection, 1198–1261', in *England and the Continent in the Middle Ages: Studies in Memory of Andrew Martindale*, ed. J. Mitchell (Stamford, 2000), pp. 75–89; but for the potential advantages to the king and English cathedral and monastic churches, see J.E. Sayers, 'Centre and Locality: Aspects of Papal Administration in England in the Later Thirteenth Century', in her *The Law and Records in Medieval England* (London, 1988), ch. 1.

Binham's appeal, when the papal auditor was persuaded that the pope had appointed a boy of eight who was not ordained and who already held a benefice with cure of souls.[44] Suffield surely knew of this case, and certainly had other direct experience. At least a dozen Italians were in possession of parochial benefices in Norwich diocese during his episcopate; to cite merely two examples, Vernacius, archbishop of Reggio in Calabria, retained the church of Loddon, while Armann Penellus, kinsman of the count of Lavagna and hence of Pope Innocent IV himself, held Bury's church of Whepstead.[45] Nor did such pressure on livings come only from the pope himself: early in 1257 King Henry III presented Master Rostand, the papal collector, and Arnald Cocetti, his kinsman, to two of the quarters of Dickleburgh church, in the royal gift due to the abbatial vacancy at Bury.[46]

Three cases illustrate the pressure which the system of provisions could place upon the diocesan bishop as well as upon the religious houses which, as patrons of so many parish churches, represented the main target. In 1249 Suffield received a mandate to make provision for Henry de Monticello, nephew of the cardinal bishop of Sabina. The bishop intended to provide him to a mediety of the well-endowed church of Walpole, until the monks of Lewes, the patrons, complained that they were already burdened by another provision;[47] in fact, they were bound to pay eighty marks a year to John Spata, papal chaplain, in compensation for his resignation in 1245 of the same priory's church of Melton Mowbray.[48] The bishop convened the interested parties, and it was eventually agreed that the provision should be waived on this occasion, but that Monticello should receive fifteen marks a year from the rector of Walpole until Lewes should grant him another benefice in Norwich diocese or he should acquire one from another source. The rector of the same mediety of Walpole was also to pay Lewes forty marks a year as a contribution to Spata's pension for life, after the first year of the rector's incumbency during which the first fruits were diverted in total, by papal command, to the subsidy payable to Archbishop Boniface to relieve the debts of the church of Canterbury.[49]

Second, in 1252 the monks of St Benet of Holme presented Giles of Stalham to the church of Potter Heigham, but Berard de Nimpha, the papal scribe who was in effect resident nuncio in England, collated the church to Peter Lena, clerk, son of Bartholomew Alexus, citizen of Rome. Suffield intervened and brokered a settlement: the Englishman was to hold the church at the monks' presentation, but the Roman was to receive five marks

---

[44] Paris, *Chronica Majora* v, pp. 177–8; BL ms Cotton Claud. D xiii, fol. 141r–v.
[45] *Reg. Innocent IV*, nos 5646, 8222; *Reg. Alexander IV*, no. 32; *CPL* i, pp. 307, 309–10.
[46] *CPR 1247–58*, pp. 536, 543.
[47] TNA, E40/14114.
[48] *Guala's Letters*, no. 67.
[49] TNA, E40/14118. Within the year the church of Bramford, normally in the gift of Battle abbey, was collated to Monticello (*Reg. Innocent IV*, no. 5355; *CPL* i, p. 272).

a year from the abbey's *camera* until they should provide him with an ecclesiastical benefice, according to the bond made between them; this sum was to be recouped from Giles or any successor as rector.[50]

The third case occurred in the same year, 1252, when the bishop found himself, and the episcopal church of Blickling, bound by papal mandate to make payment of forty marks to Petrinus, a clerk and son of the noble Hugh Blanch of Lavagna, until provision should be made to him of a benefice to that value. Suffield wished to provide him to the church of Fulmodestone, with the chapel of Croxton, in the gift of Castle Acre priory.[51] This benefice was valued in 1254 at only fifteen marks, and the whole ensuing proceedings indeed have the air of a complex fiction. Master John of Palgrave, who had been presented by the monks to the church, renounced his right therein, but the monks were to pay him five marks a year until they obtained his institution, or that of his nominee, to another of their benefices with an annual value of at least twenty marks; this annuity was to be paid out of the annual pension of ten marks for the use of the infirmary which Suffield now assigned to the monks, in addition to their customary ancient yearly pension of £2. Castle Acre now presented to the bishop, for institution to Fulmodestone, one of his own clerks, Thomas of Walcott, but this church was bound to annual payment to Petrinus of thirty marks out of those forty marks to which the bishop and his church of Blickling were obligated, until he acquired a benefice of similar value. Since the rectory of Fulmodestone was worth only half of the sum now due from its incumbent to Petrinus, the implication is that the monks of Castle Acre were in fact responsible for this payment from their general funds. Few documents can illustrate more clearly than this transaction how even the most conscientious bishop, acting in obedience to papal mandates and in accordance with canon law, was obliged to treat the parish churches of his diocese as parcels of real estate.

Yet to balance this sorry tale of papal fiscality, driven by the costs both of the Hohenstaufen war and of an ever-expanding bureaucracy, it is worth citing an instance of legal consultation which is reminiscent of the previous century. Walter Suffield had himself lectured at Paris, and owned a copy of the *Decretales*, published only in 1234 as a compendium of the 'new law' of the church. This collection did not, however, resolve every problem, and there survives a most interesting decretal of 1248 addressed by Innocent IV to Suffield relating to legitimacy, and hence to the right of inheritance in English law.[52] The uncle of Thomas of Raveningham, the putative heir, claimed that Thomas was not legitimate because a third brother had espoused his mother, Cassandra, before the heir's father had married her, although this alleged marriage had not been consummated. The son's reply

---

[50] BL ms Cotton Galba E ii, fol. 49r–v.
[51] BL ms Harley 2110, fols 135r–v.
[52] *Reg. Innocent IV*, no. 4468; *CPL* i, pp. 254–5; cf. J.A. Brundage, *Law, Sex and Christian Society in Medieval Europe* (Chicago, 1987), pp. 371, 435–6, 498.

was that this betrothal had been before his mother was seven years old, that he had been born of a marriage contracted *in facie ecclesie*, and that his legitimacy had never been questioned during his father's lifetime. The pope adjudged that to deprive the heir of his inheritance not only was it necessary to prove that his mother, when his uncle was betrothed to her, was seven or older and that the betrothal had continued after that age by the free will of both parties, but also to establish that the father knew this when he married her. Such a ruling, given in response to Suffield's request for clarification, demonstrates the continuance of that 'equity and compassion' in papal matrimonial legislation which has been noted in the twelfth century.[53]

At a time when political tension was mounting in England, and when some bishops were soon to be prominent in the growing opposition to Henry III, Suffield's relationship with his temporal sovereign seems to have been remarkably peaceful. The contrast with his two immediate predecessors is marked – Thomas Blundeville had suffered the temporary confiscation of his temporalities, while the dispute over William Raleigh's translation from Norwich to Winchester had culminated in a sustained campaign of aggression by the crown.[54] It was not that Suffield avoided contact with the royal court – his unwelcome role as collector of papal taxation in which the king had a vested interest made this impossible. He attested a few royal charters, particularly for East Anglian beneficiaries,[55] and can be seen in a moderating role as one of the arbiters, in 1252, for the assessment of Simon de Montfort's expenses in royal service in Gascony.[56] Henry's respect for the bishop is clearly revealed by the invitation to preach at the translation of the Holy Blood relic to Westminster in 1247, and in a less public way by licence to hunt in the royal forest in Essex, gifts of deer and a pardon for transgression of the forest law.[57] It was perhaps in recognition of these favours that Suffield bequeathed to the king his pack of dogs, as well as a palfrey and a cup. He was able to obtain respite of knighthood for three years for his nephew William,[58] and was granted the right to hold markets in two of the episcopal manors, for a very modest fine.[59] He was not subservient – he disregarded a royal writ of assignment drawn on the collectors in favour of the king's creditors, holding to the papal prohibition of the use of taxation before the launching of the crusade.[60] It is, however, an indication of generally good relations that the nearest to confrontation appears to have come in 1255

---

[53] C. Duggan, 'Equity and Compassion in Papal Marriage Decretals to England', in his *Decretals and the Creation of the 'New Law' in the Twelfth Century* (Aldershot, 1988), ch. IX.
[54] *EEA* 21, pp. xxvi, xxxiv–xxxvii.
[55] *CChR 1300–1326*, p. 480; *CChR 1327–41*, p. 50; *CChR 1257–1300*, pp. 315, 318, 402.
[56] *CPR 1247–58*, p. 124.
[57] *CPR 1247–58*, p. 219; *CCR 1253–4*, p. 66; *CCR 1254–6*, p. 302; *CCR 1256–9*, p. 20.
[58] *CPR 1242–7*, p. 477.
[59] *CCR 1242–7*, p. 523.
[60] *CCR 1253–4*, p. 69; *CPR 1247–58*, p. 358.

when the bishop claimed a 'monstrous fish' which had been beached on the land of a boy in his wardship, but the king ordered the sheriff to seize the carcass and sell it at the best possible price.[61]

The king had as much influence on the composition of the ranks of beneficed clergy in the diocese as did the pope. There are in Suffield's time over twenty recorded royal presentations to churches in the king's gift, in his own right or through minority, forfeiture or vacancy. These include a learned member of the Lusignan family, a kinsman of the steward of the royal household, a nephew of the Chancellor and the king's proctor at the papal curia, none of whom, despite the diocesan statute requiring the residence of rectors, was likely to be present in his benefice.[62] In one case, however, royal patronage was apparently in the church's interest: in 1246 the king presented Master Henry of Campden to Gosbeck church since the manor was in his hands because Richard of Gosbeck, who was both lord of the manor and rector, had ravished the wife of William le Bretun, against the king's peace, and contracted marriage with her.[63] The use of royal power could, of course, be requested by the church. In 1248 Suffield asked the king to liberate Bexwell church, described as 'occupied by the lay power', presumably as the result of an advowson dispute.[64] More usual was the signification to Chancery of excommunicates who had remained obdurate for more than forty days, a process which was apparently only formalised in the 1240s. Eighteen significations were made by Suffield, and in these were named 10 clerks, including 5 incumbents, and 39 lay persons, including 13 from Shouldham who had engaged in some mass transgression.[65] It is frustrating that the reason for excommunication is never given in the significations; malpractice by executors of last testaments may often have been the cause, as two near-contemporary synodal statutes refer to this.[66] Certainly, however, excommunication seems now to have been used more frequently to enforce compliance with canon law, and the effort to make the sentence effective is indicated also by a statute enjoining that excommunicates should be studiously avoided by all.[67]

In June 1256 Walter Suffield set down his last testament, a remarkable document which confirms Matthew Paris's notice of his exceptional charitable largesse.[68] It exudes good will to those who had served him in any capacity, from the cathedral cleaners through the warreners of his manors

---

[61] CCR 1254–6, p. 44; cf. F.M. Powicke, *Henry III and the Lord Edward* (Oxford, 1947), p. 334.
[62] CPR 1232–47, p. 499; CPR 1247–58, pp. 59, 121, 546.
[63] CPR 1232–47, p. 489.
[64] CCR 1247–51, p. 120.
[65] TNA, C85/130, 1–17, 86; cf. F.D. Logan, *Excommunication and the Secular Arm in Medieval England* (Toronto, 1968).
[66] C&S part ii, vol. i, 359, nos 66–7.
[67] C&S part ii, vol. i, 361, no. 77.
[68] See n. 3 above.

and his goldsmith at Lynn to his most intimate counsellors. These clerks, frequent attestors of his *acta* and his executors, were obviously held in the highest affection: William of Pakenham, from whom nothing but death could separate him; his faithful and beloved William of Whitwell; Geoffrey of Loddon, whose fidelity would ensure that he would take care to benefit the bishop's soul. Suffield's burial was entrusted to the monks of his cathedral priory, and his body was to be interred before the altar of the Lady Chapel which he had himself added to the east end.[69] To the light of St Mary there he assigned the tithes of the episcopal manor of Thornham, and to the monks themselves one hundred marks for their favour shown in his burial, with another £100 to cover their expenses. Further provision was made for a monk, on a weekly rota, to celebrate mass daily in perpetuity at his tomb.

It was, however, to his own foundation of St Giles, built for the remission of his sins and as a chantry for his soul, that he made his largest single bequest of three hundred marks, with other small legacies to be used at the discretion of the master and brethren whose hospital community he had already generously endowed during his lifetime, imposing detailed regulations for the succour of the poor.[70] His successor in the see was urged to favour the house, the inspiration and model for which was acknowledged by a bequest to the hospital of St Gilles in Provence, to which he had been on pilgrimage and to which he now left a mitre and crozier given to him by his predecessor.[71] Suffield's concern for hospital provision is emphasised by small bequests to St Mary Magdalen's and St Paul's hospitals in Norwich, St John's at Lynn, and outside the diocese to St John the Evangelist's at Oxford.

This concern for the poor and needy is reiterated in clause after clause of the will. As his funeral cortège proceeded from his deathbed, wherever that might be, to Norwich, at each resting place it should be attended by poor people of all ages, who should be rotated frequently so that more individuals might receive a penny each. One hundred marks were bequeathed to the poor of the episcopal manors, sixty marks to needy persons on those manors held in dower by Matilda, Countess Warenne, and numerous smaller sums, ranging from three to twenty marks, to the distressed of various parishes, probably those where Suffield had been parson or had frequently resided when bishop, often given on condition that they should pray for the souls of his friends already dead. All revenues due to him at the time of his death through sequestration of benefices were to be remitted and set to the use of poor parishioners. Even his nephews were bound by the terms of their lega-

---

[69] *Norwich Cathedral: Church, City and Diocese*, ed. I. Atherton et al. (London, 1996), pp. 52, 158–61.
[70] C. Rawcliffe, *Medicine for the Soul: The Life, Death and Resurrection of an English Medieval Hospital* (Stroud, 1999); the hospital statutes are translated at pp. 241–8.
[71] For his pilgrimage, *CPR 1247–58*, p. 28.

cies to feed one hundred poor people each year at the feast of the Assumption and one such in their households every day of the year.

This same commitment to the poor is reflected in a number of Suffield's *acta*. When in 1246 he resolved an advowson dispute at Ashby in Lothingland between the cathedral priory and Geoffrey of Ashby, he adjudged that, in return for lay retention of the presentation, two marks a year should in perpetuity be paid from the church to the monks' almonry.[72] When appropriating to his new hospital the church of Seething, of which he shared the advowson with the cathedral priory, he again assigned a pension of five marks for the increase of the monks' alms, supplementing this by the same amount from another source, and he insisted that in return for the grant of the church the hospital brethren should each year on his anniversary make an extra distribution of food and drink to a hundred poor people.[73] In confirming the possessions of St Paul's hospital, Norwich, he assured it a gradual small increase in income by granting it the tithe of future assarts on his manor of Thorpe.[74] In the first year of his episcopate he appropriated Great Hautbois church to the canons of Coxford for the maintenance of hospitality, and Rede church to the monks of Stoke-by-Clare in consideration of their merciful provision of lodging and aid for the poor flocking to their house.[75] In 1251, when Little Witchingham church was appropriated to Newton Longville, it was ordained that each Ash Wednesday two seams of peas should be distributed by the monks' proctor to the poor of the parish.[76] All the fruits of the church of Horning were to be divided by the almoner of St Benet of Holme between the poor at the abbey gate, except for five marks diverted to the infirmarer for the use of frail and sick monks; *ipso facto* excommunication was pronounced against any who might divert these revenues to other uses.[77] While allowance must be made for the rhetoric of petitioners which may have influenced the composition of episcopal *acta*, it does seem clear that Suffield was particularly concerned that the diversion of parochial revenues to monastic houses should have positive implications for the increase of charity.

Beyond the completion of St Edmund's shrine at Cistercian Pontigny, Suffield's bequests to male monasteries did not amount to much. Within the diocese there is only an amount of two marks to the small Bigod Augustinian foundation at Weybridge,[78] a mark to Horsham St Faith priory for the soul of

---

[72] *Norwich Cathedral Charters* i, no. 216.
[73] Arundel Castle, Duke of Norfolk's Muniments, Seething ch. 280.
[74] *Norwich Cathedral Charters* i, no. 259 (17).
[75] Norfolk Record Office, ms SUN/8, fol. 56v; *Stoke by Clare Cartulary* i, no. 93.
[76] *Newington Longville Charters*, ed. H.E. Salter (Oxfordshire Record Society 3, 1921), no. 118.
[77] BL ms Cotton Galba E ii, fol. 49r.
[78] Probably out of affection for Thomas Bigod, one of his own clerks, and for the aged John Bigod, for whom he wrote a testimonial to the archbishop of York (*Register of Walter Gray, Archbishop of York*, ed. J. Raine (Surtees Society 56, 1872), p. 103).

one of his clerks, and the mutual renunciation of debts agreed with Bromholm priory. Despite the conventional *arengae* of his *acta* emphasising the special obligations of a bishop to the religious, including in one charter a paean of praise for the Cluniac order,[79] Suffield obviously did not feel a great personal commitment to them, although it is quite possible that monastic prayers were activated by the circulation of a mortuary roll, such as survive for Bishops Wakering and Brouns in the early fifteenth century.[80] Outside the diocese, ten marks to the Master of Sempringham was apparently payment for a horse rather than a genuine bequest, while ten marks for Cistercian Warden may represent recognition of hospitality received while he was itinerating as a tax collector.

The nuns fared rather better. Small bequests were made to Carrow priory, where he had received episcopal consecration, to Campsey Ash and Blackborough, and to an unnamed house where the mother of Br John of Stamford had died a pittance was provided for the convent of Stratford. The concern for female religious is reflected in Suffield's *acta*. He was obviously solicitous for the Cistercian nuns of Marham, founded in 1249 by Isabella d'Albini, brokering beneficial arrangements between them and the canons of Westacre, proprietors of Marham parish church, regarding celebration of mass and burial within their house and receipt of the countess's demesne tithes.[81] In 1245 Suffield created a perpetual benefice of ten marks a year in the church of St Gregory, Sudbury, for the ladies of Nuneaton, the patrons, on account of their poverty, and specifically to repair the deficiency of their vestments.[82] In 1254 he granted an indulgence of twenty-five days to contributors to the upkeep of the nuns of St Radegund, Cambridge, and the construction of their church, which still largely survives as Jesus College chapel,[83] and in 1257 he mediated in a dispute between the nuns of Blackborough and their patron, Sir Robert de Scales, arranging a compromise which appears to have safeguarded the interests of both parties.[84]

Last among Suffield's bequests to the religious came five marks to each house of Franciscans and Dominicans in his diocese, and thirty marks to the provincial chapter of each order. Both had been established at Norwich twenty years before his election, and by 1244 there were Franciscans too at Ipswich and Lynn, and possibly Yarmouth. He also came into contact with the friars as preachers of the crusade for which he was the collector, and he knew the eminent Franciscan scholar Adam Marsh.[85] It is probable that the

---

[79] TNA, E40/14927.
[80] BL, Cotton ch. II, 17–18.
[81] Norfolk Record Office, ms Hare 1/232 X, fols 1r, 20r–v.
[82] BL, Add. ch. 47959.
[83] Gray, *Priory of St Radegund*, p. 79.
[84] BL ms Egerton 3137, fols 187r–88r.
[85] *Monumenta Franciscana*, ed. J.S. Brewer and R. Howlett, 2 vols (RS, 1858–82), i, p. 389, no. 221.

Dominicans were established at Dunwich and Lynn during his episcopate, as were the Augustinian friars at Clare and the Carmelites at Norwich. This last foundation was colonised from Burnham Thorpe, of which the bishop's nephew was co-founder, while his brother, the archdeacon of Norwich, was closely involved in the establishment of the city house.[86] So, although evidence is sparse, it seems that Suffield, like all the reforming bishops of his generation, was a supporter of the mendicant revolution.

In support shown for less formalised manifestations of religion, Suffield's last testament acts almost as a template for countless East Anglian wills of the later middle ages.[87] Ten pounds was left for distribution among the recluses of the diocese, and in addition 6d was to be given to every anchorite of Norwich on the day of his funeral. Bequests were made to individual recluses at Stratton, Suffield and Thornham, and to the bishop's own niece Ela in her anchorhold at Massingham. (Concern for the respectability and reputation of the increasing number of female recluses was demonstrated in a synodal statute forbidding parish priests to visit their enclosures, to the scandal of the church and the peril of their souls; they were to talk to them only at the windows of their cells about matters pertaining to salvation.)[88] The sum of £5 was to be distributed among the lepers of the diocese, living either in communities or alone, with an additional 2d to each coming to his obsequies. Finally, in an act of charity as much as for public utility, he left three marks to the repair of bridges.

A related theme which recurs frequently in Suffield's long will is restitution of money acquired in dubious circumstances. Most explicitly, he instructed his executors to distribute £100 to make recompense for all those things which he had received in his diocese, by whatever title or for whatever reason, over which he might have a bad conscience. In other clauses he remitted all that was owed to him by poor people as amercements, either of spiritualities or temporalities, and all that at the time of his death had been received or was due by sequestration. He wished 24 chaplains throughout the diocese who were to pray for his soul to intercede also for those for whom he had acted as executor or whose goods had come to him because they were intestate, or for other reasons. He also left twenty marks to those whom he had oppressed when he had acted as official in the diocese. This seems to amount to more than the conventional desire expressed in so many late medieval wills that all debts should be discharged, and to indicate a sense of guilt about extortion. It is interesting that Matthew Paris's one unfavourable reference to Suffield relates to his return from the papal curia in 1249 with

---

[86] K.J. Egan, 'The Establishment and Early Development of the Carmelite Order in England' (Cambridge University Ph.D. thesis, 1965), pp. 278–80.
[87] For Norwich city wills, see N.P. Tanner, *The Church in Late Medieval Norwich, 1370–1532* (Toronto, 1984), ch. 3.
[88] *C&S* part ii, vol. i, p. 359, no. 62.

an infamous privilege allowing him to extract money from his diocese.[89] There is no evidence of such an indult issued to Suffield, but what is certainly referred to is the right of the bishop of Norwich to receive the first-fruits of benefices which had fallen vacant and to which he had instituted new incumbents. This right, unique to Norwich among English diocesans, originated in the papal grant in 1220 to Pandulf, papal legate and still not consecrated as bishop, to take two years' revenue from all vacant churches in the diocese for the discharge of his debts;[90] in its modified form of one year, this became customary, and papal confirmation was in fact granted not to Suffield, but to his successor, Simon Walton, by Pope Alexander IV in 1260. The precise form was confirmation of the ancient laudable custom whereby the bishop should receive first-fruits of churches vacant at Easter, although there is later evidence that they were taken from every vacant church.[91] Archbishop Winchelsey, at his visitation of Norwich diocese in 1304, was horrified by the custom and sought, unsuccessfully, to have it rescinded in litigation at the court of Rome in 1310–11.[92] Embedded in his evidence then is the assertion that the Franciscan archbishop John Pecham had been similarly appalled and had confronted Ralph Walpole, elect of Norwich, when he came to him in 1289 for confirmation, calling it an evil abuse, hateful to God and man, and a clear manifestation of cupidity. Ralph was allegedly persuaded to renounce this exaction for his lifetime.[93] All that can be said is that such feelings about first-fruits may explain the resonances of guilt in Suffield's will.

Closely related to this issue was the right of rectors and vicars to dispose by will of the fruits of their benefices for the harvest season after their deaths. In the one synodal statute which can with certainty be attributed to Suffield, rather than his predecessor or successor, he decreed that, contrary to the arguments of some, in accordance with ancient custom, incumbents who were still alive on Easter Sunday but died at any time up to the Michaelmas synod might dispose by will of the revenues of their benefice, reserving to the bishop the right to the fruits of benefices vacant before Easter in which no new incumbent had been installed by then, but warning his successors that they should not defer institution until after Easter so as dishonestly to acquire the fruits of that year.[94] This statute was still cited in the wills of incumbents two and a half centuries later.[95]

---

[89] Paris, *Chronica Majora* v, p. 638.
[90] *Reg. Honorius III*, nos 2257, 2456; *CPL* i, pp. 68, 71.
[91] *Norwich Cathedral Charters* i, no. 306.
[92] J.H. Denton, *Robert Winchelsey and the Crown, 1294–1313* (Cambridge, 1980), pp. 47–8.
[93] *Registrum Roberti Winchelsey, Cantuariensis Archiepiscopi, A. D. 1294–1313*, ed. R. Graham, 2 vols (CYS, 51–2, 1952–56), ii, pp. 1179–80.
[94] *C&S*, part ii vol. i, 498–501.
[95] *The Register of John Morton, Archbishop of Canterbury, 1486–1500*, ed. C. Harper-Bill, 3 vols (CYS, 75, 78, 89, 1987–2000), iii, nos 94, 121, 125, 180.

Suffield's episcopal *acta* provide evidence to support the view that he was anxious to moderate financial pressure on the parochial clergy. In February 1253, when transmitting to the rural deans of the diocese the papal ruling that procurations at visitation should be limited to four marks (a ruling elicited by the English bishops seeking to curtail the visitatorial activity of Archbishop Boniface), he agreed to limit his own procurations to 31s 10d or less, according to the resources of the place being visited, and instructed that archdeacons should be satisfied with 7s 6d.[96] In 1251 he had persuaded the archdeacon of Norfolk to abandon his action against the monks of Wymondham and the vicars of Wymondham, Happisburgh and Snettisham for non-payment of procurations, and to agree that he and his successors would in future be content with 6s 8d from each church, exempting the monks' portions of these churches from distraint and renouncing interdict on the parish churches as a weapon to enforce payment.[97] This specific settlement is echoed by the principle established in a synodal statute that archdeacons should conduct an annual visitation, but should demand only moderate procurations and should not suspend divine office in churches, such action being declared invalid. Another related statute insisted that rectors or vicars resident at their churches should not be burdened by the bishop's servants as they moved about the countryside.[98]

The substance of Walter Suffield's *acta* is very little different from that of his predecessors and his successor, all curial bishops advanced to the see because of administrative or judicial service to the king. All operated, with the help of skilled clerks, in accordance with the new canon law which had transformed the life of the church in the twelfth and early thirteenth centuries. Yet set alongside his remarkable will, odd nuances in Suffield's *acta* reveal an extremely conscientious pastor, committed above all to the relief of poverty. His episcopate was marked by scrupulous and humane efficiency. Despite popular veneration, he probably did not merit canonisation. His character, it is true, appears more attractive than that of Bishop Thomas Cantilupe of Hereford later in the century, but if he did not display Cantilupe's litigious aggression, he failed also to furnish the impressive range of miracles which testified to Thomas's sanctity. Suffield does, however, emerge as a model diocesan, who fails to be outstanding only because he coincided in time with St Richard of Chichester and Robert Grosseteste.

---

[96] Paris, *Chronica Majora* vi, pp. 231–2.

[97] BL ms Cotton Titus C viii, fols 71v–72r; this despite the fact that the archdeacon had already received a favourable verdict from the papal auditor (the future pope Nicholas III) in 1249 when he brought a case against Wymondham priory concerning his right to visit and exercise jurisdiction in the parishes of Wymondham and Happisburgh (*Reg. Innocent IV*, nos 4645–6).

[98] *C&S* part ii, vol. i, 360, no. 71.

The Law of Charity and the English Ecclesiastical Courts

R.H. HELMHOLZ

David Smith and I first met in the fall of 1967. At the time we were graduate students. We shared an interest in the institutional history of the church and were attempting to write Ph.D. dissertations on some aspect of that subject. Although our research would eventually take us into many corners of England and require us to work in many different archives, at the time we were both in London, and we chanced to enroll in a seminar on medieval bishops' registers being given at the Institute of Historical Research by the late Professor Rosalind Hill. As I recall, we were the only students taking part, and we became friends.

This was a happy event for me, both professionally and personally. In the years that followed, I became something of a specialist in the history of the ecclesiastical courts in England, and David became (among other things) the Director of the Institute which contains the best collection of surviving records from those courts. It became my practice and my aspiration to spend at least one week each year working in the Borthwick Institute. I may have missed a summer, or perhaps two, but I have been a regular user of the Borthwick, and David has been there to greet me and to help me. The occasion of his formal retirement and his sixtieth birthday provides a fitting moment to recall some of the things that have brought us together over the years and also to attempt to fill one small gap in the history of English law: the law of charity and the ecclesiastical forum.

Introduction

It was once assumed that the English law of charity had its origins in the enactment of the Tudor statutes of charitable uses.[1] Prior to this legislation, charity had existed, but it stood largely outside the realm of regulation by law. Giving to charity was a spiritual and private matter. Charitable gifts

---

1 39–40 Eliz. I, c. 6 (1597); 43 Eliz. I, c. 4 (1601). See William Holdsworth, *History of English Law*, 4th edn (London, 1925), iv, pp. 398–400.

were undoubtedly made, but their definition was uncertain, their regulation sporadic, and their enforcement ineffective.[2] Moreover, the principal purpose of charitable giving was thought to be saving the soul of the donor, rather than benefitting the world's unfortunates. Personal piety was manifest in the gift, and that manifestation was itself the object. Thus 'indiscriminate charity', often enough coupled with crude attempts to repress vagabondage and idleness, became the order of the day.[3] The law did not much matter.

More recent scholarship has redrawn this picture. It has recognized the relevance of the medieval canon law in setting out some basic principles of the law of charity and it has shown that a more realistic attitude towards the aims and limitations of charitable giving animated medieval juristic thought.[4] Some enthusiasts have gone so far as to see the church and its law as the prime mover in creating an effective law of charity,[5] and today the medieval church often receives immediate and respectful attention as the font of organized benevolent giving. However, so far as I am aware, no one has looked at this matter from the perspective of the records of the ecclesiastical courts. These records allow us to ask how far the charitable aspirations of the people were translated into effective law prior to enactment of the Statutes of Charitable Uses. An adequate appraisal must begin, however, with the law contained in the *Corpus iuris canonici*.[6]

---

[2] This is encouraged by the preamble to the act of 1601, which asserts its necessity because of 'frauds, breaches of trust, and negligence' on the part of those responsible for administering charitable gifts.

[3] See, e.g., William Ashley, *Introduction to English Economic History and Theory*, 4th edn (London, 1925), ii, pp. 328–38; W.K. Jordan, *Philanthropy in England 1480–1660* (New York, 1959), pp. 54–6.

[4] Gareth Jones, *History of the Law of Charity, 1532–1827* (Cambridge, 1969), pp. 1–9; George W. Keeton, *The Modern Law of Charities* (London, 1962), pp. 1–12.

[5] See, e.g., R.N. Swanson, *Church and Society in Late Medieval England* (Oxford, 1989), pp. 299–308; Brian Tierney, *Medieval Poor Law* (Berkeley and Los Angeles, Calif., 1959); Eamon Duffy, *The Stripping of the Altars: Traditional Religion in England, 1400–1580* (New Haven and London, 1992).

[6] The following citations to the texts of the canon law are used hereafter:
    Dist. 1 c. 1   *Decretum Gratiani*, Distinctio 1, canon 1
    C. 1 q. 1 c. 1   ———, Causa 1, quaestio 1, canon 1
    X 1.1.1   *Decretales Gregorii IX*, Book 1, tit. 1, cap. 1
    Sext 1.1.1   *Liber sextus*, Book 1, tit. 1, cap. 1
    gl. ord.   *glossa ordinaria* (standard commentary on texts of *Corpus iuris canonici* and *Corpus iuris civilis*)
    s. v.   *sub verbo* (reference to *glossa ordinaria* or other commentary on a legal text)

The Canon Law

In some respects, beginning with the formal law leads the reader to doubt the reality of any expectation that the church was the prime mover in development of the law of charity. The *ius commune*'s contribution to the creation of a proper law of charity was an uncertain one.

The *Corpus iuris canonici*

Neither Gratian's *Decretum* (1140) nor the *Decretales Gregorii IX* (1234) contained any book or title dealing expressly with charitable institutions or with the law of charity generally. Roman law, however rudimentary its law about property given for charitable purposes,[7] did at least have a title devoted to hospitals and orphans (Cod. 1.3(6).1–55). The canon law did not have even that. The Decretals contained a title *De donationibus* (X 3.24.1–10), but it was not especially concerned with charitable gifts. There was also a section called *De testamentis* (X 3.26.1–20), but it was not devoted to charitable bequests in particular. More pointedly, there were no titles called *De causis piis*, *De pauperibus*, *De hospitalibus*, or anything similar in the classical canonical texts. Universities, schools, and eleemosynary institutions merited no special treatment. The Decretal's title *De foro competente* (X 2.2.1–20) did not assert that charitable causes belonged within the church's jurisdiction. Jurists in the tradition of the *ius commune* were thus not encouraged by the formal law to think of 'a law of charity' as a distinct head of ecclesiastical jurisdiction.

The absence of a special place for charity within the classical law made a difference in practice, but a full picture would be more complicated. Certain texts in the *Corpus iuris canonici* contained rules and principles that would become important in the history of the law of charity. The *Decretum* directed the church to take special care to succour widows and orphans (Dist. 87 c. 1) and to prevent oppression of the poor (C. 14 q. 3 c. 21). The Decretals asserted that a last will and testament made in favour of a charitable use was valid even though it did not meet the ordinary legal requirements (X 3.26.11), and the canon law placed a special responsibility on officers of the church to secure implementation of pious bequests (X 3.26.17). When we recall, moreover, that churches were themselves the most prominent objects of charitable giving during the Middle Ages, and that virtually every page of the canonical texts regulated and advanced the life of the clergy and their churches, then the absence of any special treatment of charity in the canon

---

7 Hubert Picarda, 'Charity in Roman Law: Roots and Parallels', *Charity Law & Practice Review* 1 (1992–93), p. 9.

law seems less definitive. The canon law contained many texts connected to subjects we would call charitable.

Still, the absence of a special title on charity mattered. Although treatises devoted to 'pious causes' came to be written by continental jurists, they were never produced in great numbers and their compilation in any numbers did not occur before the seventeenth century.[8] Charity never stood at the top of the canonists' agenda. By contrast, topics like the law of ecclesiastical elections or marriage and divorce – which *were* dealt with in particular titles in the Decretals – attracted commentators sooner and in greater numbers.[9]

William Lyndwood

The treatment of charity as it appeared in the commentary of England's most important late medieval canonist, William Lyndwood (d. 1446), casts a similar light upon the subject. His *Provinciale* offers an important perspective on the concept of charity as understood at the time and as put into practice by an English ecclesiastical lawyer. It dealt directly with the provincial constitutions that controlled several aspects of the English church's jurisdiction, including the law of testamentary succession, which provided a natural 'home' for what juristic treatment of the law of charity existed. The *Provinciale* contained no separate section for pious causes any more than did the Decretals, but Lyndwood dealt with the concept of charity at length in outlining the sources and nature of the English church's testamentary jurisdiction.

The immediate problem for him was the following: the medieval canon law did not claim exclusive jurisdiction over last wills and testaments. Proof and enforcement of testaments ordinarily belonged to the lay courts. The most ecclesiastical courts could claim under Decretal law was a subsidiary jurisdiction over specifically charitable bequests. Where the temporal courts failed to act, the church could step in to secure the rights of charities. That was the bishop's special duty. In England, however, custom had established a different regime. Nothing depended upon failure by one court system to protect charitable bequests. In the absence of special custom, the dividing line depended upon subject matter. Succession to real property was dealt with by secular courts; succession to goods and chattels by the courts of the church.[10] Charitable bequests were not treated as a special case.

---

[8] Andreas Tiraquellus (d. 1558) was the author of *Tractatus de privilegiis causarum piarum* (Cologne, 1597).

[9] See Martin Lipenius, *Bibliotheca realis iuridica* (Leipzig, 1757, repr. 1970) under appropriate headings.

[10] For an attempt to trace the obscure process by which this jurisdictional division was reached, see M.M. Sheehan, *The Will in Medieval England* (Toronto, 1963), pp. 164–76.

Lyndwood sought to explain this system and to bring it into tolerable harmony with the church's law.[11] One possibility was to treat it simply as a matter of local custom. Custom could be a valid source of jurisdiction under the medieval canon law,[12] although some limits were put on its scope. Lyndwood did take this route. Citing the opinions of Hostiensis and well as papal decretals, he asserted that the English system was based on a valid custom.[13] However, he was not content to leave it there. Perhaps he was dissatisfied with custom as a full justification for apparent deviation from the law of the Decretals,[14] for he also sought to show that the English system came within the jurisdictional exception made for episcopal responsibility to secure enforcement of charitable bequests. The term 'pious' was not self-defining; it had no fixed meaning in the canonical texts, and it might be said that a testamentary gift in favour of one's children was 'pious' in the larger sense of that word. And if children, why not others? Was it not a pious act to secure performance of the last wishes of a decedent who had wished his property to pass in a certain way but could no longer make sure it happened? Was it not a pious act to see to it that his debts were paid so that he could appear unspotted before the Final Judge? So, at any rate, ran the argument made by Lyndwood.[15] In support, he offered citations to one Roman law text (Cod. 1.2.1), three papal decretals (X 3.24.2, X 3.24.6, and X 3.24.17), with commentaries on them by Hostiensis and Innocent IV, and one text from the *Liber sextus* (Sext 3.11.2). None of these provided unambiguous support; they spoke, for example, of the work of a testamentary executor as a quasi-sacred duty, but they did no more. In the fashion of the day, they provided grist for legal argument. They allowed Lyndwood to argue that the canon law's solicitude for charitable bequests counted in support of the legitimacy of the English church's testamentary jurisdiction. But it was a stretch.

What of the law of charity itself? There was a potential danger. If payment of debts owed by decedents could be thought of as falling under the rubric of pious causes, so could almost any lawful activity. Lyndwood's argument proved too much. Potentially, it would have opened the jurisdiction of the church's tribunals to litigation well beyond any then current understanding of the church's proper role in society, not to speak of the jurisdictional rules of the common law's writ of prohibition. It would have tortured the concept

---

[11] See Brian Edwin Ferme, *Canon Law in Late Medieval England: A Study of William Lyndwood's* Provinciale *with Particular Reference to Testamentary Law* (Rome, 1996).
[12] See, e.g., *gl. ord.* ad X 2.13.13 s.v. *in tua*.
[13] See *Provinciale* 174 s.v. *approbatis*.
[14] See Brian Ferme, 'The Testamentary Executor in Lyndwood's *Provinciale*', *The Jurist* 49 (1989), pp. 632–78, at p. 644, speaking of 'Lyndwood's reluctance to rely merely upon the authority of English custom' as a general trait running throughout his great work.
[15] *Provinciale* 169 s.v. *residuis*.

of charity, making it perform tasks for which it was ill suited. The definition of charity might have covered everything, allowing canon lawyers to claim jurisdiction in every situation where the church's law sought to do right. Such a prospect and problem was not entirely unknown to other parts of the medieval canon law; for instance the concept that the courts of the church could take cognizance of any sort of human behaviour *ratione peccati* (X 2.1.13). That was actually more potentially subversive of settled assumptions about the reach of the church's jurisdiction. But Lyndwood's argument led to potentially subversive results, and it was not pushed that far in practice. The more immediate question was (and is) the canon law's place in the development of the law of charitable institutions.

The canon law as it stood c.1400 thus presented English ecclesiastical lawyers with an uncertain legacy and base. It included some grand claims, a short list of general rules that could be used in administering rules supporting charities, and a longer list of regulations governing the church and its governors. For example, the high duty that all fiduciaries owed to the institutions they led was stated in both contexts in the canon law.[16] Roman law also stood in reserve. It could supply rules applicable to testamentary practice in the English ecclesiastical courts, many of which were relevant to charitable institutions. However, there was no 'law of charity' either in the medieval canon law or in Lyndwood's presentation.[17] Unlike the law of marriage and divorce, or even the law of tithes, the regulation of charities lacked obvious immediate reference points in the canonical texts. Charity could claim no tradition of careful juristic commentary. The question is: what would be made of the subject in practice?

The Court Records

From the 'building blocks' of the *ius commune*, English civilians might have fashioned a class of ecclesiastical jurisdiction devoted especially to charity. This was more than a fanciful possibility. The courts of the diocese of Barcelona in Spain appear to have done so. Separate records of litigation were kept under the rubric of 'Causas pías'.[18] Some Italian dioceses also treated them distinctly.[19] This development did not happen in England, however.

---

[16] See Shael Herman, 'The Canonical Conception of the Trust', in *Itinera Fiduciae: Trust and Treuhand in Historical Perspective*, ed. Richard Helmholz and Reinhard Zimmermann (Berlin, 1998), pp. 85–109.

[17] This is broadly consistent with the conclusions of Andreas Richter, *Rechtsfähige Stiftung und Charitable Corporation* (Berlin, 2001).

[18] The file is called 'Testamentos y Causas Pías'; see Arxiu diocesà attached to the cathedral of Barcelona, 2.3.2.1, described generally in José Sanabre, *El Archivo diocesano de Barcelona* (Barcelona, 1947).

[19] See Richard C. Trexler, 'The Bishop's Portion: Generic Pious Legacies in the late Middle Ages in Italy', *Traditio* 28 (1972), pp. 397–450.

Ecclesiastical jurisdiction did come to be divided into separate categories. Very much as the jurisdiction of the royal courts was divided by forms of action (writs of trespass, debt, and so forth), in the spiritual courts there were tithe causes, matrimonial causes, defamation causes, and so on. However, there never were charitable causes *eo nomine*.[20] When English civilians came to describe the practice of the courts, they too made no special place for charitable institutions.[21] This is the first, and perhaps most important, conclusion to be drawn from the archives of the English ecclesiastical courts. Whenever a question of charitable gifts or bequests came before the consistory courts in England, it came under some other rubric than that of charity. In this, English practice faithfully mirrored the law of the *Corpus iuris canonici*.

This is not the whole story, of course. As a matter of fact, causes that involved charitable matters did often come before the spiritual courts, chiefly under the rubric of testamentary causes. Disputes over ecclesiastical offices and property devoted to charitable purposes also regularly arose in practice; they would call for the application of rules of law. There is something to study, therefore. And the records yield results. Once examined, they quickly make it apparent that some of the rules applied in practice were identical with those which became associated with the modern, secular law of charity. There is a notable, but not wholly unexpected, continuity to them. In this sense, it makes sense to reserve a place for the ecclesiastical forum in the development of an English law of charity.

Privileges of Charitable Gifts

Four special characteristics of the modern law of charity were found in law and practice as administered by the English ecclesiastical courts. First was the privilege of indefinite existence.[22] No one had yet heard of the Rule against Perpetuities, of course. No obstacle prevented the courts from upholding and enforcing burdens fastened upon lands or benefices that were meant to last in perpetuity, as for example a fifteenth-century bequest of the rents and profits of three acres of land for the maintenance of lights in a Lincolnshire parish church. In 1490, the successor in title to the three acres had (it was alleged) withheld the rents and profits accruing from the land, and he was required to appear before the bishop's court to justify his

---

[20] The 'causa subtractionis bonorum pauperum' was an exceptional entry, but it occurred in Ex officio c. Churchwardens of Newcastle (Durham, 1567), Durham University Library, DDR/EJ/CCA/3/2, fol. 97.
[21] E.g., John Ayliffe, *Parergon juris canonici Anglicani* (London, 1726), pp. 1–4.
[22] See *Tudor on Charities*, ed. S.G. Maurice and D.R. Parker, 7th edn (London, 1984), pp. 156–60; L.A. Sheridan and G.W. Keeton, *The Modern Law of Charities*, 3rd edn (Cardiff, 1983), p. 1.

actions.[23] Perpetual charitable gifts like this one were enforceable. They appeared from time to time in the act books.[24]

The Protestant Reformation would have made some of them illegal, as with perpetual trusts for masses. However, the underlying legal principle remained in force. For instance, the will of Richard Maddyson had left £5 to be set aside for the benefit of four poor men of the parish of Mablethorpe, the income to be paid 'in coals or any other commodity . . . for ever'. In 1612, the diocesan court was obliged to intervene when the sum had proved insufficient to meet the needs of the four men and a dispute had arisen about how the four men were to be selected.[25] The court ordered the executor to devise a plan to carry out Maddyson's intent, with the proviso that the money should be 'employed forever according to the true will of the decedent'. Successors to pious givers to local churches could thus find themselves obliged to respond to claims for annual payments many years after the death of the original donors.[26]

Second was the exception, carved out only in favour of charities, to the rule requiring certainty in the objects of a gift or bequest. Ordinarily, the takers under a last will and testament must be ascertainable with a reasonable degree of certainty.[27] The testator cannot leave their designation up to a third person. It is otherwise with a charitable bequest, in which a gift that would be void for uncertainty is valid so long as it is clear that the object is charitable. This was the rule in the ecclesiastical courts; as noted by one civilian: 'A legacy given to pious causes is not rendered ineffective because of [its] uncertainty'.[28] So it happened in practice. In the case just mentioned, a gift to an undesignated group of four poor men of the parish was held to be valid. The ecclesiastical courts were able to enforce an obligation to pay a sum of money *in pios usus*, leaving the specific uses to be determined by the discretion of persons appointed.[29] Just as vague were the popular bequests of money to be used 'for welfare of the soul' of the testator; the choice of the

[23] Ex officio c. Zale (1490), LAO, Act book Viv/3, fol. 15v. See also Ex officio c. Watkyn (Archeaconry of Hereford 1608), Herefordshire Record Office [hereafter HRO], Act book HD 4/1/O/83, p. 53: 'benevolence given out of certen lands in pios usus'.

[24] E.g., Ex officio c. Stole (Norwich 1593–94), Norfolk Record Office [hereafter NNRO] Act book DN/VIS 2/1 (parish of Downham): 'he deteyneth a legacie . . . given by the last will of Tho. Cranham for to continue for ever'.

[25] See LAO, Act book Vj/21, fol. 55v (1611–12).

[26] E.g., Vicar of Wadworth c. Hugh Maire (York 1526), BI, D/C.CP.1526/1, seeking dues and oblations allegedly owed from the foundation of the vicarage from the inhabitants of a house within the parish.

[27] See *Tudor on Charities*, pp. 147–52.

[28] CUL, EDR, F/5/49 (c. 1600), fol. 6v: 'Legatum ad pias causas non vitiatur propter incertitudinem'.

[29] E.g., Ex officio c. Elliot (Archdeaconry of Nottingham 1597), Nottingham University Library, Act book AN/A 11/2, p. 83.

specific use apparently being made by the executor.[30] It was possible to create a charitable remainder to take effect after the death of a widow and child, the property to be disposed of 'in works of charity and other pious uses' after the death of the last survivor.[31] Some testaments spelled this charitable purpose out at some length: the money was to be used 'according as it shall seem best to them [the executors] for the health of my soul and as they shall wish to answer before God and men at the dread day of final judgment'.[32] As in the modern law of charitable trusts, ordinarily the courts did not substitute their own judgment for that of the chosen fiduciaries, but they stood ready to supervise the suitability of the choices made. However, the records do contain occasional entries where specific provisions were made in the courts, at whose insistence is not entirely clear.[33]

Third was the availability of the doctrine now known as cy près. In its modern form, the doctrine holds that when the original purpose of a charitable gift becomes impossible or impracticable to perform, the terms of gift may be varied to reflect the spirit of the gift, so long as it appears that the donor had possessed a general intent to devote the property given to charitable uses. This doctrine had its origins in the Roman law. Under the canon law, this rule was most familiar as part of the broader concept of commutation of one form of good work to replace another. Best known today from its utility in the commutation of crusading vows into more local obligations, it was more often used in English practice in commuting penances, as where a party who had been found guilty of a public offence against the ecclesiastical law was assigned public penance, but then allowed to commute it to a money payment devoted to a charitable purpose.

The idea also had its part in testamentary law relating to charitable bequests. English civilians admitted it as a matter of principle,[34] and cy près was applied in appropriate circumstances in the ecclesiastical courts. Thus, in a case that came before the diocesan court of Ely during the 1460s, a bequest for the purpose of erecting a cross in the parish church of Leverington was varied in favour of what the record described as 'a more

---

[30] E.g., Testament of Edmond Tame (1534), BL Egerton ch. 781.
[31] See Fifteenth Century Precedent Book, BL Add. ms. 41503, fol. 87v, called a 'testamentum caritativum' in the margin.
[32] Lyndby c. Executor of Simon, rector of Bilborough (York 1382), BI, CP E. 125: 'secundum quod eis pro salute anime mee melius videbitur expedire necnon in die tremendo iudicii coram deo et hominibus voluerint respondere'.
[33] E.g., Ex officio c. Symonds (Rochester 1457), Kent Archives Office, Maidstone [hereafter KAO], Act book DRb Pa 3, fol. 337v, where an obligation to expend monies 'pro anima Johannis Davy' was stated to require the recipient to pay for the celebration of masses, to distribute 40s among poor scholars at Oxford, to purchase a cope for use in the church of Hadlow, and to help repair the church's tower.
[34] E.g., Civilian's Casebook c. 1600, Worcestershire Record Office, Worcester, ms. 794.093 BA 2470/B, fol. 170v: 'if it bee not possible to observe the saide use, then the ordinarie may convert the same to some other use'.

convenient use' at the petition of the churchwardens.[35] Another case, which arose in the diocese of Rochester, allowed a bequest for repair of a church's bell tower to be converted to one for repair of the parish church itself, apparently because of an immediate danger to the church.[36] In some situations where a decedent was declared to have died intestate, administrators were directed to take at least part of the decedent's assets 'to be converted and disposed in pious uses and charitable works' at the direction of the bishop or his agents.[37] The same rationale of amplifying charitable purposes seems to have been at work.

Underlying these three special characteristics of charitable gifts was a fourth – more general in character and applicable beyond its role in supporting these three rules. It was the law's general disposition to treat charitable gifts and bequests as valid in circumstances where similar private transactions would have been invalid. A testament *ad pias causas* was a privileged testament in Roman law and remained so in England.[38] When, for example, it was objected, against an effort to treat as a valid bequest an oral statement made by a dying man that he had given 40s to be used by the church of Bledlow to purchase a communion chalice, that it would not have been admitted as a valid codicil to his previously written testament, the court nevertheless admitted it.[39] Where a last will and testament used the vague language 'I would wish' money might be used for a charitable purpose, the wish was upheld as a valid disposition against the objection that the words were not dispositive.[40] That particular bequests had been made *in pios usus* was often noted specifically in the records,[41] a mark of the special status such bequests enjoyed in the canon and Roman laws. If charitable gifts were not placed under a special heading of ecclesiastical jurisdiction in England, they do appear to have been given preferential treatment. Many of the charitable uses that would be held good over technical objections in the common law in interpreting the Statute of Charitable Uses were 'anticipated' by the law of the church.[42]

---

35 Ex officio c. Executors of Everard (Ely 1462), CUL, EDR Liber B, fol. 20v.
36 Ex officio c. Lorkey (1459), KAO, Act book DRb Pa 3, fol. 383.
37 Ex officio promoto c. Joan, widow of Ralph Merke (Lincoln, 1545), LAO, Act book Cj/3, fol. 88: 'ad convertendum et disponendum in pios usus et opera charitativa'.
38 See Henry Swinburne, *Brief Treatise of Testaments and Last Wills* Pt 1 §16 (London, 1590), pp. 30–31.
39 Testament of John Francklin, Berkshire Record Office, Reading, MS. D/A/X/5, fol. 149 (17th century).
40 Will of Thomas Austen (Durham c. 1600), Durham University Library, DDR/EJ/CCG/2/1, fol. 156.
41 E.g., Testament of Rusby (York 1489), BI, CP F. 271: 'viginti et sex solidos et octo denarios in pios usus viz. ad fabricam dicte ecclesie de Barnby legavit et donavit'.
42 See generally John Herne, *The Law of Charitable Uses* (London, 1660), pp. 55–110.

Supervision of Charitable Bequests and Institutions

An aspect of ecclesiastical jurisdiction that most commonly involved principles that would later appear in the law of charity was the supervision of charitable administration and the enforcement of charitable gifts. Here too the texts of the canon law contained no special title covering the subject, but development of a rule of fiduciary duty was an almost inevitable consequence of texts spread throughout the *Corpus iuris canonici*. Not only did the canon law impose upon bishops and their subordinates a special responsibility to oversee the fulfilment of pious bequests;[43] it also announced as a general rule that the church's property was not to be alienated.[44] Such a rule was too strict to have been obeyed to the letter, and various ways around it were found. Many things, for example, could be done with the consent of a cleric's superiors. However, the principle that those who administered the church's patrimony had an obligation not to dissipate it was never lost sight of. The principle covered both those who unlawfully gave and those who unlawfully received ecclesiastical property. It covered both property removed from the possession of the church and property unlawfully withheld. It covered those who held offices in churches but failed to live up to the accompanying obligations.[45] Whether better considered as protection of charitable purposes or as protection of ecclesiastical assets, the principle put the ecclesiastical courts in the business of enforcing standards of fiduciary conduct that would come to characterize the law of charity.

As a matter of practical ecclesiastical administration, the result most in evidence in the court records was the requirement that fiduciaries render account for their administration of church property. They were required, for example, to 'faithfully account and pay over' whatever they had that belonged to a parish church.[46] Churchwardens were subject to charges that they had 'not made a true account of the church's goods' at the end of their term of office.[47] Vicars were required to 'restore what they had sacrilegiously taken from parochial funds' or to show legitimate cause for their action.[48] Wardens of hospitals were compelled to 'render due account of their administration of the hospital's goods'.[49] Such actions, undertaken *ex officio* or

---

[43] X 3.26.17.
[44] See X 3.13.5.
[45] E.g., Ex officio c. Rokeson (York 1532), BI, CP G. 219, an action against a parish clerk for 'leaving God's service contrary to his duty and promise'.
[46] Ex officio c. Alen and Benett (York 1438–9), BI, Act book D/C. AB. 1, fol. 100: 'quod de quibusdam receptis dictorum fructuum . fideliter computent et satisfaciant infra octo dies'.
[47] Ex officio c. Hardwell and Comer (Bath & Wells 1568), Somerset Record Office, Taunton, Act book D/D/Ca 40, s.d. 19 June.
[48] Ex officio c. Vicar of Leeds (York 1503), BI, Act book Cons. AB. 5, fol. 62.
[49] Ex officio c. John Mulsho (Ely 1380), CUL, EDR Act book D/2/1, fol. 139: 'compotum super administratione sua in bonis hospitalis predicte'.

upon complaint of other officials, were familiar parts of ecclesiastical jurisdiction in England. 'Detaining a legacy' left to charitable (normally ecclesiastical) uses was probably the most frequent form for such entries in the court act books.[50]

The records contain little or nothing to contribute to answering most of the questions that have been of moment for scholars of Roman legal traditions: the development of the concept of a foundation, enjoying the status of a *persona ficta* in the law, for example.[51] Appearances may be deceptive, but it appears that the English judges who toiled in the ecclesiastical courts were untroubled by such problems. The notebooks of English civilians contain little material on them. Disciplinary proceedings were brought to enforce the terms of charitable gifts, but they were treated as *in personam* actions against the officials involved. By virtue of either their offices or the oaths they took on admission to those offices, administrators stood under a duty to carry out the terms of charitable gifts. So, for example, Peter Symonds of the parish of Hadlow in Kent was required to appear before the consistory court of the diocese of Rochester in 1457 and to render an account (*reddere rationem*) of the proceeds received from the sale of land left for charitable purposes.[52] In 1443, similar proceedings were brought against a man in Herefordshire for failing to account for the revenue accruing from a black cow left for the benefit of the fabric of a parish church of Rushbury.[53] At Canterbury in 1420, the man who held 8s bequeathed for the purpose of buying lead for the roof of the parish church of Lyminge was required to show cause (if he had any) for failing to carry out this task properly.[54] The courts of the medieval church thus provided a forum for enforcing charitable gifts. They continued to do so after the Reformation, although no separate jurisdiction over charity emerged from the process.

From a more legal point of view, such disciplinary actions could be described as ancestors of the action for equitable accounting in the Court of Chancery and also of the rule that charitable trustees are bound to keep and present adequate accounts of their administration.[55] The formal nature of

---

50 E.g., Ex officio c. Anna Hughes (Chester 1606), Cheshire Record Office, Act book EDV 1/14, fol. 16: 'for deteyning v s given to the poore of Eccleston parish and ii s iiii d to the use of the church'; Ex officio c. Playforde (Norwich 1594), NNRO, Act book DN/VIS 2/1, s.d. 28 February: 'she deteyneth a legacie of v s given to the poore'.
51 See, e.g., Robert Feenstra, 'L'histoire des fondations, à propos de quelques études récentes', *Tijdschrift voor Rechtsgeschiedenis* 24 (1956), pp. 381–448; Patrick Duff, *Personality in Roman Private Law* (Cambridge, 1938), pp. 168–205; Richter, *Rechtsfähige Stiftung*; C.E.F. Rickett, 'Charitable Giving in English and Roman Law: A Comparison of Method', *Cambridge L.J.* 38 (1979), pp. 118–47.
52 Ex officio c. Symonds (Rochester 1457), KAO, Act book DRb Pa3, fol. 337v.
53 Churchwardens of Rushbury v. Nycoll (Hereford 1443), HRO, Act book HD 4/1/O/2, p. 65.
54 Executors of Godland c. Gylbert (Canterbury 1420), Canterbury Cathedral Archives and Library, Act book Y.1.4, fol. 18.
55 See Holdsworth, *History of English Law* vi, 650–7; *Tudor on Charities*, pp. 432–3

most of the remaining records does not permit us to say much about some of the intricate legal questions that have arisen under the modern law of charity, but on the level of giving effect to an underlying fiduciary obligation in favour of a charitable use, it can be said that Chancery was continuing to enforce a duty equally enforced in the courts of the church.

Conclusion

Taking a formal approach, a student of the law of the church must conclude that the medieval canon law possessed no text or other locus that could serve as the point of departure for the creation of a law of charity. No title in the *Corpus iuris canonici* served that function. In English law, by contrast, the Statutes of Charitable Uses would. Around these statutes, commentators could organize a proper law of charity. So we have the works by George Duke,[56] John Herne[57] and Sir Francis Moore.[58] As is shown by canonical texts, reinforced in this case by the records and other literature from the English ecclesiastical courts, the canon law lacked an equivalent focus.

Taking a functional approach, however, a student may fairly say that many of the individual characteristics of the law of charity were already in place when the Tudor Statutes were enacted. The favour shown to testamentary gifts, the doctrine of cy près, and the availability of actions for accounting against those who administered charitable properties are prominent examples of features of the *ius commune* that ultimately became the law of England. Although they were new in the sense of standing within a separate legal category, it would not be false to say they had been the law of England all along.

---

[56] George Duke, *The Law of Charitable Uses*, 1st edn (London, 1676).
[57] Herne, *Law of Charitable Uses*.
[58] See 'Reading on Charitable Uses', printed in appendix to Duke, *Law of Charitable Uses*; see also Jones, *History of the Law of Charity*, pp. 231–46.

Continuing Service: the Episcopal Households of Thirteenth-Century Durham

PHILIPPA HOSKIN

The medieval English bishop was a man of huge spiritual and temporal power. Throughout the thirteenth century, prelates ranked among some of the most powerful men in the land, often holding vast landed estates, as well as having spiritual jurisdiction, with the power to bind and loose which extended beyond even the authority of the king. In order to understand the ways in which any medieval baron's power was wielded, and the patterns of patronage he held, it is vital to understand the nature and construction of his household. That there were similarities between the households of great ecclesiastical and secular nobles is clear: in the household of Hubert Walter, archbishop of Canterbury, for example, in the late twelfth and early thirteenth centuries, Cheney notes that there was confusion and overlap between the ecclesiastical staff serving him as archbishop and those servants fulfilling their duties to him as baron and servant of the king, whilst the Countess of Lincoln in the early 1240s had the rules for her household drawn up by Robert Grosseteste, bishop of Lincoln, based on statutes for his own household.[1] The studies of noble households, however, have tended to concentrate on the secular nobility, omitting their episcopal counterparts and claiming fundamental differences in their composition and continuity, claims which have been tacitly upheld in considerations of episcopal households, focusing upon the spiritual rather than temporal jurisdiction of the bishop.

The personnel and structure of a bishop's household are always elusive. The focus upon the spiritual dimension of the episcopal *familia* results largely from the limitations of the surviving records. Quite simply, the acts of bishops have tended to survive in ecclesiastical archives and the monks who copied them carefully into their cartularies, or preserved them in their original states, saw their bishops as guarantors of spiritualities and providers of

---

[1] C.R. Cheney, *Hubert Walter* (London, 1967), p. 160; *Walter of Henley and other Treatises on Estate Management and Accounting*, ed. D. Oschinsky (Oxford, 1971), pp. 191–7, 387–416; C. Given-Wilson, *The Great Household in Late Medieval England* (London, 1999), p. 19.

indulgences to encourage visitors to their shrines. The secular estates with which these monks concerned themselves were their own, not their prelate's. And yet the majority of household members are identifiable through their presence in the witness lists to these episcopal charters. The strengths and weaknesses of these sources have been well rehearsed.[2] Those attesting three or more charters for one bishop, of differing dates and preferably granted in different locations, are held to be, at the very least, extremely likely to be members of that bishop's *familia*. This use of witness lists is not without its flaws for identification and study of both ecclesiastical and secular households. We can at least, following the work of Greenway on twelfth and thirteenth-century ecclesiastical charters and Russell and Given-Wilson on royal charters, be all but certain that witnesses were actually present on the occasions upon which they witnessed.[3] The status of individual witnesses, however, is not beyond doubt. Their roles and positions are also often uncertain. Titles may be given only intermittently if at all, whilst even those heading such lists, who are assumed to be amongst the more important household members, often appear without further explanation. The loss of many medieval documents and the abbreviation of witness lists in cartularies mean that many household members, even those from amongst groups frequently attesting charters, are never named. If we are lucky, the information from witness lists is supplemented by other references, perhaps actual mentions of an individual within episcopal grants (possibly as grantee, or a judge or a party in a dispute), in other charters – for example those of the cathedral chapter – or even in secular records, such as those of royal government. These sources can confirm what witness lists have already implied, casting new light on particular individuals or providing names otherwise unknown. However, with a frequent lack of other, consistently available documentation, such lists are a central source.

Studies of households are a vital part of the editions of episcopal *acta* of the twelfth and thirteenth centuries. Since 1973 the British Academy's English Episcopal *Acta* Project has worked to gather together and edit the surviving episcopal documents for all English dioceses before the introduction of registration in each individual see, drawing on those other, similar *acta* volumes produced under the auspices of the Canterbury and York Society or other local record societies.[4] Since 1973 this project has

---

[2] EEA ii, pp. xxix–xxxiii.

[3] Diana Greenway, 'Ecclesiastical Chronology: Fasti 1066–1300', in *Materials Sources and Methods*, ed. D. Baker, Studies in Church History 11 (Oxford, 1975), pp. 53–60; J.C. Russell, 'Attestations of Charters in the Reign of John', *Speculum* 15 (1940), pp. 480–98; C. Given-Wilson, 'Royal Charter Witness Lists 1327–1399', *Medieval Prosopography* series 2 vol. 12 (1991), pp. 35–59.

[4] These include *Acta Stephani Langton*; *Chichester Acta*; *The Letters and Charters of Gilbert Foliot*, ed. A. Morey and C.N.L. Brooke (Cambridge, 1967); *DEC*; Mary Cheney, *Roger, Bishop of Worcester 1164–1179* (Oxford, 1980); *The Acta of Hugh of Wells, Bishop of Lincoln 1209–1235*, ed. David M. Smith (LRS 88, 2000).

proceeded under the general editorship of David Smith, who has himself produced three of its volumes. As the *acta* project approaches the publication of its thirtieth volume at the time of this writing, certain elements and structures have come to be expected of episcopal households.

One of the notable features is the general, almost total change in a household's personnel with the arrival of each new prelate. It is assumed that either the new bishop arrived to discover his predecessor's household had already departed for pastures new, or that he arrived with his own men, all eager for the patronage their lord now had at his disposal, and that those left from the former regime could expect little profit. In this, bishops' *familiae* have been contrasted with the households of the secular nobility, where a great deal of continuity could be expected.[5] This contrast may well have held good in a number of sees – certainly the distinction between the secular and spiritual lord has a clear logic. The ties of patronage that held the episcopal household to their bishop were personal ones involving loyalty to one man not to, for example, a great local family. On the rare occasions when twelfth and thirteenth-century bishops were translated from one see to another,[6] members of their existing households can be seen to travel with them. Richard Poore, for example, was served by a Master Valentine, clerk in his successive sees of Salisbury, Chichester and Durham between 1215 and 1237.[7] When William Raleigh, bishop of Norwich, was translated to Winchester he sent his official, Master Geoffrey of Ferring, ahead of him.[8] New bishops were expected to use their available patronage for members of their own retinues, men who had perhaps served them when they held lesser ecclesiastical positions or who were family connections. The bishop's household was, then, unsurprisingly, officially dissolved by his death. It could be retained until after the prelate's funeral, at least in the thirteenth century, and this was clearly the case for the *familia* of Richard Gravesend, bishop of London, in 1303,[9] and for that of Edmund of Abingdon, archbishop of

5   Kate Mertes, *The English Royal Household 1250–1600: Good Governance and Politic Rule* (Oxford, 1988), p. 65.
6   There were thirteen translations in these two centuries, of which five can be accounted for by moves to the archbishoprics of Canterbury and York (to York, Walter Giffard from Bath and Wells in 1266 and Walter de Gray from Worcester in 1215; and to Canterbury, Ralph d'Escures from Rochester in 1114, Baldwin from Worcester in 1184 and Hubert Walter from Salisbury in 1193); two were moves to or from dioceses overseas (Bernard from Ragusa to Carlisle in 1203 and Walter of Coutances from Lincoln to Rouen in 1184–5) and two can be accounted for by one man, Richard Poore, who was translated from Chichester to Salisbury in 1217 and then from Salisbury to Durham in 1228. The remaining four bishops were Hervey, translated from Bangor to Ely in 1109, Gilbert Foliot from Hereford to London in 1163, William Raleigh from Norwich to Winchester in 1243 and Nicholas of Ely from Worcester to Winchester in 1268.
7   See EEA 22, p. xlviii; EEA 18, p. lxxxiii; EEA 24, p. xxx.
8   EEA 21, p. xlvi.
9   *Account of the Executors of Richard Bishop of London 1303, and of the Executors of*

Canterbury, where, although his chancellor, Richard Wich, is said to have dispersed his servants (*famuli*) at the archbishop's death, Paris's life of the archbishop separates these from the *clerici* to whom those departing said farewell (presumably the clerics of the archbishop's household) and makes it clear that the most eminent members of the household remained, even arguing with the monks of Pontigny and casting doubt on the sanctity of their previous employer.[10] However, such a delay was probably, as Woolgar notes, a practical solution to the need to organise a state funeral and was only a temporary measure:[11] the death of the bishop meant the household members were freed from their obligations. Ralph Bocking, author of the Life of Richard Wich, confirms that on Archbishop Edmund's death Wich, his former chancellor, was free to study theology at Orleans.[12] Members of other households moved from one episcopal *familia* to another, as the steward Simon de Senliz did on the death of Ralph Neville, bishop of Chichester, entering the service of Edmund of Abingdon in Canterbury.[13]

The necessity of relying upon witness lists from the surviving charters, most often from ecclesiastical grants that have been preserved in the archives of religious communities, has also placed a heavy emphasis upon the religious members of the *familia* – the bishops' clerks, chaplains and (from the early thirteenth century) their officials, whilst little, if anything, is known of the secular household. There are occasional references to episcopal servants or stewards – those responsible for the day-to-day running of the household itself – and the names of some few foresters and bailiffs responsible for the bishops' manors survive, but for the most part the secular household, and the household roles of the bishops' tenants of his temporal fief, are hidden.

The diocese of Durham in the mid thirteenth century is different in a number of ways. Most important, the wealth of medieval material surviving in the archive of the Dean and Chapter at Durham both provides extensive information about the families and networks of men who in other dioceses are just names, and also preserves many charters of a type not normally found amongst episcopal *acta* – land grants showing the bishop at work as a secular lord and landholder, and complementing the charters revealing him in his more familiar, ecclesiastical role. Amongst the thirteenth-century episcopal households examined so far this extent of information is rivalled only by that available for the household of Peter des Roches, found particularly in the Winchester pipe rolls.[14] Additionally, the large number of originals rather

---

Thomas Bishop of Exeter 1310, ed. W.H. Hale and H.T. Ellacombe (Camden Society 2nd series 10, 1874), p 100.

[10] C.H. Lawrence, *St Edmund of Abingdon: A study of Hagiography and History* (Oxford, 1960), pp. 272, 276.

[11] C.M. Woolgar, *The Great Household in Late Medieval England* (London, 1999), p. 1.

[12] David Jones, *St Richard of Chichester: The Sources for his Life* (Lewes, 1995), p. 94.

[13] EEA 22, p. lii; Lawrence, *St Edmund of Abingdon*, p. 148.

[14] EEA ix, p. xxxviii.

than cartulary copies (where witness lists are often omitted), together with the Durham chancery practice of using extensive witness lists in the 1270s, when a number of other dioceses were beginning to abandon them, means that there is an abundance of all-important witness list evidence.[15] In this large archive the surviving documentation is skewed towards grants for the cathedral priory. Other surviving information, however, and the place dates of the charters themselves, which were largely granted at episcopal manors outside either the city of Durham or the priory's own lands, suggests that this does not affect the status of the witnesses, who can still be considered members of the bishops' households.

The extant charter evidence from the episcopates of Bishops Farnham, Kirkham, Stichill and Holy Island between 1242 and 1283 provides 214 charters surviving in full texts of which 104 (nearly half) survive in originals and 97 (just over 45 per cent) include witness lists. The information gleaned from these *acta*, and from other available sources surviving both within and outside Durham, provides details about the 'clerical' component of episcopal households, but also goes further. The charters provide a far more comprehensive picture of the household, including its secular members, than is available for other contemporary bishops' households. Strikingly, it also provides a picture of household continuity between episcopates, particularly of household members whose service extends across not just two but three or more episcopates, which differs from what is known about other sees.

The mid-thirteenth-century bishops of Durham appear making grants to – and having their charters witnessed by – servants and other secular household members. In other dioceses (except again at Winchester under Peter des Roches) these men are usually either completely hidden from our view or only glimpsed briefly. According to Matthew Paris, Bishop Nicholas Farnham (1243–49) was ill towards the end of his episcopate[16] and his doctor, Alexander of Bramfield, appears as witness to two charters, one in 1245 (the year after Nicholas is said to have been cured of what is described as a tumour at Pontigny) and one after July 1247.[17] We also have details of two of Farnham's foresters, Laurence of Pontorp and Adam of Bradley, who witness charters twice and four times respectively.[18] They also receive instructions concerning the bishop's woodland.[19] Another layman, Geoffrey of Stockton, who is described as the bishop's servant, was granted land in Norton by Farnham.[20] Bishop Walter Kirkham's (1249–60) tailor, Henry, and his constable, Roger of Waltham (once described as bishop's clerk), both

---

15 EEA 29, p. lxii.
16 *Matthaei Parisiensis monachi Sancti Albani, Chronica Majora*, ed. H. Richards Luard, 7 vols (RS, 1884–89), v, p. 53.
17 EEA 29, no. 21, 29; Paris, *Chronica Majora* iv, p. 330.
18 EEA 29, nos 5, 7, 10, 41.
19 ibid., no. 2.
20 ibid., no. *43.

witnessed charters for him.[21] After Kirkham's death his successor Robert Stichill's (1261–74) valet, Laurence of Bearpark, Andrew his messenger and Walter Slator, a tailor in the bishop's service, all received land from the bishop,[22] whilst John de Ynfleth, bailiff of the episcopal manor of Howden, and Robert de Bruninghill, the bishop's constable, appear as witnesses.[23] Under Bishop Robert of Holy Island (1274–83), Henry de Middleton, witness to four charters,[24] is called bailiff of Howden in two of them,[25] whilst Hugh de Monte Alto and Walter de Bremerton both witness as bishop's foresters.[26] Amongst the most important figures in the administration and supervision of the household of any secular noble were their stewards. Bishops' stewards, whilst doubtless of equal importance, usually appear only fleetingly in the evidence for their *familia*. They are, however, clearly in evidence at Durham. Nicholas Farnham's stewards, John of Romsey and Geoffrey of Lewknor, witnessed ten and one charters respectively;[27] three of Bishop Walter's stewards – Roger de Creppint, William of Middleton and John Gylet – appear, with the latter two witnessing ten and eight times each,[28] and from the episcopates of the two bishops Robert come three more stewards, Geoffrey Russel, Richard le Chauncelor and Guichard de Charron. The last, who was witness to no fewer than twenty-six of Bishop Holy Island's charters and the recipient of several land grants from the bishop,[29] had also been the steward of the household of a secular noble, that of Peter of Savoy, in the early 1260s, when in 1262 he and the Queen had been left in charge of the administration of Peter's estate whilst the latter was abroad.[30] Also extremely frequent amongst the witnesses at Durham are the bishops' knights, men who held land of the bishops as well as attesting their documents as part of his *familia*.

Both secular and ecclesiastical household members also provide an indication of the degree of continuity amongst the personnel of the Durham *familia* from one episcopate to the next. Evidence for bishops of other thirteenth-century sees retaining some of their predecessors' staff can be found. At Worcester master Robert Clipstone acted as bishop's official through several episcopates,[31] and at Chichester, when John Climping was

---

[21] ibid., nos 47, 56, 97, 112.
[22] ibid., nos 117–18, 181.
[23] ibid., nos 163, 187.
[24] ibid., nos 196, 201, 207, 210.
[25] ibid., nos 196, 201.
[26] ibid., nos 208–9, 237, 262.
[27] ibid., no. 5–7, 10–11, 15–17, 20, 28.
[28] ibid., nos 53–4, 56, 58, 60–3, 77–8, 91–2, 97, 100–1, 103, 112, 115; DCM, SHD 1/13.
[29] EEA 29, nos 196, 198, 199–200, 206–10, 216, 221, 224, 234, 236–7, 241–3, 248–50, 253, 256, 258, 261–2.
[30] Margaret Howell, *Eleanor of Provence, Queenship in Thirteenth-Century England* (Oxford, 1998), p. 186
[31] EEA 13, p. xxv; E. Rathbone, 'The Influence of Bishops and Members of Cathedral

appointed bishop he retained several men from his predecessor's household.[32] In early thirteenth-century Hereford there are some examples of household members surviving from one episcopate to the next.[33] At Winchester, Peter des Roches kept several of his predecessor Godfrey de Lucy's clerks and at least one of his knights in his service.[34] Lawrence has also noted some continuity at Canterbury under Archbishop Edmund of Abingdon,[35] and earlier at Canterbury Professor Cheney has remarked that Hubert Walter retained some of his predecessor's servants when he became archbishop.[36] The overriding impression is not, however, of continuity. Peter des Roches's household, for example, is notable for the large number of clerks and knights whose names suggest they were drawn from France, and one of the main accusations made against him was his employment of aliens.[37] In Durham, these links from one episcopate to another were a more sustained phenomenon, occurring across all four of the mid-thirteenth century episcopates as well as looking back to Bishop Farnham's predecessors, and clearly stretching forward into the last years of the century, in the household of Bishop Anthony Bek.

It is important not to overstate this continuity by implying that a new bishop arrived in Durham to find a full complement of 'civil servants' waiting for him. Nicholas Farnham certainly did bring new blood to Durham, extending his patronage to men such as Geoffrey of Lewknor, Robert of St Albans and Martin of St Cross, whose Hampshire names suggested close personal links with the bishop, whilst John Gylet, who first appears in this episcopate, was to become an important part of more than one Durham household.[38] Some of these men are known to have left Durham and to have risen through the ecclesiastical ranks. The most famous incomer of this episcopate, Walter de Merton, was a future royal chancellor and bishop of Rochester, whose fame was to stretch far beyond the see. However, Farnham's staff also included a number of prominent men found in his predecessor's household. John of Romsey, mentioned above as steward in this episcopate, also appears as the bishop's clerk and acting as bishop's justice in 1242.[39] Farnham also made him a grant of forty acres from the episcopal manor of Stanhope with rights of pasture (a grant of land and rights made in exactly the same terms to Jordan Heyrun, a member of Bishop

---

Bodies in the Intellectual Life of England 1066–1216' (London University Ph.D. thesis, 1936), i, p. 317.

[32] *EEA* 22, pp. lvii–lviii.
[33] *EEA* vii, pp. lx–lxi.
[34] *EEA* ix, pp. xl–xli.
[35] Lawrence, *St Edmund of Abingdon*, pp. 140–2.
[36] C.R. Cheney, *Hubert Walter*, p. 160.
[37] *EEA* ix, pp. xxxix–xl.
[38] *EEA* 29, p. xliv.
[39] 'Two Thirteenth-Century Assize Rolls', *Miscellanea* (Surtees Society 127, 1916), p. 75.

Marsh's and Bishop Poore's households).[40] Yet John of Romsey had also been a prominent member of the household of Bishop Poore, possibly following him from his first see of Salisbury. He was bishop's steward as early as 1226 and justice in 1235, and acted as one of the executors of Poore's will.[41] Philip of St Helen too was clearly a member of Farnham's household, witnessing six charters, and had also been a clerk under Bishop Richard Marsh.[42] Walter of Selby's exact role in the *familia* is not clear but he attested charters for both Nicholas Farnham and Richard Poore.[43] Finally, both William of Blockley and Robert of St Meldred appear in Farnham's episcopate, as witness and bishop's justice respectively,[44] but they were both clearly in Durham by the 1240s, being household members of, or receiving grants from, earlier bishops there.[45]

Under Farnham's successor, Walter Kirkham, there is again clear evidence of new men in the diocese within the bishop's household. The most notable of these were Roger of Seaton, witness to four of Kirkham's charters and recorded as bishop's official in the close roll of 1260,[46] and Richard of Kirkham, found in ten witness lists and very possibly a relative of the bishop.[47] Much of Kirkham's *familia* was, however, comprised of men who had been members of the households of earlier bishops. Walter of Merrow was a regular witness under Kirkham, appearing eight times, and also acted as the bishop's proctor.[48] He had also witnessed documents of earlier bishops, although only attesting once in the surviving sources for Bishop Farnham.[49] Other men, such as Philip of St Helen, Martin of St Cross and Walter of Selby, clearly members of Farnham's staff and very possibly of earlier Durham households,[50] witness at least once for Kirkham.[51] It is tempting to see in all these men the signs of long-term continuity – though glimpsed only briefly at this period, due to the loss of evidence. Certainly we can say with confidence that they had all served bishops of Durham before Kirkham's succession. The evidence for continuity of service is clearer in the case of men such as Adam of Bradley, one of Farnham's foresters, who also appeared in Walter's *familia* witnessing seven documents,[52] and John Gylet, who witnessed both for Farnham (when he is once described as sheriff) and

---

[40] *EEA* 29, no. *38.
[41] *EEA* 24, p. l; DCM, SHD 3/6; *CPR 1232–47*, p. 180, *CCR 1234–37*, p. 437.
[42] *EEA* 29, nos 5, 7, 11, 15–17; *EEA* 25, nos 275, 278, 281.
[43] *EEA* 29, nos 5, 15–17, 31, 41; *EEA* 25, nos 290, 319, 326.
[44] *EEA* 29, nos 5, 7, 15–17, 20, 29, 41; 'Two Thirteenth-Century Assize Rolls', p. 1.
[45] *EEA* 25, no. 250; *EEA* 24, p. xlviii.
[46] *EEA* 29, nos 58, 77–8, 91; *CCR 1259–61*, p. 183.
[47] *EEA* 29, nos 61, 63–4, 66, 71, 98–101, 103.
[48] *EEA* 29, nos 47, 55–6, 58, 77–8, 91, 112.
[49] ibid., no. 41.
[50] See above, p. 130.
[51] *EEA* 29, nos 64, 108.
[52] ibid., nos 53, 55, 60, 62, 98, 103, 107.

on eight occasions as Kirkham's steward (a position he had already held in the household of John Fitz Philip in 1240, before entering Farnham's service),[53] also breaking the episcopal seal at Kirkham's death.[54]

Under Robert Stichill this continuity becomes increasingly obvious, with a growing number of the bishop's staff drawn from the ranks of his predecessors' households. There is also evidence that some at least of these men were slowly rising through the ranks of the *familia*. Those who are described as the bishop's knights – such as Marmaduke son of Geoffrey, witness of over twenty charters for Bishop Kirkham and seven for his successor,[55] or Thomas of Herrington, witnessing three documents for Kirkham and six for Robert[56] – in all probability owe their regular appearance to their families' positions as prominent landholders in the diocese. Certainly both these men came from families long known in Durham. Geoffrey son of Geoffrey, Marmaduke's father, appears regularly in Durham documents of the early thirteenth century and his family were lords of Horden, whilst Thomas's great-grandfather was probably closely related to Bishop Flambard.[57] This is not the case, however, for other witnesses across more than one episcopate. John Gylet, recorded above as Kirkham's steward and as first appearing at Durham under Farnham, was still receiving commissions from Bishop Stichill; for example to make inquisition with Richard of Hartburn in 1263/4.[58] Roger of Auckland still appeared in Stichill's witness lists and Roger of Seaton, previously Kirkham's official, attested six charters in this episcopate, as well as acting as the bishop's justice in 1271, and was also one of his executors.[59] William of Merrow, meanwhile, a witness across several episcopates stretching back into the early thirteenth century, was Bishop Stichill's official in 1264.[60] During Robert of Holy Island's episcopate, there are also instances of continuity of staff. A number of these are, again, household knights witnessing the charters of two or three Durham bishops. In addition, to take the most notable other examples, Alexander de Biddick, sheriff under Stichill (a position in the bishop's gift) and witness of four of his charters, appears in three witness lists;[61] Stichill's clerk Thomas of Levesham attests ten charters for Bishop Holy Island (twice still described as clerk) and

---

[53] ibid., nos 56, 58, 77–8, 91–2, 97, 112; CCR 1237–1242, p. 200.
[54] *Historiae Dunelmensis scriptores tres, Gaufridus de Coldingham, Robertus de Graystanes, et Willielmus de Chambre*, ed. J. Raine (Surtees Society 9, 1839), p. 44.
[55] EEA 29, nos 47, 53–6, 58, 60–3, 66, 77–8, 91–2, 98, 101, 103, 107–8, 114–15, 119, 121, 131, 133, 148–9, 161.
[56] ibid., nos 71, 78, 91, 119, 121, 131, 148–9.
[57] R. Surtees, *The History and Antiquities of the County Palatinate of Durham*, 4 vols (London, 1816–1840), iv, p. 33.
[58] EEA 29, no. 146.
[59] EEA 29, nos 124, 149, 178, 185, 167, 174; TNA, DURH 3/92, m. 16d; CFR 1272–1307, p. 26.
[60] EEA 29, no. 178.
[61] ibid., nos 121, 139, 148–9, 208–9, 241.

was also one of his executors,⁶² whilst Robert of Driffield, another clerk, was also a member of both households.

Just as it was possible to look back from Nicholas Farnham's episcopate and mark the connection between his household and that of Bishops Poore and Marsh, so we can look forward to Anthony Bek's household and note the continuity with his predecessors' staff. Thomas of Levesham, clerk to both Bishop Stichill and Bishop Holy Island, was sent by Bishop Bek to reclaim money deposited in Durham priory and in 1300 was still being described as an episcopal clerk.⁶³ Bishop Holy Island's steward, Guichard de Charron, who was also executor of his will and keeper of the temporalities of the see after that bishop's death, acted as steward to his successor also,⁶⁴ and Robert of Avenel, Bishop Holy Island's chancellor who broke the episcopal seal at the bishop's death was also chancellor to Bek at the start of the latter's episcopate.⁶⁵ Bishop Bek's official, Alan of Easingwold, had witnessed twenty-two charters for his immediate predecessor,⁶⁶ whilst one of the most eminent members of Bek's household, Peter de Thoresby, who served both as Bek's chancellor from 1290 to 1302 and as his receiver-general between 1303 and 1307 attested seven of Robert of Holy Island's *acta*.⁶⁷ Others of Bishop Holy Island's household also appear as witnesses to several of Bek's charters, including Henry of Holy Island and Walter de Bremerton, who also received land from Bek.⁶⁸

With such marked evidence of continuity in episcopal households within this one diocese over the space of nearly one hundred years, a continuity somewhat at odds with the accepted tradition, amongst historians of both secular and ecclesiastical administration, regarding the changeability of English ecclesiastical households, it is necessary to ask the simple question: why? Can comparisons with other dioceses and a study of the particular nature of the see of Durham provide any reasons for this apparently marked difference from other, contemporary bishops' households?

It is, of course, possible that the answer is simply that there is no actual difference between Durham and other medieval English dioceses in this respect, except for the nature and extent of the surviving evidence. Perhaps the large number of surviving Durham land grants has skewed the evidence

---

62 ibid., nos 203–4, 207, 216, 224, 248, 250, 256, 258, 261; *CFR 1272–1307*, p. 148; no. *263.
63 C.M. Fraser, *A History of Anthony Bek* (Oxford, 1957), pp. 100, 102.
64 DCM, SHD 1/18; *Records of Anthony Bek, Bishop and Patriarch*, ed. C.M. Fraser (Surtees Society 162, 1953), nos 22, 24, 28, 38, 40–1, 54, 60–2, 64, 77–8, 103, 152.
65 Fraser, *A History of Anthony Bek*, p. 101; *CChR* ii, p. 166.
66 *EEA* 29, nos 197–200, 202–4, 206, 210, 216, 221, 224, 234, 236, 242–3, 248, 250, 253, 256, 258, 262; Fraser, *A History of Anthony Bek*, p. 114.
67 ibid., p. 101; *Boldon Buke, A Survey of the Possessions of the See of Durham made by Order of Bishop Hugh Pudsey*, ed. W. Greenwell (Surtees Society 25, 1832), App. xxv–xxxix; *EEA* 29, nos 203–4, 207, 216, 249, 258, 261.
68 *Records of Anthony Bek*, nos 22, 24, 33, 38, 40–1, 60–1, 74, 76.

in favour of the secular household just as the lack of any such documentation in other dioceses may have concealed it. Certainly there is an element of this. Some of those found as frequent, and continuing, witnesses in these charters, or with titles that demonstrate they had secular roles within the bishops' households, could be expected to have continued from one episcopate to the next. The bishops' foresters, for example, unsurprisingly, often witness or appear in Durham charters related to episcopal woodland – charters rarely found in other collections of episcopal *acta* – and these men may well be expected to have retained their positions under a new bishop. Indeed, a story is told of Bishop Robert of Holy Island dismissing one of his predecessor's foresters because he was known to have been disloyal to his former master,[69] implying that in normal circumstances foresters would have continued in their positions. Bailiffs of episcopal manors, and those episcopal knights who were also tenants of the bishops' lands would be other similar examples. It would not be difficult to find examples of ecclesiastical office holders who were treated in the same way – archdeacons, for example, although they might have familial links to the bishops who appointed them or have been members of their households would, naturally, not be expected to resign at the start of a new episcopate. However, this cannot be the whole explanation. It is true that a large proportion of documents amongst the *acta* of the mid-thirteenth century bishops of Durham are land grants. However, even those with apparently secular positions within the household witness charters relating to ecclesiastical grants, for example of advowsons, and many of the land grants are also witnessed by bishops' clerks and others clerical members of the *familia*. It would even be possible to trace at least some of the continuity of staff between episcopates without any consideration of the surviving grants of land.

One of the solutions to Durham's differences could lie in the unusual nature of the holders of episcopal office. Two of the four bishops under consideration were monks, appointed from within the diocese, at a time when monastic candidates for bishoprics were rarely successful.[70] Robert Stichill and Robert of Holy Island would not have had a following of men from outside the see of Durham for whom they needed to provide patronage. A similar explanation has been offered for the continuity between the staff of John Climping – bishop of Chichester and formerly official to Bishop Neville, archdeacon of Chichester then chancellor of the cathedral in that diocese – and that of his predecessor, Ralph Neville.[71] At Hereford too, the continuity between the *familia* of Bishop Giles de Braose and his successor, Hugh de Mapenore (1216–19), could be explained by Hugh's rise from within the see, where he had been dean of the cathedral before his election.

---

[69] *Historia Dunelmensis*, p. 58.
[70] M. Gibbs and J. Lang, *Bishops and Reform 1215–1272* (London, 1962), p. 6.
[71] *EEA* 22, p. lviii.

This must have been an element in the composition of the Durham households from Robert Stichill on, but again, it cannot be the entire story. The appointment of a bishop from within his own diocese did not always lead to continuity amongst the members of episcopal households, and equally there could be continuity of staff where bishops were previously unknown within the see. The staff of Stephen Bersted, John Climping's successor at Chichester, do not noticeably appear in his predecessor's household, although admittedly Bersted's political interests and absence from his see have left us with few witness lists and therefore little information about his staff.[72] At Hereford, Hugh de Mapenore was succeeded by another member of the chapter, Hugh Foliot; but this second Hugh seems to have employed only one member of his predecessor's *familia*.[73] At Durham, although the households of Nicholas Farnham and Walter Kirkham show clear connections with those of their predecessors, the two bishops were royal appointments from within the king's household and administration; men with no strong connections with Durham before they became its diocesans. Additionally Robert of Holy Island's successor, Anthony Bek, whilst he was archdeacon of Durham at the time of his election to the episcopate there, was also a royal servant who continued in the king's service after his election:[74] he could be expected to have had his own retinue. There is also a logistical problem. If episcopal households were, as seems certain, usually dissolved at a bishop's death or at least after his funeral, even a delay of a month between one bishop's death and the appointment of his successor would be enough time for episcopal staff to move on to new employment, as indeed we know that sometimes, in other dioceses, they did.

If the continuity of the bishop's staff in Durham cannot be attributed solely to the nature of the evidence, nor to the backgrounds of the men appointed to the episcopate there, what other features of the diocese may have influenced the structure of the bishop's household? What, indeed, was that structure, and can answering this second question help to provide an answer to the first? With so little evidence it is not possible to be certain about the way in which the household at Durham worked, but it may be useful to consider Lawrence's suggestions about the household of Edmund of Abingdon, the archbishop of Canterbury, whose household also contained some men from the staff of his predecessors. Lawrence posits that there may have been a nucleus of standing civil servants, the basis of the household at Canterbury, which remained the same despite changes of archbishops.[75] In support of his theory he notes the names of several household members remaining from Stephen Langton's archiepiscopate (there is as yet no study

---

[72] ibid., p. lix.
[73] *EEA* vii, p. lxi.
[74] Fraser, *A History of Anthony Bek*, p. 3.
[75] Lawrence, *St Edmund of Abingdon*, p. 140.

of the household of Richard Grant, archbishop of Canterbury between Langton and Abingdon). Although these do include the archdeacon, Simon Langton, and also Archbishop Langton's official, Thomas of Freckenham, on the basis of only one known attestation of a charter issued by Abingdon, Lawrence also mentions Langton's steward, Elias of Dereham (a great man in his own right who was steward to a large number of bishops, even apparently serving some concurrently, but certainly worked as steward to Langton and Archbishop Grant[76]) and at least one, and very possibly three, of the archbishop's clerks. In addition, Lawrence notes the existence of an Archbishop's Council in the mid to late thirteenth century under Archbishop Boniface of Savoy, a body which is described as meeting at the archbishop's manor of Wingham when he was appointing a new prior of Christ Church.[77] In other words, the archbishop's *familia* may have been functioning in a way closer to that of a secular nobleman's or even to the king's court at this date than to the traditional bishop's household. This would have been a logical, and perhaps necessary, development for the household of the archbishop, with its central administrative position within the Church in England. Could the same thing have happened at Durham, and if so, why? There is no indication of a bishop's council at mid-thirteenth-century Durham, but the evidence for the episcopal *familia* as it stands would certainly be commensurate with the existence of a core standing household, with members serving across twenty years or more, some of whom clearly rose to prominent positions over time. In addition, each new bishop (particularly those from outside the diocese) would naturally have needed to provide for his own men: those whom he brought with him or who came to his notice during his episcopate. Some of these men would then move on in the manner of other episcopal households, but others would remain to become part of the standing household of the next bishop. This distinct *familia*, with a strong resemblance to the households of not just spiritual but also secular lords, must have arisen for a reason and to discover why we must consider another distinctive feature of the see of Durham: the palatinate and its management.

The nature of the palatinate and the power of the prince bishops of Durham has been the subject of much debate, and I do not intend to enter into a full analysis here – an analysis which would, in any case, go beyond what is necessary for this discussion. William of St Botolph's claim, as steward of Bishop Anthony Bek, that 'There are two kings in England, namely the Lord King of England wearing a crown as symbol of his regality and the lord bishop of Durham wearing a mitre in place of a crown as a

---

[76] For an extremely valuable, discussion of Elias' career see Nicholas Vincent, 'Master Elias of Dereham (d.1245): A Reassessment', in *The Church and Learning in Later Medieval Society: Essays in Honour of R.B. Dobson*, ed. Caroline M. Barron and Jenny Stratford (Donnington, 2002), pp. 128–59.

[77] Lawrence, *St Edmund of Abingdon*, pp. 140–2, 147.

symbol of his regality in the diocese of Durham'[78] was surely an exaggeration, even in the early fourteenth century when he spoke, and it was certainly not true fifty years earlier in the mid-thirteenth century. Scammell noted that the king's writ always ran in Durham and that it was often more powerful than that of the bishop, that there were definite limits to episcopal jurisdiction and that the bishop's 'subjects' were also willing to appeal to the king on frequent occasions, by-passing any secular authority inherent in the position of their spiritual lord.[79] Fraser has described the bishop of Durham as ruling in partnership with the king, but only as a very junior partner.[80] However, this does not alter the fact that within the bishop of Durham's liberty – the land between the rivers Tyne and Tees, known at this date as the land of St Cuthbert, as well as in the wapentake of Sadberge and in outlying areas around Norham and Holy Island and the manor of Bedlington – the bishop exercised considerable judicial, financial and administrative power, much of it developed for pragmatic reasons rather than by right, but none the less real for that. The bishop of Durham, more perhaps than any of his peers within the episcopate, was in fact not only a bishop but also one of the great feudal lords of England. During vacancies, such as that of four years between the episcopates of bishops Poore and Farnham, the diocese, like other English sees, was administered by royal appointees, but hearings continued to be in the bishop's court and the liberty had still to be managed in a remote area where there was little enthusiasm – in the cases of Bishops Stichill and Holy Island – even for enforcing the appointment of a suitable royal candidate or administratively important bishop. It is probably not a coincidence that so many of the bishops' men, and indeed many of those who seem to have formed the core household, had demonstrable legal expertise and experience, acting for example as proctors and justices for the bishop. Certainly under Robert of Holy Island's successor, Anthony Bek, the bishop's justices acted also as judges in the royal peripatetic courts, with sessions of the two legal institutions carefully arranged not to coincide, in order to facilitate this arrangement.[81] The standing household, in such a large, remote and powerful liberty, may have been no more than a practical necessity, albeit one which must have added to the bishop's status in the eyes of his contemporaries and furthered his appearance and claims to be the equivalent not just of his fellow diocesans but also of the great secular lords of the kingdom.

The palatinate of the medieval see of Durham has been described as a 'crude mixture of diocesan administration and baronial household':[82] an

---

[78] Quoted in Fraser, *A History of Anthony Bek*, p. 98.
[79] Jean Scammell, 'The Origins and Limitations of the Liberty of Durham', *EHR* 81 (July 1966), pp. 449–73.
[80] Constance M. Fraser, 'Prerogative and the Bishops of Durham, 1267–1376', *EHR* 74 (July 1959), pp. 467–76.
[81] Fraser, *A History of Anthony Bek*, p. 83.
[82] Scammell, 'The Origins and Limitations of the Liberty of Durham', p. 471.

administrative centre in which the bishop managed to combine the ecclesiastical and the lay in a unique way and thus enabled the holding of a large franchise peacefully and with appearance of power. This combining of spiritual and secular rule is also reflected in the episcopal households at Durham through the thirteenth century. The staff of the bishops of this see included the expected elements of the episcopal household, as revealed principally through the extant *acta* and witness lists of twelfth and thirteenth-century bishops, with both those holding ecclesiastical roles and those with secular positions within the household (more obvious at Durham, but not unknown elsewhere) appearing. In addition, however, the continuity in the membership of these households, with individuals appearing over twenty years or more under more than one bishop, reflects the great secular households of the middle ages, reminding us that if the bishop of Durham was less than a king within the palatinate, he was still more than just a bishop.

The Acta of English Rural Deans in the Later Twelfth and early Thirteenth Centuries

BRIAN KEMP

This article brings together for the first time a substantial selection of the earliest known *acta* and charters of English rural deans, from the mid twelfth century to c.1220. The aim is to illustrate from documents issued by them some aspects of their role in English diocesan administration and jurisdiction at this early and important stage of their existence.[1] Of the twenty-two texts included here, most survive as more or less full copies, but four are originals. The small number of ruridecanal letters surviving from this period, some quite lengthy, have been omitted for reasons of space,[2] as have the few *acta* issued by deans in conjunction with others, such as when acting as papal judges-delegate,[3] but the total of individual *acta* so far discovered is still pitifully small, considering the hundreds of deans who operated in England at this time. The rural deans of the later twelfth and early thirteenth centuries are mostly shadowy figures about whom, as individuals, we know next to nothing. It is not that we hear little of rural deans, or do not know their

---

1 On the role of rural deans in this period, see F. Barlow, *The English Church 1066–1154* (London, 1979), pp. 49–50, 137, 155–6; M. Brett, *The English Church under Henry I* (Oxford, 1975), pp. 211–15; C.R. Cheney, *From Becket to Langton* (Manchester, 1956), pp. 146–7; and in a broader perspective, A. Hamilton Thompson, 'Diocesan organization in the Middle Ages: Archdeacons and Rural Deans', *Proceedings of the British Academy* 29 (1943), especially pp. 167–194.
2 E.g., *The Cartulary of Oseney Abbey*, ed. H.E. Salter, 6 vols (Oxford Historical Society, 89–91, 97–8, 101, 1929–36), v, no. 556; *Select Cases (from the Ecclesiastical Courts of the Province of Canterbury c. 1200–1301)*, ed. N. Adams and C. Donahue (Selden Society 195, 1981), Appendix 1, p. 106, no. 19; Cheney, *From Becket to Langton*, pp. 196–8.
3 E.g., *(Twelfth-century English) Archidiaconal (and Vice-archidiaconal) Acta*, ed. B.R. Kemp (CYS 92, 2001), nos. 66, 305–6; *Select Cases*, Appendix 1, p. 106, nos 20–1; *The Cartulary of Cirencester Abbey, Gloucestershire*, ed. C.D. Ross and M. Devine, 3 vols (Oxford, 1964, 1977), ii, no. 610; *Two Cartularies of Abingdon Abbey*, ed. C.F. Slade and G. Lambrick, 2 vols (Oxfordshire Historical Society, new series 32–33, 1990, 1992), i, no. L 505; *The Cartulary of Worcester Cathedral Priory*, ed. R.R. Darlington, (Pipe Roll Society new series 38, 1968), no. 129. See also J.E. Sayers, *Papal Judges Delegate in the Province of Canterbury, 1198–1254* (Oxford, 1971), pp. 128–9, 137–40, 149–50.

names – quite the reverse, for they occur frequently in the charters and other legal documents of the period. Most commonly they appear as witnesses to gifts (particularly to monasteries), settlements and the like, but deans are also fairly often referred to in other people's charters as playing some part in the legal processes recorded therein.[4] A major limitation of the surviving evidence, however, is its almost total silence on the inquisitorial and corrective powers of the rural deans. Among the *acta* printed below the only such case is the precious reference to the rural dean of Pirehill (or Stafford) exacting a penalty of ten shillings from a wife convicted of adultery, presumably in his rural chapter (no. 11). Other types of record show rural deans carrying out a variety of legal and administrative duties,[5] but the extreme rarity of such references in their *acta* is due to the fact that the overwhelming bulk of the evidence surviving from this early period concerns the rights of individuals or monasteries to possess lands, churches and the like, since it was generally only documents which fortified those rights that were preserved.

A fundamental relationship in this period was that between rural deans and their archdeacons or the deputies of the latter, the vice-archdeacons and archdeacons' officials. Out of 146 twelfth-century archidiaconal *acta* with surviving witness-lists, rural deans occur as witnesses in over a third; of 13 vice-archdeacons' *acta* with such lists, deans witness two-thirds.[6] Although a few of these are private deeds, the great majority are official acts. Again, there is a significant scattering of references to deans acting with archdeacons or their deputies on official business, while a number of notifications by archdeacons, etc., to all the deans of their archdeaconries, or of mandates to individual deans, likewise testify to the cooperation between the two authorities.[7] Occasionally, too, rural deans might act on behalf of archdeacons or serve as vice-archdeacons or the equivalent.[8] It is equally clear that bishops maintained a direct relationship with the deans of their dioceses, and archbishops or papal judges-delegate might similarly address deans directly.

---

[4] E.g., *EYC* i, no. 70; *The Coucher Book of Furness Abbey*, ed. J.C. Atkinson and J. Brownbill, 6 parts (Chetham Society new series, 1886–1919), iii, pp. 734–5; *Two Cartularies of . . . Bruton and . . . Montacute*, ed. anon. (Somerset Record Society 8, 1894), Bruton no. 81.

[5] E.g., *Select Cases*, Appendix 1, p. 105, no. 7; p. 108, no. 30; *The Earliest Northamptonshire Assize Rolls A. D. 1202 and 1203*, ed. D.M. Stenton (Northamptonshire Record Society 5, 1930), nos 59, 78; *Rolls of the Justices in Eyre . . . for Lincolnshire 1218–9 and Worcestershire 1221*, ed. D.M. Stenton (Selden Society 53, 1934), no. 324.

[6] These figures are calculated from *Archidiaconal Acta* (see note 3).

[7] E.g., *Archidiaconal Acta*, nos 91, 162, 208, 210, 247, 261, 271, 296.

[8] See the cases of Robert, dean of [West] Bergholt, acting for the archdn of Colchester; Nicholas of Tadcaster, dean of Tadcaster and vice-archdeacon of York; and Reiner, dean of Cleveland ?and sub-archdn (ibid., 203 and n. 5; ibid., 199, and *Cartularium Prioratus de Gyseburne*, ed. W. Brown, 2 vols (Surtees Society 86, 89, 1889, 1894), ii, no. 720).

The *acta* printed below illustrate the changes in the way deaneries were named in this period. In the twelfth century a dean might not name his deanery at all, calling himself simply 'X the dean', as in no. 1, but generally deans used the name of either their own church within the deanery (nos 2, 5–7, 9, 14, 19 and perhaps 4) or, in some areas, the local hundred or wapentake where the latter was roughly co-extensive with the deanery (nos 3 and 10–11). In 1205 x 1208 the dean of Elford (no. 19) was still using the name of what was evidently his own church within the deanery later called Tamworth (and this practice can be found in some places until the mid thirteenth century[9]), but most of the *acta* after 1200 show that deanery names were soon generally to become fixed, entirely divorced from those of deans' churches, and derived in some places from the hundred or wapentake names.

Among the official activities recorded in the *acta*, the majority are concerned with parish churches. No fewer than nine concern inductions of incumbents (individual or corporate) into parochial benefices, following their admission and institution by the bishop.[10] These show that, while inductions might equally be performed by the archdeacon or his deputy, rural deans were often called upon to act. The mandate for induction usually came from the bishop, but in particular circumstances from a variety of other ecclesiastical superiors. The diplomatic of decanal *acta* of induction likewise varied considerably over the period, although the process it described remained essentially the same. The earliest of the present collection, dating from 1173 x 1182, uses the verb 'introducere' for the act of induction (no. 5), but others opt for 'putting into corporal possession' or a variant, and in two cases the deans speak of having 'instituted' corporate incumbents (nos 9 and 16), which from other evidence we know refers to induction.[11] Standardisation of diplomatic was slow to arrive, but what was to become the normal expression, 'induction into corporal possession', was reached in the case of 1205 x 1208 (no. 19) and recurred in our final example, probably soon after December 1220 (no. 22).[12]

The rural chapter was the main focus of the rural dean's activities and provided the context for various kinds of inquests relating to parish churches, in which the dean presided over recognitions by the clergy and others of the deanery who were present.[13] The place of meeting varied,

---

[9] J. Foster, 'The Activities of Rural Deans in England in the Twelfth and Thirteenth Centuries', unpublished M.A. thesis, Manchester, 1955, pp. 14–16.

[10] Below, nos 5, 7, 9, 13, 15–17, 19, 22.

[11] In each case the institution proper had already been carried out by, respectively, the vice-archdn of Lincoln and the archdeacon of Richmond (*Archidiaconal Acta*, no. 289; BL, Cotton ms Claudius D xi, fol. 61r–v).

[12] However, in another case in 1220 the dean of Waddesdon used the older form 'introduced' (*Cartulary of the Monastery of St Frideswide at Oxford*, ed. S.R. Wigram, 2 vols (Oxford Historical Society 28, 31, 1895–6), ii, no. 821).

[13] For the rural chapter in general, see J. Scammell, 'The Rural Chapter in England from the Eleventh to the Fourteenth Century', *EHR* 86 (1971), pp. 1–21.

however, according to the principal matter before the chapter. The earliest recognition, dating from ?1176 x 1181 and made by dean Nicholas and the chapter of Maidstone in the presence of John, vice-archdeacon of Canterbury, concerned the status of the church of Chart Sutton as a parish church belonging to Leeds priory and not as a chapel dependent on another church (no. 6). The record of an inquest concerning the vicarage of Henlow (Beds.), held in 1200 by the dean and chapter of Langford, is interesting for the information it gives on the income and obligations of two successive vicars, Haco and Hugh, both now dead, and of their respective deacons, and for its statement that after Hugh's death the rural dean found among his records ('in scriniis eius') the charter from Lanthony priory defining the terms of his vicarage (no. 14).

The final two *acta* in this group represent early examples of inquests *de iure patronatus*, which show something of how such inquests may have evolved into their final form.[14] It became a regular part of diocesan procedure for the bishop, on receipt of a letter of presentation to a parochial benefice from the patron, real or alleged, to initiate an enquiry in the relevant rural deanery as to the facts about the benefice (whether it was vacant, etc.) and as to the suitability of the clerk presented. The inquest might be held by the archdeacon, who might alternatively pass the task on to his official or to the local dean, but the bishop might equally commission the dean direct. If a satisfactory return was made, the bishop would normally proceed to admit and institute the presented clerk, the whole process being clearly devised to avoid improper institutions. By the mid thirteenth century such enquiries followed a fairly standard form, with a recognized series of questions to be answered by the chapter,[15] but in the early thirteenth century considerable variation seems to have prevailed in the range of matters covered. Both these points are illustrated by the notification by I., dean of Tendring (Essex), to his archdeacon in c.1218 x 1228 that from an inquest of clergy and laity he affirms that a particular church is vacant and that the abbot of Bury St Edmunds is its patron (no. 20) – whether any more aspects were investigated we do not know. By contrast, an example from 1220 concerning a vacancy in Hillingdon church (Middx) reflects a more advanced state of the inquest, for the dean of Middlesex reports to the bishop of London the findings of the chapter at Hounslow on whether Hillingdon church was

---

[14] See in general J.W. Gray, 'The Ius Praesentandi in England from the Constitutions of Clarendon to Bracton', *EHR* 67 (1952), pp. 481–509. For other early inquests *de iure patronatus* (not all conducted by rural deans), see *Calendar of Charters and Documents relating to . . . Selborne and its Priory*, ed. W.D. Macray, 2 vols (London, 1891–4), ii, p. 1 (?1204 x 05); *CRR* vii, p. 136 (1213 x 14); *Eynsham Cartulary*, ed. H.E. Salter, 2 vols (Oxford Historical Society 49, 51, 1907–8), i, p. 17, no. XVIII (?1221).

[15] See the list of seven matters to be enquired into concerning the benefice, and six concerning the person presented, in an early fourteenth-century formulary (Gray, 'Ius Praesentandi', p. 509).

vacant, whether it was the subject of dispute, to whom the patronage belonged, its value and whether it owed a pension (no. 21). This is virtually the complete range of what were soon to be regarded as the standard questions on the benefice, although nothing was said (nor asked for in the bishop's mandate) about the suitability of the clerk presented to the benefice.

Two of the *acta* testify to, and reinforce, gifts to religious houses made in the presence of the rural dean and chapter (nos 2 and 3). In each case the dean is Ingelram, dean of what would become known as the deanery of Ryedale, but in one case called dean of Ryedale and Pickering Lythe and in the other dean of Welburn, enabling us to identify him with Ingelram the priest of Welburn, who witnessed charters from the 1140s to the 1160s.[16] Since the deanery comprised the wapentakes of Pickering and Ryedale, the two documents show the dean choosing on different occasions to refer to his deanery by the name of his church or by that of the local wapentakes.

Two *acta* are *sui generis*, being testimonials by successive rural deans of Pirehill (later Stafford) as to the ecclesiastical liberties of Burton abbey, in particular its exemption from being obliged to send a person, male or female, to synods and chapters, a privilege which was the subject of repeated episcopal and archidiaconal grants and confirmations (nos 10 and 11).[17] The dean's title in these acts is that of the local hundred.

Finally, four private deeds of rural deans are included (nos 1, 4, 8 and 18). Although such deeds usually throw no light on deans' official activities, they are valuable in enabling us, with other information, to build up a picture of how individual deans fitted into local society. Almost invariably drawn from among the beneficed clergy of the deanery (except in the diocese of Norwich after 1240), the rural dean at this time might also be a local man with local landed interests and possibly married.[18] All these aspects are illustrated particularly by the cases of Hamelin the dean and Nigel, dean of Oxford (1 and 8), but space permits detailed examination of the first only.

Hamelin's gift to the Gilbertine nuns of Alvingham (Lincolnshire) of three-quarters of his parish church of Alvingham, to add to the fourth quarter which they had already been given by Roger son of Jocelin, one of their founders, reveals him not only as the former parson of the church, whose benefice he had already surrendered into the diocesan's hands, but also as its patron and a landholder there. He later resigned his deanery and entered Alvingham priory as a canon, when he made a further gift of lands in the nearby parish of Grainthorpe.[19] Moreover, he was presumably married, for he had at least five sons, of whom the eldest, Brian, succeeded to his

---

[16] *EYC* ix, nos 124, 150, 158.
[17] *EEA* 14, nos 5, 48; *EEA* 16, no. 10; *Archidiaconal Acta*, no. 28.
[18] For Norwich diocese, see *EEA* 21, pp. xxxiii–xxxiv.
[19] *Transcripts of Charters relating to Gilbertine Houses*, ed. F.M. Stenton (LRS 18, 1922), p. 107, no. 9.

lands in Alvingham and Grainthorpe.[20] The identity of his deanery is uncertain; he is once referred to as dean of Yarburgh, and once as Hamelin of Yarburgh,[21] but these probably indicate not his deanery, but some other association with the place (possibly the church), since Yarburgh was not in the wapentake or later deanery of Yarborough, but in the wapentake of Louthesk and later deanery of Ludborough, as was Grainthorpe.[22] Since Alvingham, whose church he certainly held, also lay in the wapentake of Louthesk and was subsequently in that deanery, he was probably dean of what became the deanery of Louthesk, later to be combined with Ludborough.[23]

These *acta* have been edited in accordance with the principles established for the British Academy's *English Episcopal Acta* series. The siglum A indicates an original *actum*, the sigla B and C indicating copies in approximate chronological order. I am very grateful to His Grace the Duke of Rutland for permission to print no. 9 from an original act at Belvoir Castle, and to all corporate owners of manuscripts for permission to publish material in their collections. I am also much indebted to Professor Nicholas Vincent for kindly bringing no. 6 to my attention.

1. *Gift in pure alms by Hamelin the dean to the nuns of Alvingham of the three parts of St Adelwold's church, Alvingham (Lincs.), that belonged to the land he held of the fee of the count of Brittany; the fourth part the nuns have by gift of Roger son of Jocelin with his consent, he having once been parson of the church and surrendered the* personatus *into the hands of Robert de Chesney, bishop of Lincoln, who invested the nuns with the church in the chapter of Sempringham.* [1148 x 1166; ?c.1155]

    B = Bodl. ms Laud. misc. 642 (Alvingham cartulary), fol. 10r. s. xiii; C = TNA, E159/185 (King's Remembrancer's Roll 10 Hen. IV), Communia, Easter term, m. 13r.
    Pd from B, *Mon. Ang.* vi (2), p. 958, no. 1; pd and transl. from C, *Charters to Gilbertine Houses*, ed. F.M. Stenton (LRS 18, 1922), p. 103, Alvingham series, no. 2.

Sciant omnes tam futuri quam presentes quod ego Hamelinus decanus assensu et consilio heredum meorum dedi et concessi et hac presenti carta[a] confirmavi deo et ecclesie sancte Marie de Alvingham et sanctimonialibus ibidem deo servientibus in puram et perpetuam elemosinam possidendam totam partem ecclesie sancti Adelwoldi[b] de Alvingham que pertinet ad terram quam teneo de feudo comitis Brictannie[c] in eadem villa, scilicet tres

---

[20] Ibid., pp. 106–7, nos 8–9.
[21] Ibid., p. 105, no. 5; *Archidiaconal Acta*, no. 140.
[22] *The Lincolnshire Domesday and the Lindsey Survey*, ed. C.W. Foster and T. Longley (LRS 19, 1924), pp. lxxxi–lxxxii; *Taxatio Ecclesiastica Angliæ et Walliæ auctoritate P. Nicholai IV*, ed. J. Caley (Record Commission, 1802), p. 58.
[23] *Lincolnshire Domesday*, p. lxxxi; *Taxatio*, p. 58; *V CH Lincolnshire* ii, map between pp. 78 and 79.

partes eiusdem ecclesie cum omnibus pertinentiis suis. Hanc elemosinam ego et heredes mei contra omnes homines warantizabimus. Quartam vero partem eiusdem ecclesie tenent*d* prescripte sanctimoniales de donatione Rogeri filii Gocelini per concessum meum, qui aliquo tempore persona eiusdem ecclesie extiterim, set dimissionem personatus in manu Roberti de Chenei Lincolnien' episcopi feci. Facta dimissione pontifex memoratus sanctimoniales predictas de prefata ecclesia cum pertinentiis suis integre et plenarie investivit in capitulo de Sempingham.*e* [Huius rei testes sunt: Robertus archidiaconus Lincoln' et Rogerus frater eius, Robertus capellanus, magister Iohannes, magister Robertus Scrope, Ricardus frater decani, Galphridus de Wythecall', Gilbertus de Beseby, Hugo de Halei, Reginaldus sacerdos, Iohannes de Cunyngesholme et Hugo de Richebroke et David frater eius, Osbertus sacerdos de Saltfletby et Robertus magister, Robertus de Suine, Thomas de Brachenbergh'.]

a Insert mea *C*   *b* Adelwodi *C*   *c* Britannie *C*   *d* Om. in *C*   *e* B ends; the remainder from *C*

After the earliest possible date for the foundation of the priory and before the death of bp Robert of Lincoln (D. Knowles & R.N. Hadcock, *Medieval Religious Houses England and Wales*, 2nd edn (London 1971), p. 194; *Fasti* iii, 2); c.1155 is the date suggested by F.M. Stenton, *Gilbertine Charters*, p. 103. For Hamelin's deanery, see above, p. 144.

2. *Notification by Ingelram, dean of Welburn [= Ryedale], and the chapter of Ryedale that in their presence Theobald son of Pain of Wykeham (Yorks.) gave to the nuns of Wykeham two bovates of land there, with his daughter whom he handed over to the religious life, in perpetual alms and free of all secular service save that of the king.*   Normanby [?c.1160 x Nov. 1181]

B = Bodl. ms Dodsworth 7 (transcripts of charters formerly in St Mary's Tower, York, 1644), fol. 292v; C = Bodl. ms Top. Yorks. e. 11 (transcripts of charters by John Burton), fols 77r–v (pp. 145–6). s. xviii med.
Pd, incompletely, from B, *Mon. Ang.* v, p. 670, no. 3.

Ingelram decanus de Welebrun et capitulum de Ridala omnibus sancte matris ecclesie filiis ad quos littere iste pervenerint in domino salutem. Notum vobis facimus quod Tedbaldus filius Pagani de Wicham in presentia nostra dedit et concessit atque fide in manu nostra affirmavit ecclesie sancti Michaelis de Wicham et*a* sanctimonialibus ibidem deo servientibus duas bovatas terre in campis de Wicham cum pertinentiis suis, cum filia sua religioni in ibidem tradita, in perpetuam elemosinam et liberam *b*et quietam ab omni humana consuetudine et seculari servitio quod ad eum et ad heredes suos attinet,*b* excepto servitio regis. Hanc autem elemosinam ipse Tedbaldus et heredes sui ad opus predicte ecclesie warantizabunt *c*supradictis sanctimonialibus ab omnibus calumniantibus eam.*c* His testibus: Roberto de Bruntun, Gervasio sacerdote*d* de Mideltun,*e* Willelmo clerico de Kirkabi,*f* magistro Willelmo de Maltuna, Samson de Slingesbi, Rainaldo de Staingrifa,

Nicolao de Nunnigtun,^g magistro Ricardo de Hotun,^{h i}Willelmo cler(ico) de Nortmanbi, Hugone sacerdote de Laistingham, Waltero capellano de Oswald', Roberto sacerdote de Hedestom,^j Willelmo capellano de Abatun, Alano capellano de Siflingtuna, Hermero capellano de Matania, Roberto capellano de Oviham,^k capellano de Salatuna, Gerardo capellano de Levezaim,ⁱ Ingenaldo de Furnais, Gaufrido de Chiltona,^l Willelmo de Staintuna, Radulfo de Wath, Huberto mercatore de Maltuna, Paulino de Wintrigishaim,^m Petro clerico de Kircabi, et multis aliis. Hec carta facta fuit aput Nortmanbi.ⁿ

> a Interlined in B   b–b &c. *C*   c–c Om. in *C*   d Om. in *C*   e Midletun *C*
> f Kircabi *C*   g Numigtun B; Nunington *C*   h Hoton *C*   i–i Om. in *C*   j Reading uncertain   k Followed by gap for name   l Chiltonia *C*   m Wintrigeshai *C*
> n Normanbi *C*

> Dating very uncertain, but Wykeham priory was founded by Theobald's father in or before 1153 (S. Thompson, *Women Religious* (Oxford, 1991), p. 231), Theobald was a tenant of William de Percy in 1166 (*The Red Book of the Exchequer*, ed. H. Hall, 3 vols (RS 1896), i, p. 425), and Ingelram had been succeeded as dean of Ryedale (see above, p. 143) by Robert of Helmsley by Nov. 1181 at the latest (*EEA* 20, no. 9).

3. *Notification by Ingelram, dean of Ryedale and Pickering Lythe, that Sunnive, wife of Lambert of Hoveton (Yorks.), and her two daughters quitclaimed to Rievaulx Abbey a bovate of land and two assarts which they had held of the monks, and swore to maintain this in the dean's hand in Helmsley church (Yorks.).*

[1164 x 1171]

> B = BL, Cotton ms Julius D i (Rievaulx cartulary), fol. 163r (146r). s. xii ex.
> Pd, *Cartularium Abbathiæ de Rievalle*, ed. J.C. Atkinson (Surtees Society 83, 1887), p. 174, no. 239; *EYC* ix, pp. 217–18, no. 131.

Omnibus sancte matris ecclesie filiis Engelrammus decanus de Ridale et Pikeringalith salutem. Notum sit vobis quod Sunnive uxor Lamberti de Hovetun et due filie eius Sigerith et Orenge coram fratribus capituli nostri et multis aliis quieta clamaverunt deo et sancte Marie Rievall' et monachis ibidem deo servientibus unam bovatam terre et duo sarta que continent v. acras terre que de eisdem monachis tenuerant cum omnibus earum pertinentiis libera et quieta sine omni reclamatione in posterum de se et de omnibus heredibus suis. Et hoc legitime et firmiter tenendum in manu mea coram omnibus affidaverunt in ecclesia omnium sanctorum apud Helmeslai in presentia duorum archidiaconorum, Iohannis scilicet filii Lethold' et Radulfi del Alnai. Monachi vero propter hoc dederunt eisdem mulieribus sex marchas argenti et unam vaccam. His testibus: Roberto filio Willelmi subarchidiacono, Hugone de Ruddebi et Waltero fratre eius, Willelmo de Laceles, Waltero decano de Bulemer, Willelmo clerico de Kirkebi, Roberto capellano de Helmeslai, Roberto clerico de Martun, Roberto de Bruntun, Petro de Surdevals et Willelmo fratre eius, Alano de Buleford', Radulfo filio Margar(ete), Petro de Hovetun.

The date is determined by the archdns mentioned. Ralph d'Aunay became archdn of York not earlier than 1164, and John son of Letold had ceased to be archdn of Cleveland (the local archdn) before late 1171 (*Fasti* vi, pp. 32, 37).

4. *Gift by Henry, dean of Haddon (Northants.), to the canons of Sulby of one mark of silver [annually] in his church of Guilsborough.* [1155 x 1185]

> A = BL, Add. Ch. 21866. 157 x 76 + 16/20 mm; endorsed: H' decan' de marca (s. xii ex.); seal missing, tag surviving (method 1).

Notum sit omnibus ecclesie sancte fidelibus quod ego Henricus decanus de Hadun' do et hac mea carta confirmo et sigilli testimonio consigno deo et sancte Marie et canonicis de Sulebi unam marcam argenti in ecclesia mea de Gildesburc in puram elemosinam inperpetuum. Teste^a Nicholao presbitero de Turnebi, et Radulfo capellano de Gaham, Radulfo milite de Aissebi, Henrico de Mundevilla, Herberto silvano, Willelmo carpent(ario).

> *a* Sic

> After the foundation of Sulby abbey (H.M. Colvin, *The White Canons in England* (Oxford, 1951), pp. 78–9) and before the latest date for Henry's resignation as parson of Guilsborough (*Archidiaconal Acta*, no. 149).

5. *Notification by Adam, dean of Titchmarsh [= Oundle], that, on a mandate of G(eoffrey), elect of Lincoln, he has inducted prior H(erbert) and the monks of St Neots into the church of Hemington (Northants) in the chapter at Oundle.*
[c.May 1173 x 6 Jan. 1182]

> B = BL, Cotton ms Faustina A iv (St Neots cartulary), fol. 40v. s. xiii med.
> Pd, *Mon. Ang.* iii, p. 474, no. 20; G.C. Gorham, *The History and Antiquities of Eynesbury and St Neot's*, 2 vols (London, 1824), i, p. 307, no. R.

Universis sancte matris ecclesie filiis Adam decanus de Tichemer' salutem in domino. Universitati vestre notificetur me ex suscepto mandato G. Lincol' ecclesie electi in capitulo apud Undele H. priorem et monachos sancti Neoti in ecclesiam de Hemmingeton' introduxisse et ipsius auctoritate eos in plenariam misisse possessionem; ita quod Rog(erus) presbiter de Hemmingeton' in vita sua illam nomine monachorum possidebit cum omnibus que ad illam pertinent, reddendo annuatim ecclesie sancti Neoti de vicaria ii. solidos ad vincula sancti Petri. Post decessum vero ipsius in subiectionem et dispositionem monachorum predictorum quieta prefata reddibit ecclesia. Hiis testibus.

> While Geoffrey was elect of Lincoln (*Fasti* iii, p. 2); for his mandate to induct, see *EEA* i, no. 292.

6. *Testimony by Nicholas, dean, and chapter of Maidstone [= Sutton] that the church of Chart [Sutton] (Kent) has never been a chapel of [?East] Sutton church, but a 'mother' church in the possession of Leeds priory, the truth of which they have declared in the presence of John, vice-archdeacon [of Canterbury].*

[?1176 x 1181]

> A = Canterbury Cathedral Library, ms Chartae Antiquae C408. 149 x 82 + 29 mm; endorsed: Inquisicio ecclesie de Chert (s. xiii ex.); seal missing, tag surviving (method 1).

Nicholaus decanus et capitulum de Meidestane omnibus sancte matris ecclesie filiis salutem. Noverit sancta fraternitas vestra quod iuniores cum senioribus capituli nostri omnes unanimiter contestamur nos nunquam vidisse ecclesiam de Chert capellam fuisse de Suttune, set maiores nostri ab ineunte etate in eadem provincia commorati pro certo asseruerant ecclesiam de Chert a diebus antiquis semper matricem ecclesiam extitisse et eam viros religiosos scilicet canonicos de Ledes continue xl. annis et multo amplius canonice et inconcusse possedisse. Huius itaque rei veritatem prout dictum est de ecclesia de Chert in presentia magistri Iohannis vicearchidiaconi nostri adiurati in verbo veritatis confessi sumus.

> Certainly after 1168, when vice-archdn Robert occurs, and before 1189, when R. (probably = Ralph) occurs (*Archidiaconal Acta*, p. 200); and probably, as suggested to me by Prof. Nicholas Vincent, contemporary with *EEA* ii, nos. 145–6, of 1177 x 81, especially since a Nicholas the dean witnesses an act of archbp Richard of Canterbury in 1176 x 80 (ibid., no. 59).

7. *Notification by Peter, dean of Asfordby [= Goscote], that, on the orders of Baldric, archdeacon of Leicester, and the abbots of Rievaulx and Welbeck, judges-delegate of Pope Lucius [III], he has put the canons of Sempringham and the Premonstratensian canons of St John de Valle [i.e., Croxton] into corporal possession of separate moieties of the church of South Croxton (Leics.).*

[6 Sept. 1181 x 1185]

> B = BL, Cotton ms Claudius D xi (Malton cartulary), fol. 218v. s. xiii med. Mentioned in Belvoir Castle, Add. ms 71 (Croxton Abbey register), fol. 85r. s. xiii med.; whence transcripts (s. xviii) in BL, Add. ms 4934, fol. 173r, and BL, Stowe ms 928, fols 72v–73r.

Universis sancte matris ecclesie filiis Petrus decanus de Asfordeby salutem in domino. Noverit universitas vestra me ex officio decanatus mei misisse canonicos ordinis de Sempingeh' in corporalem possessionem medietatis ecclesie de Suth Croxt' que est de feudo Belvarie et canonicos ordinis Primonstracens' de Valle sancti Iohannis in aliam medietatem eiusdem ecclesie, ex precepto domini Baldrici tunc temporis archidiaconi nostri Laycestrie et ex precepto dominorum abbatum de Rievall' et de Wellebec qui, a domino Lucio papa in causa que super eadem ecclesia vertebatur iudices delegati, predictam ecclesiam per diffinitam sententiam eis adiudicaverunt. Et ne huius veritas rei processu temporis in preiudicium iuris predictorum canonicorum a memoria hominum aliqua possit oblivione deleri, presens scriptum, et c'. Hiis testibus, et c'.

During the pontificate of Lucius III, who seems here still to be alive.

8. *Restitution by Nigel, dean of Oxford, to St Frideswide's priory of the land which the canons had acquired by gift of his father and which they had promised that he might hold for life for twenty pence [annually], which he no longer wishes to do.*
[?1184 x Sept. 1199]

> B = Oxford, Corpus Christi College Library, ms CCC 160 (St Frideswide's cartulary), p. 102, no. 156. ss. xiii ex.–xiv in.; C = Oxford, Christ Church, D. & C. Library, vi. c. 1 (St Frideswide's cartulary), p. 79. s. xv med.; D = Ibid., p. 475. s. xv med.
> Pd from B and D, *Cartulary of the Monastery of St Frideswide* (see above, p. 000, n. 00) i, p. 421, no. 599; from C, ibid., ii, p. 28, no. 719.

Sciant ^{a}omnes tam^a presentes quam^b futuri quod ego Nigellus decanus Oxenf'^{c} reddidi deo et ecclesie sancte Frid' terram illam quam tenuit Radulfus Croulec,^{d} quam canonici ^{e}eiusdem ecclesie,^{e} ex donatione patris mei consecuti [sunt],^{f} ut eam tenerem in vita mea pro viginti denariis promiserunt. Set eandem ^{g}diutius nolens^g tenere, ut potius anime patris mei et mee consulerem, eam^h eisdem canonicis salvo servitio domini regis omnino quietam restitui. Hiis testibus:^{i} Iohanne Kepharm, et c'.

> a–a Om. in C   b et C   c Oxon' C, D   d Croulek C   e–e ecclesie eiusdem C
> f Om. in B, D; supplied from C   g–g nolens diutius C   h eandem C   i C ends; D ends with et c'

> For the dates of Nigel as dean of Oxford, see *Facsimiles of Early Charters in Oxford Muniment Rooms*, ed. H.E. Salter (Oxford, 1929), no. 77 n., but he may have succeeded his father, Ralph of St Martin's, some time after Hugh became abbot of Osney in 1184 (*Heads* i, p. 180) rather than after Ralph's death.

9. *Notification by A., dean of Swinderby [= Graffoe], that on the order of R(obert) of Hardres, vice-archdeacon of Lincoln, who was acting on a mandate of B(aldwin), archbishop of Canterbury, he has instituted the prior and convent of Belvoir in the church of Auboum (Lincs.) and received them into corporal possession as parson.*
[prob. Oct. 1185 x 1186]

> A = Belvoir Castle, Leicestershire, ms 171. 132 x 67 + 17 mm; endorsed: Carta A. decani de Swiderbi (s. xii ex.), and post-medieval; seal missing, fragment of tag surviving (method 2).
> B = Belvoir Castle, Add. ms 105 (Belvoir cartulary), fol. 27r. s. xv in.
> Pd (calendar) from A and B, *HMCR Rutland* iv, p. 114.

Universis sancte^a ecclesie filiis ad quos littere iste pervenerint A. decanus de Swinderbi perpetuam in domino salutem. Noverit universitas vestra quod eo tempore quo decani fungebamur officio, et sedulo rebus intendebamus ecclesiasticis pertractandis per provinciam quam iurisdictioni nostre novimus fuisse subiectam, ex precepto R. de Hardr'*b* vicearchidiaconi Lincoln' secundum quod preceperat ei B. dominus Cant(uariensis), priori de Belveer et conventui eiusdem loci institutionem fecimus in ecclesia de Alb(ur) et domibus et terris ad ecclesiam pertinentibus et in plenariam et corporalem possessionem recepimus sicut personam, salvo iure Lincoln' ecclesie. Volentes quod hanc institutionem cunctis in posterum temporibus stabilem et inconvulsam permanere, presenti scripto confirmavimus et sigilli nostri appensione corroboravimus. His*c* testibus: Huberto presbitero de Higam, Herberto presbitero de Swinderbi, Ricardo*d* clerico de Hicham, Alexandro*e* presbitero de Turlebi,*f* Roberto presbitero de eadem villa, Gaufrido filio Sim' (?)*g* de Alb(ur), et Gaufrido preposito eiusdem ville.

a B inserts matris   *b* Haydr' B   *c* Hiis B   *d A has* [ ]ic', *the first letter being lost because of a small hole; supplied from B*   *e* Allex' B   *f B ends with* cum c(eteris) aliis   *g Reading uncertain:* ? Lini

Shortly after the vice-archdn's act, which can be dated 29 Sept. 1185 x 21 Sept. 1186 (*Archidiaconal Acta*, no. 289).

10. *Testimony by A. of Stone, dean of Pirehill [= Stafford], that the abbot and convent of Burton are not obliged to send a man or woman from their land to chapters or synods, but hold their own chapters, as he saw in the parish of [Abbots] Bromley (Staffs.) in the time of bishops Richard, Gerard and Hugh of Coventry.*

[1188 x 27 Mar. 1198]

B = BL, ms Loans 30 (Burton cartulary), fols 59v–60r (39v–40r). s. xiii med.
Pd, incompletely 'The Burton Chartulary', ed. G. Wrottesley, in *Staffordshire Historical Collections* (William Salt Archaeological Society V, 1884), p. 54.

Omnibus Cristi fidelibus ad quos presens scriptum pervenerit A. de Stanes decanus de Pirhul' salutem. Quoniam non in vitio impares iudicantur qui falsum asserit quam qui verum occultat, nec minus peccat qui verum subprimit quam qui falsum intendit, que de libertatibus Burton' ecclesie audivimus et vidimus ad notitiam vestram volumus pervenire. Noverit igitur universitas vestra quod abbas et conventus Burth' hominem vel feminam de tota terra sua ad capitula vel sinodos mittere non tenentur, set capitula sua tenere debent quousque a recto non defecerint, prout privilegia sua tes[fol. 60r]tantur. Nos vero temporibus dominorum Ricardi, Gerardi, Hugonis Coventrensium*a* episcoporum abbates et monachos de Burton' in parochia de Bromleia hac vidimus gaudere libertate. Igitur, testimonium veritati perhibentes, presens scriptum sigilli nostri appositione dignum duximus roborare. Valete in domino.

a Ms Coventransium

Probably while Hugh de Nonant was bp of Coventry (*EEA* 16, p. 110); just possibly (but unlikely in view of no. 11 below) during the vacancy before his successor was consecrated, 21 June 1198.

11. *Notification by A. of Chebsey, dean of Pirehill [= Stafford], that the monks of Burton have established before Mr Godfrey de Insula in Lichfield cathedral their right not to send a man or woman from their land to chapters or synods, but to hold their own chapters; and that he [the dean], by the witness of the chapter of Pirehill, has restored to Hubert, the monks' proctor, ten shillings which he had taken from a wife of [Abbots] Bromley convicted of adultery.* [?27 Mar. x 21 June 1198]

> B = BL, ms Loans 30 (Burton cartulary) fol. 60r (40r). s. xiii med.
> Pd, very incompletely 'The Burton Chartulary' (see no. 10), p. 54.

Omnibus Cristi fidelibus ad quos presens scriptum pervenerit A. de Iebbeseia, successor A. de Stanes, decanus de Pirhul salutem. Cum verba sacerdotis vera sint aut sacrilega, nos qui sacerdotis officio licet indigni fungimur maxime veritati testimonium perhibere tenemur. Icirco^a que super libertatibus Burthon' ecclesie vidimus et audivimus notitiam vestram latere non permittimus. Noverit universitas vestra quod monachi de Burth' in maiori ecclesia de Lich' coram magistro Godefrido de Insula, privilegiis suis utentes et ius suum instantius protestantes, obtinuerunt quod de tota terra sua hominem vel feminam ad capitula vel sinodos mittere non tenentur, set ipsi capitula sua tenere debent iuxta quod privilegia sua testantur. Preterea decem solidos quos de quadam uxore de Bromleg' super adulterio convicta percepimus, attestationi capituli de Pirhul necnon et privilegiis Burth' ecclesie deferentes, Huberto tunc temporis monachorum procuratori refudimus. Et ut hiis indubitatam fidem adhibeatis, presens scriptum sigilli nostri inpressione roboravimus. Valete in domino.

> a Sic

> Dating uncertain, but perhaps during the vacancy at Coventry between bps Hugh de Nonant and Geoffrey Muschamp (EEA 16, p. 110), when Godfrey de Insula was apparently official of Coventry diocese (EEA iii, no. 636 and n.); an 'A. dean of Chebsey' witnessed a Coventry episcopal act in 1198 x 1201 (EEA 17, no. 127).

12. *Testimony by the dean and chapter of Pontefract to the bishops of Lincoln and Ely and the abbot of Reading that Richard of Birstal is true possessor of a moiety of [Kirk]burton (Yorks.) church and was instituted at the presentation of the prior and convent of Lewes by the officials of the archbishopric of York, and that I., Richard's brother, has no right in the moiety save as Richard's proctor and custos.*
[June 1199 x Jan. 1229]

> B = BL, Cotton ms Vespasian F xv (Lewes cartulary), fol. 300r (337r), in notification (before Jan. 1229) by Richard of Birstal, rector of a moiety of Kirkburton church, that he has this document. s. xv med
> Pd, EYC viii, pp. 218–20, no. 157; (calendar), C.T. Clay, 'The Yorkshire portion of the Lewes Chartulary', *Yorkshire Archaeological Journal* 31 (1932–3), p. 311.

Lincol(niensi) et Elyensi dei gratia episcopis et abbati de Rading' decanus et capitulum de Pontefr(acto) salutem in vero salutari. Veritatis amatores veritati testimonium perhibere tenentur. Hinc est ut^a rei veritatem super causa que vertitur inter magistrum W. de Summere et Ricardum clericum de Burstal vobis significamus. Noveritis itaque prefatum Ricardum clericum medietatis ecclesie de Birton' verum esse possessorem et eam canonice esse adeptum, et ad presentationem prioris et conventus de Lewes per magistros L(aurentium) quondam archidiaconum Bedef'[b] et Ricardum Arundell', qui tunc officiales archiepiscopatus Ebor' curam gerebant spiritualium, institutum fuisse; et omnia episcopalia ad medietatem prefate ecclesie Birthon pertinentia archidiac(onis) et decanis capituli illius persolvisse eumque longo tempore possidisse;[c] ita quod I. frater predicti Ricardi nichil iuris habuit in prefata medietate ecclesie predicte nec eam nunquam possedit nisi tanquam procurator et custos ipsius Ricardi. Nec etiam vos lateat ut,[a] quando decimationes exigebantur ab ecclesiis totius Angl(ie) tempore Henrici regis qui tunc temporis crucis caractizare signitus erat, prefata medietas cum aliis suis redditibus ab tali exactione libera et soluta fuit, quia signum crucis gerebat; et hoc testimonio nostro et sigillorum nostrorum appositione[d] vobis significamus. Valeat sanctitas vestra in domino.

a Ms et   *b* Ms Bedelf'   *c* Sic   *d* Ms apposiscione

After Laurence's successor as archdn of Bedford was in office (*Fasti* iii, p. 42) and before the vacancy in Richard of Birstal's moiety of Kirkburton church (*EYC* viii, no. 157 n.); however, since the institution took place in 1181 x 87 (while the officials of York were active and before the grant of exemption from the Saladin tithe for those who took the cross: ibid.), the later terminus was probably in reality much earlier than 1229.

13. *Notification by Calixtus, dean of Kidderminster, that, at the mandate of Mauger, bishop of Worcester, he has put the leper sisters of [Maiden] Bradley into corporal possession of the* personatus *of Kidderminster church (Worcs.) by Andrew, their proctor.* [4 June 1200 x 1 July 1212]

A = TNA, E210/2246. 143 x 114 + 27 mm (turn-up folded out; endorsed: Kalixtus (s. xiii); seal and tag missing (method 1).
B = TNA, E326/10051 (copy of 6 deeds concerning Maiden Bradley's possession of Kidderminster church). s. xiii in.; C = BL, Add. ms 37503 (Maiden Bradley register), fols 30v–31r (21v–22r). s. xiv med.
Pd from C collated with B, B.R. Kemp, 'Maiden Bradley Priory, Wiltshire, and Kidderminster Church, Worcestershire', in *Reading Medieval Studies* 11 (1985), p. 109, no. 4.

Universis sancte matris ecclesie filiis ad quos presens scriptum pervenerit Calixtus decanus de Kiderminist'[a] salutem in domino. Universitati vestre innotescat me ad mandatum domini Maugeri Wigornensis episcopi in corporalem possessionem personatus ecclesie de Kideminist'[a] soro[res lepro]sas[b] de Brad'[c] per Andream procuratorem suum misisse. Et ut hoc omnibus in[d] presenti et futuris temporibus notum fiat, scripto presenti sigillum meum apposui. His[e] testibus:[f] Ricardo capellano de Kideminist', Roberto capellano de Wlferdesl', Laurencio capellano de Chedesl',[g] Waltero capellano de Stanes, Philippo capellano de Mutton', Roberto diacono de Chedesl', Roberto de Dunchelt,^h Rogero diacono de Kiderminist', Thoma sacrista de Kidemin', Hamone clerico, Hugone Spiring, et multis aliis.

<small>*a* Kedeministr' B   *b* Passage in square brackets destroyed by a hole in A   *c* Bradel' C
d Om. in C   *e* Hiis B, C   *f* B ends   *g* Chedest' C   *h* Chedeston' C</small>

While Mauger was bp of Worcester (*Fasti* ii, p. 100).

14. *Record of the inquest held at Warden by R., dean of Langford [= Shefford], and the chapter, concerning the income and obligations of successive vicars of Henlow (Beds.), Haco and Hugh, the latter according to the terms of a charter of the canons [of Lanthony], which charter the dean said he had found among Hugh's records after his death; the chapter decided that the dean should affix his seal to the present writing.*   25 Oct. 1200

    B = TNA, C115/74 (Llanthony cartulary), fol. 160r–v. s. xiii med.; C = TNA, C115/77 (Llanthony cartulary), fols 227v–228r. s. xiv med.; apparently copied from B, with reduced witness-list.
    Pd from C, C.R. Cheney, *From Becket to Langton* (Manchester, 1956), pp. 192–3, App. III, no. x.

[H]ec est inquisitio facta per R. decanum de Langeford et totum capitulum sui decanatus super vicaria de Henlowe apud [fol. 160v] Wardon' in festo sanctorum Crispini et Crispiniani proximo post consecrationem Egidii Hereford' episcopi. Scilicet quod quidam capellanus Haco tenuit et habuit quoad vixit nomine vicarie tertiam partem oventionum^a totius ville de Henl', excepto de dominio canonicorum unde habuit tertiam partem tertie partis decimationum et unam acram et dimidiam ad mesuagium. Diaconus vero qui ecclesie deserviebat procurabatur duabus septimanis in mensa canonicorum et tertia septimana in mensa ipsius Haconis. Ipse vero Haco de senodalibus^b et auxiliis archidiaconi et de omnibus aliis consuetudinibus que ad ecclesiam pertinent [respondebat],^c excepto quod si episcopus posuisset auxilia per episcopatum suum canonici responderent pro duabus partibus, Haco vero pro tertia parte. Cui de medio sublato Hugo capellanus successit presentatus in sinodo^d apud Bedeford per magistrum^e Moysen tunc procuratorem canonicorum in partibus illis et per cartam illorum eandem vicariam continentem quam Haco habuit, preter quod ipse Hugo habuit totum panem altaris et totum caseum, et ipse debebat diaconum suis sumptibus totaliter exhibere, quam etiam cartam in morte ipsius Hugonis predictus R. decanus in scriniis eius presentibus multis clericis et laicis dixit se invenisse. Quod ne cuiquam longevitate veniret in dubium, voluit capitulum hoc scriptum ad petitionem canonicorum conficere et ei sigillum R. decani apponere. Huic inquisitioni faciende interfuerunt Robertus de Potton', Fulco de Tamifeford,^f Hugo de Kerdinton',^g ^hIohannes de Camelton', Henricus de Clifton', Rad(ulfus) de Hatteleie, Hugo de Sandeie, Helias de Wrastlingword', Regin(aldus) de Dunton', Nicholaus de Wardon', Silvester de Stand',^h et plures alii.

a oventium B, C (probably in error)   b Sic B, C   c Om. in B, C; supplied to complete the sense   d Altered from senodo B   e Preceded by mr marked for deletion B   f Sic B, C; ? for Tamiseford   g Herdinton' C   h–h Om. in C

15. *Notification by R. of Kirkby [?Malzeard], dean of 'Boroughshire' [= Boroughbridge] (Yorks.), that, on a mandate from R(oger), dean, Mr W(illiam), chancellor, and W(illiam), subdean of Lincoln, judges-delegate of Pope Innocent III, he has inducted the prior and canons of Malton as parsons of the church of Marton in 'Boroughshire'.* [? c.Aug. x Sept. 1201]

B = BL, Cotton ms Claudius D xi (Malton cartulary), fol. 60v (58v). s. xiii med.

Omnibus ad quos presens scriptum pervenerit R. de Kyrcheb' decanus de Burgesire salutem. Noverit universitas vestra me ad mandatum domini R. decani, magistri W. cancellarii et W. subdecani Linc', iudicum a domino papa Inocentio iii° delegatorum, induxisse priorem et canonicos de Malt' personas in corporalem possessionem ecclesie de Marton' in Burgesire, et illis liberam ipsius ecclesie quam canonice adepti sunt dispositionem tradidisse perpetuo possidendam. Test'.

For the date, see C.R. and M.G. Cheney, 'Letters of Innocent III: Additions and Corrections', *Bulletin of the Institute of Historical Research* 44 (1971), p. 102, no. 1208 n.

16. *Notification by Henry of Staveley, dean of 'Boroughshire' [= Boroughbridge], that by order of Honorius, archdeacon of Richmond, he has inducted and instituted the prior and canons of Malton as parsons of the church of Marton.* 20 July 1203

B = BL, Cotton ms Claudius D xi (Malton cartulary), fol. 61r (59r). s. xiii med.

Universis sancte matris ecclesie filiis presentibus et futuris Henricus de Stavele decanus de Burg'sire salutem. Noverit universitas vestra me, auctoritate et precepto Honorii archidiaconi Richemund', induxisse priorem et canonicos de Malton' et personas instituisse ecclesie de Mart(ona) et in corporalem possessionem posuisse, et illis liberam ipsius ecclesie in proprios usus dispositionem tradidisse, die sancte Marie Magdalene anno incarnationis domini M°. CC°. iii°. Teste capitulo Burg'sire.

17. *Notification by John of Sutton, dean of Holland, that at the mandate of H(ubert), archbishop of Canterbury, and R(oger), dean of Lincoln and official sede vacante, he has put abbot R(ichard), as parson, and the canons of Waltham into corporal possession of the church of Wrangle (Lincs.).*

[May 1201 x 6 July 1203]

B = BL, Harley ms 391 (Waltham cartulary), fol. 105v. s. xiii in.; C = BL, Cotton ms Tiberius C ix (Waltham cartulary), fols 143r–v. s. xiii med.

Pd, *The Early Charters of . . . Waltham Abbey*, ed. R. Ransford (Woodbridge 1989), pp. 299–300, no. 436.

Universis*a* sancte matris ecclesie filiis ad quos presens scriptum pervenerit Iohannes de Sutton' decanus Hoilaund'*b* salutem. Noverit universitas vestra me, ad mandatum domini H. Cant(uariensis) archiepiscopi et magistri R. decani ecclesie Linc(olniensis) officialis eiusdem ecclesie *c*sede vacante,*c* misisse dominum R. abbatem de Waltham tanquam*d* personam et canonicos eiusdem loci in corporalem possessionem ecclesie de Wrengle vacantis. Et ut maior fides omnibus adhibeatur, presentem paginam sigilli mei appositione communivi. Hiis testibus:*e* Luca persona de Lech, magistro Gerardo persona de Benigthon', Giliberto capellano de Buteswich, Roberto capellano de Levertona, Waltero capellano de Lech, Simone le Bret advocato eiusdem ecclesie, et multis aliis.

a Omnibus C   *b* Hoyland' C   *c–c* sedis vacantis B; sede vacantis C   *d* tamquam C
e C ends with et c'

During the vacancy at Lincoln between bps Hugh of Avalon and William of Blois (*Fasti* iii, p. 3) and after Richard became abbot of Waltham: his predecessor died 2 May 1201 and he himself was blessed 29 Dec. 1201 x 10 June 1202 (*Heads* i, pp. 188, 287).

18. *Gift in perpetual and pure alms by John, dean of [Droit]wich (Worcs.), to the nuns of Westwood of the land formerly held by Hathulf in [Droit]wich next the land which William, the donor's father, held of Deerhurst priory, for an annual render to Deerhurst of three halfpence and two cakes of salt.*   [?early 13th cent.]

    B = BL, Cotton ms Vespasian E ix (Westwood cartulary), fol. 6v. s. xiii.
    Pd, *Mon. Ang.* vi (2), pp. 1007–8, no. 26.

Sciant presentes et futuri quod ego Iohannes decanus de Wich' dedi et concessi et hac presenti carta mea confirmavi et quietam clamavi deo et ecclesie beate Marie de West(wode) et sanctimonialibus ibidem deo servientibus, pro anima mea et animabus Hathulf' et Cristiane uxoris sue et pro animabus aliorum antecessorum meorum, totam terram illam quam predictus H. tenere consuevit in Wich', que scilicet terra est iuxta terram illam quam Willelmus pater meus tenuit de ecclesia de Derhurst'; habendam et tenendam*a* in perpetuam et puram elemosinam libere et quiete, honorifice, in bono et in pace in perpetuum, reddendo inde annuatim ecclesie de Derhurst' tres obolos et duos panenios*b* salis, videlicet ad Nativitatem sancti Iohannis iii. quadrantes, et ad festum sancti Michaelis ii. pan(enios) salis, et ad festum sancti Andree iii. quadrantes, pro omni servitio et exactione. Et ut hec mea donatio et concessio perpetuam optineat firmitatem, presentem cartam sigilli mei appositione duxi roborandam. His testibus.

    a Followed in ms by et marked for deletion   *b* Sic

Dating very uncertain, but a charter in *The Cartulary of Haughmond Abbey*, ed. U. Rees, Shropshire Archaeological Society (Cardiff, 1985), p. 235, no. 1295, which the editor tentatively dates to the early thirteenth century, is witnessed by John, dean of

'Wiche', and Richard the chaplain 'de Monte', the latter of whom occurs as the recipient of a gift of rent in 'Gosford' (a lost name) in Droitwich (BL, Cott. Vesp. E ix, fol. 7r) and seems likely to have become the Richard, chaplain of Dodderhill, who made a final concord in 1226 (ibid., fol. 7v) and who later, as Richard, 'sacerdos' of St Augustine's, Dodderhill, made a gift to Westwood (*Mon. Ang.* vi (2), p. 1008, no. 30).

19. *Notification by Henry, dean of Elford [= Tamworth], to G(eoffrey), bishop of Coventry, that in execution of a mandate of the bishop, who has granted the church of Shenstone (Staffs.) to the abbot and convent of Osney in proprios usus on the resignation of Roger of Bray and has instituted the canons as parsons, he has inducted Mr W. de Meisam, canon of Osney, into corporal possession of the church in the name of the whole community.* [1205 x 7 Oct. 1208]

    B = BL, Cotton ms Vitellius E xv (Osney cartulary), fol. 38r. s. xiii in.; damaged by fire; C = BL, Add. Ch. 20472(2) (copy of three charters concerning this institution). s. xiii.
    Pd from B and C, *Cartulary of Oseney Abbey*, ed. H.E. Salter, 6 vols (Oxford Historical Society 89–91, 97–8, 101, 1929–36), v, p. 64, no. 573A; (bp's mandate only) from B and C, *EEA* 17, pp. 106–7, no. 123.

Venerabili patri et semper reverendo G. dei gratia Coventr(ensi) episcopo Henricus decanus de Elleford[a] salutem et debitam reverentiam. Mandatum vestrum ea qua decuit devotione in hec verba suscepi. [G.][b] dei gratia Coventr(ensis) ecclesie humilis minister dilecto filio [decano de] Elleford[c] salutem et benedictionem. Dedimus et concessimus [dilectis filiis] et amicis nostris abbati et conventui de Osen', ad resig[nationem] Rogeri de Brai, in proprios usus suos ecclesiam de Sen[estan cum] omnibus pertinentiis suis habendam, et eos in eandem ecclesiam [canonice] instituimus personas. Quocirca tibi mandamus et precipimus quatinus [canonicum] suum quem ad te destinaverint in corporalem possessionem eiusdem [ecclesie nomin]e universitatis inducas. Hoc mandatum vestrum [obedientia et re]verentia debita exsecutus sum, [et magistrum W. de Meisam, Osen' canonicum,] in corporalem [possessionem prefate ecclesie nomine uni]versitatis in[duxi. Valeatis.[d]]

    a Oxeneford' C   b *Words in square brackets lost in B through fire; supplied from* C
    c Oxen'ford' C   d C *reads* Valeat' *followed by a few unintelligible characters*

After the election of abbot Clement of Osney (1205), who was present at Roger of Bray's resignation, after which the bp immediately instituted the abbot in the church, and before the bp's death (*Heads* i, 180; *Cartulary of Oseney* v, no. 573B; *EEA* 16, p. 110).

20. *Notification by I., dean of Tendring, to R(oger), archdeacon of Colchester, that from an inquest carried out by clergy and laity he has learnt that the church of Wrabness (Essex) is vacant and the abbot of Bury St Edmunds is its true patron.*
[c.1218 x 1228]

B = London, Guildhall Library, ms 25501 (St Paul's Liber A), fol. 43v (21a), no. 200. s. xiii med.
Pd, *Early Charters of . . . St Paul's*, ed. M. Gibbs (Camden 3rd series 58, 1939), pp. 160–1, no. 204.

Venerabili domino suo in Cristo^a R. archidiacono Colec' suus I. decanus de Tedring' salutem et tam debitum quam devotum famulatum. Noverit discretio vestra sicut ex diligenti inquisitione facta tam a clericis quam a laicis audivi quod ecclesia de Wrabenes' vacans est et sine litigio et dominus abbas Sancti Eadmundi verus est patronus. In cuius rei testimonium presentes litteras meas patentes vobis transmitto. Valete.

a Followed in ms by karissimo *marked for deletion*

While Roger Niger was archdn of Colchester (*Fasti* i, p. 19). The inquest evidently followed the presentation to the church by Hugh, abbot of Bury (*Early Charters*, no. 203).

21. *Notification by H., dean of Middlesex, and W., chaplain of Harmondsworth, to W(illiam), bishop of London, of the results of an inquest held in the chapter of Hounslow on the bishop's mandate concerning the church of Hillingdon (Middx), to which the abbot and convent of Evesham have presented Mr Walter of Longdon.*
[prob. shortly before 9 Dec. 1220]

B = BL. Cotton ms Vespasian B xxiv (Evesham cartulary), fol. 35v. s. xiii.
Pd (bp's mandate only), *EEA* 26, pp. 107–8, no. 114.

Reverendo patri et domino in Cristo karissimo W. dei gratia London' episcopo H. fidelis suus decanus Midilsex et W. capellanus de Hermodeswith' tam debitam quam devotam obedientiam et reverentiam. Literas sanctitatis vestre in hec verba suscepimus. W. dei gratia Lond' episcopus dilectis in Cristo filiis . .^{a} decano Middelsex' et capellano de Hermodesworh' salutem et benedictionem. Presentarunt nobis dilecti filii abbas et conventus Evesham latorem presentium magistrum Walterum de Longedon' ad ecclesiam de Hillendon' vacantem sicut dicitur. Ideoque vobis mandamus quatinus an ipsa ecclesia vacans sit et sine lite, quante etiam estimationis et ad quam eiusdem pertineat patronatus, diligentius et evidentius inquiratis, quam^b etiam pensionem dicti monachi perceperint de eadem si quam perceperunt, et quo iure, et quid super hiis inquisieritis^c nobis significetis per literas vestras festinanter. Huius igitur auctoritate mandati facta diligenti^d inquisitione in pleno capitulo de Hondeslae super premissis, invenimus ecclesiam de Hillend'n vacantem esse et sine lite, eiusdem etiam patronatum ad^e abbatem et conventum Evesham pertinere. Estimatio etiam eiusdem ecclesie xx. marc(arum) est, et est antiqua et debita pensio unius marce. Valeat sancta paternitas^f vestra in domino.

a Sic in ms; ? for insertion of initial   *b Sic in ms; ? for* quantam   *c Followed in ms by* super h *deleted*   *d Ms* diligendi   *e Repeated in ms*   *f Ms* fraternitas *(in error)*

The bp's letter of institution, following receipt of this return, is dated London, 9 Dec. 1220 (EEA 26, no. 115).

22. *Notification by H., dean of Middlesex, that in response to a mandate of W(illiam), bishop of London, who has admitted and instituted Mr Walter of Longdon as parson of Hillingdon church, he has inducted him into corporal possession of the same.* [prob. not long after 9 Dec. 1220]

B = BL, Cotton ms Vespasian B xxiv (Evesham cartulary) fol. 35v. s. xiii
Pd (bp's mandate only), *EEA* 26, p. 109, no. 116.

Omnibus sancte matris ecclesie filiis ad quos presens scriptum pervenerit H. ^{a}dei gratia^a decanus Middelsex' salutem in auctore salutis. Mandatum domini Lond' in hec verba suscepi. W. dei gratia Lond' episcopus dilecto in Christo filio . .^{b} decano Middelsex' salutem et benedictionem. Noveris nos ad presentationem dilectorum in Christo filiorum abbatis et conventus Evesham dilectum filium magistrum Walterum de Longad'n ad ecclesiam de Hildend'n cum omnibus ad eam pertinentibus admisisse, ipsumque in eadem personam instituisse. Quo circa tibi mandamus quatinus ipsum sine dilatione inducas in possessionem eiusdem ecclesie corporalem. Valete. Ne igitur istud inposterum devocari possit in dubium, universitati vestre significo me^c predictum magistrum Walterum induxisse in corporalem possessionem ecclesie de Hildendun' cum omnibus ad eam pertinentibus. Valeat universitas vestra semper in domino.

a–a *Sic in ms, but it is unlikely that the dean was so-called in the original letter*   b *Sic in ms; ? for insertion of initial*   c *Interlined*

After the bp's mandate to induct, which was probably issued at the time of the institution (see no. 21 n.), but exactly how long would have elapsed before the induction is unknown.

The Court of Arches and the Bishop of Salisbury

F. DONALD LOGAN

Roger Martival was consecrated bishop of Salisbury on 28 September 1315 and served as bishop until his death on 14 March 1330. Entries were made in his episcopal register as early as 18 July 1315 (as bishop elect and confirmed) and continued to be made for the rest of his pontificate. Martival's is among the fullest and best kept of medieval English bishops' registers.[1] Although we speak of the register of Bishop Martival, there were, in fact, four registers, which are now bound in two volumes. The present volume 1 contains the register of presentations and institutions to benefices and the register of royal writs received by the bishop, and the present volume 2 contains the register of diverse letters and the register of inhibitions of the Court of Canterbury (i.e., the Court of Arches) and the acts of the bishop's consistory court. It is this last of the four registers which provides the historian of the Court of Arches with an exceptionally rich source, an unrivalled cache of records concerning the most important ecclesiastical court in medieval England.[2]

The Court of Arches was the provincial court of appeal, the archbishop's court as metropolitan of the province of Canterbury, not to be confused with other courts of the archbishop: his two other metropolitan courts (the Court of Audience and the Court of Prerogative) and his Consistory Court for the diocese of Canterbury. His provincial court of appeal sat from at least the mid-thirteenth century at the church of St Mary le Bow, Cheapside, in the city of London, in the deanery of the Arches, an extra-territorial part of the diocese of Canterbury. *Ecclesia beate Marie de arcubus* – so named because of the remarkable arches in the church's structure – was known familiarly as

---

[1] The register has been published in four volumes under the general editorship of Kathleen Edwards for the Canterbury and York Society: *The Register of Roger Martival, Bishop of Salisbury, 1315–1330*, vols. 1 (1959), 2 (1963–72), 3 (1965), 4 (1975); hereafter cited as *Reg. Martival*. Volume 4 was edited by Dorothy M. Owen, and all references hereafter having only item numbers are to items in Volume 4. The manuscript of Martival's register in two volumes is Wiltshire County Record Office, Register of Roger Martival; hereafter all references here simply to folios are to vol. 2 of the manuscript register. For Martival see *BRUO* ii, 1232–33.
[2] For the court generally see F. Donald Logan, *The Medieval Court of Arches* (CYS vol. 95, 2005); hereafter, Logan, *Arches*.

ecclesia de arcubus, and the *curia Cantuariensis* that sat there became known familiarly as *curia de arcubus* (Court of Arches).

The Great Fire of London of 1666 destroyed the records then kept in the church of St Mary le Bow, although about a dozen post-Reformation volumes, apparently kept elsewhere, have survived.[3] The central archive for the medieval period does not survive, and what is known about the court has to be pieced together from external sources such as statutes, customs, treatises, formulary books kept by notaries and others, writs of prohibition and signification in the public records and out-letters from the Arches, which were kept in bishops' archives. Among the records occasionally found in episcopal registers are inhibitions sent by the court to the local bishops. Although inhibitions were inserted in many registers, only Bishop Martival undertook to keep a separate register of inhibitions.[4] The earliest inhibition which it records is dated 2 January 1316 and the latest 1 January 1330.[5]

Nature of an Inhibition

A word must be said about the inhibition. Direct appeals could be made to the Arches only from the jurisdiction of a local bishop. These could be judicial (i.e., from his court) or extra-judicial (i.e., from an administrative decision). In addition, appeals (called 'provocations') could be made in anticipation of a prejudicial action, judicial or extra-judicial. Besides direct appeals, judicial or extra-judicial, there were tuitorial appeals, which, in fact, were two appeals: an appeal of the principal matter to the pope, which could be made by anyone at any time from any jurisdiction, and an appeal to the provincial court for protection (*pro tuicione*) for a year while prosecuting the principal appeal. Also, we shall encounter *querele* (i.e., complaints) issued by subjects of the bishop of Salisbury against alleged injustices done in the bishop's name; these were appeals only in a broad sense of that word. Whatever the type of appeal – direct or tuitorial or as a *querela* – it was initiated by the appellant sending a written instrument to the Court of Arches. If the Court of Arches accepted to hear the appeal (i.e., to 'rescribe' to it), the

---

[3] See generally M. Doreen Slatter, 'The Records of the Court of Arches', *JEH* 4 (1953), pp. 139–53, and 'The Study of the Records of the Court of Arches', *JSA* 1 (1955), pp. 29–31; Melanie Barber, 'Records of the Court of Arches in Lambeth Palace Library', *Ecclesiastical Law Journal* 3 (1993–95), pp. 10–19. For the post-Restoration period see Jane Houston, ed., *Index of Cases in the Records of the Court of Arches at Lambeth Palace Library* (Index Library, 85; British Record Society, 1972).

[4] For descriptions of the contents of episcopal registers see David M. Smith, *Guide to Bishops' Registers of England and Wales: A Survey from the Middle Ages to the Abolition of the Episcopacy in 1642* (London, 1981) and *Supplement to Guide to Bishops' Registers of England and Wales* (CYS Centenary Supplement, 2004).

[5] Nos 5, 181.

court issued an inhibition to the relevant bishop.[6] It is these inhibitions that Roger Martival systematically enregistered.

The inhibition – apart from its salutation and dating clause – fell into four parts.

> *Narration.* The Official of the Court of Arches related the cause of appeal. This narration was taken directly from the *appellacio* submitted by the appellant. It began, 'ex parte . . . nobis extitit intimatum quod' and normally concluded, 'unde ex parte eiusdem sencientis se ex hoc [or ex hiis et eorum quolibet] per uos indebite pregrauari ad [in *tuitorial appeals* sedem apostolicam et pro tuicione ad] curiam Cantuariensem extitit ut asseritur appellatum'.
>
> *Inhibition.* The actual inhibition required the bishop (if he were the appealed party) or through him the appealed party to refrain from attempting or causing to be attempted anything prejudicial to the appellant while his appeal was pending in the Court of Arches so that he could freely prosecute his appeal.
>
> *Citation.* The Official peremptorily cited the appealed party to appear before him or his commissary on a specific day and place to proceed and act in the appeal and to receive what justice will demand.
>
> *Certification.* The Official required the bishop to certify in letters patent to him that he had received the inhibition and to indicate what action he had taken on it; the certificatory should contain a copy of the inhibition ('harum seriem continentes'). The response of the bishop to the inhibition took the form of a certificatory which, addressed to the Official of the Arches, reported what action had been taken.

Subject matter of appeals

Martival's register of inhibitions indicates 60 cases which were appealed to the Arches from the jurisdiction of the bishop of Salisbury during his almost fifteen-year pontificate:

Year	Appeals
1316	9
1317	4
1318	6
1319	1
1320	2
1321	8
1322	4
1323	1
1324	4
1325	5
1326	4
1327	8
1328	1
1329	3

---

6   For procedure in the Court of Arches, see Logan, *Arches*, pp. xxxviii–xlviii.

What were the basic matters with which these 60 appeals were concerned? The vast majority (47) had to do with benefices, and of these 42 were the appeals of unsuccessful presentees, who appealed 'a non amissione'; the 5 others were made by incumbents who claimed to have been molested in possession of their benefices or actually deprived.[7] The 13 non-benefice appeals ranged over a variety of matters. There were two each concerning marriage and defamation. One dealt with a disputed monastic election, another with tithes and one with an allegedly adulterous cleric. Also one – and probably two – concerned testaments. In the remaining four cases the subject-matter of the case under appeal is unclear. To these 60 should be added five *querele*, which were appeals in a broad sense of the word.

Manner of Appeal

How did these 60 appeals come to the Court of Arches? In other words, which sorts of appeals were used? Of the 60 appeals, 47 came to the Arches by direct appeal, whereas only 12 came by way of tuitorial appeal, and one is uncertain. Let us look, in the first place, at the direct appeals.

Direct appeals

Of the 47 direct appeals, 42 were extra-judicial appeals and 5 were judicial appeals. All of the extra-judicial appeals were from disappointed presentees to benefices, whereas the 5 judicial appeals concerned various matters.

First, with respect to the 42 cases of direct extra-judicial appeals, a pattern is quite clear: they appealed the administrative decision of the bishop not to admit them to a benefice to which they believed themselves entitled. For example, in April 1317 Master Richard Trenchard appealed, claiming that he was presented to the church of Corton by the true patron but the bishop, at the instance of the de facto incumbent, refused to admit him.[8] Or, again, William, son of Lapyn Roger, in a dispute over the parish church of Brightwell, appealed to the Arches and succeeded in having his rival, William Inge, cited to appear before the court.[9] And in yet another case, John Fylongele was presented by the prior of the Hospital of St John of Jerusalem in England to the church of Speen, but Martival refused to admit him, citing his insufficient knowledge; on 1 March 1324 the presentee appealed

---

[7] Reference here is to the matter which first came to the attention of the Court of Arches; in some cases there were repeated appeals and counter appeals.
[8] No 21. The certificatory (dated 26 May 1317) stated that because of the shortness of time it was not possible to cite the incumbent.
[9] No. 51; inhibition dated 15 December 1319.

the bishop's decision to the Arches.[10] These are typical of the direct appeals made extra-judicially.

The 5 direct appeals which were made judicially have no single pattern and will be described individually.

> There was the marriage case between Lord Alan Plokenet, knight, and his wife, Lady Sybil, which at her instance in 1321 was heard by the court of Bishop Martival. Since her husband said that he was unable to be represented by an advocate, he petitioned for a delay. When this was denied him, he appealed to the Arches. Notwithstanding the appeal, according to Alan Plokenet, the bishop imposed a sentence of alimony on him. Plokenet appealed again. Four years later Plokenet's matter was still being treated in the Arches.[11]
>
> Sir Walter de Momesey, knight, appealed directly to the Arches, claiming that he had been cited by Bishop Martival at the instance of Robert, vicar of Chapelayston (Chapel Easton?) to an unsafe place at a term too short and peremptory to respond to unknown articles – reasons frequently asserted in appeals. The principal matter at issue was not mentioned. The parties came to a peaceful settlement, and the appeal was not prosecuted.[12]
>
> Master John Borkgrave appealed from the bishop's audience, alleging that he had been presented to the prebendal church of Wantage and, the vicar general of the dean of Salisbury cathedral refusing to admit him, he had appealed to the bishop's audience and that court refused to hear his appeal.[13]
>
> In a defamation case John Lotewyk, clerk of Lambourne, appealed directly to the Arches, claiming that, although he had been cited by the bishop's commissary at the instance of Richard de Cleet, also of Lambourne, to an unsafe place and to a time too brief and peremptory, he appeared with great difficulty but was refused copies of documents; he appealed to the bishop's audience, yet, despite his appeal, the bishop's commissary gave a definitive sentence against him. He appealed again, this time to the bishop's audience, but the bishop refused to hear his appeal. Whence to the Arches.[14]
>
> Sir John Latymer, knight, using usual language, appealed from a citation to

---

[10] No. 109. Fylongele later withdrew his appeal and later still entered another appeal (no. 127). For the early stages of this case see *Reg. Martival* i, p. 298.

[11] See nos 101 (i and ii), 105, 111, 115 and 130–1.

[12] No. 96; inhibition dated 13 November 1322.

[13] No. 133; inhibition dated 2 May 1325: 'Et licet idem magister Iohannes, ad uos congruis loco et tempore competentibus accedens et premissa uobis exponens, ad huiusmodi suam appellacionem per uos instanter rescribi in forma iuris petiuisset, uos tamen ipsam partem sic petentem exaudire et iusticiam sibi in hac parte debitam facere non curastis set express denegastis minus iuste' (fol. 339v).

[14] No. 141; inhibition dated 27 February 1326. The Court of Arches on 25 February 1328 remitted the case to Salisbury because the appeal had not been prosecuted (no. 166).

a time too soon and peremptory to answer to unknown articles; the matter radically at issue is not mentioned in the inhibition.[15]

These, then, are the 5 direct judicial appeals appearing in Martival's register of inhibitions.

Tuitorial appeals

There were 12 tuitorial appeals, 9 of which had been preceded by tuitorial provocations. Typically in these 9 cases party X, fearing prejudice will be done to him, tuitorially provoked (i.e., appealed in anticipation of a prejudicial act to the apostolic see and for protection to pursue that appeal to the Court of Arches). Despite this provocation, he claimed that something prejudicial to him was done, and from this prejudicial act he tuitorially appealed. Of these 9, 4 concerned incumbents threatened and then disturbed in the holding of their benefice; one each concerned tithes, testaments, adultery, defamation and spoliation. For example in 1320, Master Roger de Kington, rector of Bridport, claiming that the chapel of Little Bredy was a dependent chapel of his parish and fearing prejudicial action to his possession of it, tuitorially provoked. Despite this provocation, he said, the bishop gave the chapel to William Ayston.[16] A similar case in 1324 concerned the church of Corfe Castle. The rector, Master Peter de Compton, fearing prejudice to his rights, provoked tuitorially. Nonetheless, Bishop Martival at the instance of William Bradenstock instituted Bradenstock to the portion of Alfrington in his parish. Compton, claiming that Alfrington pertained to his parish since time immemorial and that his provocation had been violated, appealed tuitorially.[17] In yet another case, in 1326, the priest John de Dagenhale, fearful of action being taken against him for alleged adultery with Isabella Fynk, wife of John de Hartham, provoked tuitorially. Despite this provocation he was convicted and assigned a public penance for his crime. This conviction and penance Dagenhale tuitorially appealed as violations of his provocation.[18] In the event, Dagenhale failed to pursue his appeal and it was dismissed by the Arches on 11 October 1326.[19] What was being appealed in all such cases was the violation of the provocation by the bishop.

The three tuitorial appeals which were not preceded by tuitorial provocations were all judicial appeals. Hugh de Sapy was cited to appear in the bishop's court related to his possession of the parish church of Langworth, but, claiming the citation required him to appear at an unsafe place, he

---

[15] No. 142; inhibition dated 10 March 1326, which may be in error since it was received at Salisbury on 9 March.
[16] No. 61.
[17] Nos 114, 116.
[18] No. 145; inhibition dated 12 July 1326.
[19] No. 148.

appealed tuitorially.[20] In another case, Alexander de la Hook was brought to trial *ex officio* at the promotion of his wife, Margery, and others at what he considered too short notice – hardly a day – for his alleged ill-treatment of her. The bishop's commissaries, he claimed, refused to accept certain documents, and he appealed tuitorially; he was then excommunicated by the bishop's court and appealed this excommunication.[21] In the third case, some parishioners of East Hendred had their rector, Thomas de Insula, cited to appear in the bishop's court; claiming that he had been given insufficient notice, he appealed tuitorially to the apostolic see and the court of Canterbury.[22]

Querele

Besides direct appeals and tuitorial appeals actions came to the Court of Arches from Salisbury *per modum querele*. A *querela* was a complaint brought to the Arches against the actions of a diocesan bishop.[23] Five *querele* appear in Martival's register, and they are instructive about this way of proceeding.

1. A mandate from the Arches of 9 May 1316 relates the *querela* of the Official of the prebendal jurisdiction of Bedwyn, who complained that the bishop had delayed executing his request for a writ of signification for the arrest of William Miller of East Bedwyn, whom he had excommunicated. The Court of Arches commanded the bishop, if the complaint was true, to show the petitioner justice within fifteen days. If for some reason the bishop was unwilling to do this, he should cite the excommunicate, William Miller, to appear in the Arches, which, in fact, the bishop did.[24]
2. According to a mandate of 23 March 1322, John le Devenysch, tailor, claimed to have been named executor of the testament of William de Taunton and that, although the testament was duly proved and approved by the Official of the archdeacon of Berkshire, the same Official refused to make him executor. Devenysch further claimed that he had petitioned Bishop Martival for justice and that the bishop refused to hear him.

---

[20] No. 3; inhibition dated 20 March 1316. At about the same time Sapy was cited to appear regarding his failure to be ordained priest (*Reg. Martival* ii, pp. 62–4). The two matters were undoubtedly related.

[21] No. 14; inhibition dated 24 January 1317. Hoo's appeal was remitted to Salisbury for his failure to prosecute it (no. 19). His proctor was excommunicated at the same time.

[22] No. 154; inhibition dated 2 April 1327. The appellant failed to prosecute his appeal at the Arches, and the case was remitted to Salisbury on 9 May 1327 (ibid.).

[23] *Querele* were among the issues raised by suffragan bishops against Archbishop Pecham in 1282. The bishops held that the archbishop should not rescribe to *querele* from their subjects. For this dispute see Decima L. Douie, *Archbishop Pecham* (Oxford, 1952), pp. 192–213; on the issue of *querele* see Logan, *Arches*, pp. xxii–xxiv.

[24] No. 2.

3 Hence, he issued a *querela* to the Court of Arches, requesting a suitable *remedium*. In response, the Arches required the bishop to give Devenysch justice within thirty days; failing that, the bishop and the archdeacon of Berkshire were to appear in the Arches on the eighth juridical day after the thirty-day period. The bishop replied that, since there was doubt about the legal status of the deceased at the time of his death, an executor was not appointed; he agreed to appear in the Arches and to cite the archdeacon to appear.[25]

4 In November 1325, Sybil, daughter of Roger le Palmere, citizen of London, and wife of Adam de Bydic of Bookham, complained that her husband deserted her and was guilty of adultery and that she had sued restitution of marital rights in the bishop's court but was denied a hearing. The Official of the Court of Arches ordered the bishop to give justice to Sybil and, failing that, to appear in the Arches at a given date. The bishop responded that Sybil had not sought justice in his court. He, however, had wished to obey the mandate to cite Adam to appear in the Arches, but the latter could not be found in his diocese and Sybil said that he was living in London.[26]

5 In 1325 the prior and convent of the Carmelite house in London and, in particular, Henry de Peccheford and Roger de Werketon, friars of that order, complained to the Court of Arches that, although they had been bequeathed certain goods by Master Richard de Abindon, none the less the sole executor, Master Robert de Glonteston, *locum tenens* of the absentee dean of Salisbury, refused to hand over those goods to them and the bishop of Salisbury failed to cite the executor to appear in his court. The Official of the Court of Arches instructed Bishop Martival to give justice within a fortnight or otherwise cite the executor to appear in the Arches.[27]

In 1326 John de Froyle, prebendary of the church of Urchfont, complained to the Arches that the executors of the estate of his predecessor had not taken responsibility for money due for repairs to the church and that the bishop's court refused to cite them. The Court of Arches gave the bishop one month to do justice or else to cite the executors to appear in the Arches. The response from Salisbury was that the plaintiff had not made such a request.[28]

In all of these *querele* the party querelant complained to the Arches that the bishop had failed to provide justice to that party. The Arches, in turn, wrote to the bishop, saying that the party had 'acceded to us' for an 'opportune remedy'. In every case the bishop was told to give the party justice

---

[25] No. 83. The bishop and archdeacon were not expected to be present personally and would have been represented by proctors.

[26] No. 140; mandate dated 29 November 1325 and the bishop's response 18 January 1326.

[27] No. 138; mandate dated 6 November 1325. For Abindon see *BRUO* I, 4–5; he died by March 1322, over three years before this *querela*.

[28] No. 147; mandate dated 7 July 1326. Froyle had been in previous litigation (in 1321–22) about his presentation to the church (nos 70, 79).

within a specified period or the matter would be withdrawn from his jurisdiction. A *querela*, then, was an appeal only in the broadest sense. It differed from appeals strictly so called in that it did not automatically withdraw the matter from the lower jurisdiction. The Arches responded to the *querela* not with an *inhibitio* but with a *mandatum*. It gave the bishop the option of doing what the complaining party wanted or explaining himself in the Arches. If we can judge from the Salisbury cases, a *querela* was used only in cases where it was alleged that the judge of the bishop's court had failed to provide justice. It was simply a complaint to a superior about an inferior, combined with a request for help.

Non-Prosecution and Failure to Cite

It would be wrong for us to conclude that the 60 cases of appeals found in Martival's register led to litigation in the Court of Arches. Two factors must be taken into account. In the first place, about one-third of the appeals were probably not prosecuted in the Arches by the appellants. In at least three of these cases the parties came to a mutual agreement not to proceed;[29] in one of these three the scribe noted 'non fuit certificatum, quia partes pacificati fuerunt et ulterius prosequi noluerunt'.[30] In the remainder of such cases the appellants simply did not pursue their appeals in the Court of Arches. One can only speculate about the reason for failure to pursue an appeal. The appellant might have reconsidered and concluded that his chances of being successful were not propitious or that the expenses involved were not worth the risk. Also, the appeal might have been frivolously conceived in the first place as a tactic to intimidate an adversary. The prospect in cases of tuitorial appeal of having a year's respite from whatever was being appealed might have led to appeals which the appellants had no intention of bringing to the apostolic see.[31] The time between notification of the appeal and the remission from the Court of Arches to Salisbury or the notice of the renouncing of the appeal varied considerably. On 4 March 1318 the two contending parties for possession of the parish church of Cricklade issued appeals to the Arches, and on the following 20 June the parties agreed to withdraw their appeals.[32] More commonly the appellant failed to appear and, as was its procedure, the court, after waiting three juridical days, cited the appellant under threat of remission and, when he still failed to appear, the case was remitted.[33] One

---

[29] Nos 24, 41, 98.
[30] Fol. 317v; no. 98.
[31] In two further cases the Arches remitted the cases to Salisbury because the appellants failed to prove their appeals for tuition (nos 60 (iii), 136). This could mean that the appellants actually brought the matters to the Arches and did not prove that their appeals were not frivolous.
[32] Nos 29, 31, 41.
[33] See Logan, *Arches*, p. xliv.

suspects that this happened in the case concerning possession of the church of Boyton. In this case notice of the appeal was sent to Salisbury on 6 August 1327 (during the court's vacation) and parties were to be cited to appear in the Arches on 7 October, the first day of the next session. On 9 October the court remitted the matter because the appellant had failed to appear to prosecute his appeal.[34] In several cases, however, a much longer period elapsed between an appeal and its remission. For example, in February 1326 John Lotewyk, clerk of Lambourne, appealed against conviction for defamation by the bishop's court, and only in the following February did the Court of Arches remit the matter to Salisbury because of Lotewyk's failure to prosecute.[35] It is clear, then, that a very large number of appeals to the Court of Arches did not proceed in that court.

In another way appeals might not go forward to full process in the Court of Arches: in cases where the bishop certified that he could not find the appealed party to cite him to appear in the Arches. This happened in 12 cases.[36] For example, in a testamentary case in 1329 the court sent a mandate to Martival to cite the four executors of the estate of John de Wodeford, prebendary of Broad Chalke. Martival or, more precisely, his Official referred the matter to the archdeacon of Salisbury, who reported that the executors could not be found.[37] The case left no further trace in the register. Or, again, it was probably late in 1326 or early in 1327 that an appeal concerning possession of the parish church of Bishopstrowe came to the Court of Arches at the instigation of David Wauter, calling himself rector, against John de Bradeford; on 2 February 1327, a certificate was sent to the Arches, reporting that Bradeford could not be cited because he could not be found in the diocese.[38] On one occasion the bishop said that there had not been enough time to cite the party: the inhibition was dated 29 April 1317 but was not received at Salisbury until 26 May, and the party was expected to appear in London on 29 May.[39] In two cases, both concerning possession of benefices, it was reported that the appealed party could not be found and the citation was made at Sunday mass at the party's parish church, and in one of these cases the apparitor affixed a copy of the citation to the rector's house.[40] Yet

---

[34] Nos 160, 162.

[35] Nos 141, 166. It is not known whether he did not appear at all, using delaying tactics to justify his absence, or simply dropped the matter after one or several appearances.

[36] Nos 5, 21, 30, 31, 78, 81, 85, 103, 140, 151, 171, 176.

[37] No. 171.

[38] No. 151.

[39] No. 21.

[40] Nos 65, 88. The latter case concerned the church of Trowbridge. The certificate, dated 1 July 1322, reported, 'dictum uero Henricum [de Morely], partem, ut premittitur, appellatam, personaliter non inuentum, coram clero et populo in ecclesia de Trowbrigg predicta intra missarium solempnia et postea in manso ipsius ecclesie rectorie huius citacionis edicto publice proposito citari fecimus peremptorie . . .' (fol. 314r).

even beyond these dozen cases there are others where a further step was taken: the bishop issued the citation to the party's proctor. In 1321, Roger de Parys, the appealed party in a dispute over a benefice, could not be found in the diocese and, in addition to the publication of the citation at mass in the parish church, it was issued to Parys's proctor.[41] Two other similar citations of parties appear in the register.[42] If the appealed party failed to appear in the Court of Arches on the assigned day, the court would usually wait three juridical days for his appearance, after which the appeal would go forward unopposed, probably in a fairly summary fashion.[43]

The conclusion must be that in the 21 cases which were remitted to the bishop's court at Salisbury and in a dozen or more cases in which the cited party was not found the appeal did not go forward to the Court of Arches for full procedure. Thus, more than half of the 60 appeals from Salisbury to the Arches probably did not lead to litigation in the appellate court.

Alia notabilia

There remain several other matters to be gleaned from this register of Arches inhibitions. In the first place, in the course of an appeal in the Arches the appellant frequently needed copies of documents in the bishop's archives. When this happened, the presiding judge in the appellate court, at the request of the appellant, sent to the bishop of Salisbury a mandate to search his register and perhaps the register of his predecessor for certain information and to send a copy to the Arches. In 15 of the 60 appeal cases found in Martival's register of inhibitions the Arches sent such mandates for information. In three of these cases an additional mandate was issued and in one case three mandates were sent.[44] And in another case that had come to the Court of Arches from another diocese (Lincoln) Bishop Martival was asked to search his archives for a needed document.[45]

Another point to be noted is that all of the inhibitions, save two, were

---

[41] No. 65.
[42] Nos 72, 169. In one case, where the party could not be found, it was reported that the proctors of the party were not known (no. 103).
[43] See Logan, *Arches*, p. 87.
[44] The 15 cases are nos 7, 15, 20 (and 23), 45 (and 46, 47), 48, 49, 67, 76, 71, 79, 97, 113, 117 (and 124), 153 (and 168) and 178.
[45] The case concerned possession of the church of Beaconsfield (Bucks.), Lincoln diocese. Edmund Hauberdyn claimed that on 21 May 1322 he had exchanged the church of White Waltham (Berks.), Salisbury diocese, for Beaconsfield. His possession of Beaconsfield was challenged by Thomas de Eltesdon, and the case came to the Arches, which requested Martival to certify Hauberdyn's admission to White Waltham (no. 125). The case turned on the question whether Hauberdyn had been validly admitted to White Waltham. Martival replied that Hauberdyn had been admitted on 24 March 1301 by his predecessor, Simon of Ghent (no. 128).

sent in the name of the Official of the Court of Arches. By way of exception, on 22 June 1329, under the seal of the Arches, Henry Idsworth, dean of the Arches, sent an inhibition to Bishop Martival.[46] Also, in an instrument dated 3 November 1329 at Dorchester the dean of Dorchester, claiming to be acting by authority of the court of Canterbury (i.e., the Arches), inhibited the bishop of Salisbury and his commissaries as well as the monks of Sherborne Abbey from acting prejudicially against Brother Thomas le Gildene, monk of Sherborne. The bearer of the inhibition, when asked for a document giving such authority to the dean of Dorchester, replied that he did not have such a document. With the authority of the dean of Dorchester under suspicion, the matter probably ended at that point.[47] It is quite possible that there was no Official of the court in the hiatus between the death of Dean Bloyhou (1328) and the appointment of Idsworth (possibly not till 1330 or later), and that Idsworth acted as the principal officer of the court during this period and the dean of Dorchester had a temporary commission.[48]

The inhibitions are mostly dated at London, although a significant number are from elsewhere. For example, between 10 May 1316 and 12 July 1326 fifteen inhibitions are dated at Yeoveney in Middlesex.[49] Other places outside of London are Leighton Buzzard (Beds.), Winchester, Sundridge (Kent), Barton, Stanton (Oxon.), Little Harwoods (Lancs.), Edington (Lincs.), Thame (Oxon.), Dallington (Northants), Bromley (Kent), Wimbledon (Surrey), Potterspurty (Northants), Canterbury, East Barnet (Herts.), Catherston Leweston (Dorset), Graston (Dorset) and Mears Ashby (Northants). They were clearly sent by the Official from wherever he happened to be, and not by a clerk of the court in London.

The amount of time allowed between the issuance of the inhibition and the expected appearance in London varied somewhat but was normally between three and four weeks, occasionally less, but in no instance under two weeks.[50] If the inhibition was issued within three weeks or so of the end of a session, the date for appearance was invariably early in the next session. Thus, John de Dagenhale, a priest accused of adultery, was ordered by an inhibition dated 12 July 1326 to be cited to appear on the following 9

---

[46] No. 172.
[47] No. 177.
[48] For the Officials of the court see Logan, *Arches*, pp. 197–200.
[49] Yeoveney was a manor of Westminster Abbey (*VCH Middlesex* iii, p. 1819). Barbara Harvey has kindly suggested that there might have been a friendship between the abbot, William de Curtlington, and the Official, Master Gilbert de Middleton, both of whom held their respective offices during these years.
[50] In only three cases were there less than three weeks: 16, 17 and 19 days (nos 172, 10, 22). In the case mentioned above (p. 168), when the inhibition arrived only three days before the date of appearance in the Arches, it had taken four weeks for the inhibition to arrive at Salisbury, a most unusual occurrence (no. 21).

October.⁵¹ When inhibitions were granted to *querele*, the bishop, if he failed to remedy the complaint within a certain stated period (usually either a fortnight or a month), was cited to appear, generally one week or a fortnight after the expiration of that period.

A related question in this matter is how long it took for the inhibition from the Court of Arches to reach the bishops of Salisbury. The answer is that it varied widely from same-day delivery – when Martival was in or near London – to as many as twenty-nine days, but three-quarters of the inhibitions were delivered within a week.⁵²

A final matter concerns the place where the Court of Arches actually sat during the period of Martival's pontificate (1315–30). We learn from the register of inhibitions that for much of this period the court sat not in the church of St Mary le Bow but nearby at the church of St Mary Aldermary, which was also in the peculiar jurisdiction of the deanery of the Arches. For the first five years of Martival's pontificate, citations were for appearance in St Mary le Bow. Inhibitions sent to Martival on 25 and 26 July 1320 ordered parties to appear in St Mary le Bow on the following 10 October.⁵³ These were the last such citations to Bow Church in Martival's register of inhibitions. Beginning with the inhibition dated 5 February 1321, which ordered the appealed party's appearance on 28 February, all citations were for appearance in St Mary Aldermary.⁵⁴ A notarial instrument dated 20 March 1321 refers to the reading of a letter from the archbishop by his Official 'in ecclesia beate Marie de Aldermariecherche Londonia in pleno consistorio'.⁵⁵ From February 1320 the inhibitions for the remainder of Martival's pontificate – thirty-eight in number – required appearance in the church of St Mary Aldermary. Not only were parties to appear there but documents were to be sent there too.⁵⁶ The annals of London note that in 1326 the dean of the Arches was sitting in the same church.⁵⁷ Absence from the church of St Mary le Bow continued until 1335, as we learn from other sources.⁵⁸ The court returned to St Mary le Bow by the Hilary session of 1337.⁵⁹ During this period of absence building works were almost certainly going on at the

---

51 No. 145. For the calendar of the Court of Arches, see Logan, *Arches*, pp. 225–9.
52 For the despatch of instruments from royal chanceries see James F. Willard, 'The Dating and Delivery of Letters Patent and Writs in the Fourteenth Century', *Bulletin of the Institute of Historical Research* 10 (1932–33), pp. 1–11.
53 Nos 61, 62.
54 No. 66.
55 *Reg. Martival* i, p. 199.
56 No. 78.
57 *Chronicles of the Reigns of Edward I and Edward II*, vol. 1, Annales Londonienses, ed. William Stubbs (RS 76, 1882), p. 310.
58 See T.S. Holmes, ed., *The Register of Ralph of Shrewsbury, Bishop of Bath and Wells, 1329–1363* (Somerset Record Society 9–10, 1896), no. 933, and *Calendar of the Register of Simon de Montacute, Bishop of Worcester, 1334–1337*, ed. Roy M. Haines (Worcestershire Historical Society n.s. 15, 1996), no. 105.
59 *Reg. Montacute*, no. 1052.

northern side of Bow Church, which would have required the transfer of the court to the nearby site.[60]

The diocese of Salisbury, extending over three counties – Wiltshire, Berkshire and Dorset – and having four archdeaconries and in excess of three hundred parishes can hardly be seen as an atypical English diocese. While one should be slow to extrapolate findings from a single diocese onto the larger English ecclesiastical scene, nonetheless from the Salisbury records we can learn much about the type of business that came to the Court of Arches and how that court proceeded. Moreover, we can, at the very least, suggest that what we learn here may be more widely representative and not peculiar to this diocese and that these records indicate how the larger picture would probably appear, should we be as fortunate elsewhere as we are in the records kept by Bishop Martival.

---

[60] From information kindly provided by Professor Derek Keene; for the history of the church building of St Mary le Bow see D. Keene and V. Harding, *Historical Gazetteer of London before the Great Fire*, I, *Cheapside* (Cambridge, 1987), no. 104/20.

Bishops' Registers and Political History: a Neglected Resource

A.K. McHARDY

It is a truth insufficiently acknowledged that the registers of medieval English bishops are a rich quarry for the political historian. Historians of secular events overlook this material because they do not imagine that church records will contain anything useful for their enquiries, and it is the purpose of this essay to urge them to look more carefully at bishops' registers, for in this class of record will be found rich and unexpected rewards, the 'Uncovenanted Blessings of Ecclesiastical Records', of which the late Professor Rosalind Hill (a warm admirer of David Smith) so eloquently spoke.[1] In this article I will not attempt to give a complete catalogue of such material, but rather, by drawing examples from a number of different dioceses, hope to encourage students of English political history in the later middle ages to investigate this class of record for themselves. It will be immediately obvious that any such collection of examples will owe much to the editors of bishops' registers, those unsung heroes and heroines whose work is published by such learned societies as the Canterbury and York Society and the Lincoln Record Society, to both of which David Smith has given, and continues to give, such distinguished service.

Medieval bishops were, in every sense, public figures and public servants, and many had previous or concurrent experience in secular administration. Helping to administer the realm and putting into execution crown policy was part of their job, and there is no evidence that they resented this or regarded their secular administrative duties as an imposition; nor is this surprising, for good order and respect for authority were the goals of both crown and church governments. The bulk of this secular work, as recorded in their registers, was of a local nature. Yet what would seem to be purely local matters could sometimes have wider implications. For example, John le

---

[1] This was the title of her presidential address to the Ecclesiastical History Society in 1973. *The Materials, Sources and Methods of Ecclesiastical History*, ed. Derek Baker (Studies in Church History 11, 1975), pp. 135–46. Generous tribute is paid to David Smith's *Guide to the Archive Collection in the Borthwick Institute of Historical Research* (York, 1973), on p. 140.

Breton, bishop of Hereford, was also sheriff of Hereford, and a servant of the Lord Edward; he was bailiff at Abergavenny and keeper of Montgomery castle in 1257, but by 1261 had become keeper of the prince's wardrobe. He died in 1275 and over the next two years his executors filed a series of accounts which were copied into the register of his successor.[2]

There were three main aspects of bishops' public work. One was the execution of writs. The recording of this material in registers began in the late thirteenth century and probably coincided with an increase in the amount of documentation generated and retained by royal government. The systematic recording of these local tasks reached its high point during the first quarter of the fourteenth century. After that, though the number of orders received probably did not decrease, copying them all became an overwhelming task so rigorous exclusion practices were employed.[3]

Collections of writs in registers are always worth investigating, for among the routine and repetitive material can be found valuable nuggets of political information, as well as occasional ecclesiastical gems.[4] For example, one of the tasks which bishops were sometimes called upon to undertake for the crown was the swearing-in of local officials; John Buckingham of Lincoln, for example, received the oath of a customs collector in the port of Boston in 1385, and later those of the sheriffs of Rutland (1388), and of Lincoln (1396). These were apparently routine occasions, and the interest for the historian lies in the fact that, in the first two cases, the form of the oath (both were in French) was entered into the writ register.[5] The situation was very different when Thomas Milling of Hereford was ordered to receive the oath of the new sheriff of Herefordshire early in 1491. The writ ordering the bishop to receive the oath was dated 6 January 1491 and received by the bishop on 22 January. Two forms of the oath were recorded, one in Latin, the other in English. Two letters patent were also included: the general

---

[2] *The Register of Thomas de Cantilupe Bishop of Hereford 1275–1282*, ed. W.W. Capes and R.G. Griffiths (Cantilupe Society, 1, 1906), pp. 35, 172–5. All the Hereford registers were published jointly with the Canterbury and York Society. For [le] Breton's administrative career see T.F. Tout, *Chapters in the Administrative History of Medieval England*, 6 vols (Manchester, 1920–33), vi, p. 115, and Michael Prestwich, *Edward I* (London, 1988), pp. 18–20. I owe to Dr Julia Barrow the information that the prince's servant and the bishop were indeed the same person.

[3] The identification of collections of writs in registers is made easy by David M. Smith, *Guide to Bishops' Registers of England and Wales* (London, 1981). For the history of recording these orders see *Royal Writs addressed to John Buckingham Bishop of Lincoln 1363–1398*, ed. A.K. McHardy (CYS 86 and LRS 86, 1997), pp. xii–xvi, hereafter *Lincoln Writs*.

[4] For treasures encountered by the present writer in the course of systematic reading of a writ collection see 'Bishop Buckingham and the Lollards of Lincoln Diocese', in *Schism, Heresy and Religious Protest*, ed. Derek Baker (Studies in Church History 9, 1972), pp. 131–46; 'John Wycliffe's Mission to Bruges: A Financial Footnote', *Journal of Theological Studies* 26 (1973), pp. 521–2.

[5] *Lincoln Writs*, nos 294, 347, 489.

notice of the appointment of Sir Thomas Monington as the new sheriff, and a mandate to clergy and laity to obey and assist him in every matter relating to his office. Both were dated 5 November 1490, and on the same day an order was addressed to the outgoing sheriff, Sir Thomas Devereux, to hand over to his successor everything relating to the office, along with rolls, writs, and memoranda. This belt-and-braces approach is perhaps to be explained by the sensitive nature of the parties involved. If Devereux was connected to Walter Devereux, Lord Ferrers of Chartley, he had powerful Yorkist connections, especially in Wales, and the government of Henry VII was taking no chances in relieving him of his office.[6]

An example of a writ collection which yields rich political matter is to be found in the large register of Roger Martival of Salisbury.[7] It has much to say about the domestic crises of the 1320s, in a collection which contains orders not only to the bishop but to sheriffs, and in which not all the orders came from the king. Both the rebellions of 1321–22 and Isabella's invasion and Edward II's deposition, from 1326 to 1328, can be followed in this material. There are orders to the sheriff of Berkshire to assemble troops for the king at Cirencester late in 1321, and early in 1322 for the bishop to move north against the rebels in south Yorkshire and the invading Scots.[8] Here can be found notice of the revocation of the younger Despenser's banishment (15 December 1321), and a publication of the names of the Marcher rebels, along with a call for prayers on the king's behalf; Martival seems to have obeyed this with energy and enthusiasm.[9] As well as high policy – the pardon to Thomas of Lancaster's adherents, and the confiscation of the bishop of Hereford's property[10] – a number of writs convey vividly the effects of this civil war, not only the administrative consequence of the land confiscation of 1322, but the high level of crime and insecurity felt far from the field of Boroughbridge.[11]

The final phase of Edward's reign can also be charted among these writs. A proclamation instructed the correct response to the expected return of Isabella and Prince Edward (8 February 1326), while three months later the bishop was to prepare for a full invasion, and the younger Despenser was put in charge of defence of the south of England.[12] From the other camp come

---

6 *The Register of Thomas Myllyng Bishop of Hereford 1474–1492*, ed. A.T. Bannister (Cantilupe Society x, 1919), pp. 132–5. For Walter Devereux see Rosemary Horrox, *Richard III: A Study in Service* (Cambridge, 1989), and Charles Ross, *Richard III* (London, 1981). For Monington as a military personage in the run-ups to the expeditions of 1488 and 1491, see *CPR 1485–94*, pp. 281, 282, 354.
7 The register was edited by a committee of four; details may be found in *Guide to Bishops' Registers*, p. 189; the writs are in vol. iii, ed. S. Reynolds (CYS 59, 1965).
8 Ibid., nos 310–11, 323.
9 Ibid., nos 320, 321 (15 January 1322).
10 Ibid., nos 328, 537–8.
11 Administration of rebels' lands which had been seized by the crown 5 October 1323–5 October 1324, ibid., nos 400, 403, 455, 482; roads which were unsafe for transporting clerical tax revenues, nos 324, 327, 351.
12 Ibid., nos 624, 647, 644.

two writs from the queen: a call to arms against the king, and an order to keep safely the Despenser's treasure which she had heard was in Salisbury cathedral.[13] By October the functioning of the law courts had broken down, and clearly Martival was not bothering to execute all writs, though by March 1327 government was getting back to some semblance of efficiency.[14]

This collection of administrative documents is exceptionally rich in political information, thanks not only to the interesting times in which Bishop Martival lived, but also the very high standard of record-keeping in his chancery. But political matters could sometimes reverberate in local administration long after the event, and so appear in writ collections. The fall of Roger Mortimer in 1330 had local and financial repercussions which were still being felt over forty years later, and Edward III's ill-fated scheme to manipulate the wool trade in 1337 also cast a long shadow.[15]

The second aspect of bishops' public duties lay in what we might call national, as opposed to strictly political matters, as they and their subordinates implemented public policy decisions. Pre-eminent in this area was taxation. Taxation was voted in the two convocations, institutions which are under-researched compared with the lay equivalent, parliament. Even the names of those attending convocation are usually unknown; a list of members of the lower house of Canterbury convocation in February 1473 is a rare survival.[16] Although the records of deliberations are often laconic, they do form a neglected counterpart to the Rolls of Parliament, so that even the briefest account – of the length of time needed to agree a grant, or the identities of lay spokesmen the king felt obliged to despatch to put his case – can be useful. When asked for taxation, convocations were usually compliant, if grudging, but refusals and protests can be found, and these deserve scrutiny as rare examples of medieval public opinion. In 1338, for example, the convocation of York was asked to make a grant of wool, following the lead of a recent parliament, but the northern clergy refused, both at provincial and at diocesan level, to comply.[17] The following year the same body was again in uncooperative mood when the king asked for a further grant beyond the triennial tenth granted in 1337. Its refusal of a further tenth was not outright, but any further grant was made upon five conditions, including the extension of the term for paying the triennial tenth.[18] The years 1337–40 are

[13] 15 and 25 October 1326, ibid., nos 679–80.
[14] Ibid., nos 673, 678 n, 692.
[15] *Lincoln Writs*, Mortimer: nos 112, 126, 149. The last of these was dated 24 January 1373. The wool trade scheme: nos 21, 29, 36, 59, 138–9.
[16] *The Registers of Robert Stillington Bishop of Bath and Wells 1466–1491 and Richard Fox Bishop of Bath and Wells 1492–1494*, ed. H.C. Maxwell-Lyte (Somerset Record Society 52, 1937), no. 576. There are forty-five names on the list.
[17] *The Register of John Kirby Bishop of Carlisle 1332–352*, ed. R.L. Storey, 2 vols (CYS 79, 81, 1993, 1995), i, nos 456, 480, 500. For background see W.M. Ormrod, *The Reign of Edward III* (Yale, 1990), pp. 11, 62, 128, 135, 164–5, 239.
[18] *The Register of William Melton Archbishop of York 1317–1340, vol. iii: Divers Letters*, ed. Rosalind M.T. Hill (CYS 76, 1988), no. 293.

traditionally seen as an exciting turning-point in English history, with the start of the Anglo-French war and Edward III's claiming of the French crown. Contemporaries, however, may have experienced it differently, as a time when distrust of the king, and resentment of his financial demands, brought the country to the brink of insurrection. Archbishop Melton's plea for a charitable view of the king's exactions accords well with a political poem which alleged that only the lack of a leader prevented a popular uprising.[19]

The major part of the taxation task was the collection of the money which the convocations had voted. The mechanism for collecting the tax grants was already well established by the early fourteenth century (so that there was no need to record the forms of such documents in later years), and tax grants are by their nature ephemeral matters: the moneys are paid and the matter is ended – until the next grant is imposed. It is therefore somewhat surprising that episcopal registers are so full of such routine procedures as the commissions to collectors within each diocese, and the recording of the fact that the collectors' names had been notified to the exchequer. Typical of the care with which this was done was the practice in Coventry and Lichfield under William Booth, who was responsible for appointing the collectors of two grants during his tenure of the see.[20] His register records, not simply the names of those appointed to collect the moieties of the two tenths (the same collectors were not invariably chosen to levy each half), and the 'poll tax' of 6s 8d from each unbeneficed priest which was part of the first grant, but the exceptions to the grants of tenths. By the middle years of the fifteenth century these exceptions were very numerous, and they had become traditional, yet these long lists were carefully entered in the register each time a set of collectors was commissioned.[21]

In the course of the fifteenth century taxation material assumed a greater importance in many registers as the keeping of memoranda declined. An extreme case can be found in London, a diocese whose memoranda sections are generally disappointing: from Thomas Kemp's episcopate the only

---

[19] *Reg. Kirby* i, no. 430. The letter, in response to a writ of 28 March, was dated 10 April 1338. It is not found in *Reg. Melton*. For political protest in these years see *Thomas Wright's Political Songs of England: From the Reign of John to that of Edward II*, ed. P.R. Coss (Cambridge, 1996), pp. 185–6.

[20] He was consecrated in July 1447, just too late to be responsible for appointing collectors for the tenth whose terms were 24 June 1447 and 24 June 1448, CFR 1445–52, pp. 61–4. For the list of taxes in the fifteenth century see the appendices to A. McHardy, 'Clerical Taxation in Fifteenth-Century England', in *The Church, Politics and Patronage in the Fifteenth Century* ed. R.B. Dobson (Gloucester, 1984), pp. 179–89. A new and improved list is being prepared by Dr Maureen Jurkowsky.

[21] For example, there were twenty-two exempt benefices in the archdeaconry of Derby, and ten in the archdeaconry of Stafford, J.C. Bates, 'The Episcopate of William Bothe Bishop of Coventry and Lichfield 1447–1452, with an Edition of his Register' (unpublished M.Phil. thesis, Nottingham, 1981), nos 248, 255.

subject, apart from promotions to benefices, is the clerical subsidy of 1489, covering six folios; it was of £25,000 and this was the first time since 1371 that a specific sum had been granted. At Hereford the memoranda of such bishops as Stanbury and Milling are heavily weighted with taxation material.

It is of course true that taxation was not, in practice, the temporary matter which it was in theory, because the crown might spend years, or even decades, trying to recover arrears from individual clerics,[22] but it remains curious that most bishops, even those who had no love for their particular monarch,[23] felt obliged to record the details of tax grants, and their collection, with such assiduity. The increasing number of exemptions and exceptions which were the main feature of clerical taxation in the fifteenth century, and the need to record these, may be one answer, but the subject is puzzling and certainly deserves further study.

The second of the national efforts about which registers inform us are the prayers which were organised for the English realm, especially in war time; from 1295 England was beset by hostile states to north and south. In the north the Scots, both by their 'official' invasions, and even more, by their constant raiding, did a great deal of damage and disrupted daily life both east and west of the Pennines, especially during the reign of Edward II. From the south the French did not invade, but they might have done, and for two centuries French invasion fleets allegedly massing across the Channel were the 'weapons of mass destruction' used to persuade the English that the realm was in peril. In this propaganda exercise the place of the church was central, and no aspect of the impact of politics upon registers has been the object of so much enquiry as this. The national prayers ordered for foreign wars by Edward I, and those ordered by his son and grandson in the same cause, the prayers of one diocese (Lincoln) during the entire Hundred Years' War, and the role of liturgy in general in that conflict, as well as a general account of the church's propaganda role – all have been the subjects of published studies.[24] Yet there has been no comprehensive coverage; Dr Burton's list of

---

[22] Numerous examples can be found among the writs addressed to Buckingham of Lincoln. Debts more than 15 years old were common, *Lincoln Writs*, passim, but no. 15 is a vivid example of the crown's problems. Cf. Henry VII's attempts to gather arrears of taxes granted to Edward IV and Richard III, *The Episcopal Registers of the Diocese of St David's 1397 to 1518, vol. II (1407–1518)*, ed. R.F. Isaacson (Cymmrodorion Record series 6, 1817), p. 530.

[23] The register of Langton of Salisbury, a strong supporter of Richard III, contains none of the mandates to pray for Henry VII which are known to have been issued, but has abundant material for the collection of taxation for the crown, *The Register of Thomas Langton Bishop of Salisbury 1485–93*, ed. D.P. Wright (CYS 74, 1985), see subject index.

[24] D.W. Burton, 'Requests for Prayers and Royal Propaganda under Edward I', in *Thirteenth Century England III*, ed. P.R. Coss and S.D. Lloyd (Woodbridge, 1991), pp. 25–35; J. Robert Wright, *The Church and the English Crown 1305–1334: A Study based on the Register of Archbishop Walter Reynolds* (Pontifical Institute of Medieval Studies, Toronto, 1980), pp. 348–60; A.K. McHardy, 'Some Reflections on Edward III's Use of

prayers ordered by Edward I does not include prayers for the royal family, nor those requests for prayers sent to the chapters of religious orders, especially the Dominicans and Franciscans, while Professor Wright's list of prayers during the archiepiscopate of Walter Reynolds is comprehensive; Burton, Jones and McHardy were mainly concerned with foreign warfare.

This has left considerable gaps. The threat of foreign invasion did not cease in 1453, the year now seen as the effective end of the Hundred Years' War, and prayers for later expeditions were organised,[25] though during the fifteenth century the Turkish menace, and consequent need for a crusade, could be said to have replaced the Anglo-French war as the international concern of many. Prayers for the royal family, for national emergencies like the plague, for bishops' patrons, and for political crises at home, remain unstudied. Even a few examples indicate how rewarding further investigation would be. John Gynewell of Lincoln issued mandates for prayers on behalf of Henry of Grosmont, duke of Lancaster, and his successor performed the same service for the soul of Thomas Beauchamp, earl of Warwick, both demonstrating the strength of affectionate feeling towards their former employers.[26] On becoming archbishop of Canterbury in 1382 one of William Courtenay's first acts was to instigate a burst of liturgical activity designed to pacify the province following the upheavals of the previous year, and to brace the community against other troubles, both foreign and domestic, including wars and a recent plague. One letter was issued from Otford on 30 May 1382, transmitted by Braybrooke on 5 June, and executed by Buckingham of Lincoln on 12 July.[27] Another similar mandate was issued by Courtenay from Lambeth on 8 June, while a further command to pray, which appears to have been a local initiative, and which mentioned the evils of heresy and error, was dated by Buckingham from Buckden, his Huntingdonshire manor house, on 14 December.[28] Courtenay's successor as primate, Thomas Arundel, played a crucial part in ensuring Richard II's

---

Propaganda', in *The Age of Edward III*, ed. J.S. Rothwell (York and Woodbridge, 2001), pp. 171–92; 'Liturgy and Propaganda in the Diocese of Lincoln during the Hundred Years War', in *Religion and National Identity*, ed. Stewart Mews, Studies in Church History 18 (Oxford, 1982), pp. 215–27; 'Religious Ritual and Political Persuasion: The Case of England in the Hundred Years War', *International Journal of Moral and Social Studies* 3 (1988), pp. 41–57; W.R. Jones, 'The English Church and Royal Propaganda During the Hundred Years War', *Journal of British Studies* 19 (1979), pp. 18–30.

25 The latest occasion was early in 1489, *The Register of John Morton Archbishop of Canterbury 1486–1500 I* (CYS 75, 1987), no. 108.

26 Mandate to pray for Henry duke of Lancaster going abroad to fight Otto duke of Brunswick, his enemy, in 1352, LAO Reg. 8 (Gynewell, Memoranda), fol. 21v. Prayers were ordered for the soul of Warwick, who died in 1369 during the siege of Calais, LAO Reg. 12 (Buckingham, Memoranda), fol. 82v.

27 Ibid., fol. 240v.

28 Lambeth Palace Library, Reg. Courtenay, fols 11v–12; LAO Reg. 12, fol. 253. Buckingham spent Christmas at Buckden (the only time in his long episcopate when

deposition and Henry IV's succession, and the mandate which he issued on 16 October 1399, ordering prayers for the new king ('a second Maccabaeus') is a piece of pure political propaganda.[29]

During the fifteenth century the scope of public and national prayers became, if anything, wider. There was one problem after another which needed divine help: heresy, epidemics, the menace of Owain Glyndwr's rebellion,[30] and then – leaving aside the self-induced matter of the renewed war with France – attempts to end the schism, first at Pisa,[31] then Constance.[32] The Turkish offensive of 1480, in which Rhodes was besieged, provoked a national effort, both royal and ecclesiastical,[33] and in 1490 Archbishop Morton ordered prayers against unspecified 'external enemies'.[34] A systematic study of such mandates for processions, prayers, and the homilies which accompanied them would be revealing, and would contribute greatly to the study of political persuasion in late-medieval England when it comes to be written.

No clear distinction divides the subject of taxation from that of politics. Not only did each tax grant have to be argued for and justified to the convocations, but, even when taxes had been granted, the sums which could be collected could be modified by political circumstances, both internal and external. The depredations of the Scots considerably reduced the amounts of taxation which could be collected during the 1320s and 1330s from the northern province, and the registers of that province are eloquent in proclaiming the clergy's sufferings, as well as vividly illustrating how disruptive the war was, and over how wide an area. Numerous examples can be found in, for example, the registers of Melton of York and Kirby of Carlisle. The effect of the war upon the tax values of the archdeaconry of Richmond is one perspective on this problem,[35] while the complaint of Kirby of

he did so) following the convocation held at Oxford, to discuss heresy, 18–26 November 1382.

[29] Issued from Lambeth, the letter was received by the bishop of London on 24 October and transmitted to the other bishops the next day. It was executed by Guy Mone, bishop of St Davids, on 2 November while he was still in London, *Registers of St David's, vol. I (1397–1407)* (Cymmrodorion Record series 6, 1917), pp. 132–6.

[30] *The Register of Richard Clifford Bishop of Worcester, 1401–1407: A Calendar*, ed. Waldo E.L. Smith, Subsidia Medievalia 6 (Toronto, 1976), pp. 26, 50–1.

[31] *The Register of Thomas Langley Bishop of Durham 1406–1437*, ed. R.L. Storey (Surtees Society 164, 1956), vol. i, nos 91–3; *The Register of Robert Hallum Bishop of Salisbury 1407–17*, ed. Joyce M. Horn (CYS 72, 1982), no. 939.

[32] Ibid., no. 922.

[33] LAO, Reg. 22 (Russell), fols 55–7. Otranto was taken in August, but Edward IV's writ was dated 17 of that month.

[34] *Reg. Myllyng*, pp. 128–30. This was not entered in Morton's register.

[35] *The Register of William Melton Archbishop of York 1317–1340, vol. i*, ed. Rosalind M.T. Hill (CYS 70, 1977), nos 7, 8, 396. For other problems caused in this part of the diocese see Rosalind Hill, *The Labourer in the Vineyard: The Visitation of Archbishop Melton in the Archdeaconry of Richmond* (St Anthony's Hall Publications 35, 1969).

Carlisle, that almost all his sheep had been taken by the Scots, is another.[36] A century later the bishop of St Davids diocese was to argue, successfully, that the damage caused by Owain Gyndwr's rebellion made tax collection impossible.[37]

The same lack of clear demarcation between ecclesiastical and political matters is true of prayers for national causes. Not only was the health and well-being of members of the royal family a matter of practical political importance,[38] so too the schism and the need for defence against the Ottomans were important for international relations, even though Englishmen were slow to appreciate the Muslim menace. Liturgy, and more particularly the observance of saints' days, had political importance. We could point to Henry V's promotion of the cults of St George, the patron of chivalry, and of St John of Beverley, on whose feast day the battle of Agincourt was fought, reflecting precisely his military ambitions.[39]

Third, last, and most important, we come to the impact of internal politics on the registers. In matters of 'pure' politics the rewards are less easy to find and have to be quarried from essentially ecclesiastical material. Nor are they in the expected places. For example, when Edward III was embarking upon his war with France in 1337, one of his diplomats was Henry Burghersh of Lincoln, yet no material relating to the start of the war exists in his register. Nearly a century later, when John Catterick of Coventry and Lichfield was a leading envoy of Henry V, his register is similarly barren of political entries. Robert Braybrooke of London was far from being a constant traveller to foreign parts. His itinerary shows a man who rarely left his diocese, and quitted England only for brief diplomatic excursions,[40] but he was closely in touch with the government of his kinsman Richard II, even joining the king on both his Irish expeditions.[41] It is, therefore, disap-

---

[36] In reply to a writ to collect wool for the king's benefit, Kirby answered that his clergy had been almost ruined by Scots incursions, 'The bishop's own few sheep have almost totally perished in enemy raids. He has not collected any wool, nor could he, and no one is holding any; there is none to be collected', 21 May 1339, *Reg. Kirby* i, no. 500.

[37] '. . . we have not been able to depute or appoint any collector in our diocese for levying or collectin because all the benefices are destroyed, as we are fully informed by faithful men. . . .', *Reg. St David's* i, pp. 312–16.

[38] Mandate, with precise instructions for the prayers from the Sarum Mass for the Infirm, issued by Buckingham of Lincoln 8 October 1376, during Edward III's last illness, LAO, Reg. 12, fol. 133r. The same register also records prayers for the prince of Wales (1367), and for the souls of Lionel duke of Clarence (1368) and of Queen Philippa (1369), fols 41r, 71r, 81v.

[39] *The Register of Henry Chichele Archbishop of Canterbury 1414–1443*, ed. E.F. Jacob, 4 vols (Oxford, 1943–7), iii, pp. 8, 28.

[40] To Amiens in February 1391, and Calais in July 1394 and September 1396, L.H. Butler, 'Robert Braybrooke, Bishop of London (1381–1404), and his Kinsmen' (unpublished D.Phil. thesis, Oxford, 1951) ii, pp. 587, 602, 608.

[41] He was at Drogheda 14–19 March 1395, though not earlier in the expedition, and again in Ireland on 1 June 1399, ibid., ii, pp. 603, 617.

pointing to find that his register contains no memoranda section, since this surely would have included material of a political nature. Even when interesting material exists in registers it is not always to be found in the expected place. Thus the writs ordering the saying of prayers in connection with Edward III's foreign campaigns were, in every case examined, entered in the memoranda sections of bishops' registers, and not among the other writs.[42]

Despite such difficulties the rewards are considerable. A very basic source of political information can be arrived at by constructing episcopal itineraries; for example, Professor Dobson was able to pinpoint the very moment when Alexander Neville, until the summer of 1385 known merely as a greedy and quarrelsome archbishop of York, turned into a member of Richard II's hated inner circle.[43] It is also true that the number of English sees, and the duplication of political material in registers, means that, if the searcher draws a blank in the most likely place, another register may provide the material sought. Thus, although the register of the diplomat Burghersh of Lincoln has nothing to say about the start of the Anglo-French war in 1337, there is detailed information on this very subject in the register of the scholar and stay-at-home, Ralph Shrewsbury of Bath and Wells.[44]

In the later thirteenth century, when the first registers were being assembled, political England had quite recently been riven by civil war, and was still turbulent. Late in 1277 Thomas Cantilupe of Hereford was directed by a bull of Nicholas III to enquire about the dispensations for plurality supposedly granted by a previous pope to Geoffrey de Aspall, keeper of Queen Eleanor's wardrobe; these had been kept in a house in London, but lost during 'the general turbulence of the kingdom of England'. Aspall was a notorious pluralist and had still not produced his dispensations in 1286.[45]

It was also in Henry III's reign that Llywelyn ap Gruffudd had been recognised as Prince of Wales and given lordship over 'extensive parts of the March of Wales'.[46] This no doubt explains his aggression towards his episcopal neighbour, for he occupied three villages – Chastroke, Astone, and Muletone – near, and belonging to, the bishop's property (Bishop's Castle) of Lydbury North. Cantilupe wrote a series of letters to Llywelyn asking for the return of these settlements, and even enlisted the help of his colleague

---

[42] McHardy, 'Edward III's use of Propaganda', pp. 179–80.
[43] R.B. Dobson, 'Beverley in Conflict: Archbishop Alexander Neville and the Minster Clergy, 1381–8', in *Medieval Art and Architecture in the East Riding of Yorkshire*, ed. C. Wilson (British Archaeological Association, IX, 1989), pp. 149–64.
[44] *Register of Ralph of Shrewsbury Bishop of Bath and Wells 1329–1363*, ed. T.S. Holmes, 2 vols (Somerset Record Society, 9, 10, 1896), i, nos 1276–9. There was considerable duplication of entries between, for example, the registers of Melton of York and Stapledon of Exeter, and between Hallum of Salisbury and Chichele of Canterbury.
[45] *Reg. Cantilupe Bishop*, pp. 203–4; Tout, *Chapters* v, pp. 236–8.
[46] In 1267; E.B. Fryde, D.E. Greenway, S. Porter, and I. Roy, eds., *Handbook of British Chronology*, 3rd edn (London, 1986), p. 51.

the bishop of Bangor.⁴⁷ The Prince was not the bishop's only Welsh problem, for instructions to his seneschal in late 1276 paint a picture of the Marches as a war zone.⁴⁸

In the Welsh Marches there was continuing civil strife between Cantilupe and Gilbert Clare, earl of Gloucester. At the time of Cantilupe's accession, 1275, the earl, whose record of loyalty to the crown had been, in Henry III's reign, very patchy, had recently made his peace with the new king. Perhaps because of a new confidence in his status as loyal subject, Clare made a determined effort to take possession of the Bishop's Chase of Colwall and Eastnor. The dispute seems to have started in 1275, for the earl was in trouble for trespass that year, and it continued until December 1279 when three of the earl's foresters, agents of his wrongdoing, submitted to the bishop and were absolved from a sentence of excommunication. The case was largely fought in the king's courts, both at Westminster, and in Gloucestershire and Herefordshire. The earl was unscrupulous, using procrastination, intimidation of juries, bullying of tenants, and chicanery in unsuccessful efforts to defeat the bishop,⁴⁹ but Cantilupe too was prepared to use any means at his disposal, including the power of his curses, and the employment of his champion in single combat.⁵⁰

An example of the depths to which the earl would go to harass the bishop was the squabble over lodgings for a meeting of the king and his magnates. The gathering was planned for 1 July 1277 at Worcester, and the bishop was assigned (by the marshal of the household, Geoffrey de Everle) to the house of the rector of Powick. Subsequently he was informed by Ralph Bluet, the temporary marshal, that all the lodgings from 'Henle' to Powick (three miles south-west of Worcester) had been assigned to the earl, by the king's special order. Cantilupe complained to Bluet in the king's presence, and Edward ordered Powick rectory to be given to him immediately. Meanwhile, however, his baggage had been sent to Whitbourne, so the bishop was bereft of many of his staff and belongings; a memorandum of the incident was entered into Cantilupe's register.⁵¹ Gilbert de Clare and Thomas Cantilupe had both been active in the troubled reign of Henry III⁵² and it is surely not

---

⁴⁷ All but one of these (1 January 1276) is undated. *Reg. Cantilupe*, pp. 29–30, 42, 103.
⁴⁸ Ibid., pp. 108–11.
⁴⁹ Ibid., pp. 23, 34, 36, 52–6, 59–62, 104–5, 227–8.
⁵⁰ Ibid., pp. xxix, 104–5. The bishop's champion, Thomas Bridges (de Bruges) was paid a retainer of 6s 8d a year. For a portrait of a personal champion and discussion of the role see Giles Waterfield, Anne French, Matthew Craske, *Below Stairs: 400 years of Servants' Portraits* (London, 2004), pp. 30–3.
⁵¹ *Reg. Cantilupe*, pp. 123–4.
⁵² For Clare see F.M. Powicke, *King Henry III and the Lord Edward*, 2 vols (Oxford, 1947); for Cantilupe, David Carpenter, 'St Thomas Cantilupe: His Political Career,' in *St Thomas Cantilupe Bishop of Hereford: Essays in his Honour*, ed. Meryl Jancey (Hereford, 1982), pp. 57–72.

fanciful to see at least part of the reason for their quarrel in old enmities which remained in the reign of Henry's son.

Both foreign warfare and domestic political strife made an impact on the register of the bishop of Hereford from 1317 to 1327, Adam Orleton. It was perhaps Orleton's career as a diplomat which resulted in the number of entries about Anglo-French relations which appear in his Hereford register.[53] Chronologically, the first entry dated from the episcopate of his predecessor, Richard Swinfield, to whom Edward I had addressed a writ on 10 November 1290. This ordered the bishop to summon the clergy of his diocese – deans, archdeacons, prebendaries, rectors, vicars, and all other beneficed men – who were of the lordship, power, affinity or confederacy of the king of France to appear before the treasurer and others of the king's council at Westminster on a day to be assigned by the bishop at his discretion according to the distance they would have to travel, there to hear what the king had decided to do about these men. The bishop was to certify the names, and benefices, of those concerned.[54] Clearly, some five years before he seized the benefices of French clergy, Edward I was already thinking of ways to control, and to benefit from, the clerical subjects of the king of France within his realm.[55]

The mounting troubles of Edward II, at home and abroad, in the 1320s are clearly reflected in Orleton's register. In 1322 a national effort was demanded in the propaganda war against Thomas of Lancaster: a writ dated from Coventry on 1 March was directed to the archbishop of Canterbury, who ordered processions for the king's success in the forthcoming northern campaign in an order dated from Lambeth on 7 March.[56] Notwithstanding his success at Boroughbridge, Edward's troubles soon took on an international dimension and these are also evident in this Hereford register. Writing from Limoges shortly after Christmas 1322, Charles IV pressed Edward II to perform the act of homage he owed – a duty which, he urged, could be deferred no longer – and named the following 1 July at Amiens as the date and place for this ceremony. Even in December 1322 the question of the *bastide* St Sardos was causing friction between the two monarchs, though Charles sought to distance the problem of the border dispute from the matter of homage. The *bastide* was the sole subject of a letter from the French king to Antonin Pasquin, his sergeant at arms, written on 1 January 1323. These letters are very early documents about what would later become

---

[53] Roy Martin Haines, *The Church and Politics in Fourteenth-Century England: The Career of Adam Orleton c.1275–1345* (Cambridge, 1978), pp. 5–26.
[54] *The Register of Adam de Orleton Bishop of Hereford A.D. 1317–1327*, ed. A.T. Bannister (Cantilupe Society 2, 1907), pp. 309–10. The writ was not entered in Swinfield's register.
[55] Marjorie Morgan, *The English Lands of the Abbey of Bec* (Oxford, 1946) and Donald Matthew, *Norman Monasteries and their English Possessions* (Oxford, 1962).
[56] *Reg. Orleton*, pp. 218–20.

known as the War of St Sardos, and perhaps the most remarkable aspect of their inclusion in Orleton's register is that by 1322 the bishop had lost Edward II's confidence and ceased to be employed by him on diplomatic missions.[57]

By the spring of 1326 Edward II's home and foreign problems had combined; his wife, sent to the French court as a peacemaker in 1324, along with their eldest son, deputed to do homage on his father's behalf, had not returned home, and rumours were circulating that they had been banished, and that the two papal envoys were afraid to approach the king's presence. Walter Reynolds, archbishop of Canterbury, once again proved the king's confidence in him by directing that these rumours should be scotched by public refutations during Mass on Sundays and feast-days in all the churches which seemed suitable; also that prayers should be offered for the queen's speedy return to England with joy and exultation. The command, issued at Otford on 25 April, was forwarded by the bishop of London from Fulham on 6 May.[58] Interestingly, and perhaps significantly, there is no evidence that Orleton, a long-time adherent of Roger Mortimer, took steps to carry out either this, or Reynolds' earlier order to vilify Lancaster.

Meanwhile, those in the north of the country were more concerned with the Scottish war. This made a significant impact on the register of Archbishop Melton, which contains an unsurpassed collection of entries about both the War of Independence and its impact on the north of England. The English portrayed Robert Bruce, king of Scots, as a traitor who had violated his oath of fealty to his overlord, and during the pontificate of John XXII (1316–24) Anglo-Scottish relations were conducted within an ecclesiastical framework. For papal envoys and messengers the road to the Scottish court was a perilous one, and the dangers were not confined to Scotland; in the autumn of 1317 two cardinals and the bishop-elect of Durham were attacked in Northumberland.[59] Letters beginning 'To Robert Bruce governor of Scotland' were returned as being 'incorrectly addressed'. Since the Scottish higher clergy were strong supporters of Bruce the problem of finding a suitable messenger to deliver sentences of excommunication and interdict was difficult, but the nuncios eventually chose Adam, the guardian of the Franciscans of Berwick. The unfortunate friar had an unpleasant time in Scotland, where he was mishandled by Bruce's men. The sentence of excommunication, drawn up in May 1318, was apparently published throughout England that autumn.[60] It failed to bring Bruce to heel, and was reissued in

---

[57] Ibid., 334–7. *The War of Saint-Sardos (1323–1325): Gascon Correspondence and Diplomatic Documents*, ed. Pierre Chaplais (Camden Society Third Series lxxxvii, 1954); Haines, *Church and Politics*, p. 26.
[58] *Reg. Orleton*, pp. 359–61.
[59] Geoffrey W.S. Barrow, *Robert Bruce and the Community of the Realm of Scotland*, 3rd edn (Edinburgh, 1988), pp. 246–50.
[60] *Reg. Melton* iii, nos 21, 26.

July 1320 – from the safety of France – and was now to have yet wider publicity, for it was to be published not only in England, Scotland, Ireland, and Wales, but also throughout France, Brabant, and Flanders.[61] Meanwhile, papal summonses to Bruce and the bishops of St Andrews, Dunkeld, Aberdeen, and Moray, and safe-conducts for their passage to the curia were issued by John XXII in the spring of 1320 and transmitted, in an ecclesiastical game of 'pass the parcel', from Avignon northwards, and involving the archbishop of York and the bishops of Hereford, Norwich, and Durham. Each time the sequence seems to have ended with the luckless Franciscan, Adam, in Berwick. It is clear that everyone concerned was anxious to show that he was a loyal subject of both pope and king, but wanted others to take responsibility for carrying out this dangerous mission.[62] The recognition of Bruce as king of Scots by John XXII in 1324 may have eased one problem for Archbishop Melton, but it brought no respite for the people of his province from the menace of Scottish raiding, which had been a problem since the accession of Edward II.[63] Melton said as much in a letter to the pope in 1327.[64]

In contrast to Edward III's reign, which was seen even in his lifetime as a golden age,[65] Richard II's reign produced all too many similarities to that of his great-grandfather. For these stormy twenty-two years registers offer important material both to complement and to reinforce the admittedly copious evidence of chronicles and crown records. An area in which this can be demonstrated is the so-called 'Norwich Crusade'. With the French war going badly, and the political establishment traumatised by the Peasants' Revolt, the parliament which met in February 1383 decided to mount a campaign in the form of a crusade against one of England's schismatic enemies. This would have the advantage that funds would be raised by public donations, and not by taxation, which, two years after the Great Revolt, was felt to be politically dangerous. The only question was, should the campaign be against the king of Castile, John of Gaunt's political adversary, or France's ally the count of Flanders? The decision to opt for the 'Way of Flanders', with an army led by the bishop of Norwich, Henry Despenser, was taken after brisk discussion, yet already some two months earlier the bishop of Lincoln had begun to organise and support fund-raising efforts on

---

[61] Ibid., no. 141.
[62] Ibid., nos 54–7, 63–5, 230.
[63] Barrow, *Robert Bruce*, p. 389. Colm McNamee, *The Wars of the Bruces: Scotland, England and Ireland 1306–1328* (Edinburgh, 1997), especially chapters 2 and 3 on the raiding and defence of northern England 1311–22. The maps are especially helpful. Dr McNamee lists four registers in his bibliography, though the use he made of them is unclear.
[64] 7 November, *Reg. Melton* iii, no. 154,
[65] D.A.L. Morgan, 'The Political After-Life of Edward III: The Apotheosis of a Warmonger', *EHR* 112 (1997), pp. 856–81.

behalf of this army, on the bishop of Norwich's prompting.[66] It was not until 10 April 1383 that Archbishop Courtenay ordered province-wide prayers on behalf of the bishop of Norwich and his army. As was common in such cases, the order followed a long preamble in which the cause of the campaign, in this case the schism in the church, was explained.[67]

The success of the subsequent fund-raising on the bishop's behalf is well known from the sour comments made by Henry Knighton. The results of these efforts brought to light the secret treasure of the realm, he said, which existed in the form of women's jewels, and the success of appeals for money lay in the unscrupulous methods of the bishop's agents, who promised that, in return for a sufficiently generous donation, 'angels would descend from the skies at their bidding, and snatch souls in purgatory from their places of punishment, and lead them to heaven without delay'.[68] The collectors were evidently better at collecting money than they were at passing it on to Despenser, for on 26 August 1383 Courtenay wrote directly to his suffragans to explain that the initial success of the Flemish crusade was now being threatened by shortage of money, caused, he was afraid, by the detention and concealment of funds by those same collectors. He ordered his colleagues to accelerate the hand-over of donations, forwarding the money to Master Walter Douell and John Mascall esquire.[69] Following the failure of his campaign Despenser was widely criticised for a variety of reasons: failure to take advice, to defer to lay commanders, and for cowardice, but the evidence of Courtenay's register suggests that we should view his record more sympathetically.[70]

Meanwhile, although Gaunt's Castilian project had been snubbed by parliament, it had not been forgotten by the church. On 21 March 1383 privileges and indulgences to the crusading Gaunt were granted by Urban VI,[71] and on 10 September Courtenay again wrote to Braybrooke ordering him to organise province-wide masses, sermons, processions, and prayers on behalf of the duke, as well as for his colleague the bishop of Norwich, whose crusade, though the order does not mention this, was even then collapsing in ignominy.[72]

As tension mounted between Richard II and his domestic opponents in the mid 1380s the political situation was sufficiently remarkable to make an impact upon some bishops' registers. Thus the commission of government,

---

[66] 15 December 1382, LAO, Reg. 12, fol. 253v.
[67] Lambeth Palace Library, Register of William Courtenay (Canterbury), fol. 36r.
[68] *Knighton's Chronicle 1337–1396*, ed. and trans. G.H. Martin (Oxford, 1995), p. 325.
[69] Reg. Courtenay (Cant.), fol. 44r.
[70] Margaret Aston, 'The Impeachment of Bishop Despenser', *Bulletin of the Institute of Historical Research* 38 (1965), pp. 127–48.
[71] *CPL iv 1362–1404*, pp. 264–5; they were withdrawn in January 1389, having, it seems, been abused, pp. 270–1.
[72] Reg. Courtenay (Cant.), fol. 44v.

issued on 19 November 1386, was copied into the register of William of Wykeham, though this was perhaps not surprising since the bishop of Winchester was among the commissioners.[73] A year later relations between king and critics descended into a brief civil war, in November–December 1387 and the subsequent 'Merciless Parliament' from February 1388. This period of crisis, from autumn 1386 to the summer of 1388, provoked a remarkable example of the impact of politics on an episcopal register. It occurs in the register of Henry Wakefield of Worcester. Folios 124–8 not only contain a systematic record of royal commands – to attend parliament, appoint collectors of a subsidy, proceed against heretics, and to pray for a naval expedition – but also comments by the bishop's clerk which are so extensive and so forthright that they form a mini-chronicle. These entries have been in print for some years, and their content and significance have been subjected to close scrutiny.[74]

Dr Davies, who has discussed these most fully, speculated on the motive behind this vigorous pro-appellant commentary, and sought to discover the political affiliation of Wakefield, a former treasurer who left crown service at the start of Richard's reign. A further suggestion may be offered here, with the aid of a similar 'chronicle' from one of Wakefield's neighbours. *The Stoneleigh Leger Book*[75] also contains a short political account, from the advent of Robert de Vere and his army from Cheshire, until the exiling of the judges in the Merciless Parliament, but this is almost entirely factual, save that he says of de Vere that 'he came with a great army from Cheshire into Oxfordshire, in breach of the king's peace'. It seems plausible that it was the passage of this army through the West Midlands which stirred the imaginations of the two men and provoked them to composition. As for any political affiliations, the simplest explanation is that the earl of Warwick, a leading appellant, was the largest landowner in the neighbourhood of these secret authors.

There was nothing secret about the part played in the Merciless Parliament by Archbishop Courtenay. A forthright and confident leader of his flock since his days as a young bishop of Hereford,[76] William Courtenay took advantage of the legal uncertainties of the start of this gathering to insist

---

[73] *Wykeham's Register*, ed. T.F. Kirby, 2 vols (Hampshire Record Society, 1896–9), ii, pp. 396–400. The commission was enacted as a statute on 1 December, *Statutes of the Realm*, 11 vols (Record Commission, 1810–28), ii, pp. 39–43.

[74] *A Calendar of the Register of Henry Wakefeld Bishop of Worcester 1375–95*, ed. Warwick Paul Marett (Worcester Historical Society new series 7, 1972), nos 820, 824, 826, 829; Richard G. Davies, 'Some Notes from the Register of Henry de Wakefield, Bishop of Worcester, on the Political Crisis of 1386–1388', *EHR* 86 (1971), pp. 547–58. This material is located in the writ section of the register.

[75] Ed. R.H. Hilton (Dugdale Society 24, 1960), 95–6.

[76] For Courtenay's protest against the taxation of himself and the clergy of Hereford diocese, recorded in Reg. Wittlesey fol. 65, see Joseph Dahmus, *William Courtenay Archbishop of Canterbury 1381–1396* (Pennsylvania, 1966), pp. 12, 282 n. 57.

first, that the prelates be recognised as peers of the realm, and second, that they could not take part in person in the judgement likely to lead to the death penalty. There is some doubt about the date of this protest, the Rolls of Parliament giving 5 February, and the version in the *Westminster Chronicle* giving 11th. Those who wish to know the true date, the place where the protest was made, and in whose presence, must consult Courtenay's register, which tells us that it took place on 5th.[77]

The next parliament, that of September–October 1388, was held at Cambridge. The reasons for using this small town are obscure (it may have been the choice of Thomas Arundel, now archbishop of York and chancellor, but formerly bishop of Ely) but it was certainly an inconvenient location for many; the trouble and expense which the London MPs incurred in pursuit of suitable lodgings is well known.[78] Bishops were in a better position to ask for accommodation, and Courtenay apparently lodged at the Carmelite friary, where he conducted business on 14 October. The place was so unusual that his registrar made a marginal note that at that time parliament was being held at Cambridge.[79] Where did the other bishops stay? A systematic study of their registers might well provide the answer.

It was on 3 May 1389 that Richard suddenly announced to a meeting of his council that he was now fully of age and would in future make his own decisions. As reported by Thomas Walsingham, this event took those present completely by surprise. Was it a sudden decision, or had it been planned, and, if so, who knew of the king's intentions? The register of John Waltham of Salisbury may provide the answer. Waltham, a Lincolnshire native and one of a dynasty of leading chancery clerks, had been the appellants' choice for promotion to Salisbury, but seems quickly to have won the king's trust. He was almost continuously in London from Christmas 1388 until late May 1389. On 1 March 1389 he commissioned a suffragan bishop to celebrate general orders on Ember Saturday in Lent (13 March) in Cerne abbey, and at a similar time (the entry is undated but is surrounded by letters issued January–March 1389) Waltham issued a commission which enlarged the existing powers of his vicar-general, indicating, perhaps, a coming change in his circumstances as king's adviser.[80]

---

[77] Reg. Courtenay (Canterbury), fol. 174. Cf. *Rotuli Parliamentorum*, ed. J. Strachey et al., 6 vols (Record Commission, 1767–77), iii, pp. 236–7, where Courtenay's (carefully-prepared intervention) is said to have been recorded at the king's particular command; *The Westminster Chronicle 1381–1394*, ed. L.C. Hector and Barbara F. Harvey (Oxford, 1982), p. 280.

[78] Translated from City of London Letter-Book H in H.T. Riley, *Memorials of London Life in the XIII, XIV & XV Centuries* (London, 1868), pp. 511–12, and repr. (though wrongly dated) in A.R. Myers, *English Historical Documents IV* (London, 1969), pp. 451–2.

[79] Reg. Courtenay (Cant.), fol. 286v.

[80] *The Register of John Waltham Bishop of Salisbury 1388–1395*, ed. T.C.B. Timmins (CYS 80, 1994), nos 30, 32, and p. 219.

For the fifty years and more after Richard's eventual deposition, opposition to the crown was more often physical than constitutional, and much of the 'political' material in registers could better be described as 'international affairs', for which prayers were needed. It is during this period that registers contain more heresy cases than ever before, and we do well to remember that, for the early Lancastrians, Lollardy was not a purely theological matter, but had serious security implications too.

Historians of the fifteenth century and its political troubles have chronicle evidence which is much less full than it had been a century earlier, while official records are nothing like as informative as they became during the sixteenth century, and they turn gratefully to other sources of information and comment.[81] But while letter collections have been used by generations of scholars, bishops' registers have been generally ignored. Despite the decline in episcopal record-keeping there are still gems to be found from this time. One example comes from John Kemp's brief tenure of the archbishopric of Canterbury. Shortly before he died Kemp issued to his province a mandate to make processions for the state of the realm. Disasters were crowding in on the nation: there was the 'serious illness and bodily weakness of the king', and the French conquests, the plague, famines, and dissensions.[82] Though his letter adds no new information, the sense of desolation and bewilderment is eloquently expressed. 'We don't know what we ought to do', confessed Kemp, before enjoining processions on Sundays and feast-days. The effort was to last for a full year, a remarkable, and possibly unique instruction. Dated from Lambeth on 2 March 1454 the instruction was forwarded to the other bishops by Thomas Kemp of London on 6 March.[83]

From the last year of Henry VI, and throughout the Yorkist period, the archbishop of Canterbury was Thomas Bourgchier, scion of an aristocratic family which consistently supported the Yorkists, a man so much involved in political and public affairs that his register records several times that he was too busy to deal with routine ecclesiastical matters.[84] Bourgchier's register is

---

[81] There is an eloquent lament for the lack of contemporary sources in Charles Ross, *Edward IV* (London, 1974), p. 429, including the judgement that 'For no other reign in English history since Henry III do we possess less strictly contemporary information, save perhaps that of Henry VI.'

[82] The king lost his reason in August 1453 shortly after the English had been driven from south-west France. Even without Cade's rebellion (1450) political dissension was bitter. Parliament, which had been called to Reading in early November 1453, was prorogued on the grounds that the town was riddled with plague; R.A. Griffiths, *The Reign of King Henry VI* (London, 1981), p. 719.

[83] LAO, Reg. 20 (Chedworth), fols 15v–16v. There is no record of how of the bishop of Lincoln executed the order. John Kemp died on 22 March 1454.

[84] In February 1455 pressure of business prevented him from being at Canterbury, and the prior was commissioned to deputise for him, while in May 1460 he commissioned the bishops of London and Salisbury to continue holding convocation in his absence;

incomplete,[85] and for only three (1460/1, 1463 and 1481) of the thirteen convocations held during his primacy are there records in his register. These three accounts are, however, both extensive – filling eighteen folios[86] – and of considerable political interest. The first two chart the change of dynasty from the mad Henry VI to the martial Edward IV; the convocation record of 1463 shows with particular vividness the lengths to which Edward had to go in order to placate or curry favour with the clergy of Canterbury province, a powerful interest group with considerable financial muscle. Not only did he send a high-powered delegation (to this as to other meetings of convocation) to argue for the grant of a subsidy to the king, but he also conceded a charter to the clergy, confirming their rights, especially in respect of the actions of local royal officials like sheriffs, coroners, and escheators. The clergy were not the only groups which were able to wring concessions from the Yorkist kings; minstrels (1469) and heralds (1484) too, were able to benefit from their need of allies,[87] but the clergy, who were both ubiquitous and powerful in all but the military sense, had to be courted and pacified to a considerable degree. It is perhaps because the business of each of these meetings included strictly ecclesiastical matters – heresy in 1460, forgery in 1463, and the observance of certain feasts in 1481 – that their proceedings have been ignored by political historians, but there is a good case to be made that they are as significant as a chronicle or as the Rolls of Parliament.

Clergy, of course, are especially important at the beginnings and endings of life, and Archbishop Bourgchier's seizure of Edward IV's good, seals, and jewels on 7 May 1483, and his instructions to the king's executors later that month to pay the funeral expenses, show just how great was the political and administrative vacuum left by Edward's sudden death.[88] The register also contains what appears to be the coronation oath of Richard III, the king's responses being identified as 'R. Rex', though it is unheaded and undated in the register. It was in English and contained four clauses: to uphold the ancient laws going back to St Edward (the Confessor), to preserve the church in peace and concord, to do right and justice to his subjects, and to defend 'suche lawes as to the worship of God shalbe chosyn by your people'. Then followed a petition from the clergy to uphold the church's privileges and canon law, which the king agreed to do.[89] This oath raises a number of

---

Registrum Thome Bourgchier Cantuariensis Archepiscopi 1454–1486, ed. F.R.H. du Boulay (CYS 54, 1957), pp. 17–18, 83.

[85] On its deficiencies see ibid., pp. xxiii–xxvi.

[86] The printed version runs to seventy-three pages, pp. 77–150 inclusive.

[87] C.A.J. Armstrong, 'The Inauguration Ceremonies of the Yorkist Kings', *Transactions of the Royal Historical Society* 4th series 30 (1948), p. 51 and n. 2.

[88] *Reg. Bourgchier*, pp. 52–3, 54–5. Instructions for paying the funeral expenses were issued on 23 May.

[89] Ibid., pp. 60–1.

questions.⁹⁰ The process by which the Yorkist kings attained the throne has been studied in detail,⁹¹ but still some mysteries remain. Was this the oath which Edward IV had sworn? And when precisely had he sworn it?⁹² What is known, though, is that Richard III followed his brother in many aspects of his ascent to the kingship, since both, in their different ways, were usurpers trying to put a veneer of right onto a position caused by military might.

On the other hand, there is good evidence that Richard III used an English form of the oath, and may have been the first king to do so.⁹³ It has been suggested that he was keen to have the wording of his oath understood by as many of his subjects as possible, given the unusual circumstances of his accession; also that his own grasp of French – the traditional language in which the oath was taken – may have been poor, for unlike his brother Edward he had not spent time in France when young. What is certain is that his coronation oath was important to Richard, for he referred to it on several subsequent occasions. There survives a document called the *Little Device* which seems to be a coronation programme prepared for Richard III, and its form of the oath is very similar to, though not exactly the same as, that preserved in Bourgchier's register. Which form was actually used on the day? Possibly the *Little Device* contains a draft form of the oath, while the register gives us the final form used at the coronation. Thanks to widespread public interest in this brief reign all the evidence for its commencement has been scrutinised, even if some uncertainties still remain.

It is pleasing to be able to end this essay on a positive note. No churchman was more closely concerned with politics than was John Morton, the archbishop of Canterbury who was so deeply involved with the establishment and maintenance of the Tudor regime that his fiscal devices earned him a place in *1066 and All That*.⁹⁴ Two matters of political import feature in Morton's register. One was the king's marriage. The dispensation for the marriage between Henry Tudor and Elizabeth of York was given by the papal legate on 16 January 1486, and the ceremony itself took place two days later.⁹⁵ Confirmations by Innocent VIII of the dispensation, dated 27 March and 23 July 1486, were entered in Morton's register, as was also a papal commission, issued at the king's request, to absolve those who had incurred

---

90 H.G. Richardson, 'The English Coronation Oath', *Transactions of the Royal Historical Society* 4th series 23.
91 Armstrong, 'Inauguration Ceremonies', pp. 51–73.
92 Ibid., p. 58.
93 For what follows, see *The Coronation of Richard III: The Extant Documents*, ed. Anne F. Sutton and P.W. Hammond (Gloucester, 1983), especially pp. 11–15, 39.
94 W.C. Sellar and R.J. Yeatman, *1066 and All That* (London, 1930), 'Henry VII's Statecraft' in chapter 29, describes Morton's Fork in detail. For further and more sober detail see C.S.L. Davies, 'Bishop John Morton, the Holy See, and the Accession of Henry VII', *EHR* 102 (1987), pp. 2–30.
95 Ibid., p. 15.

excommunication by their opposition to the king's succession and marriage.[96]

Quite how dangerous that opposition could be may be seen from the items relating to rebellions against Henry VII. Early in 1487 (17 February), there was produced before Canterbury convocation a priest called William Symonds who confessed his part in the conspiracy to put Lambert Simnel on the throne; he had kidnapped the son of an organ-maker of Oxford University and taken him to Ireland where he had been presented as though he was the earl of Warwick. His confession was made before the Lambert Simnel rebellion took place, and the fact that it was made in convocation, to which London's civic dignitaries had been invited, indicates how closely Morton was committed to the survival of the Tudor regime, as well as the effectiveness of his intelligence-gathering.[97]

By coincidence, the part of Morton's register which contains this report was published in 1987, five hundred years after Simnel's rebellion, and it was to mark this anniversary that Michael Bennett's *Lambert Simnel and the Battle of Stoke* was written, in which attention was forcefully drawn to the importance of this item in Morton's register, not only in the text, but also by printing it as the first of the 'Key Documents' which illuminate the rebellion.[98] Dr Bennett found his text in an eighteenth-century compilation,[99] and made his own translation. The work of publishing societies, especially those associated with David Smith, like the Canterbury and York Society and the Lincoln Record Society, ensures that these important sources are available across the globe, and, increasingly, in forms which make them accessible to those with widely varying levels of skill. Now it is up to historians, including students of English and international politics, to make use of them.

---

[96] *The Register of John Morton Archbishop of Canterbury 1486–1500*, ed. Christopher Harper-Bill, 3 vols (CYS 75, 78, 89, 1987–2000), i, nos 8, 12; Rome, 6 August 1487, no. 11.

[97] Ibid., no. 89. Morton was also to be involved in the military suppression of the Perkin Warbeck rebellion on 1495, ibid., no. 195.

[98] Michael Bennett, *Lambert Simnel and the Battle of Stoke* (Gloucester, 1987), pp. 12, 44, 121.

[99] *Conciliae Britanniae et Hiberniae A.D. 466–1718*, ed. D. Wilkins, 4 vols (London, 1737), iii, p. 618.

The Vatican Archives, the Papal Registers and Great Britain and Ireland: the Foundations of Historical Research

JANE SAYERS

No one today can contemplate writing serious medieval history, or carrying out any major research project, certainly from the thirteenth century onwards, without recourse to some part of the Vatican Archives. The Vatican Archives is the oldest and the largest collection of archives in Europe, the major fount of knowledge and the most important (from a European point of view) for the last millennium. Here are major sources for the political, religious, and social history of the countries of Europe. It should not be thought that the information here contained is restricted only to matters of political and diplomatic interest, to foreign affairs and religious disputes. There is in fact a wealth of material on social subjects and ordinary people, on education, on hospitals, on marriage, divorce, illegitimacy, on occupations and industries, on violence, excommunication, and heresy.

The story of the opening of the papal 'Archivio Segreto' in 1883 has already been robustly told by Owen Chadwick.[1] It had much to do with the events of the previous seventy years: the transport of the papal archives to Paris by Napoleon in 1810–11 and the more recent event of the calling of the Vatican Council in 1870. Such secret archives and sensitive papers as those concerning the trial of Galileo and the Trial of the Templars disappeared in Paris at this time, and were only recovered in part. The minutes of the sixteenth-century Council of Trent survived and were duly returned with the rest, but the sojourn of the archives in Paris had opened up sensitive papers to public, and possibly hostile, gaze. When the Vatican Council was called in 1870, the procedure of the great Council of Trent was examined and found to be much more liberal than that proposed. The archivist was accused of leaking this information and consequently his entrance to the Archives was walled up. The Secret Archives remained exactly that, secret to all but a very few.

---

[1] O. Chadwick, *Catholicism and History. The Opening of the Vatican Archives* (Cambridge, 1978).

It is at this point that some comments are needed on the role of the archivist. Primarily the archivist's function was to protect the archive of the employer, and this has continued to be so. A question frequently put to archives candidates concerns the priority of the archivist's responsibility: whether it is to the employer or the public at large. The early notion of the archivist was as a protector of the collection, a censor, who transcribed material for certain searchers and users, and who did not allow access to collections.

The earliest of the scholars who began work on the Vatican Archives in the nineteenth century was Joseph Stevenson (1806–95) a remarkable man, who was both historian and archivist. As a schoolboy he was put in the charge of the Rev. James Raine at Durham, and, as the *Dictionary of National Biography* (*DNB*) records, 'for more than sixty years from 1831 his pen was never idle'.[2] He was first engaged in arranging the public records in the Tower of London. He then obtained a post in the manuscripts department of the British Museum. Appointed a sub-commissioner of the public records, he worked on the proposed new edition of Rymer's *Foedera*. Later he returned to Durham, was ordained priest and succeeded James Raine as librarian and keeper of the records of the Dean and Chapter. His output was formidable. The Rolls Series was largely due to his vision and he contributed four titles. For the Maitland Club, he edited 8 volumes; for the Bannatyne Club, 2 volumes; for the English Historical Society, 4 volumes; for the Roxburghe Club, 4 volumes; for the Surtees Society, 7 volumes; for the 'collection of Church Historians of England', 7 volumes; and the *Calendar of State Papers, Foreign Series*, of the reign of Elizabeth, 7 volumes. Nor was this the totality of his work. He reported on no less than twenty-four manuscript collections for the newly formed Historical Manuscripts Commission.

On converting to Rome in 1863, Stevenson resigned as vicar of Leighton Buzzard and accepted employment in the Public Record Office (PRO). Religious difficulties resulted in his leaving the Record Office, but in 1872 he secured the government post of making an examination of the Vatican Archives.[3] The fruits of his labours in those Archives are contained in thirteen volumes of transcripts, now in the National Archives (formerly the PRO). With his long experience as an editor, his instructions from the Deputy Keeper seem somewhat otiose, and showed a totally inadequate grasp of the size of the task required, let alone any appreciation of the difficulties of access. Stevenson was to begin by transcribing material relating to the reign of Henry VIII; he was then to cover the period from Edward VI to James II; only finally was he to cover the period between 1066 and Henry VII. Any documents already published were to be noted only. Stevenson was sixty-

---

[2] *DNB* 18 (1909) pp. 1127–9.
[3] On Stevenson in general, see *DNB* as above; and J.H. Pollen in *The Month* (May 1895). On his contribution to the Rolls Series, see especially D. Knowles, *Great Historical Enterprises* (London, 1963), pp. 104, 105–6, 108, 112, and 117.

three at the time of his appointment, sixty-seven when he finished. His work depended both on what he was able to find from the existing lists and also on what he was allowed to see. Here he was extraordinarily fortunate. His extensive privileges in using the Archives ('the roaming Englishman' as Chadwick describes him),[4] before they were declared open for public use by Pope Leo XIII in 1881, can only be put down to one of the chance happenings of history. It was Pio Nono who, at the request of the PRO, had first given Stevenson permission in 1872 to work in the Vatican Archives 'but secretly, in order to keep Austrian and German scholars, then out of favour, at bay'.[5] And it was Stevenson, and later Elie Berger, a Frenchman (who was given permission to edit the registers of Innocent IV and allowed to occupy the table in the Library nearest to the Archives), and finally Pastor, a German, who prised 'open the door inch by inch' before Leo XIII appointed Cardinal Hergenröther as archivist with a specific brief to draw up a system for providing regular and easy access to accredited scholars.[6]

W.H. Bliss was to assume the mantle of Stevenson in 1887. Bliss had worked in the Bodleian Library, and he was to continue Stevenson's work in collecting copies of documents relating to British history. Bliss had problems of access that were not confronted by his more fortunate predecessor. His other main problem was the lack of support from home and the niggardlyness of the Treasury. It was now thought that a calendar would be a more useful tool, and it was apparent that a start should be made with the papal registers.

Here a consideration is needed of the immense series of the papal registers. In imitation of the emperors, the popes began to keep copies of their letters from at least the time of Pope Simplicius (468–83). Gregory the Great had made records on papyrus rolls. An eleventh-century copy of the fifth to the tenth years of the register of John VIII (872–82), and registers of letters for the first eleven years of Gregory VII (1073–85) have survived, and we have references to registers of the twelfth-century popes,[7] but the main series, without major interruptions, begins with Pope Innocent III in 1198. This series, the Regesta Vaticana, to 1590 (Sixtus V), consists of about two thousand volumes. The Regesta Lateranensia, from 1389 to 1892, comprises 2467 volumes: they contain 'common' letters, and the editor's approach to them can be swift; as they are formulaic in construction it is not necessary to record more than the details, in a succinct way. The third series of papal registers, the Regesta Avignonensia, extend from John XXII to Benedict XIII. There are some 350 volumes, and they are on paper, not parchment. The Avignon 'common' registers remained at Avignon during the Great

---

[4] Chadwick, *Catholicism*, p. 136.
[5] Leonard Boyle in *JEH* 31 (1980), p. 265, reviewing Owen Chadwick's *Catholicism*.
[6] Boyle, ibid., and Chadwick pp. 89–90.
[7] On these see Uta-Renate Blumenthal, 'Papal Registers in the Twelfth Century', *Proceedings of the 7th International Congress of Medieval Canon Law*, ed. P.A. Linehan, Monumenta Iuris Canonici Series C: Subsidia, vol. 8 (Città del Vaticano, 1988).

Schism, and the Roman obedience opened its own registers. At the end of the Great Schism in 1404 they were transferred to the datary. There were also additional series of more specialist registers: the register of the imperial question (the famous RNI), registers of supplications or petitions to the pope from 1342 to 1899 (7365 volumes), and registers of briefs (from 1417 onwards). In 1896, the supplications to the pope from British and Irish petitioners, made between 1342 and 1419 and entered in the first 99 registers of supplications, were published by W.H. Bliss.[8]

Bliss's task was to commence the calendaring of the papal registers, starting with the registers of Pope Innocent III. The Deputy Keeper of the Public Records, Henry Maxwell Lyte, went to Rome in 1890 and drew up the rules for the formation of the Calendar (PRO 1/55/216). The rules were not printed at the beginning of the Calendar, and no reference was made to where they might be found. This was unfortunate, and on that matter the Deputy Keeper (Maxwell Lyte) is very much to blame. This was one of the main criticisms made by reviewers. Mary Bateson, reviewing the first two volumes in the *English Historical Review* 11 (1896),[9] surmised, for example, that the principle had been to calendar all personal and place- names, but nowhere was this stated, and it had not been adhered to in every case. As every editor and calendarer knows, decisions have to be made, and whether right or wrong, maintained consistently throughout the work.

The second criticism concerned the lack of an introduction. Here it is necessary to make a comparison with other contemporary record publications. Not till later did introductions reach the standards that one has now come to accept as necessary for the complete understanding of the text.[10] First of all, details of editorial principles and decisions are vital. Second, the manuscript needs to be set in context, both archival and historical. The Preface to the first volume, a matter of only five pages, gives only the briefest account of what is to be found in papal registers. It referred to what had already been published. For Innocent III, Baluze's edition of 1682, reproduced by Migne in the 1890s, was old and inaccurate. For Honorius III, only the first volume of Pressutti's calendar had so far been published.[11] Reference was also made to the work of the French School at Rome, which was undertaking complete calendars of the popes for the period covered by Bliss's first volume (excluding Honorius III, because of the Abbé Pressutti's calendar).[12]

---

[8] *CPL, Petitions to the Pope* vol. i, *Clement VI to the Anti-Pope Benedict XIII* (HMSO London, 1896).

[9] *EHR* 11 (1896), pp. 562–4.

[10] One might cite here as exemplary the introductions of C.W. Foster to *Final Concords of the County of Lincoln* and of F.M. Stenton to *Transcripts of Charters Relating to Gilbertine Houses*, both published in the 1920s (Lincoln Record Society 17 and 19); and Sir Cyril Flower, *Introduction to the Curia Regis Rolls* (Selden Society 62, 1944).

[11] P. Pressutti, cal. *Regesta Honorii III*, 2 vols (Rome, 1888–95).

[12] It was Pope Leo XIII himself who had entrusted the edition of the register of Honorius III to the Abbé Pressutti and that of Pope Clement V to the Benedictines of St Paul

These were to be published in fascicules (a distinct advantage where there are demands for signs of progress from sponsoring institutions or governments) and started to come out from 1883. We will reserve comments on this series for a moment, and first return to Bliss and the Introduction. In the short account so far given by Bliss, one cannot help but notice that the names of Pressutti and Auvray are misspelt.

Another major criticism concerned the Index, especially the cross-referencing of proper names. On the question of place-name identification, some of the Irish reviewers went to town – this was to remain a major complaint until the Irish were closely involved in the project – and a peculiarly vitriolic attack was made not only on Bliss but also on Bateson by the Reverend Bernard MacCarthy in the following issue of the *English Historical Review*, on the translation of a passage in a letter of Gregory IX concerning Scotland.[13] To establish the text MacCarthy used Theiner's *Vetera monumenta Hibernorum et Scotorum*.[14] MacCarthy had already reviewed Bliss's Calendar in the *Irish Ecclesiastical Record*.[15] While some of his points of criticism were not without foundation – the lack of any kind of diplomatic discussion of the documents or of any explanation of technical terms, and the omissions and mistranslations – the charge that the work was the 'outcome of culpable apathy' which was to be 'more reprehended than sheer incapacity' was, to say the least, uncharitable.[16] From this point onwards, the management and financing of the *Calendar of Papal Letters* (CPL) became a political football between the English and the Irish, who were joined enthusiastically by the Welsh, in no less a person than Lloyd George, in English-bashing. On 22 August 1895, Hansard reported the questions that were raised in Parliament concerning the first two volumes of the Calendar. The summaries were said to be 'seriously imperfect', the translations of Latin contain 'gross blunders', and the arrangement is 'not chronological, *as the instructions to the editors require*'. The impossibility of this procedure was realized at least by 1897, when further questions in the House drew the response that 'the extract order' (that is, the order of the letters in the register) was pursued by other scholars of different nationalities who worked on similar

---

outside the Walls; B. Galland, 'La publication des registres de lettres pontificales par l'Ecole française de Rome', *Bibliothèque de l'Ecole des Chartes* 154 (1996), pp. 627, 628.

[13] *EHR* 11 (1896), pp. 813–14. MacCarthy himself was apparently not clear about the significance of the phrase *nullo medio* (without intermediary) for which he had castigated both Bliss and Bateson, the point being that the Scottish church was regarded as a daughter church of Rome, answerable directly to the papacy without any intermediary in the shape of a metropolitan. See *CPL* i, p. 161 for Bliss's erroneous précis.

[14] Augustin Theiner, *Vetera monumenta Hibernorum et Scotorum historiam illustrantia . . . a. d. 1216–1547* (Rome, 1864), no. xc, pp. 34–5.

[15] *Irish Ecclesiastical Record* 3rd series 16 (4), April 1895, pp. 329–43.

[16] Ibid., p. 339. He had, however, pointed out that Bliss was 'a solitary summarist', as opposed to the twelve French scholars at work on Gregory IX's register. Cf. below p. 201.

projects in the Vatican Archives. More to the point was the desirability of providing a chart, giving the dates of the documents in sequence, as supplied by the French, while printing the entries in their registered sequence. Many of the allegations were grossly offensive and unfair. One salient point raised in 1895 was 'whether it is the case that the Record Department employ only 1 person on this important historical work at a total cost of £380, whereas the French Government employ 12 scholars for the same purpose'.[17] Mary Bateson had also pointed out an omission from the register of Honorius III (referred to by Shirley as in the Marini Transcripts) and two omissions from the registers of Innocent IV, which appear in a printed source, Matthew Paris's Additamenta, edited by Luard in 1882 as volume vi of the *Chronica Majora*. She had also drawn attention to the irregular printed references.[18] Another decision that was not acceptable was the omission of all letters sent out 'in eundem modum', that is to say letters sent to multiple recipients such as crowned heads, religious orders and so forth, many of these letters being of great historical value. Bateson also drew attention to the maintenance of the Roman calendar, without provision of the English equivalents; a decision which has caused great aggravation to users of the Calendar over the years.

The fact of the matter was that too much had been expected of Bliss in a very short time. He had been engaged to work on another project, not just the registers. He had been forced to prepare material at great speed, and without much support, and worst of all he became the victim of vicious sectarian and nationalist attack. Realization that too much had been required of Bliss resulted in Charles Johnson, an Assistant Keeper in the Record Office, being sent to Rome to help him with the necessary corrections to volumes 1 to 3. Johnson provided the index to volume 2, which covered the years 1305–42, and collaborated with Bliss in the production of volume 3 (1342–62). Johnson's appointment was only temporary, until a permanent assistant could be found. This assistant was Jesse Twemlow, appointed in 1896, and Bliss and Twemlow together produced volume 4 (1362–1404) which came out in 1902. Twemlow drew up a list of Addenda and Corrigenda to the previous volumes, which was printed here, and also a section showing the chronological arrangement of the *litterae secretae*, and a list of English and Welsh papal auditors. He, too, provided the subject index. Bliss was assisted in the identification of Irish place-names by Fr M. Costello, OP, of San Clemente – so was to begin a happy association between the Calendars and San Clemente, culminating in the appointment of Fr Leonard Boyle as general editor in 1970. By 1902, the volumes covered the period of the papacy at Avignon (1309–76). Twemlow was from Christ Church, Oxford. He had also been at the Ecole des Chartes. Relations between

---

[17] *Hansard* vol. 36 (22 Aug. 1895), cols 560–1, and (26 Aug.) cols 838–48; vol. 52 (2 Aug. 1897), cols 89–91.

[18] *EHR* 11, pp. 562–4, at p. 563. Bateson's own reference to Shirley no. 145 is incorrect: it is in fact Appendix V no. 11, pp. 536–7 that she is referring to.

Twemlow and Bliss were not exactly cordial, attributed by some to Bliss's dislike of Twemlow's French wife (who was related to one of the French editors, Maurice Prou), but more likely due to the fact that Twemlow's standards of accuracy were closer to those of the French scholars engaged on fully inclusive calendars of the registers of the thirteenth-century popes. After producing two volumes with Bliss, Twemlow then produced nine further volumes on his own, published between 1904 and 1960, bringing the project up to 1492. He was lecturer, and then professor of Palaeography, at the University of Liverpool until 1949, and remained editor of the *CPL* after the death of Bliss in 1909. Twemlow's long involvement with the Calendar – his final volume, 14, appearing posthumously in 1960 – allowed for addenda and corrigenda and for improvements and additions to be made. Experts were called in to help with the Irish place-names and with the indices of persons and subjects. A papal itinerary was provided in volume 10 for Nicholas V, but volume 11 noted 'Itineraries of popes Calixtus III and Pius II were compiled by the Editor from the marginal dates in this volume, similar to the Itinerary of Pope Nicholas V ... They have been omitted, by direction of the Deputy Keeper of the Public Records, as not directly bearing on the history of Great Britain and Ireland.'

The Avignon popes had therefore been covered for the British entries, but the problem was that the editors had confined their work to the Vatican Registers for the common letters and had not used the Avignon Registers (so named because they remained in Avignon until 1783), which contain much more material. Indeed, the Vatican registers for this period are parchment copies of the Avignon paper volumes, and much less inclusive. Patrick Zutshi estimates the ratio to be 10 to 1 in favour of Avignon, and he makes the point that therefore the calendars cannot be relied upon to include all the information.[19] No doubt if they had consulted the Avignon registers the rate of progress would have been slower, but without the careful work of the French editors, the researcher would be thrown back on an examination of the originals to be sure of getting all the relevant material. This lacuna in the British Calendars is pointed out by Leslie Macfarlane and Leonard Boyle. Additional criticisms are made by Dr Zutshi in his 'Letters of the Avignon Popes (1305–78)'.[20] In assessing the use of the fourteenth-century calendars for Scottish searchers, D.E.R. Watt pointed to certain faults in volume 3 (1342–62): no cross-references between the Calendar of Petitions and the Calendar of Papal Letters (or Theiner's *Monumenta*, a work of importance for Scotland),[21] wrong Christian names, surnames not always correctly tran-

---

[19] P.N.R. Zutshi, 'The Registers of Common Letters of Pope Urban V (1362–1370) and Pope Gregory XI (1370–1378)', *JEH* 51 (2000), pp. 497–508, at p. 499.

[20] In *England and her Neighbours 1066–1453. Essays in honour of Pierre Chaplais*, ed. Michael Jones and Malcolm Vale (Hambledon, 1989), pp. 259–75, at p. 262.

[21] See above n. 14. Theiner had been prefect of the Vatican Archives from 1855 to 1870.

scribed, omission of entries and of details about petitioners, and occasionally, inaccurate marginal dates. While some inaccuracy was to be expected, Watt clearly thought the percentage of errors still too high. He did, however, record some improvement to volumes 3 and 4 and noted the calendarers' inclusion of the headings to the different sections: the letters 'secrete', issued by the Chamber, and the letters 'communes', issued by the Chancery, and the letters 'de curia', from the decisions taken in the Consistory.[22]

The National Schools

The Ecole Française in Rome was created in 1874. The cardinal librarian at the time was J.B. Pitra, a Frenchman and a Benedictine from the abbey of Solesmes.[23] In the following year the Ecole was installed in the magnificent Palazzo Farnese, and most significantly its head, Auguste Geoffroy, was a historian who wished the Ecole to pursue historical as well as archaeological research.[24]

By 1891 all the thirteenth-century papal registers from Gregory IX onwards had been assigned to French editors and between 1884 and 1960 the French completed editions of all the papal registers from Gregory IX (1227–41) to Benedict XI (1304), the so-called 2nd series.[25] In 1960 Robert Fawtier signalled the achievement in an article published in *Mélanges d'Archéologie et d'Histoire*, drawing attention to 'the type of disinterested research much praised now, but practised as little as possible'.[26] A comparison between the Bliss Calendar's entries for Pope Gregory IX and the four volumes edited by Lucien Auvray (the first was published in 1896) shows the strength of the French series on the grounds of layout and completeness, but it was not until 1955 that the registers of Gregory IX were completed by other members of the French School, Mme Vitte-Clémencet and M. Louis Carolus-Barré, with the indexes (1) chronological, (2) of Incipits, (3) of names and places, and (4) of subjects, together with a concordance to Potthast. If two cheers are raised for the Auvray edition on the grounds of the inclusion of the address, incipit, dating clause, and date translated, together with the folio number, year and cap. number for each entry, one can be raised for Bliss, who identified the place-names and their counties,

---

[22] D.E.R. Watt, 'Sources for Scottish History of the Fourteenth Century in the Archives of the Vatican', *Scottish Historical Review* 32 (1953), pp. 101–22, mainly pp. 104–10. The 'de curia' headings had been noticed from their occurrence under Innocent IV; see *CPL* i, p. 227.
[23] Bruno Gallard, 'La publication des registres de lettres pontificales par l'Ecole française de Rome', *Bibliothèque de l'Ecole des Chartes* 154 (1996), pp. 625–34, at pp. 625–6.
[24] Chadwick, *Catholicism*, pp. 88–9.
[25] See Appendix, p. 206.
[26] 'Un grand achèvement de l'Ecole française de Rome: la publication des registres des papes du xiiie siècle', vol. 62 (1960), pp. i–xiii. The quote is on p. ix (my translation).

while the French were content to leave them in their registered form.[27] Clearly Bliss had the advantage here. The English user is, therefore, fortunate in being able to sail the larger text of Auvray with the aid of the steering of Bliss in some instances, and when we consider that Bliss enabled many searchers to begin their work as early as 1893, we have cause to be grateful. Auvray himself had remarked 'Les *Calendars* de M. W.-H. Bliss, *tout utiles qu'ils sont*, ne sont pas un Bullaire et ne sauraient en tenir lieu'.[28] Unlike Bliss, the French editors were fortunate in that they were given the time to pause, reflect, and compile the full indices, detailed introductions, and Tables.

They also undertook the editing of the registers of the Avignon popes: the 3rd series. Between 1902 and virtually the present they have been concerned with the pontificates from John XXII (1316–34) to Gregory XI (1370–78).

The Austrian Contribution

It was clear that the scholarly world was the poorer without a proper and modern edition of Innocent III's registers. The Abbé Migne's *Patrologia Latina*, volumes 214–16, was the first full edition of Innocent's register, published in Paris in 1855. It relied heavily on the work of scholars of previous centuries, the seventeenth-century Baluze and the eighteenth-century La Porte du Theil. Migne did a great service in bringing all the material together, but basically the existence of his volumes slowed up the work of editing, with Leo XIII commissioning the Roman cleric Paolo Pressutti to edit the registers of Innocent's successor, Honorius III, and the French picking up the baton with Honorius's successor, Pope Gregory IX. A new edition of the registers of Pope Innocent III, in spite of his importance, was not commenced until the Austrian Kulturinstitut in Rome decided to undertake a complete critical edition in 1952, following important ground-clearing work by the late Fr Friedrich Kempf. Their first volume appeared in 1964, and at the time of writing (2003) eight volumes have been completed. These are the registers for the first (1198–99), second (1199–1200), fifth (1202–3), sixth (1203–4), seventh (1204–5) and eighth years (1205–6). Volumes 3 and 4 for the incomplete third and the lost fourth years (1200–1, 1201–2) will be reconstructed. There is no register for the pope's seventeenth year (1214–15). Anyone not convinced of the importance of an entirely new text only has to take a look at the old, unexplained, and corrupt text of the pope's register in Migne volume 215, cols 277–554 for the seventh year, or at the pages for 7 Innocent III in the *CPL* and compare it with this edition for the same year.

[27] A comparison can be made, for example, between the presentation of a grant of protection to the bishop of Exeter, Auvray vol. i, col. 12, no. 18, and *CPL* i, p. 117; and for the place-names between Auvray, vol. 4, Index, 'Cathefel', and Bliss, p. 117 and Index, 'Catfield'.

[28] My italics. Auvray, vol. 1, p. iii n. 2.

The British and Irish Editors

One of the main difficulties for the British editors was that they did not have the support of a national school. The British School in Rome did not come into existence until 1901 and it had little interest in medieval research until 1931. The founding committee had had a meeting with Maxwell Lyte, who promised support, but there was no suggestion that the PRO should be involved or the editors of the *CPL* project.[29] When medieval research began to be promoted after 1931, Geoffrey Barraclough was to do some fine work but he was not concerned with the Calendar. After the Second World War, the names of Shirley Bridges, Research Student in 1948, Leslie MacFarlane (1949), Donald Bullough (1951) and Peter Partner (1952), were added to those medievalists who were concerned primarily with written sources. At the risk of disfavour, it would not be incorrect to say that the British School's emphasis has remained strongly on archaeological research, though the use of written evidence has not been neglected in recent years when medieval sites have been excavated.

After the war, in times of austerity and saving, the PRO decided to discontinue all the calendars of material – no matter its importance – that was not actually in Chancery Lane. That was in 1947: it took twenty-three years to revive the *CPL*, and then in other hands. When the PRO ceased to publish in 1960 (the last volume came out in 1960 as volume 14) the Irish Manuscripts Commission took over the responsibility of publishing future volumes in the series. There was a backlog of material collected by Twemlow, and volume 14 was his last volume, posthumously published. The foreword by Sir David Evans, then Deputy Keeper, recorded that the index of persons and places had been compiled by the Rev. John Brady and that of subjects by Mr R.L. Storey of the Record Office.

Great changes were on the way. The British School at Rome was sounded out but it was reluctant to take over the project. In the end the enthusiasm of the Irish Manuscripts Commission won the day, and after discussions it was decided to run the series in future with an editor appointed and paid for by the Irish government. The PRO was to approve the selection and provide for training in palaeography, diplomatic, and editorial procedure. When a suitable candidate was finally found in 1952, the notion that the editor would work from transcripts and microfilms proved unworkable. It was not until 1967 that a new initiative resulted in the appointment by the Irish Manuscripts Commission in 1970 of an editor, Dr Michael Haren, to be paid as an Irish civil servant. Two years later in 1972 an English editor, Mrs Anne Fuller, was appointed. She was to be supported by annual grants from the

---

[29] On the history of the School, see Andrew Wallace-Hadrill, *The British School at Rome: One Hundred Years* (Rome, 2001), pp. 20–2 on the foundation, pp. 219–20 for the list of Scholars mentioned.

British Academy. The editors were appointed to edit the volumes for a specific papacy, not to divide the work according to the type of register, whether Vatican registers or Lateran registers.

The Catalogues

Two persons closely connected with the British editorial project for the papal registers provided guides or catalogues. The first was Dr Leslie Macfarlane. His splendid outline for British users has not been supplemented or bettered for its purpose. This was published in *Archives* volume IV for 1959, pp. 29–44, and 84–101,[30] and then as a separate pamphlet. The second was Leonard Boyle. As professor at Toronto, he taught a course on 'The Vatican Archives'. This guide, from another first-rate scholar, who knew the archives so well as a user, lived up to all that was to be expected. It came out in 1972 and covers the Archives from a general point of view.[31] A ten-year project of the University of Michigan to provide a new catalogue was completed in 1998 and published by the Oxford University Press.[32] This has not replaced earlier printed guides.[33]

The Revised Series

In any editorial project, the general editor is all-important. None was better suited to the task than Leonard E. Boyle, OP, who from February 1955 to June 1957 had been employed by the National Library of Ireland together with the PRO to continue the *CPL*. He was probably the foremost palaeographer of his day, with a unique knowledge of medieval manuscripts. As professor at Toronto from 1961, each summer he returned to San Clemente in May, and spent July and August in England and Ireland working on the Calendar at the PRO and the National Library. From 1970 until his death Leonard Boyle acted as General Editor. He continued to hold the post (by no means a sinecure) after his appointment as Prefect of the Vatican Library in 1984. J. Ambrose Raftis, writing an obituary of Leonard Boyle in the journal of the Pontifical Institute, *Mediaeval Studies* volume 62 (2000), said

---

[30] 'The Vatican Archives, with Special Reference to Sources for British Medieval History, I', and 'The Vatican Archives, with Special Reference to Sources for British and Irish Medieval History, II'.

[31] L.E. Boyle, *A Survey of the Vatican Archives and of its Medieval Holdings*, Pontifical Institute of Mediaeval Studies, Subsidia Mediaevalia i (Toronto, Canada, 1972).

[32] Francis X. Blouin, general editor, Leonard A. Coombs and Elizabeth Yakel, archivists, and Claudia Carlen and Katherine J. Gill, historians.

[33] It was reviewed by the Prefect of the Archives, Fr Sergei Pagano, and described as 'discutibile' (questionable), 'Una Discutibile "Guida" degli Archivi Vaticani', *Archivum Historiae Pontificiae* 37 (1999), pp. 199–201.

'Almost as a sequence to the Second Vatican Council, this appointment "opened the doors" to this vast literary treasure'. Under Leonard Boyle's general editorship, volumes 15, 16, 17 pt 1, and 18 appeared, and he himself provided an introduction 'The Papal Chancery at the end of the Fifteenth Century' and an Appendix, 'List of Bulls lost from the Lateran Registers of Innocent VIII', to volume 15, the first of the Revised Series.[34]

The Revised Series, covering both Vatican and Lateran Registers, has taken into account the varying requirements of calendaring the different types of register. Dr Haren's first volume of Innocent VIII's Lateran Registers allowed a formulaic approach. He provided a frontispiece photograph of an entry, the full transcription, and then the English calendared entry. The letter chosen is a faculty to Donald, elect of Derry, to be consecrated by the bishop of his choice, with an instruction concerning his oath to the pope. The reader can therefore swiftly and easily follow the editor's process. The calendar is well set out on the page and is easy to use, with a number for each entry, the date, and the reference to the Lateran Register, with folio number.

New Techniques of Reproduction

It is now possible to gain access to the Registra Vaticana 1–136 (John VIII to Benedict XII (876–1342) on CD ROM. These can be purchased from the Archivio Segreto Vaticano for a sum that is not outside the range of research libraries. However, in spite of the advantages of 'microfilmage' as the French call it, the palaeographical difficulties of the later registers are clear for all to see from the frontispieces of volumes 14 and 15, and of course there is much more to the understanding than simply reading the letter.[35] While no one is against formularization and the simple listing of information, where possible, and a more streamlined approach for the common letters, the same is not true for the Vatican series. Short cuts must be found, where appropriate, but not at the expense of compromising the understanding of the documents. Web sites will be needed and the provision on-line of all the printed volumes will be a great step forward.[36] For the French, the hope is that their 3rd series will be completed; for the British and Irish, the hope must be that the work can be continued at least up to the Reformation.

---

[34] Many of the details of this paragraph have been taken from J. Ambrose Raftis's obituary, pp. vii–xxvi, which includes a photograph of Boyle and a bibliography of his works. The quotation is on p. x.

[35] For the British and Irish entries in the papal registers, the National Library of Ireland holds microfilm copies of the relevant material in the Lateran Registers from 1484 and in the Vatican Registers from 1492 onwards. For Scotland there is microfilm material from the Vatican Archives in Glasgow.

[36] The French (the Ecole Française de Rome and the Institut de Recherche et d'Histoire des Textes) have produced CD ROMs of all the volumes so far published, 32 for the thirteenth-century popes and 48 for those of the fourteenth century, published by Brepols (Turnhout).

Appendix

Registers of the Thirteenth-Century Popes
(published in the 2nd series of the BEFAR =
Bibliothèque des Ecoles françaises d'Athènes et de Rome)

1. *Les registres de Grégoire IX* (1227–41), ed. L. Auvray, S. Clémencet and L. Carolus Barré, 4 vols in 13 fasc., BEFAR 2nd ser. ix: Paris, 1890–1955
2. *Les registres d'Innocent IV* (1243–54), ed. E. Berger, 4 vols in 13 fasc., BEFAR 2nd ser. i: Paris, 1884–1921
3. *Les registres d'Alexandre IV* (1254–61), ed. C. Bourel de la Roncière, J. de Loye, P. Hellouin de Cénival and A. Coulon, 3 vols in 8 fasc., BEFAR 2nd ser. xv: Paris, 1895–1959
4. *Les registres d'Urbain IV* (1261–64), ed. J. Guiraud and S. Clémencet, 4 vols in 11 fasc., BEFAR 2nd ser. xiii: Paris, 1892–1958
5. *Les registres de Clément IV* (1265–68), ed. E. Jordan, 1 vol. in 6 fasc., BEFAR 2nd ser. xi: Paris, 1893–1945
6. *Les registres de Grégoire X et de Jean XXI* (1272–77), ed. J. Guiraud and E. Cadier, 1 vol. in 6 fasc., BEFAR 2nd ser. xii: Paris, 1892–1960
7. *Les registres de Nicolas III* (1277–80), ed. J. Gay and S. Vitte, 1 vol. in 5 fasc., BEFAR 2nd ser. xiv: Paris, 1898–1938
8. *Les registres de Martin IV* (1281–83), ed. F. Soehnée, G. de Puybaudet, R. Poupardin and F. Olivier Martin, 1 vol. in 8 fasc., BEFAR 2nd ser. xvi: Paris, 1901–35
9. *Les registres d'Honorius IV* (1285–7), ed. M. Prou, 1 vol. in 4 fasc., BEFAR 2nd ser. vii: Paris, 1886–88
10. *Les registres de Nicolas IV* (1288–92), ed. E. Langlois, 2 vols in 9 fasc., BEFAR 2nd ser. v: Paris, 1887–93
11. *Les registres de Boniface VIII* (1294–1303), ed. A. Thomas, M. Faucon, G. Digard and R. Fawtier, 4 vols in 17 fasc., BEFAR 2nd ser. iv: Paris, 1884–1939
12. *Le registre de Benoit XI* (1303–4), ed. Ch. Grandjean, 1 vol. in 5 fasc., BEFAR 2nd ser. ii: Paris, 1883–1905

Registers and Letters of the Fourteenth-Century Popes
(published in the 3rd series of the BEFAR, unless otherwise noted)

13. Clement V (1305–14)
    Les registres de Clément V, ed. the Benedictines, 8 vols (Rome, 1884–94). Tables by R. Fawtier, Y. Lanhers, C. Vogel and G. Mollat, 2 fasc. (1948–57)

14. John XXII (1316–34)
    Lettres communes, ed. G. Mollat, 16 vols in 31 fasc. and 1 fasc. introduction (1904–47)
    Lettres secrètes et curiales se rapportant à la France, ed. A. Coulon and S. Clémencet, 10 fasc. (1900–)

15. Benedict XII (1334–42)
    Lettres communes, ed. J.-M. Vidal, 3 vols in 6 fasc. (1902–11)
    Lettres closes, patentes et curiales se rapportant à la France, ed. G. Daumet, 1 vol. in 3 fasc. (1899–1920)
    Lettres closes et patentes intéressant les pays autres que la France, ed. J.-M. Vidal and G. Mollat, 2 vols in 6 fasc. (1913–50)

16. Clement VI (1342–52)
    Lettres secrètes et curiales se rapportant à la France, ed. E. Déprez, J. Glénisson and G. Mollat, 3 vols in 6 fasc. (1925–61)
    Lettres secrètes et curiales intéressant les pays autres que la France, ed. E. Déprez and G. Mollat, 1 vol. in 3 fasc. (1960–61)

17. Innocent VI (1352–62)
    Lettres closes, patentes et curiales se rapportant à la France, ed. E. Déprez, 1 fasc. (1909)
    Lettres secrètes et curiales, ed. P. Gasnault and M.-H. Laurent, 4 vols (1959–)

18. Urban V (1362–70)
    Lettres secrètes et curiales se rapportant à la France, ed. P. Lecacheux and G. Mollat, 1 vol. in 4 fasc. (1902–55)
    Lettres communes, ed. M.-H. Laurent, P. Gasnault and M. Hayez, 11 vols including 2 index vols (1954–86)
    Les registres d'Urbain V (1362–3). Recueil des bulles de ce pape, ed. M. Dubrulle (Paris, 1926)
    Lettres d'Urbain V (1362–70), ed. A. Fierens and C. Tihon, 2 vols, Analecta Vaticano-Belgica ix, xv (Brussels, 1928–32)

19. Gregory XI (1370–78)
    Lettres secrètes et curiales se rapportant à la France, ed. L. Mirot, H. Jassemin, J. Vielliard, G. Mollat and R. Labande, 1 vol. in 5 fasc. (1935–57)
    Lettres secrètes et curiales intéressant les pays autres que la France, ed. G.

Mollat, 1 vol. in 3 fasc. (1962–65)
Lettres communes, ed. A.-M. Hayez, 3 vols (1992–93)
Lettres de Grégoire XI (1371–1378), ed. C. Tihon, 4 vols, Analecta Vaticano-Belgica xi, xx, xxv, xxviii (Brussels and Rome, 1958–75)

The Calendar of Papal Letters
(Calendar of Entries in the Papal Registers relating to Great Britain and Ireland)

Vol. 1.	Innocent III to Benedict XI 1198–1304, ed. W.H. Bliss, HMSO (London, 1893)
Vol. 2.	Clement V to Benedict XII 1305–1342, ed. W.H. Bliss, with an index by C. Johnson (London, 1895)
Vol. 3.	Clement VI (1342–1352) and Innocent VI (1352–1362) 1342–1362, ed. W.H. Bliss and C. Johnson (London, 1897)
	Urban V (1362–1370), Gregory XI (1371–1378), Urban VI (1378–1389), Clement VII, anti-pope (1378–1394), Boniface IX (1389–1404)
Vol. 4.	1362–1396, ed. W.H. Bliss and J.A. Twemlow (London, 1902)
Vol. 5.	1396–1404, ed. W.H. Bliss and J.A. Twemlow (London, 1904)
	Innocent VII (1404–1406), Gregory XII (1406–1415), Alexander V (1409–1410), John XXIII (1410–1415, deposed)
Vol. 6.	1404–1415, ed. J.A. Twemlow (London, 1904)
Vol. 7.	Martin V (1417–1431) 1417–1427, ed. J.A. Twemlow (London, 1906)
Vol. 8.	Martin V (1417–1431), Eugenius IV (1431–1447) 1428–1437, ed. J.A. Twemlow (London, 1909)
Vol. 9.	Eugenius IV (1431–1447) 1438–1447, ed. J.A. Twemlow (London, 1912)
Vol. 10.	Nicholas V (1447–1455) 1447–1455, ed. J.A. Twemlow (London, 1915)
Vol. 11.	Calixtus III (1455–1458), Pius II (1458–1464) 1455–1464, ed. J.A. Twemlow (London, 1921)
Vol. 12.	Pius II (1458–1464) and Paul II (1464–1471) 1458–1471, ed. J.A. Twemlow (London, 1933)

Sixtus IV (1471–1484)
Vol. 13. Part 1, 1471–1475, ed. J.A. Twemlow (London, 1955)
Part 2, 1474–1484, ed. J.A. Twemlow (London, 1955)

Innocent VIII (1484–1492)
Vol. 14. Vatican and Lateran Registers (1st year), ed. J.A. Twemlow (London, 1960)
Vol. 15. Lateran Registers (1484–1492), ed. Michael J. Haren (Dublin, 1978)

Alexander VI (1492–1503)
Vol. 16. Lateran Registers part i (1492–1498), ed. Anne P. Fuller (Dublin, 1986)
Vol. 17. Part 1, Lateran Registers part ii (1495–1503), ed. Anne P. Fuller (Dublin, 1994)
Part 2, Vatican Registers (1492–1503), ed. Anne P. Fuller (Dublin, 1998)

Pius III (1503) and Julius II (1503–1513)
Vol. 18. Vatican Registers (1503–1513), Lateran Registers (1503–1508), ed. Michael J. Haren (Dublin, 1989)

Julius II
Vol. 19. Lateran registers (1505–1513), ed. Michael J. Haren (Dublin, 1998)

Postscript

No account dealing with the British Isles would be complete without reference to the Scottish material, in the publication of which the Scottish History Society has been the rock. C. Burns and F. McGurk have calendared the letters of Clement VII (1378–94) and Benedict XIII (1394–1419) of Avignon to Scotland. And no roll call of work on fifteenth-century Scottish sources in the Vatican Archives would be complete without reference to the immense contribution over many years of Annie I. Dunlop (née Cameron). With others she has been the driving force behind the Calendars of Scottish Supplications to Rome between 1418 and 1447,[37] and on the Apostolic Camera.[38]

---

[37] *Calendar of Scottish Supplications to Rome, 1418–22*, ed. E.R. Lindsay and Annie I. Cameron; *1423–1428*, ed. Annie I. Dunlop; *1428–1432*, ed. A.I. Dunlop and I.B. Cowan; *1433–1447*, ed. A.I. Dunlop and D. MacLauchlan (Scottish History Society 3rd series xxiii, xlviii (Edinburgh, 1934, 1956, 1970, and Glasgow, 1983).
[38] The Apostolic Camera and Scottish benefices 1418–1488, ed. A.I. Cameron (Oxford, 1934).

Bibliography of the Writings of David Smith

From 1973 to 2003 David Smith was sole general editor of the British Academy English Episcopal Acta series (from 2003 joint General Editor with Dr Philippa Hoskin). He was also general editor of the Lincoln Record Society from 1996 to 2002 and founding editor of the *Monastic Research Bulletin* from 1995 to 2001 (joint editor with Dr Martin Heale in 2002). From 1974 to 1979 he contributed an annual report entitled 'The British Archival Scene' in *Archives et Bibliothèques de Belgique*. Reviews are not included in this list of publications, and similarly excluded are his contributions to *Lexicon des Mittelalters* (Munich), the *Dictionnaire d'Histoire et de Géographie Ecclésiastiques* (Louvain) and *The Oxford Dictionary of National Biography*.

1972

'The Rolls of Hugh of Wells, Bishop of Lincoln 1209–35', *Bulletin of the Institute of Historical Research* 45, pp. 155–195.

1973

A Guide to the Archive Collections in the Borthwick Institute of Historical Research (Borthwick Text and Calendar 1).

1974

Calendar of the Register of Robert Waldby, Archbishop of York 1397 (Borthwick Text and Calendar 2).
'The episcopate of Richard, Bishop of Asaph: A Problem of Twelfth-Century Chronology', *Journal of the Historical Society of the Church in Wales* 24, pp. 9–12.

1975

Fasti Ecclesiae Anglicanae 1541–1837 iv: York Diocese (with J.M. Horn) (London).
'Archivists and Historical Research: A Personal View of the English Scene', *Archives et Bibliothèques de Belgique* 46, pp. 158–63.
'Lost Archiepiscopal Registers of York: The Evidence of Five Medieval Inventories', *Borthwick Institute Bulletin* 1, pp. 31–7.
'Archives of Genealogical Interest at the Borthwick Institute', *Genealogist's Magazine* 18, pp. 7–13, 83–7.

1976

'The Archivist's Personal Involvement in Historical Research', *Archives* 12, pp. 167–9.

'A Reconstruction of the York *sede vacante* Register, 1352–3', *Borthwick Institute Bulletin* 1, pp. 75–90.

1978

'The York Institution Act Books: Diocesan Registration in the Sixteenth Century', *Archives* 13, pp. 171–9.

1979

Medieval Latin Documents, series 1: Diocesan Records (Borthwick Palaeography Wallet 6).

1980

English Episcopal Acta i: Lincoln 1067–1185 (Oxford University Press for the British Academy).

A Supplementary Guide to the Archive Collections in the Borthwick Institute of Historical Research (Borthwick Text and Calendar 7).

1981

Guide to Bishops' Registers of England and Wales: A Survey from the Middle Ages to the Abolition of Episcopacy in 1646 (Royal Historical Society Guide and Handbook 11).

1982

'Thomas Cantilupe's Register: The Administration of the Diocese of Hereford 1275–1282', in *St Thomas Cantilupe, Bishop of Hereford: Essays in his Honour*, ed. M. Jancey (Hereford), pp. 83–101.

'Suffragan Bishops in the Medieval Diocese of Lincoln', *Lincolnshire History and Archaeology* xvii (1982), pp. 17–27.

1983

'A Reconstruction of the Lost Register of the Vicars-General of Archbishop Thoresby of York, part 1', *Borthwick Institute Bulletin* 3, pp. 29–61.

1984

Medieval Latin Documents, series 2: Probate Records (Borthwick Palaeography Wallet 8).

1985

'A Reconstruction of the Lost Register of the Vicars-General of Archbishop Thoresby of York, part 2', *Borthwick Institute Bulletin* 3, pp. 102–13.

1986

Fasti parochiales V: Deanery of Buckrose (Yorkshire Archaeological Society Record Series 143): completely revised and seen through the press, the original compiler N.A.H. Lawrence having died in 1973.
English Episcopal Acta iv: Lincoln 1186–1206 (Oxford University Press for the British Academy)

1987

'Hugh's Administration of the Diocese of Lincoln', in *St Hugh of Lincoln*, ed. H. Mayr-Harting (Oxford), pp. 19–47.
'The House of Crutched Friars at Farndale', *Borthwick Institute Bulletin* 4, pp. 16–17.

1988

Ecclesiastical Cause Papers at York: The Court of York 1301–1399 (Borthwick Text and Calendar 14).

1990

A Guide to the Archives of the Company of Merchant Adventurers in York (Borthwick Text and Calendar 16).

1991

(general editor) *Studies in Clergy and Ministry in Medieval England* (Borthwick Studies in History 1).
'The Conventual Seal of the Dominican Friary at Edinburgh', *Proceedings of the Society of Antiquaries of Scotland* 121, pp. 331–3.

1992

'Alexander Hamilton Thompson', *Some Historians of Lincolnshire* (Occasional Papers in Lincolnshire History and Archaeology 9), pp. 61–6.

1994

A Guide to the Archives of the Company of Merchant Taylors in the City of York (Borthwick List and Index 12)
Mashamshire Records: A Collection of Documents Relating to Masham and Mashamshire in the 17th and 18th centuries (Masham Workers' Educational Association).

1995

'The "Officialis" of the Bishop in Twelfth- and Thirteenth-Century England: Problems of Terminology', in *Medieval Ecclesiastical Studies in Honour of Dorothy M. Owen*, ed. M.J. Franklin and C. Harper-Bill (Woodbridge), pp. 201–220.

1996

The Company of Merchant Taylors in the City of York: Register of Admissions 1560–1835 (Borthwick List and Index 16).
The Parish Register of Masham 1599–1716 (Yorkshire Archaeological Society, Parish Register Section 161).
The Company of Merchant Adventurers in the City of York: Register of Admissions 1581–1835 (Borthwick List and Index 18).

1997

Archdeacons' Records (with C.C. Webb) (Historical Association Short Guide to Records).

1999

'The Exercise of the Probate Jurisdiction of the Medieval Archbishops of York', in *Life and Thought in the Northern Church c.1100–c.1700*, ed. D. Wood (Studies in Church History subsidia series 12).
Fasti Ecclesiae Anglicanae 1541–1837 ix: Lincoln Diocese (with J.M. Horn) (London).
(general editor) *The Church in Medieval York: Records Edited in Honour of Professor Barrie Dobson* (Borthwick Text and Calendar 24).
'The foundation of Chantries in the Chapel of St William on Ouse Bridge, York', in *The Church in Medieval York: Records Edited in Honour of Professor Barrie Dobson*, ed. D.M. Smith (Borthwick Text and Calendar 24).

2000

Bolton Priory Compotus 1286–1325 (with Ian Kershaw) (Yorkshire Archaeological Society Record Series 154).
The Acta of Hugh of Wells, Bishop of Lincoln 1209–1235 (Lincoln Record Society 88).
'Addenda and Corrigenda to David Knowles and Neville Hadcock, Medieval Religious Houses, England and Wales' (with C.N.L. Brooke), *Monastic Research Bulletin* 6, pp. 1–37.

2001

Heads of Religious Houses: England and Wales ii: 1216–1377 (with V.C.M. London) (Cambridge).

2003

The Court of York 1400–1499: A Handlist of the Cause Papers and an Index to the Archiepiscopal Court Books (Borthwick Text and Calendar 29).

2004

Fasti Ecclesiae Anglicanae 1541–1857 xi: Carlisle, Chester, Durham, Manchester, Ripon and Sodor and Man Dioceses (with Joyce Horn and Patrick Mussett) (London).

Supplement to the Guide to Bishops' Registers of England and Wales: A survey from the Middle Ages to the Abolition of Episcopacy in 1646 (Canterbury and York Society).

2005

English Episcopal Acta 30: Carlisle 1133–1292 (Oxford University Press for the British Academy).

Index

A. dean of Swinderby, 149
Abatun, chaplain of, see William
Abbots Bromley (Staffs), church of, 150
Aberdeen, bp of, 186
Abindon, master Richard de, 66
Abingdon, Edmund of, archbp of Canterbury, 84, 95, 106, 126–7, 130, 135–6
Ad', William de, canon of Ellerton on Spalding Moor, 65
Adam, dean of Titmarsh, 147
Adel (W.R. Yorks), rector of, see John
Adrian IV, pope, 67
Adwick on the Hill (W.R. Yorks), church of, 67
Agincourt (France), 181
Aissebi, knight of, see Ralph
Alan, chaplain of Siflingtuna, 146
  son of Henry earl of Brittany, 45
Albur', see Aubourn
Alexander III, pope, 4
  IV, pope, 100, 109, 206
  VI, pope, 209
  priest of Turlebi, 150
Alexus, Bartholomew, 101
Alford (Lincs), 40, 47
Alfrington (Devon), 164
Alice, wife of William of Willoughby, 47
Alnai, Ralph del, 146
Alvingham (Lincs), church of, 143–4
  land in, 144
  priory (Gilbertine) of, 143–4
Amiens (France), 184
Amwell, John de, rector of West Rasen, 53
Anagni (Italy), 4
Andrew the messenger, 129
  proctor of Maiden Bradley priory, 152
Arches, Osbern de, 29
Arundel, Thomas, bp of Ely, archbp of York, archbp of Canterbury, 179, 189
Arundell, Richard, 152
Asfordby (Leics), dean of, see Peter
Ashby, Geoffrey of, 106
Ashby cum Fenby (Lincs), rector of, see Barton, John de

Ashby in Lothingland (Suffolk), church of, 106
Askeby, John de, vicar of Great Limber, 61
Aspall, Geoffrey de, 182
Astone, 182
Aubourn, Albur' (Lincs), 149–50
  priest of, see Geoffrey
Aubourn, Sim' of, son of, see Geoffrey
Auckland, Roger of, 132
Aughton (E.R. Yorks), church of, 69–70
Autby (Lincs), church of, 50
  rector of, see Tynton, Robert de
Auvray, Lucien, 201–2
Avalon, Hugh of, bp of Lincoln, see Lincoln, Hugh of
Avenel, Robert of, 133
Avignon (France), 4, 58, 186, 196, 200, 209
Aylesby (Lincs), church of, 40
  rector of, see Clifford, Thomas; Falle, Nicholas de; Francisci, Palmer; Ludda, master Simon de; Ludda, Thomas de; Lughton, Alan de
Ayston, William, 164

Baldric, archdn of Leicester, 148
Baldwin, archbp of Canterbury, 78, 149–50
Baluze, Etienne, 197
Bangor, bp of, 183
Barcelona (Spain), 116
Bardney (Lincs), abbey (Benedictine) of, 44
Barker, Robert, 70
Barlow, Frank, 21
Barmer (Norfolk), church of, 98
  rector of, see Sydestone, William of
Barnet, East (Herts), 170
Barnoldby (Lincs), rector of, see Colston, William de; Ragenhall, Richard de; Skelet, William
Barnoldby, John of vicar of West Ravendale, 47
Barnoldswick (Lancs), 38
Barnstaple (Devon), priory (Cluniac)of, 23, 32, 37

Barnwell (Cambs), priory (Augustinian) of, 37
Barraclough, Geoffrey, 203
Barton, 170
Barton, John de, rector of South Kelsey, 54
　John de, rector of Ashby cum Fenby, rector of Eastnor, archdn of Hererford, 51, 54
Barton upon Humber (Lincs), St Mary's chapel at, 44
　St Peter's church at, 44, 46
Bath (Som), cathedral priory of, 24, 32, 37
　bp of, see Lewes, Robert of
Bath and Wells, bp of, see Shrewsbury, Ralph of
Bartholomew, bp of Exeter, 26
Bateson, Mary, 197–99
Battle (Sussex), abbey (Benedictine) of, 24, 35–7
Bayeux (France), 53
　bp of, see Odo
Bearpark (Co. Durham), chapel of, 95
Bearpark, Laurence of, 129
Beauchamp, family of, 86
　Guy, earl of Warwick, 89
　Thomas, earl of Warwick, 88–9, 179
　William, earl of Warwick, 87
Beaumont, Isabella, Lady Vescy 54–5
Beauport (Brittany), abbey of, 45, 48, 50
Becket, Thomas archbp of Canterbury, 26, 28, 84
Bedford (Beds), 153
Bedford Minor, prebend of, 56
Bedfordshire County Record Office, 11
Bedlington (Co. Durham), manor of, 137
Bedwyn, East (Wilts), 165
Bek, Anthony, bp of Durham, 47, 130, 133, 135–7
Belvoir (Leics), castle, 144
　priory, 149
Benedict XI, pope, 201, 206, 208
　XII, pope, 205, 207, 208
　XIII, pope, 196, 209
Benigthorn', priest of, see Gerard
Bentley, Richard, 5
Berger, Elle, 196
Berkshire, 172
　archdn's of, official of, 165
　sheriff of, 175
Bernai (France), abbey of, 37
Bersted, Stephen, bp of Chichester, 135
Berwick (Northumb), Franciscans at, 185
Beseby, Gilbert de, 145

Betun, Hugh de, rector of Linwood, 54–5
Beverley (E.R. Yorks), collegiate church of, 88
Beverley, St John of, 181
Bexwell (Norfolk), church of, 104
Biddick, Alexander de, 132
Bigby (Lincs), rector of, see Wacelyn, John; Wacelyn, William
Billesby, William de, rector of Wrawby, 60
Binbrook (Lincs), church of St Gabriel, 43
　church of St Mary, 43, 49
　rector of, see Copgrave, Robert
Binham (Norfolk), priory (Benedictine) of, 100
Birstal, Richard of, rector of Kirkburton, 151–2
　I., his brother, 151–2
Bishopstrowe (Wilts), church of, 168
Bitham, William de, rector of Thoresway, 54
Blackborough (Norfolk), priory (Benedictine nuns) of, 107
Blanch, Hugh, 102
　son of, see Petrinus
Blickling (Norfolk), church of, 102
Bliss, W.H., 196–202
Blockley, William of, 131
Blois, William of, bp of Lincoln, 155
Bluet, Ralph, 183
Blundeville, Thomas, bp of Norwich, 103
Blyborough (Lincs), rector of, see Bocking, Ralph, 127
Bolton, priory, 5
Bolyngton, John, canon of Ellerton on Spalding Moor, 66, 70
Bonaparte, Napoleon, 194
Boniface VIII, pope, 51, 206
Bookham (Surrey), 166
Booth, William, bp of Coventry and Lichfield, 177
Borkgrave, master John, 163
Boroughbridge (W.R. Yorks), 175, 184, and see Boroughshire
Boroughshire, dean of, see Kirkby Malzeard, R. of; Staveley, Henry of
Boston (Lincs), 174
Boteler, John, 39
Bourgchier, Thomas, archbp of Canterbury,
Boyle, Leonard, 199–200, 204–5
Boyton (Suffolk), church of, 168
Brabant (Belgium), 186
Brachenbergh, Thomas de, 145
Bradeford, John de, 168

Bradenstock, William, 164
Bradley, Adam of, 128, 131
Brady, John, 203
Bramfield, Alexander of, 128
Braundeston Robert de, rector of South Ferriby, 49
Bray, Roger of, 156
Braybrooke, Robert, bp of London, 179, 181, 187
Brayton, Thomas de, rector of South Kelsey, 53
Breay, Claire, 8, 16
Bredy, Little (Dorset), chapel of, 164
Bremerton, Walter de, 129, 133
Bret, Simon le, 155
Breton, Guy, rector of Wold Newton, rector of Hatton, 53, 55, 57
  John le, bp of Hereford, 174
  William le, 104
Brewer, William, bp of Exeter, 92
Brian, son of Hamelin, 143
Bricett, Great (Suffolk), priory (Augustinian) of, 31, 38
Bridges, Shirley, 203
Bridlington (E.R. Yorks), priory (Augustinian) of, 37, 62
Bridport (Dorset), rector of, see Kington, master Roger de
Brigsley (Lincs), rector of, see Kirmington, Richard of; Kirmington, Robert of
Brind (E.R. Yorks), 65, 74
Brittany, earl of, 144, and see Henry
Broad Chalke (Wilts), prebendary of, see Wodeford, John de
Brockhole (W.R. Yorks), wood called, 66–7
Brocklesby (Lincs), 48
  church of, 43, 44
Broghton, Alice, nun of Thicket, 65
Bromholm (Norfolk), priory (Cluniac) of, 107
Bromley (Kent), 170
Brooke, Christopher, 15–17, 24
Broun, Thomas, bp of Norwich, 107
Bruce, Robert, king of Scots, 185–6
Bruninghill, Robert de, 129
Bruntun, Robert de, 145–6
Bubwith (E.R. Yorks), church of, 74
  rector of, Stanford, Robert de
Buckden (Hunts), 179
Buckingham, John, bp of Lincoln, 174, 179
Buckland (Devon), knights hospitallers at, 23

priory (Cistercian) of, 37
Buildwas (Shrops), priory (Cistercian) of, 37
Buleford, Alan de, 146
Bullough, Donald, 203
Bulmer (N.R. Yorks), dean of, see Walter
Burghclere (Hamps), rector of, see Ragenhall, Richard de
Burghersh, Henry, bp of Lincoln, 42, 49, 51, 54–5, 58–9, 181–2
Burns, C., 209
Burton (Staffs), abbey (Benedictine) of, 99, 143, 150–1
  proctor of, see Hubert
Burton, Robert de, canon of Ellerton on Spalding Moor, 65
Burton Joyce (Notts), Church of, 57
Bury St Edmunds (Suffolk), abbey (Benedictine) of, 101
  abbot of, 156–7
  prior of, 142
Buslingthorpe (Lincs), church of, 45
Buslingthorpe, Richard de, 45
Bydic, Adam de, 166
Byspham, William, 69

Cabourne (Lincs), vicar of, see Limberg, Thomas de
Cadney (Lincs), 43
Caistor (Lincs), church of, 43
Caistor, Lambert of, vicar of West Ravendale, 47
Calixtus, dean of Kidderminster, 152
  III, pope, 200, 208
Cambridge, 8, 37, 99, 189
  St Radegund priory (Benedictine nuns) of, 107
  University of, 52
  Jesus College, 107
  Trinity College, 2
Camelton, John de, 153
Campden, master Henry of, rector of Gosbeck, 104
Campsey Ash (Suffolk), priory (Augustinian nuns) of, 107
Canons Ashby (Northants), priory (Augustinian) of, 99
Canterbury (Kent), 122, 170, 176
  archbp of, 20, 184, and see Arundel, Thomas; Baldwin; Becket, Thomas; Bourgchier, Thomas; Courtenay, William; Dover, Richard of; Grant, Richard; Kemp, John; Lanfranc; Langton, Stephen;

Canterbury (Kent), *cont.*
  archbp of, *cont.*
    Morton, John; Pecham, John; Reynolds, Walter; Savoy, Boniface of; Theobald; Walter, Hubert; Winchelsea, Robert
  archdn of, see Langton, Simon
  Arches, court of, 159–72
    dean of, 87, and see Idsworth, Henry
  Christ Church priory (Benedictine) of, 22, 25, 29, 37, 79, 95, 101, 136
  diocese of, 159
  St Augustine, priory (Benedictine) of, 22
  St Gregory, priory (Augustinian) of, 37
  St John the Baptist, hospital of, 21, 37
  vice-archdn of, see John; Ralph; Robert
Cantilupe, Nicholas de, 54
  Thomas, bp of Hereford, 110, 182–3
  Walter de, bp of Worcester, 86, 92
Cantley (W.R. Yorks), parish of, 67
Capes, Canon William, 4
Caples, William de, rector of Laceby, 59
Carlisle (Cumbria), 46
  bp of, see Kirby, John
  diocese of, 3
Carolus-Barré, Louis, 201
Carrow (Norfolk), priory (Benedictine nuns) of, 107
Carter, William, 74
Castile, king of, 186
Castle Acre (Norfolk), priory (Cluniac) of, 98, 102
  vicar of, see Walton, John of, vicar of Castle Acre, Walton, John of
Catesby (Northants), priory (Cistercian nuns) of, 23, 37
Catherston Leweston (Dorset), 170
Catterick, John, bp of Coventry & Lichfield, 181
Cecily, prioress of Hampole, 67
Cerne (Dorset), abbey (Benedictine) of, 189
Chaddesley, Chedesl' (Worcs), dean of, see Robert
Chadwick, Owen, 194, 196
Chanter, Hugh the, 83
Chapel Easton (Wilts), vicar of, see Robert
Charles IV, king of France, 184
Charron, Guichard de, 129, 133
Chart Sutton (Kent), church of, 142, 148
Chastroke (Wilts), 182
Chaucer, Geoffrey, 41

Chauncelor, Robert le, 129
Chauncy, Gerard de 45
  William, rector of Scartho, 60
Chebsey, A. of, dean of Pirehill, 151
Chedesl' see Chaddesley
Cheney, Christopher, 4, 67, 130
  Mary, 67
Cheshire, 186
Chesney, Robert de, bp of Lincoln, 144–5
Chester (Ches), abbey (Benedictine) of, 37
Chichester, bps of, 18, and see Bersted, Stephen; Climping, John; Hilary; Luffa, Ralph; Neville, Ralph; Poore, Richard; Seffrid I; Wich, Richard
  cathedral, 35–6, 96
  chapter, 37, 20, 96
  diocese of, 24
Chiltern, Geoffrey of, 146
Chippenham (Wilts), church of, 97
Cirencester (Glos), 175
  rural dean of, 99
Clare, Bogo de, 2
  Gilbert, earl of Gloucester, 183
Claxby by Normanby (Lincs), rector of, see Daubeney, Philip; Rasen, John de, rector of
Cleet, Richard, 163
Clerfai, William de, 68
  wife of, see Tany, Avice de
Clement, abbot of Osney, 156
  IV, pope, 206
  V, pope, 207–8
  VI, pope, 207–8
  VII, pope, 209
Cleveland, archdn of, 11
Clifford, Thomas, rector of Aylesby, 56
Clifton, Henry de, 153
  William de, canon of Malton, 65, 75
Climping, John, bp of Chichester, 129, 134–5
Clinton, Geoffrey de, sheriff of Warwickshire, 80–1
Clipstone, master Robert, 129
Cocetti, Arnald, 101
Colby, William de, dean of York, 58
Colchester (Essex), abbey (Benedictine) of, 37
  archdn of, see Niger, Roger
Colne, Earls (Essex), priory (Benedictine) of, 37
Colston, William de, rector of Barnoldby, 59
Colwell (Northumb), 183

Combermere (Ches), abbey (Cistercian) of, 37
Compostella (Spain), 53
Compton, master Peter de, 164
Confessor, Edward the, 191
Constance, 180
Copgrave, Robert, rector of St Mary Binbrook, 58
Corfe Castle, 164
Costello, M., 199
Cotes, Great (Lincs), rector of, see Stanford, Robert de; Walmesford, Hugh de
Cotes, North (Lincs), church of, 45
  rector of, see Wadenho, Simon de
Cottingwith, East (E.R. Yorks), chapel of, 69
Cottingwith, West (E.R. Yorks), 70
Courtenay, William, archbp of Canterbury, 179, 187–9
Coventry (Warws), 184
  archdn of, 80, 87
  bp of, see Muschamp, Geoffrey; Nonant, Hugh de; Peche, Richard; Pucelle, Gerard
  cathedral, 79, 90
Coventry and Lichfield, bp of, see Booth, William; Catterick, John; Durdent, Walter; Pattishull, Hugh de
Coxford (Norfolk), priory (Augustinian) of, 98, 106
Crathorne, William of, lord of Ness, 73
Craucumb, John de, rector of Goxhill, 57
Crediton (Devon), collegiate church of, 78, 92–3
  canons of, 21
  minster of, 37
Creppint, Roger de, 129
Cricklade (Wilts), church of, 167
Crimplesham (Norfolk), church of, 97
Cross, Claire, 15
Croulec, Ralph, 149
Croxby (Lincs), 48
Croxton (Leics), abbey (Premonstratensian) of, 148
  chapel of, 102
Croxton (Lincs) church of, 43
  rector of, see Dalton, master William of
Croxton, South (Leics), church of, 148
Cumpton, Hugh de, 61
Cunyngesholme, John de, 145
Cuxwold (Lincs), church of, 47
  vicar of, see Habrough, Thomas of; Kirmington, Thomas of

D'Albini, Isabella, 107
Dagenhale, John de, 164, 170
Dalderby, John, bp of Lincoln, 42, 49, 54
Dallington (Northants), 170
Dalton, master William of, rector of Croxton, 49, 55–7
D'arcy, Nicholas, 44
Darel, Nicholas, 70
Darley (Derbs), abbey (Augustinian) of, 37
Daubeney, Philip, rector of Claxby by Normanby, 51
Daventre, Philip de, rector of Wold Newton, 56
Davis, Godfrey, 8, 16
Deerhurst (Glos), priory (Benedictine, alien), 155
Denton, Jeffrey, 50
Derby, 37
Dereham, Elias of, 84, 136
Derry (Armagh), bp of, see Donald
Despenser, Henry, 186
  Hugh, 175
Devensych, John le, 165–6
Devereux, Sir Thomas, 175
  Walter, lord Ferrers of Chartley, 175
Dickleburgh (Norfolk), church of, 101
Dodderhill (Worcs), chaplain of, see Richard
Dodsworth, Roger, 67
Donald, bp of Derry, 205
Donnesburgh, Richard de, canon of Ellerton on Spalding Moor, 65
Donyngton, John de, rector of North Thoresby, 54
Dorchester (Dorset), dean of, 170
Dorset, 172
Douell, master Walter, 187
Dover, Richard of, archbp of Canterbury, 148
Driffield, Robert of, 133
Droitwich (Worcs), 155
  dean of, see John
Dublin, Christ Church, 79
Duc, Richard le, 85
Duke, George, 123
Dunchelt, Robert de, 153
Dunham, Joel de, rector of Somerby, 60
Dunkeld (Perth and Kinross), bp of, 186
Dunlop, Annie I., 209
Dunmow (Essex), deanery of, 3
Dunton, Reginald de, 153
Dunwich (Suffolk), Dominicans at, 108
Durdent, Walter, bp of Coventry & Lichfield, 21

Durham, 99, 132, 195
  bp of, 18, 20, 57, 185–6, and see Bek, Anthony; Flambard, Ranulf; Farnham, Nicholas; Holy Island, Robert of; Kirkham, Walter; Marsh, Richard; Poore, Richard; Puiset, Hugh de; St Calais, William of; Sainte Barbe, William of; Stichill, Robert
  priory of, 22–4, 26, 37, 127, 133
    prior of, 95

Earls Colne, see Colne, Earls
Easington, Ranulph of, 71
Easingwold, Alan of, 133
East Barnet, see Barnet East
East Bedwyn, see Bedwyn, East
East Cottingwith, see Cottingwith, East
East Halton, see Halton, East
East Hendred, see Hendred, East
East Ravendale, see Ravendale, East
East Sutton, see Sutton, East
Eastnor (Heref), 183
Eastnor (Lincs), church of, 54
  rector of, see Barton, John de
Edelington, William de, vicar of Thornton Curtis, 53, 59
Edington (Lincs), 170
Edward I, king of England, 178–9, 184
  II, king of England, 58, 175, 178, 184–6
  III, king of England, 89, 175–7, 181, 186
  IV, king of England, 191–2
  VI, king of England, 195
Ela, anchorite of Massingham, 108
Eleanor, queen of England, 182
Ellerton (E.R. Yorks), church of, 69
Ellerton on Spalding Moor (E.R. Yorks), priory, 65, 69–70
  canon of, see Ad' William de; Bolyngton, John; Burton, Robert de; Donnesburgh, Richard de
Elford (Staffs), dean of, 141, and see Henry
Elsham (Lincs), priory (Augustinian) of, 45–6
Ely (Cambs), bp of, 151, and see Arundel, Thomas
  diocese of, 99–100
Emmison, Frederick, 13
England, king of, see Confessor, Edward the; Edward I; Edward II; Edward III; Edward IV; Edward V; Henry I; Henry III; Henry IV; Henry V; Henry VI; Henry VII; Henry VIII; Richard I; Richard II; Richard III
  queen of, see Isabella
Essex, 103
  County Record Office, 12–13
Eugenius IV, pope, 208
Evans, Sir David, 203
Everard, bp of Norwich, 31
Everle, Geoffrey de, 183
Evesham (Worcs), abbey (Benedictine) of, 157–8
Exeter (Devon), bp of, 24, and see Bartholomew; Leofric; Warlewast, William de
  cathedral, 78, 83
    chapter of, 21
  St Nicholas priory, 24–5, 37
Eye (Suffolk), priory (Benedictine alien) of, 37
Eynsham (Oxon), 99

Falle, Nicholas de, rector of Aylesby, 54–6
Farnham, Nicholas, bp of Durham, 128, 130–3, 135, 137
Fautier, Robert, 201
Fécamp (Normandy), 96
Fenby (Lincs), 48
Ferriby, South (Lincs), church of, 43
  rector of, see Braundeston Robert de
Ferring, master Geoffrey of, 126
Fillingham, Thomas of, rector of West Ravendale, 47
Fisher, John, bp of Rochester, 7
FitzJohn, Eustace, 75
FitzPhilip, John, 131
Fitzralph, Richard, dean of Lichfield, 58
Flambard, Ranulf, bp of Durham, 39, 132
  Richard, his nephew, 39
Flanders (Belgium), 186
  count of, 186
Florence, 48
Foliot, Hugh, bp of Hereford, 135
Folward, Hugh, 66
Fonge, Charles, 16
Fontevrault (France), abbey, 38
Fosseton, Thomas, proctor of Thicket priory, 69
Fountains (W.R. Yorks), abbey (Cistercian) of, 38
Fowler, G.H., 11
  R.C., 6
France, 53, 130, 181, 186
  king of, see Philip V
Francisci, Palmer, rector of Aylesby, 48

INDEX 223

Frank, Philip rector of Waltham, 51–2
Fraser, Constance, 137
Freckenham, Thomas of 136
Froyle, John de, 166
Fulham, 185
Fuller, Anne, 203
Fulmodestone (Norfolk), church of, 102
Furness, Ingenald of, 146
Fynk, Isabella, 164

Gaham, chaplain of, see Ralph
Galeway, William de, 73
Galilei, Galileo, 194
Gant, Maurice de, 30
    Walter de, 44
Gascony, 103
Gaunt, John of, 186–7
Geoffrey, bp of Coventry, 156
    priest of Aubourn, 150
    son of Geoffrey, 132
    son of Sim' of Aubourn, 15
    son of, see Marmaduke
Geoffrey, Auguste, 201
Gerard, bp of Hereford, 26
    chaplain of Levezairn, 146
    parson of Benigthorn', 155
Gervais, priest of Middleton, 145
Giffard, Godfrey, bp of Worcester, 79, 85–7
Gilbert, chaplain of Buteswich, 155
    son of Lecia, 71
    son of, see John
Gildene, Thomas le, monk of Sherborne, 170
Glanville, Gilbert, bp of Rochester, 84
Glasney (Cornw), collegiate church of, 92–3
Glastonbury (Soms), abbey (Benedictine) of, 22, 38
Glatton (Cambs), rector of, see Walmesford, Hugh de
Glonteston, master Robert de, 166
Gloucester, abbey (Benedictine) of, 21–2, 24, 26, 38
    abbot of, see Serlo
    earl of, 2, and see Clare, Gilbert
Gloucestershire, 183
Glyndwr, Owain, 180–1
Goldberg, Jeremy, 63
Goldcliff (Monmouth), priory (Benedictine alien) of, 38
Gosbeck (Suffolk), rector of, see Campden, master Henry of; Gosbeck, Richard of

Gosbeck, Richard of, rector of Gosbeck, 104
Goscote (Leics), dean of, see Ashfordby
Goxhill (Lincs), rector of, see Craucumb, John de
Goxhill, Peter of, 44
Graffoe, dean of, see Swinderby
Grainsby (Lincs), church of, 45
Grainthorpe (Lincs), 143–4
Grant, Richard, archbp of Canterbury, 136
Grasby (Lincs), vicar of, see Hotoft, Alan de
Graston (Dorset), 170
Gratian, 113
Gravesend, Richard, bp of Lincoln, 41, 48, 62
    bp of London, 126
Grayve, William, 70
Great Bricett, see Bricett, Great
Great Coles, Richard of, vicar of West Ravendale, 47
Great Cotes, see Cotes, Great
Great Hautbois, see Hautbois, Great
Great Limber, see Limber, Great
Greatrex, Joan, 7
Greenfield (Lincs), priory (Cistercian nuns) of, 40
    prioress of, see Owmby, Christine of
    prioress-elect of, see Harington, Elizabeth of
Greetwell (Lincs), church of, 67
Gregory the Great, 197
    VII, pope, 196
    IX, pope, 69, 198, 201–2, 206
    X, pope, 206
    XI, pope, 202, 207
Gresseby, Alan de, rector of Nettleton, 55
Grimsby (Lincs), 48
    deanery of, 43–4, 46, 62
    priory, 45, 60
    rector of, see Grimsby, Edmund
    St James, church, 44
    St John de la Boure, chapel, 44
    St Mary, church, 44
Grimsby, Edmund, rector of Grimsby, 56
Grosseteste, Robert, bp of Lincoln, 92, 110, 124
Grosmont, Henry, duke of Lancaster, 179
Gruffudd, Llywelyn ap, 182
Guilsborough (Northants), church of, 147
Guisborough (N.R. Yorks), priory (Augustinian) of, 30, 38
Gurney, Norah, 4, 6, 12–13

Guthmundham, John de, rector of
    Thoresway, 54
Gylet, John, 129–32
Gynewell, John, bp of Lincoln, 179

H., dean of Middlesex, 157–8
Habrough (Lincs), church of, 44
Habrough, Thomas of, vicar of Cuxwold, 47
Hackington (Kent), college of, 78, 90
Hackness (N.R. Yorks), 39
Haco, vicar of Henlow, 142, 153
Haddon (Cambs), dean of, see Henry
Hadisay, Alice, nun of Thicket priory, 65, 70
Hadlow (Kent), parish of, 122
Haines, Roy Martin, 50–1
Hale, master William de, 61–2
Halei, Hugh de, 145
Halifax, earls of, 18
Halton, Ralph de, 44
Halton, East (Lincs), church of, 44
    vicar of, 60
Hamelin, dean of Yarburgh, 143–4
    brother of, see Richard
    son of, see Brian
Hamo the clerk, 153
Hampole (W.R. Yorks), parish of, 67
    priory (Cistercian nuns) of, 66–8, 70
    prioress of, see Cecily
Handale (N.R. Yorks), priory (Cistercian nuns) of, 71–2
    prioress, see Ivetta
Happisburgh (Norfolk), vicar of, 110
Hardres, Robert of, vice-archdn of Lincoln, 149–50
Haren, Dr Michael, 203, 205
Harington, Elizabeth of, prioress-elect of Greenfield, 40
Harlow (Essex), deanery of, 3
Harmondsworth (Middsx), chaplain of, see W.
Hartham, John de, 164
Harton, William de, rector of South Kelsey, 53, 55
Harvington, Adam de, 89
Harwoods, Little (Lancs), 170
Hastings (Sussex), collegiate church of, 88
Hatcliffe (Lincs), rector of, see Kirmington, Richard of
Hathulf, 155
Hattelie, Ralph de, 153
Hatton (Lincs), rector of, see Breton, Guy
Hautbois, Great (Norfolk), church of, 106

Healing (Lincs), church of, 45
    rector of, see Healing, William of
Healing, John of, 47
    William of, rector of Healing, 47
Hedingham (Essex), deanery of, 3
Helmholz, Richard, 63, 65
Helmsley, Helmeslai (N.R. Yorks), church of, 146
    chaplain of, see Robert
Helmsley, Robert of, dean of Rydale, 146
Hemingbrough (E.R. Yorks), parish of, 74
Hemington (Northants), church of, 147
    priest of, see Roger
Hempstead (Norfolk), church of, 98
Hendred, East (Oxon), rector of, see Insula, Thomas de
Hengham, Ralf de, 85
Henlow (Beds), church of, 142, 153
    vicar of, see Haco; Hugh
Henry, dean of Elford, 156
    dean of Haddon, 147
    earl of Brittany, 45
    son of, see Alan
    I, king of England, 80, 152
    III, king of England, 103, 182–3
    IV, king of England, 180
    V, king of England, 181
    VI, king of England, 190–1
    VII, king of England, 175, 192–3
    VIII, king of England, 2, 195
    the tailor, 128
Herbert, priest of Swinderby, 150
    prior of St Neots, 147
    the *silvanus*, 147
Hereford, 4, 174
    archdn of, see Barton, John de
    bp of, 54, 175, 186, and see Cantilupe, Thomas de; Foliot, Hugh; Gerard; Mapenore, Hugh de; Milling, Thomas; Orleton, Adam; Stanbury, John; Swinfield, Richard
    cathedral, 83
    chapter, 21
    St Ethelbert's hospital, 21
    St Guthlac's priory, 38
Herefordshire, 183
    sheriff of, see Mornington, Sir Thomas
Hergenröther, Canon, 196
Herigettus, vicar of Westley Waterless, 100
Herne, John, 123
Henle, 183
Hermerus, chaplain of Matonia, 146
Herpeswell, John de, vicar of Tealby, 51

Herrington, Thomas of, 132
Hertfordshire, 3
Hewyk, John de, 75
Heyling, John de, 45
Heyrun, Jordan, 130
Hicham, clerk of, see Richard
Higam, priest of, see Hubert
Hilary, bp of Chichester, 26
Hill, Rosalind, 111
Hillam, Hillum (W.R. Yorks), 29
Hillingdon (Middlesex), church of, 142, 157–8
Hillum, see Hillam
Hindringham (Norfolk), vicar of, see Sydestone, William of
Hitler, Adolf, 5
Hoccleve, Thomas, 41
Holland (Lincs), dean of, see Sutton, John
Holme, Henry, 66
Holmes, Sherlock, 40
Holy Island (Northumb), 137
Holy Island, Henry of, 133
    Robert of, bp of Durham, 128–9, 133–5, 137
Honorius, archdn of Richmond, 154
    III, pope, 197, 199, 202
    IV, pope, 206
Hood, Robin, 41
Hook, Alexander de la, 165
    Margery, his wife, 165
Horden (Co. Durham), lords of, 132
Horn, Joyce, 3
Horning (Norfolk), church of, 106
Horsham (Sussex), St Faith, priory, 106
Hoskin, Philippa, 8, 16
Hostiensis, 115
Hotoft, Alan de, vicar of Grasby, 51
Hounslow (Middx), chapter of, 142, 157
Hoveton, Lambert of, 146
    Sunnive, his wife, 146
    Peter of, 146
Hovingham (N.R. Yorks), church of, 72–4
Howden (E.R. Yorks), bailiff of, see Ynfleth, John de
    parish of, 74
Howsham (Lincs), 43
Hubert, merchant of Malton, 146
    priest of Higam, 150
    proctor of Burton abbey, 151
Hueson, Robert, 70
Huggate, Nicholas de, rector of Scartho, 53, 60
Hugh, abbot of Osney, 149
    priest of Lastingham, 146

vicar of Henlow, 142, 153
Humber, river of, 43
Hurford, John de, rector of West Rasen, 51
Hutton, master Richard of, 146
Hutton Lowcross (N.R. Yorks), 72

I., dean of Tendring, 142, 156–7
Idsworth, Henry, dean of Arches, 170
Inge, William, 162
Ingelram, dean of Welburn, 143, 145–6
Innocent, II, pope, 50, 67–8, 154, 197, 202, 208
    IV, pope, 68, 97, 100–2, 196, 199, 206
    VI, pope, 207–8
    VII, pope, 208
    VIII, pope, 192, 205, 209
Insula, master Godfrey de, 151
    Thomas de, rector of East Hendred, 165
Ipswich (Suffolk), Franciscans at, 107
Irby (Lincs), church of, 45
Ireland, 186, 193
    National Library of, 204
Isabella, queen of England, 175
Ivetta, prioress of Handale 71–2

James II, king of England, 195
Jocelin, bp of Bath, 84
    son of, see Roger
John, dean of Droitwich, 155
    father of, see William
    master, 145
    VIII, pope, 196, 205
    XII, pope, 196
    XXI, pope, 206
    XXII, pope, 185–6, 202, 207
    rector of Adel, 64
    son of Gilbert, 74
    son of Lethold, 146
    vice-archdn of Canterbury, 142, 148
Johnson, Charles, 199
Julius II, pope, 209

Keelby (Lincs), rector of, see Malekak, Roger; Stallingborough, Thomas of
Kelsey, South (Lincs), church of, 43, 53
    rector of, see Barton, John de; Brayton, Thomas de; Harton, William de
Kemp, John, archbp of Canterbury, 190
    Thomas, bp of London, 177, 190
Kempf, Frederick, 202
Kepharm, John, 149
Kerdinton, Hugh de, 153
Kershaw, Ian, 5

Kidderminster (Worcs), church of, 152
  clerk of, see Richard
  dean of, see Calixtus; Roger
  sacrist of, see Thomas
Killingholme (Lincs), church of, 44
Kington, master Roger de, rector of Bridport, 164
Kintbury (Berks), 38
Kirkburton (W.R. Yorks), rector of, see Birstall, Richard of
Kirby, John, bp of Carlisle, 180–1
Kirkby, clerk of, see Peter; William
Kirkby Malzeard, R. of, dean of Boroughshire, 154
Kirkeby, William de, 71
Kirkham, Richard of, 131
  Walter, bp of Durham, 128–9, 131–2, 135
  William de, rector of Nettleton, 51
Kirkstall (W.R. Yorks), abbey (Cistercian) of, 38
Kirmington (Lincs), 48
  church of, 44
Kirmington, Richard of, rector of Brigsley, rector of Hatcliffe, 60
  master Robert of, rector of Brigsley, 49
  Thomas of, vicar of Cuxwold, 47
Knighton, Henry, 186
Knowles, David, 7–8
Kyme, family of, 46

La Charité-sur-Loire, abbey (Cluniac) of, 38
Laceby (Lincs), church of, 52
  rector of, see Caples, William de
Laceles William de, 146
Lambeth (Surrey), 184, 190
  college of, 87–9, 90
Lambourne (Essex), 163
  clerk of, see Lotewyk, John
Lancaster, Thomas of, earl, 45, 54, 175, 184–5
Lanfranc, archbp of Canterbury, 21
Lange, John, 70
Langford (Beds), dean of, see R.
  dean and chapter of, 142
Langland, William, 41
Langton, Simon, archdn of Canterbury, 136
  Stephen, archbp of Canterbury, 3, 18, 84, 135–6
Langworth (Lincs), church of, 164
Lanthony, see Llanthony
Lasseles, John de, 45

Lastingham (N.R. Yorks), 39
  priest of, see Hugh
Latymer, Sir John, 163
Launde (Leics), priory (Augustinian) of, 38
Laurence, archdn of Bedford, 152
  chaplain of Chedesl', 152
Lavagna (Italy), 102
  count of, 101
Lech', chaplain of, see Walter
  parson of, see Luke
Leeds (Kent), priory (Augustinian) of, 38, 142, 148
Leeds (W.R. Yorks), church of, 30
Leicester, archdn of, see Baldric
  church of, 49
Leicester, Peter of, 86–7, 89
  Robert of, 81
Leighton Buzzard (Beds), 170
  vicar of, see Stevenson, Joseph
Lena, Peter, 101
Leo XIII, pope, 196, 202
Leofric, bp of Exeter, 26
Lethold, son of, see John
Leversham Thomas of, 132–3
Leverton, Levertona (Lincs), chaplain of, see Robert
Levezairn, chaplain of, see Gerard
Lewes (Sussex), priory (Cluniac) of, 23–4, 26, 38, 101, 151–2
Lewes, Robert of, bp of Bath, 20, 32
Lewknor, Geoffrey of, 129–30
Lichfield (Staffs) cathedral, 151
  chapter of, 21, 38
  dean of, see Fitzralph, Richard
Limber (Lincs), 48
Limber, Great (Lincs), vicar of, see Askeby, John de
Limberg, Thomas de, vicar of Cabourne, 60
Limoges, 184
Lincoln, 1, 4, 174
  archdn of, see Robert; Stratford, John
  archdnry, 43
  bp of, 1, 151, 186, and see Blois, William of; Buckingham, John; Burghersh, Henry; Chesney, Robert de; Dalderby, John; Gravesend, Richard; Grosseteste, Robert; Gynewell, John; Lincoln, Hugh of; Plantagenet, Geoffrey; Sutton, Oliver; Wells, Hugh of
  cathedral, 56, 78
    chancellor of, see William
    chapter, 21

subdean of, see Maydenstan, Walter de; William
countess of, 54, 128
dean of, see Roger
diocese, 3, 18, 41, 43–4, 48, 56, 99, 178
Diocesan Archive, 12
sheriff of, 174
vice-archdn, see Hardres, Robert of
Lincoln, Hugh of, bp of Lincoln, 6, 84, 155
Linwood (Lincs), rector of, see Stanford, Robert de; Welleford, Geoffrey de
Liskeard (Cornw.), St Mary Magdalene hospital, 21, 38
Little Bredy, see Bredy, Little
Little Harwoods, see Harwoods, Little
Little Witchingham, see Witchingham, Little
Liverpool (Lancs), 5
Liverton (N.R. Yorks), 71
Llanthony (Glos), priory (Augustinian) of, 38, 142, 153
proctor of, see Moyse
Lloyd George, David, 198
Loddon (Norfolk), church of, 101
Loddon, Geoffrey of, 105
Lofthus (N.R. Yorks), 71–2
Loftsome, (E.R. Yorks), 65, 74
London, 3, 159, 166, 189
archdnry, 99
bp of, 185
and see Braybrooke, Robert; Gravesend, Richard; Kemp, Thomas; Niger, Roger
diocese, 99
New Temple, 99
St Mary Aldermary, 171
St Mary le Bow, 160, 171
St Paul's, 21, 95
London, Vera, 6–7
Longdon, master Walter of, 157–8
Losinga, Herbert, bp of Norwich, 31
Lotewyk, John, clerk of Lambourne, 163, 168
Louthesk (Lincs), deanery of, 144
wapentake of, 144
Loxwell (Wilts), 39
Lucius, III, pope, 148–9
Lucy, Godfrey de, bp of Winchester, 130
Ludborough (Lincs), deanery of, 144
Ludda, master Simon de, rector of Aylesby, 40, 60, 62
Thomas de, rector of Aylesby, 53–4
Luffa, Ralph, bp of Chichester, 26, 35–6

Lughton, Alan de, rector of Aylesby, 54
Luke, parson of Lech', 155
Lusceby, Henry de, rector of Blyborough, rector of Wold Newton, rector of Wooler, 54, 57
Lusignan, family of, 104
Lydbury North (Shrops), 182
Lyminge (Kent), church of, 122
Lydwood, William, 114–16
Lynn (Norfolk), 105
church of, 25, 31
Dominicans at, 108
Francsiscans at, 107
St John's hospital, 105
Lyons (France), 48–9, 97, 99
Lyte, Henry Maxwell, 197, 203

Mabillon, John, 5
MacCarthy, Bernard, 198
Macfarlane, Leslie, 200, 203–4
McGurk, F., 209
Maddyson, Richard, 118
Maiden Bradley (Wilts), priory (Augustinian) of, 152
proctor of, see Andrew
Maidstone (Kent), chapter of, 142, 148
Malekak, Alan, 47
Roger, rector of Keelby, 47, 54, 60
Mallet, John, 45
Malling, South (Sussex), college, 78
Malmesbury (Wilts), abbey (Benedictine) of, 22, 27
Malmeyns, Nicholas, 45
Malton (N.R. Yorks), priory (Gilbertine) of, 65, 74–75, 154
canon of, see Clifton, William de; Rygby, Henry de
merchant of, see Hubert
Malton, master William of, 145
Manneby, John de, rector of Saxby, 60
Mapenore, Hugh de, bp of Hereford, 134–5
Margaret, son of, see Ralph
Marham (Norfolk), abbey (Cluniac nuns) of, 96, 107
parish church, 107
Markby (Lincs), priory (Augustinian) of, prior of, 40
Marmaduke, son of Geoffrey, 132
Marmoutier (France), abbey (Benedictine), of, 39
Marsh, Adam, 107
Richard, bp of Durham, 131, 133
Marshal, Henry, bp of Exeter, 91

Marsham (Norfolk), church of, 98
Marske, Nicholas of, 71
Martin IV, pope, 206
 V, pope, 208
Martival, Roger, bp of Salisbury, 159–72, 175–6
Marton, Martun (E.R. Yorks), church of, 154
 clerk of, see Robert
Mascall, John, 187
Masham (N.R. Yorks), 2–3, 7, 15
Matilda, countess of Warenne, 105
Matonia, chaplain of, see Hermerus
Mauger, bp of Worcester, 152
Maydenstan, Walter de, subdean of Lincoln, 55
Mayr-Harting, Henry, 4
Mears Ashby (Northants.), 170
Meisam, master W. de, canon of Osney, 156
Melton, William, archbp of York, 53–4, 177, 180, 185–6
Melton on the Hill (W.R. Yorks), church of, 67
Melton Mowbray (Leics), rector of, see Spata, John
Melton Ross (Lincs), church of, 45
Mendlesham, (Suffolk) church of, 96
Merrow, Walter of, 131–2
Merton, Walter de, bp of Rochester, 130
Meulan, Waleran of, 81
Michigan, University of, 204
Middlesex, archdeaconry of, 3
 dean of, 142
 and see H.
Middleton [in Pickering Lythe] (N.R. Yorks), priest of, see Gervais
Middleton, Henry de, 129
 William of, 129
Migne, Abbé, 202
Miller, William, 165
Milling, Thomas, bp of Hereford, 174, 178
Mitton (Worcs), chaplain of, see Philip
Momesey, Sir Walter de, 163
Mornington, Sir Thomas, sheriff of Herefordshire, 174
Monk Bretton (W.R. Yorks), priory (Benedictine) of, 23, 38
Monk Fryston (W.R. Yorks), 29
Monte Alto, Hugh de, 129
Montfort, Simon de, 103
Monticello, Henry de, nephew of cardinal bp of Sabina, 101
Moore, Francis, 123

Moorman, J.R.H., 41, 48
Moray (Scotland), bp of, 186
Morland, William, 69
Mortimer, Roger, 176, 185
Morton, John, archbp of Canterbury, 192–3
Motekan, family of, 46
Mowbray, Roger de, 2
Moyse, proctor of Llanthony priory, 153
Muletone, 182
Mundevilla, Henry de, 147
Muschamp, Geoffrey, bp of Coventry, 151
Mussett, Patrick, 3
Mutton, see Mitton

Nedham, William de, rector of Thoresway, 54–5
Ness (N.R. Yorks), chapel of, 72–4
 lord of, see Crathorne, William of
Nettleton (Lincs), church of, 43
 rector of, see Gresseby, Alan de;
  Kirkham, William de; Thoresby, John de
Neville, Alexander, archbp of York, 182
 Ralph, bp of Chichester, 127, 134
New Malton, Robert of, canon of Malton, 65, 75
Newburgh priory, 72, 74
Newcastle, St Bartholomew priory, 38
Newhouse (Lincs), abbey (Premonstratensian) of, 44–6
Newhouse, Geoffrey de, 44
Newminster (Northumb) abbey (Cistercian) of, 38
Newsholme (Yorks, E.R.), 65, 74
 reeve of, 75
Newton, Isaac, 5
Newton by Toft (Lincs), church of, 46
 rector of, see Suthriston, Gilbert de
Newton Longville (Bucks), priory (Cluniac) of, monks of, 106
Nicholas, dean of Maidstone, 142, 148
 II, pope, 182, 206
 IV, pope, 45, 206
 V, pope, 200, 208
 priest of Turnebi, 147
Nigel, dean of Oxford, 143, 149
Niger, Roger, archdn of Colchester, bp of London, 95, 156–7
Nimpha, Berard de, 101
Nonant, Hugh de, bp of Coventry, 79, 150–1
Norfolk, archdn of, 110
Norham (Northumb), 137

Normanby (N.R. Yorks), 146
  clerk of, see William
North Cotes, see Cotes, North
North Thoresby, see Thoresby, North
Northumberland, 185
Norton (Co. Durham), 128
Norwich (Norfolk), anchorites at, 108
  archdn of, 108
  bp of, 186–7, and see Blundeville, Thomas; Broun, Thomas; Everard; Losinga, Herbert; Marshal, Henry; Raleigh, William; Suffield, Walter; Wakeryng, John; Walople, Ralph; Walton, Simon
  Carmelites at, 108
  cathedral priory, 22, 25, 31, 38
  diocese, 99
  Dominicans at, 107
  Franciscans at, 107
  St Giles' hospital, 95, 105
  St Mary Magdalene hospital, 105
  St Paul's hospital, 105–6
Nostell (W.R. Yorks), priory (Augustinian) of, 38
Nottingham, 1
Nun Cotham (Lincs), priory (Cistercian nuns) of, 46, 60
Nuneaton (Warws), priory (Fontevrault) of, 23, 38, 107
Nunnington, Nicholas of, 146

Odo, bp of Bayeux, 29
Orleans, 127
Orleton, Adam, bp of Hereford, bp of Worcester, 89, 184, 185
Osbert, parochial chaplain of Lofthus, 72
  priest of Saltfletby, 145
Osney (Oxon), abbey (Augustinian) of, 156
  abbot of, see Clement; Hugh
  canon of, see Meisam, master W. de
Oswaldkirk (N.R. Yorks), chaplain of, see Walter
Oundle (Nothants), dean of, see Titmarsh
Oviham, chaplain of, see Robert
Owen, Dorothy, 12
Owmby (Lincs), chapel of, 44
Owmby, Christine of, prioress of Greenfield, 40
Oxford, Christ Church, 199
  dean of, see Nigel; St Martins, Ralph of
  St Frideswide's priory, 149
  St John the Evangelist's hospital, 105
  University, 52, 58

Oxfordshire, 188

Packenham, William of, 105
Palmore, Roger le, 166
  Sybil, his daughter, 166
Pandulf, 109
Pantin, W.A., 41
Paris, 102, 194
Paris, Matthew, 32, 94–5, 100, 104, 108, 127–8, 199
Partner, Peter, 203
Pasquin, Antonin, 184
Pattishull, Hugh de, bp of Coventry and Lichfield, 33
Paul II, pope, 208
Peccheford, Henry de, 166
Pecham, John, archbp of Canterbury, 41, 50, 109
Peche, Richard, bp of Coventry, 150
Pennellus, Armann, 101
Penryn (Cornwall), 92–3
Percy, William de, 29, 146
Peret, John, rector of Wressell, 73–5
Peter, clerk of Kirkby, 146
  dean of Asfordby, 148
Peterborough (Cambs) abbey (Benedictine) of, abbot of, 100
Petrinus, 102
Pex, Humphrey, 71–2
Philip, chaplain of Mitton, 153
  V, king of France, 58
Pickering (N.R. Yorks), wapentake of, 143
Pirehill (Staffs), dean of, 140, 143, and see Chebsey, A. of
Pisa (Italy), 180
Pitra, J.B., 201
Pius II, pope, 200, 208
  III, pope, 209
Plantagenet, Geoffrey, bp of Lincoln, 147
Plesset, John de, 86
  Robert de, dean of Warwick collegiate church, 87
Plessis, John du, earl of Warwick, 86–7
Plokenet, Lord Alan, 163
  Lady Sybil, his wife, 163
Pontefract (W.R. Yorks), collegiate church, 88
  dean and chapter of, 151
  priory (Cluniac) of, 23, 38
Pontigny (France), abbey (Cistercian) of, 95, 106, 127–8
Pontorp, Laurence of, 128

Poore, Richard, bp of Chichester, bp Durham, bp Salisbury, 84, 126, 131, 133, 137
Pottespurty (Northants), 170
   rector of, see Welleford, Geoffrey de
Potton, Robert de, 153
Potter Heigham (Norfolk), church of, 101
   rector of, see Stalham, Giles
Powick (Worcs), 183
   rector of, 183
Pressutti, Paulo, 197, 202
Prou, Maurice, 200
Provence, hospital of St Gilles, 105
Public Record Office, 9, 197–204
Pucelle, Gerard, bp of Coventry, 150
Puiset, Hugh de, bp of Durham, 86
Purvis, Canon John, 10–12
Pylks, Richard, 73

Quarr (Isle of Wight), abbey (Cistercian) of, 39
Quatford (Shrops), 83

R. dean of Langford, 153
Raftis, J. Ambrose, 204
Ragenhall, Richard de, rector of Barnoldby, rector of Burghclere, 51, 57–9
Raine, James, 195
Raleigh, William, bp of Norwich, bp of Winchester, 99, 103, 126
Ralph, chaplain of Gaham, 147
   knight of Aissebi, 147
   son of Margaret, 146
   vice-archdn of Canterbury, 148
Rasen, West (Lincs), rector of, 60, and see Hurford, John de; Rasen, William de
Rasen, John de, rector of Claxby by Normanby, 60
   William de, rector of West Rasen & Gedney, 57
Ravendale, East (Lincs), church of, 45
Ravendale, [West] (Lincs), priory (Premonstratensian) of, 45
   rector of, see Caistor, Lambert of; Fillingham, Thomas of
   vicar of, see Great Coles, Richard of
Raveningham, Thomas of, 102
Rede (Suffolk), church of, 106
Redman, John, 2
Reggio (Italy), archbp of, see Vernacius
Reginald, the priest, 145

Reynolds, Walter, archbp of Canterbury, 179, 185
Rhodes, 180
Rich, Edmund, see Abingdon, Edmund, of, archbp of Canterbury
Richard, abbot of Waltham, 154–5
   brother of Hamelin, 145
   chaplain of Dodderhill, 156
   chaplain of Kidderminster, 152
   clerk of Hicham, 150
   I, king of England, 78
   II, king of England, 179, 181–2, 186–90
   III, king of England, 191–2
   son of Azar, dean of Warwick collegiate church, 80
   son of Simon, 72
Richebroke, Hugh de, 145
   David his brother, 145
Richmond (N.R. Yorks), archdn of, see Honorius
   archdnry of, 180
Rieti (Italy), 69
Rievaulx (N.R. Yorks), abbey (Cistercian) of, abbot of, 68, 146, 148
Ripon, diocese of, 16
Robert, archdn of Lincoln, 145
   his brother, see Roger
   the chaplain, 145
   chaplain of Helmsley, 146
   chaplain of Leverton, 155
   chaplain of Oviham, 146
   chaplain of Wlferdesl', 152
   clerk of Marton, 146
   dean of Chaddesley, 153
   master, 145
   priest of Hedeston, 146
   priest of Turlebi
   son of William, 146
   vicar of Chapel Easton, 163
   vice-archdn of Canterbury, 148
Robinson, David, 50
Roche (W.R. Yorks), abbey (Cistercian) of, 68
Roches, Peter des, bp of Winchester, 127–8, 130
Rochester (Kent), bp of, 19, And see Fisher, John; Glanville, Gilbert; Merton, Walter de
   cathedral priory of, 22, 26, 38, 84
   diocese of, 20, 120, 122
Roger, brother of Robert, archdn of Lincoln
   dean of Kidderminster, 153

dean of Lincoln, 154
earl of Warwick, 80–1
priest of Hemington, 147
royal chancellor, 31
son of Jocelin, 143–5
Roger, Lapyn, son of, see William
Rome, 153, 55m 101, 109, 197, 201–2, 209
Romney (Kent), church of, 95
Romsey, John of, 129–31
Rostand, master, papal nuncio, 100–1
Rotcy, John, canon of Ellerton, 66, 70
Rothwell (Lincs), church of, 45
  rector of, see Rothwell, Alan of
Rothwell, Alan of, rector of Rothwell, 49
Ruddebi, Hugh de, 146
  Walter, 146
Rushbury (Herts), 122
Russel, Geoffrey, 129
Rutland, duke of, 144
  sheriff of, 174
Rydale, chapter of 145
  dean of, see Welburn
  and see Helmsley, Robert of
Rydale & Pickering Lythe, dean of, 143
  deanery of, 143
  wapentake of, 143
Rygby, Henry de, canon of Malton, 65, 75

Sabina, cardinal-bp of, 101
  nephew of, see Monticello, Henry de
Sadberge (Co. Durham), wapentake of, 137
St Albans (Herts), abbey (Benedictine) of, 20, 39, 99
St Albans, Robert of, 130
St Andrews, bp of, 186
St Benet of Hulme (Norfolk), abbey (Benedictine) of, 101, 106
St Botolph, William of, 136
St Calais, William of, bp of Durham, 23
St Cross, Martin of, 130–1
St Davids, bp of, 181
St George, 181
St Helen, Philip of, 131
St-Léonard-de-Noblat (France), abbey (Augustinian) of, 31, 38
St Martins, Ralph of, dean of Oxford, 149
St Meldred, Robert of, 131
St Michaels Mount (Cornwall), priory (Benedictine alien) of, 26, 38
St Neots (Hunts), priory (Benedictine alien) of, 38, 147

prior of, see Herbert
St Valéry (France), abbey (Benedictine) of, 38
Sainte Barbe, William of, bp of Durham, 23
Salatuna, chaplain of, 146
Salisbury (Wilts), bp of, see Martival, Roger; Poore, Richard; Waltham, John
  cathedral, 83–5
  chapter, 21
  dean, 166
Salfletby, priest of, see Osbert
Samson, bp of Worcester, 78
Sandeie, Hugh de, 153
Sapy, Hugh de, 164
Savage, Walter, rector of Scartho, 60
Savoy, Boniface of, archbp of Canterbury, 95–6, 100–1, 110, 136
  Peter of, 129
Saxby (Lincs), rector of, see Manneby, John de
Scales, Sir Robert de, 107
Scamblesby (Lincs), prebend of, 45
Scammell, Jean, 137
Scartho (Lincs), church of 48, 53
  rector of, see Chauncy, William; Huggate, Nicholas de; Savage, Walter
Schalby, John de, 42
Scot, William, 73
Scotland, 185–6, 209
Scots, king of, see Bruce, Robert
Scremby, Peter de, 55, 60
Scrope, master Robert, 145
Searby (Lincs), church of, 44
Seaton, Roger of, 131–2
Seffrid I, bp of Chichester, 20, 36
Selby (W.R. Yorks), 29
  abbey (Benedictine) of, 23, 25, 29–30, 39
Selby, Walter of, 131
Senliz, Simon de, 127
Serlo, abbot of Gloucester, 22
Shadeworth, William de, 59
Shelford, dean of, see Langford
Sherborne (Dorset), abbey (Benedictine) of, 170
  monk of, see Gildene, Thomas le
Shenstone (Staffs), church of, 156
Shrewsbury (Shrops), abbey (Benedictine) of, 39
Shrewsbury, Ralph of, bp of Bath & Wells, 182

Shropshire, 7
  earl of, 83
Siddington, Thomas de, dean of Warwick collegiate church, 85
Sifflingtuna, chaplain of, see Alan
Simnel, Lambert, 193
Simon, bp of Worcester, 82
Simplicius, pope, 196
Sixhills (Lincs), priory (Gilbertine) of, 43, 46
Sixtus IV, pope, 209
Skelet, William, rector of Barnoldby, 51
Slator, Walter, 129
Sleightholme, Richard of, 74
Sleightholme Dale (N.R. Yorks), 74
Slingsby, Sampson of, 145
Slinn, Sara, 15
Smith, Margaret E., 15
Snettisham (Norfolk), vicar of, 110
Solesmes (France), abbey (Benedictine) of, 201
Somerby (Lincs), rector of, see Dunham, Joel de
Sonnebury, Thomas de, rector of Bubwith, rector of Linwood, 54, 57
South Croxton, see Croxton, South
South Ferriby, see Ferriby, South
South Kelsey, see Kelsey, South
South Malling, see Malling, South
Southampton (Hamps), God's House, 21, 39
Southwark (Surrey), St Mary Overy, priory (Augustinian) of, 39
Spata, John, rector of Melton Mowbray, 101
Speen (Berks), church of, 163
Spring, Hugh, 153
Stafford, dean of, 99
  and see Pirehill
  priory (Augustinian) of, 39
  canons of, 107
Staingrifa, Reinald de, 145
Stainton, William of, 146
Stainton-le-Vale (Lincs), church of, 43, 45
Stalham, Giles of, rector of Potter Heigham, 101
Stallingborough (Lincs), vicar of, 60
Stallingborough, Thomas of, rector of Keelby, 61
Stamford, John of, 107
Stanbury, John, bp of Hereford, 178
Stand, Silvester de, 153
Stanes, chaplain of, see Walter

Stanford, Robert de, rector of Great Cotes, 54
Stanhope (Co. Durham), manor of, 130
Stanley (Wilts), abbey (Cistercian) of, 39
Stanton (Oxon), 170
Staveley, Henry of, dean of Boroughshire, 154
Stenton, Frank, 3–4
Stephen, king of England, 26–7
Stevenson, Joseph, vicar of Leighton Buzzard, 195–6
Stichill, Robert, bp of Durham, 128–9, 132–5, 137
Stillingfleet, John, 70
Stockton, Geoffrey of, 128
Stoke-by-Clare (Suffolk), priory (Benedictine alien) of, 97, 106, 108
Stone, A. of, dean of Pirehill, 150
Storey, Robin, 203
Stratford, John, archdn of Lincoln, bp of Winchester, 51, 58
Stratton (Norfolk), recluse at, 108
Stretton, John de, 52
Stuteville, Burga de, 75
Sudbury (Suffolk), church at, 107
Suffield (Norfolk), recluse at, 108
Suffield, Walter, bp of Norwich, 94–110
Sulby (Northants), 99
  abbey (Premonstratensian) of, 147
Summere, master W. de, 152
Sundridge (Kent), 170
Surdevals, Peter de, 146
  William de, 146
Suthriston, Gilbert de, rector of Newton by Toft, 55, 60
Sutton, John of, dean of Holland, 154
  Oliver, bp of Lincoln, 40, 42, 48–9, 62
Sutton, East (Kent), church of, 148
Suyne, Robert de, 145
Swallow (Lincs), church of, 45
Swanland, John de, rector of Thoresway, 53
Swinderby, Swinderbi (Lincs), dean of, see A.
  priest of, see Herbert
Swine (E.R. Yorks), priory (Cistercian nuns) of, 66
Swinfield, Richard, bp of Hereford, 184
Swinhope (Lincs), church of, 45
Sydestone, William of, rector of Barmer, vicar of Hindringham, 98
Symonds, Peter, 122
  William, 193

INDEX 233

Tamifeford, Fulco de, 153
Tamsworth, dean of, see Elford
Tamworth (Staffs), church of, 141
Tankersley, James of, 48
Tany, Avice de, 68
Taunton, William de, 165
Tavistock (Devon), abbey (Benedictine) of, 26, 39
Tendring (Essex), dean of, I.
Tees, river, 137
Thame (Oxon), 170
Thames, river, 43
Theiner, Augustin, 200
Theobald, archbp of Canterbury, 78
  son of Pain of Wykeham, 145
Thetford (Norfolk), priory (Augustinian) of, 23, 31, 39
Thicket (E.R. Yorks), priory (Benedictine nuns) of, 65, 69, 70
  nun of, see Broghton, Alice; Hadisay, Alice
  proctor of, see Fosseton, Thomas; Thomson, Robert
Thomas I, archbp of York, 29
  II, archbp of York, 30
  sacrist of Kidderminster, 153
Thomson, Robert, proctor of Thicket priory, 69
Thoresby, North (Lincs), church of, 45
  rector of, see Donyngton, John de
Thoresby, John de, archbp of York, rector of Nettleton, 53, 55
  Peter de, 133
Thoresway (Lincs), rector of, see Bitham, William de; Guthmundham, John de; Nedham, William de; Swanland, John de
Thorganby (Lincs), church of, 43, 46
Thornham (Norfolk), manor of, 105
  recluse at, 108
Thornholme (Lincs), priory (Augustinian) of, 45, 54
Thornton [Curtis] (Lincs), abbey (Augustinian) of, 45–6
  vicar of, see Edelington, William de
Thorpe (Norfolk), manor of, 106
Thurgarton (Notts), priory (Augustinian) of, 39
Thurstan, archbp of York, 30
Titmarsh, dean of, see Adam
Trenchard, master Richard, 162
Turlebi, priest of, see Alexander
Turnebi, priest of, see Nicholas
Twemlow, Jesse, 199–200, 203

Twynham (Hants), priory (Augustinian) of, 24, 39
Tyne, river, 137
Tynton, Robert de, rector of Autby, 52, 59

Uffington, master John of, 95
Urban, IV, pope, 206
  V, pope, 56, 207–8
  VI, pope, 187
Urchfont (Wilts), church of, 166

Valentine, master, 126
Vatican, 194–209
Vere, Robert de, 188
Vernacius, archbp of Reggio, 101
Vesci, Beatrice, 75
  Eustace de, 74–5
  William, 75
Vincent, Nicholas, 8, 38, 144
Vitte-Clémencet, Madame, 201

W., chaplain of Harmondsworth, 157
Wacelyn, family of, 48
  John, rector of Bigby, 47, 60
  William, rector of Bigby, 48, 60
Wadenho, Simon de, rector of North Cotes, 54
Wakefield, Henry, bp of Worcester, 188
Wakeryng, John, bp of Norwich, 107
Walcott, Thomas of, 102
Walden (Essex), abbey (Benedictine) of, 97
Waldric, royal chancellor, 31
Waleran, earl of Warwick, 80
Wales, 186
Walesby (Lincs), church of, 48
Wallingford (Berks), priory (Benedictine) of, 39
Wallingwells (Notts), priory (Benedictine nuns) of, 66
Walmesford, Hugh de, rector of Glatton, rector of Great Cotes, 57, 61
  Peter de, 61
Walpole (Norfolk), church of, 101
Walople, Ralph, bp-elect of Norwich, 109
Walshcraft (Lincs), deanery of, 43–4, 46, 62
Walsingham, Thomas, 189
Walter, Hubert, archbp of Canterbury, 78–9, 84, 87, 124, 154–5
Walter, chaplain of Lech', 155
  chaplain of Oswaldkirk, 146
  chaplain of Stanes, 152–3
  dean of Bulmer, 146

Waltham (Essex), abbey (Augustinian) of, abbot of, see Richard
    rector of, see Frank, Philip
Waltham (Essex), collegiate church of, 88
Waltham (Lincs), 48
Waltham, John, bp of Salisbury, 189
    Roger of, 128
Walton, John of, vicar of Castle Acre, 98
    Simon, bp of Norwich, 109
Wanley, Humphrey, 5
Wantage (Oxon), church of, 163
Warden (Beds), 153
Warden, Nicholas of, 153
Warlewast, William de, bp of Exeter, 21, 32
Warminster, William of, 48
Warenne, countess of, see Matilda
Warwick, All Saints minster, 82
    earls of, 77, 85, 193, and see Beauchamp, Guy; Beauchamp, Thomas; Beauchamp, William; Plessis, John du; Roger; Waleran
    St Mary's college, 77, 80–1, 85–9, 92
        dean of, see Plesset, Roger de; Richard son of Azar; Siddington, Thomas de
    St Nicholas church, 80
Warwickshire, sheriff of, see Clinton, Geoffrey de
Wath, Ralph of, 146
Wauter, David, 168
Welbeck (Notts), abbey (Premonstratensian), abbot of, 148
Welburn (N.R. Yorks), dean of, see Ingelram
Welleford, Geoffrey de, rector of Linwood, rector of Potterspury, 53, 57
Welles, Robert, 45
Wellow by Grimsby (Lincs), abbey (Augustinian) of, 45–6
Wells (Soms), 32
    cathedral, 32
        canons of, 20, 39
Wells, Hugh of, bp of Lincoln, 1, 3–4, 6
Wendover, Roger of, 32, 39
Werketon, Roger de, 166
West Cottingwith, see Cottingwith, West
West Rasen, see Rasen, West
Westacre (Norfolk), priory (Augustinian) of, canon of, 107
Westbury on Trym (Glos), collegiate church of, 78–9, 85–6, 89
Westley Waterless (Cambs), vicar of, see Herigettus

Westminster, 183
    abbey, 22, 27, 94, 96, 103
Westwood (Worcs), priory (Fontevrault) of, 155–6
Weybridge (Norfolk), priory (Augustinian) of, 106
Wheldrake (E.R. Yorks), parish of, 70
Whepstead (Suffolk), church of, 101
Whitbourne (Heref), 183
Whitby (N.R. Yorks), abbey (Benedictine) of, 23, 25, 39
Whitwell, William of, 105
Wich, Richard, bp of Chichester, 95–6, 99, 110, 127
Wicklewood (Norfolk), church of, 98
William, carpenter, 147
    chancellor of Lincoln, 154
    chaplain of Abatun, 146
    clerk of Kirkby, 145–6
    clerk of Normanby, 146
    father of John, 155
    nephew of Bp Suffield, 103
    son of Roger, Lapyn, 162
    son of, see Robert
    subdean of Lincoln, 154
Willoughby (Lincs), 47
Willoughby, Hugh, rector of Wold Newton, 47
    Philip, rector of Wold Newton, 47
    William of, 47
        wife of, see Alice
Willoughby in the Marsh (Lincs), church of, 47
Wiltshire, 172
Wimbledon (Surrey), 170
Winchelsea, Robert, archbp of Canterbury, 109
Winchester (Hants), 170
    bp of, see Lucy, Godfrey de; Raleigh, William; Roches, Peter des; Stratford, John
    cathedral, 25, 39, 83
Windsor (Berks), 31
Wingham (Kent), manor of, 136
Wintrigsham, Paulinus of, 146
Wintringham (E.R. Yorks), church of, 75
Witchingham, Little (Norfolk), church at, 106
Wix (Essex), priory (Benedictine nuns of), 23–4, 26, 39
Wlferdesl', chaplain of, see Robert
Wodeford, John de, prebendary of Broad Chalke, 168

Wold Newton (E.R. Yorks), church of, 47, 54–5
  rector of, see Breton, Guy; Daventre, Philip de; Lusceby, Henry de; Willoughby, Hugh; Willoughby, Philip
Wolf, William, 73–4
Wolverhampton (Staffs), church of, 30
Woodbrook (Worcs), church of, 86–7
Wooler (Northumb), rector of, see Lusceby, Henry de
Worcester, 183
  bp of, 19, and see Cantilupe, Walter de; Giffard, Godfrey; Mauger; Orleton, Adam; Samson; Simon; Wakefield, Henry; Wykeham, William of,
  cathedral priory, 30, 39, 85
  diocese, 20
Worstead (Norfolk), church of, 98
Wrabness (Essex), church of, 156–7
Wrangle (Lincs), church of, 154–5
Wrastlingword, Elias de, 153
Wrawby (Lincs), church of, 45
  rector of, see Billesby, William de
Wressell (Yorks E.R.), parish of, 65, 74
  rector of, 75, and see Peret, John
Wyclif, John, 41
Wykeham (N.R. Yorks), priory (Cistercian nuns) of, 145–6
Wykeham, Pain of, son of, see, Theobald
  William of, bp of Worcester, 188

Wymondham (Norfolk), 97
  priory (Benedictine) of, 110
  vicar of, 110
Wythecall, Geoffrey de, 145

Yarborough (Lincs), deanery of, 43–4, 46, 60, 62, 144
Yarburgh (Lincs), dean of, see Hamelin
Yarmouth (Norfolk), Franciscans at, 107
Yeoveney (Middlesex), 170
Ynfleth, John de, bailiff of Howden, 129
York, 8, 58, 69, 176
  archbp of, 6, 20, 23, 186
  and see Arundel, Thomas; Melton, William; Neville, Alexander; Thomas I; Thomas II; Thoresby, John de; Thurstan
  diocese, 10, 23–5, 27, 69
  Holy Trinity priory (Benedictine alien) of, 23, 25, 30, 39, 54, 64
  Minster, 2, 78
    chapter, 20–1
    dean of, see Colby, William de
  The Retreat, 16
  St Mary's abbey (Benedictine) of, 39, 58
  University of, 4
    Borthwick Institute, 1, 4, 6, 8–9, 13, 15–17, 63, 111
York, Elizabeth of, 192

Zutshi, Patrick, 200

Tabula Gratulatoria

Rod Ambler
Margaret Aston
Melanie Barber
Julia Barrow
Nicholas Bennett
Nick Bird
Helen Birkett
Margaret Blount
Julia Boorman
Dr Paul Brand
Gerald Bray
Martin Brett
Reg Brocklesby
Rosalind and Christopher Brooke
Michael Burger
Janet Burton
Stephen Chater
Dr Peter D. Clarke
Professor Compton Reeves
Claire Cross
Peter Cunich
Professor Anne Curry
Elizabeth Danbury
David D'Avray
Jeffrey Denton
Barrie Dobson
Gwilym Dodd
Charles Donahue, Jr
Dr R.W. Dunning
C.R.Elrington
Richard Emms
Charles Fonge
Gordon C.F. Forster
Dr M.J. Franklin
Judith Frost
Joan Greatrex
Christopher Harper-Bill
Kathryn Harris
Barbara Harvey
Paul D.A. Harvey
Dr Rosemary Hayes
John Hayward
Martin Heale
Peter Heath
R.H. Helmholz
Michael Hicks
Roger Highfield
Sir James Holt
Philippa Hoskin

Michael Jones
Dr Maureen Jurkowski
Bronach Kane
Nicholas Karn
Brian Kemp
Right Reverend Dr E.W. Kemp
Ian Kershaw
Martyn Lawrence
Rachel Leech
Christian and Lisa Liddy
F. Donald Logan
Dr Peter Mackie
J.R. Maddicott
Henry Mayr-Harting
A.K. McHardy
Ileana and Roger McMeeking
Peter Meadows
Patrick Mussett
Falko Neininger
Dr J.A. Nigota
Christopher Norton
Professor W. Mark Ormrod
Arthur Owen
Professor David M. Palliser
Revd G.A. Plumb
Dr Nigel Ramsay
J.E. Redford
Felicity and John Riddy
David Robinson
Dr Michael Robson, OFMCONV
Peter and Ann Rycraft
Jane Sayers
Richard Sharpe
Norman F. Shead
Sara Slinn
M.G. Snape
R.N. Swanson
T.C.B. Timmins
Nigel Tringham
Tore H. Vigerust, Oslo
Sethina Watson
The Rev Dr C.A. Weale
C.C. Webb
Edward Wheatley
Bob Wood

Lincoln Cathedral Library
Salisbury Cathedral Library